Plenty and Want

The subtitle on the front cover should read:
A social history of food in England from 1815 to the present day.

JOHN BURNETT

Plenty and Want

————— ✤ ✤ —————

*A social history of food in England
from 1815 to the present day*

THIRD EDITION

ROUTLEDGE

London and New York

First published by Thomas Nelson in 1966
Revised edition published by Scolar Press in 1979

University Paperback edition published in 1983 by
Methuen & Co. Ltd
Reprinted 1985

Third edition published in 1989 by
Routledge
11 New Fetter Lane, London EC4P 4EE

© John Burnett 1966, 1979, 1989

Typeset in 11/12pt Cheltenham Light by Colset Private Limited, Singapore

Printed in Great Britain
by T.J. Press (Padstow) Ltd Cornwall

British Library Cataloguing in Publication Data
Burnett, John, *1925*
Plenty and want: a social history of food
in England from 1815 to the present day. —— 3rd ed.
1. England. Man. Diet, 1815–1987.
Socioeconomic aspects
I. Title
306′.3

ISBN 0-415-00862-X Pbk

Contents

Illustrations

The illustrations appear between pages 240 and 241.

The author and publishers would like to thank all copyright holders for their permission to reproduce the illustrations.

Preface to the third edition

Since the first edition of *Plenty and Want* in 1966 food history has come of age, and it is no longer true to say, as in the earlier Preface, that 'little or no serious attempt has ever been made to study the changes that have taken place in man's basic needs since Britain became an industrial society'. Food history is now an accepted area of scholarly research, and no serious account of the economic and social transformation of Britain during the past two centuries now omits reference to the changing ways in which food has been grown, manufactured, distributed, and consumed.

This new edition allows me to do two things. First, it enables me to acknowledge and incorporate some of the more important research findings of the last twenty years by scholars who have worked over neglected areas of this wide terrain: they range from studies of individual firms and commodities to methods of transport and marketing, patterns of consumption, and nutritional evaluations. Much of this research was first presented in the form of papers to the Historians and Nutritionists Seminar at Queen Elizabeth College, University of London, which began in 1963 and has met regularly ever since. Historians and nutritionists have both benefited from acquaintance with the other's discipline, and three valuable volumes of papers have resulted to which my debt will be obvious. Of the many scholars who have contributed to the success of this seminar, special mention should be made of Professor John Yudkin and the late Dr Derek Miller who led the nutritionists' 'side', and Professors Theo Barker and Derek Oddy who have represented the historians.

Second, this edition brings the account of dietary changes up to 1985, the latest date for which official statistics are available: readers who are especially interested in current trends can update Table 49 as future Annual Reports of the National Food Survey Committee are published. For the recent period my particular thanks are due to Dr Dorothy Hollingsworth, former Director General of the British Nutrition Foundation, and to Dr D.H. Buss of the Nutrition Section of the Ministry of Agriculture, Fisheries, and Food. It is scarcely necessary to say that no one is responsible for opinions expressed in this book except myself, but it is necessary for me warmly to thank Valerie Radford who battled so success-fully and uncomplainingly with my illegibility.

Although the title of this book still seems appropriate, there has been a small change to the sub-title from 'A social history of diet' to 'A social history of food'. The word 'diet' was technically correct, but was some-times interpreted in a particular, narrow way – so much so that some public libraries catalogued the book under 'cookery', 'domestic science', and even 'slimming'. Though it relates to all and more of these, it properly belongs to history.

Part One

1815–50

⇛1⇚
England in transition

The basic feature of English life during the first half of the nineteenth century was that of change – change from a small, mainly agricultural society to a large, industrial population which lived and worked in towns rather than villages. Population had first begun to grow noticeably in the middle of the eighteenth century, although at the first official census, taken in 1801, England and Wales could still only muster 8,900,000 inhabitants, scarcely more than one-third those of France, with whom we were now in mortal conflict. Within the next decade, however, nearly another million and a half were added to the English population, and by 1851 it had doubled to reach eighteen million. Various theories were advanced, and are still being advanced, in explanation of this phenomenal growth. The view that the main factor was a fall in the death rate, and particularly in child mortality, has recently come under attack, and opinion now generally favours a rise in births due to a higher rate and earlier age of marriage. The important point here is that a population which doubled in the remarkably short space of fifty years had somehow to be fed.

The problem was complicated by the fact that the increase in total numbers was accompanied by a marked shift in the balance between town and country. In 1815, England was already in the process of transition into an industrial society: factories, coal mines, and iron works were beginning to exert a magnetic effect, attracting men and women into the industrial midlands and north, and from rural areas into towns and suburbs. Urbanization was the most important and most easily recognizable social consequence of the Industrial Revolution. In 1801 only one-fifth of the population were town-dwellers, four-fifths rural; by 1851 the proportions were evenly balanced, while by 1911 they were completely reversed. During the first fifty years of the nineteenth century, Manchester grew from a town of 75,000 to a bustling city of 303,000 at the centre of the Lancashire cotton industry. The mechanization of cloth weaving raised Leeds from 53,000 to 172,000 and Bradford from 13,000 to 104,000.[1] Hardware trebled the size of Birmingham, steel nearly quadrupled that of Sheffield. Throughout the industrial areas of the country people were, in

3

the dramatic words of Ruskin, 'thrown back in continually closer crowds upon the city gates'. Thus, not only had an ever-growing population to be fed, but it was one which, as the century progressed, became more and more divorced from the land which had formerly supplied it. Even if the England of 1850 had still been able to feed itself, there would have been half the nation – the new nation of town-dwellers – necessarily dependent on others for the supply of its daily bread. Factory workers and coal-miners, nail-makers and framework-knitters, had neither land nor leisure to grow food for themselves.

These demographic changes had highly important food consequences. The growth of urban life encouraged competition and social imitation among all classes, leading ultimately to far more sophisticated tastes and eating habits. The outstanding examples of this are white bread and tea, both of which were, in the eighteenth century, the luxuries of the well-to-do. The labourer had eaten brown household bread made, in the south, of wheat, but over wide areas of the north and west more frequently of barley, rye, and oats, and had drunk home-brewed beer when he could afford it. Already by 1815, however, wheat had become the almost universal bread corn of England. Sir William Ashley's estimate that in 1795 wheat constituted 95 per cent of the nation's bread[2] is almost certainly premature, for mixtures of grains continued to be used regularly in country districts for many years to come, especially in years of scarcity and high prices. But townspeople, however poor, ate wheat bread in the nineteenth century, and, it seems, no other. Moreover, they ate *white* bread – the product of 'high milling' and total removal of the bran. This change in public taste had originated in fashionable London society early in the previous century, reaching provincial towns like Norwich by about 1745:[3] by the time of Waterloo the object of every baker was to produce the whitest possible loaf, and household bread had all but disappeared. The history of tea-drinking shows a similar progress, from the occasional luxury of the urban rich in the early eighteenth century to the national beverage of all classes by 1850. Sir Frederic Eden noted in 1797 that small quantities had already found their way into the poorest labourer's diet in the south and east of England,[4] and by the 1840s tea had taken its place alongside white bread in the poverty-line dietaries described by Engels and other contemporary writers. The apparent contradiction is easily explained. What had been mere adjuncts at the tables of the wealthy now often constituted virtually the total diet of those who could afford no more. White bread was more palatable and easily digestible than the coarser household bread, and, when necessary, could be eaten without meat, cheese, or even butter: in this case, tea became even more important, because it converted a cold meal into the semblance of a hot one.

In the new urban environment, traditional rural skills, of which

4

domestic baking and brewing were economically the most important, gradually decayed and ultimately disappeared over wide areas of the country; where they did survive – often in the households of those who could afford to employ domestic servants – it was for reasons of pre-ference, not cost. This was, no doubt, an inevitable consequence of industrialization and the division of labour. Baking and brewing were long, tedious operations, the materials sometimes hard to come by in small quantities, and the results often uncertain. In the towns there was the permanent temptation of the nearby baker's shop or public house selling, often at little greater cost and on credit terms, an apparently more attractive article than could be produced at home. Where the housewife was also engaged in paid work and had little time to spare in the kitchen, these arguments against domestic baking and brewing became compelling.

Oddly enough, the midlands and north of England clung longer to home baking than the south. Almost certainly, the main reason for this was the easier availability of fuel for the oven, still prohibitively dear in the south, even after the railways had begun to bring down costs in the 1840s. Whereas in Berkshire in 1831 there was one baker to every 295 inhabi-tants, in Cumberland the ratio was only one to every 2,200.[5] In Manchester, in 1804, there had not been a single public baker,[6] although professional baking subsequently made rapid progress, for eleven years later only 'half the population was said to prepare its own bread'. The use of public ovens in some northern industrial towns was a compromise which persisted for some time, but as the century progressed the majority of the urban working classes came to rely entirely on the baker for their daily bread. In rural areas, too, home baking was declining, though less rapidly. Bakers had first appeared in the villages of southern England in the middle of the eighteenth century, and enclosures and the Speenhamland system of poor relief soon contributed to their growth. Traditionalists and domestic economists thereafter complained in vain at the advance of a system which was essentially linked with loss of indepen-dence and increasing rural poverty: 'How wasteful,' thundered Cobbett, 'and, indeed, how shameful, for a labourer's wife to go to the baker's shop: and how negligent, how criminally careless of the welfare of his family must the labourer be who permits so scandalous an use of the proceeds of his labour.'[7] By mid-century, it would appear, the art of home baking was almost forgotten in Kent, Surrey, Middlesex, and Sussex, and of the southern counties only Suffolk and Devonshire still retained a reputation for their cottage bread.[8] Among northern counties, Yorkshire housewives in particular resisted the temptations of bought bread and continued their laborious twice-weekly bakings.

The fate of domestic baking was shared by that of home brewing. In

5

earlier times the housewife brewed as naturally as she baked, and prided herself on her skill in producing different varieties, strengths, and flavours of beer. The demise of domestic brewing is part of the wider story of the collapse of the economic position of the rural labourer which occurred during the latter half of the eighteenth century. Brewing, even more than baking, presupposed a standard of living above mere subsistence. To provide the necessary equipment of vats, mash-tuns, pails, and barrels was an initial expense which even the partial Cobbett put in the region of £10, and thereafter to buy regular supplies of costly malt and hops throughout the year placed a strain on resources which very few labourers in the pauperized parishes of the south and east could hope to meet. Even if these difficulties could be overcome, there remained one which could well be insuperable – scarcity of fuel. By the end of the eighteenth century many labourers went fireless on occasion, unable to afford the fuel for ordinary heating or cooking, let alone the large quantities necessary for brewing. As acre after acre of common land was enclosed the fuel of the poor grew ever scarcer: whereas in the past the labourer had been able to gather sticks, logs, and brushwood merely for the trouble of it, he now had to buy, or risk pilfering from the hedgerows. The disappearance of free fuel, and the high cost of coal in many areas, had profound effects on the labourer's diet and standard of living generally, and it was useless for philanthropists, however well-meaning, to criticize the poor for not baking their own bread or brewing their own beer. Actual observers, like the Rev. David Davies, who carried out a survey of poverty in his Berkshire parish, saw the difficulty clearly enough: 'Where fuel is scarce and dear, poor people find it cheaper to buy their bread of the baker than to bake for themselves . . . but where fuel abounds, and costs only the trouble of cutting and carrying home, there they may save something by baking their own bread.'[9] What was true of baking was even more true of brewing, where initial costs were higher, and the length of firing considerably longer.

Already, by 1815, regular domestic brewing by the cottager had ceased over most of the country. It tended to survive only in parts of the north, where coal was available, and in the more heavily wooded south-west; for the rest, it continued only sporadically, where local conditions were favourable. Dr Clapham has noticed the interesting fact that the normal cottage in the Dudley iron district in the 1830s contained a kitchen, two bedrooms, and what was still described as a 'brewhouse', but this was rapidly changing into the Victorian scullery. No Dudley iron worker still brewed, although there remained a memory of brewing.[10] Again, a Sussex farmer told a House of Commons Committee in 1819 that forty years ago every labourer in his parish had brewed – now not one did so. Cobbett and others were refusing to accept the inevitable when they tried to persuade the labourer to give up the tea-kettle and the beer-shop and go back to the home-brewed ale of the 'good old days'.

Domestic brewing continued to be important well into the nineteenth century in larger households, as well as in institutions ranging from hospitals to public schools and colleges. It seems likely that around 1800 about half the total national production of beer was domestic,[11] and the amount of malt used must have been well over this, for private brewers favoured strong beer, 'a single horn of which will make a man drunk'.[12] But from this time, the decline was both continuous and rapid. Dr Wilson has calculated that over the period 1801–30 private brewing accounted for some two million barrels a year out of a total production of 9,430,000. By 1850 one-seventh of the national total was home brewed, and by 1870 only one-fortieth. There was no subsequent recovery from this insignificant contribution.[13]

Rapid urbanization also created difficult problems of food supply and transport. The small market towns of the past had been able to draw most of their food easily enough from the surrounding countryside: only London had had to go into Kent and Surrey for its vegetables, to Wales for its mutton, and to Scotland for its beef. But by 1850 what had been necessary for London was now necessary for Manchester and Birmingham, Leeds and Nottingham, and a dozen more cities. For a time waggons on the turnpike roads managed to bring the produce in to the great markets of London and the provinces – the new canals were not used to any great extent for the movement of food other than grains. Scottish cattle were still driven down from Forfar to be fattened in Norfolk before sale at Smithfield; milk was still supplied from town dairies where animals fed on brewers' dregs lived in filthy sheds from which they never saw the light of day.

But many town markets, which in the past had sold foods directly to the consumer, were transformed in the first half of the century under the pressures of increased population, traffic, overcrowding, and accompanying pollution. Sheffield was not untypical of the changes to be seen in an industrial town.[14] Here, the butchers took up a large part of the old market, causing chaos and inconvenience with their live animals, carts, noise, and refuse. Already, at the beginning of the nineteenth century, a separate live cattle market was built and the slaughter-houses removed from the former site, so crystallizing a growing separation of functions between farmers and butchers. As the city expanded outwards, a further division occurred, the new residential areas being served by their own retail shops, supplied by wholesale butchers with slaughtering and distributive facilities. Similar developments took place somewhat later in the supply of fruit and vegetables. By mid-century the little farms and small-holdings which had supplied local needs had been squeezed out of the town itself; the new railways now became crucial for bringing in perishable fresh fruit and vegetables from increasingly distant sources. The Manchester, Sheffield, and Lincolnshire Railway was especially important in this connection and, incidentally, largely revived the fortunes of Grimsby as a fishing port now that its hinterland was greatly extended. In 1847 and 1851 Sheffield built two new covered markets for fruit and vegetables, one for wholesale and the other for retail trade.

The railways arrived just in time in the 1830s, and quickly brought about a revolution in the supply of food to the towns. Without their powers of rapid, cheap distribution England might not have survived the mounting pressure of demand on local sources of food supply and the social discontent which flared up at times of high prices and cyclical depression. The railways created a national market in food, levelling out regional variations in price, quickly supplying local scarcities and, at the same time, making locally produced foods available throughout the land. Within a few years they were carrying livestock to the town slaughter-houses, and country-killed meat was arriving in fresh condition from distant counties. Fish caught on the east coast in the morning was on sale in Birmingham the same evening, and Scottish salmon, packed in ice, now reached London in perfect condition at all seasons. Highly perishable foods like green vegetables, eggs, and milk benefited especially from the new mobility. Milk was first dispatched by rail to Manchester in 1844, and to London shortly afterwards; during 1854 the Eastern Counties Railway Company alone brought in over three million quarts. More important still, the railways cut costs as well as time. For many years, St Thomas's Hospital had a contract with a neighbouring town dairyman for the supply of milk at 1s a gallon: in 1846 they exchanged this for one with a Romford farmer a dozen miles away, at a price varying from 9d to 10d a gallon, including transport on the Eastern Counties Railway.[15]

Fruit and fresh vegetables benefited similarly, with special vans attached to the trains bringing apples, pears, cherries, strawberries, and raspberries to London from Kent, the Vale of Evesham, and the Sandy area of Bedfordshire. Loaded at a station in the late afternoon, they would be sold within hours at Covent Garden and on display at suburban greengrocers the next morning. From further afield in the Channel Islands early potatoes, tomatoes, and green salads now reached London in good condition within a day.[16] There can be little doubt that the new means of transport – fast, cheap, and unaffected by most vicissitudes of the weather – played an immensely important part in lowering costs and so extending food consumption from the 1840s onwards.

Although by 1850 the individual household had become dependent on professional food suppliers, the nation as a whole was still largely able to feed itself, at least in the basic items of bread and meat. Down to the 1790s, indeed, we had regularly exported wheat to France and other countries, until the outbreak of war interrupted normal trade; thereafter, as the population mounted, England became a wheat-importer, although still in quite inconsiderable quantities until the mid-century. The average annual import between 1801 and 1810 was only 600,000 quarters, rising to 1,900,000 in the 1840s:[17] it varied greatly from one year to another, and was only sizeable in times of bad harvest, such as 1817–18, 1829–31, and 1838–41 – in normal seasons we could still supply ourselves. Unfortunately, no official statistics of domestic wheat production exist against which one can compare the quantities imported. Contemporaries calculated that the average Englishman consumed between six and eight bushels of wheat a year, and on this basis imports contributed one-seventeenth of total consumption at the beginning of the century, rising to one-ninth in the 1840s.

This ability of English agriculture practically to keep pace with a population growth of unprecedented speed and size was a remarkable achievement, made possible by more intensive methods of farming, the employment of new rotational systems, and the cultivation of wide areas of formerly waste or common land. The disappearance of the commons was the hard price the labourer had to pay for the maintenance of his dietary standard at something like a constant level, at a time when the growing pressure of population upon the land could have been as disastrous for England as it was for Ireland. Wheaten bread remained the staple diet of most English people throughout this period, the Rev. David Davies reporting in 1795 that 'bread makes the principal part of the food of all poor families, and almost the whole of the food of . . . large families'.[18] This was more true of the south of England than of the north, where barley bread and 'hasty pudding' made of oatmeal boiled with milk were still major constituents of the diet at the beginning of the century, though soon in retreat in the face of the white loaf.

But the overwhelming importance of cereals generally is demonstrated by Professor Derek Oddy's calculation that, at this period, at least 70 per cent of the energy value of the national diet was derived from carbohydrate, and only about 20 per cent from fat.[19] Whether *per capita* bread consumption increased, declined, or remained roughly stationary in the years up to 1850 is impossible to know with certainty. Dr R.N. Salaman has estimated, on somewhat dubious evidence, that 'wheat availability' fell continuously from 1.6 lb per head per day in 1825 to 1.25 lb in 1846, the year of repeal of the Corn Laws: thereafter, it increased to 1.6 lb in 1851 and then gradually climbed to 2 lb by 1879.[20] It is certain that there were individual years of great scarcity when the harvest failed and wheat prices temporarily trebled or even quadrupled, though these especially hard times were more frequent during the French wars (1793–1815) than subsequently. At such periods some people necessarily had to turn to substitutes – either to the cheaper grains which they had been in the process of abandoning or, more especially, to the newer food of potatoes – and it may well be that once such a modification in the dietary pattern had occurred, it continued after the necessity had been removed, either for reasons of cost or preference. Writing in the crucial decade of the 1840s, the contemporary statistician, G.R. Porter, no doubt summed up the change correctly: 'Unless in years of scarcity, no part of the inhabitants of England except perhaps in the extreme north, and there only partially, have now recourse to rye or barley bread, but a larger and increasing number are in a great measure fed upon potatoes.'[21]

Potatoes were already an established part of the northern diet by the later eighteenth century, and consumption there expanded with the waves of Irish immigrants. Their use also spread to southern England during the scarcities of the French wars, and continued to grow in the years after 1815, Dr Salaman estimating a rise in *per capita* consumption in England and Wales from 0.4 lb a day in 1795 to 0.6 lb in 1838.[22] Unlike wheat, potatoes could be grown by the labourer on small garden plots and allotments, and therefore tended to restore something of the sense of self-sufficiency which his forefathers had enjoyed: unlike bread, a dish of potatoes provided a hot meal and, with some addition, a reasonably appetizing one. Here was the difficulty, however, for as David Davies pointed out:

> Wheaten bread may be eaten alone with pleasure; but potatoes require either meat or milk to make them go down; you cannot make many hearty meals of them with salt and water only. Poor people indeed give them to their children in the greasy water in which they have boiled their greens and their morsel of bacon.

In that respect potatoes were not a total substitute for bread, and in the south at least were regarded as a low-status food well into the nineteenth century: for Cobbett they were 'the lazy root' because they could sustain life at a low level with little expenditure of effort, for James Caird they were 'the lowest species of human food', while in the opinion of less polite commentators they were fit only for pigs and Irish. It is difficult, therefore, to assess whether the increase in potato consumption represented improvement or deterioration in the diet. Probably the southern labourer, substituting potatoes for a portion of his white bread, regarded them as a reduction in his living standard, whereas in northern towns and villages potato-pie, potato-cakes, Lancashire hot-pot and Irish stew were welcome additions to the diet, providing variety and nutriment at low cost, but not displacing traditional foods. Whether their widespread adoption as human food in England was benign or malignant, a blessing or a curse, must depend on regional and individual circumstances, and the place they came to occupy in a family's total diet alongside other foods. The historian of the potato, Dr Salaman, makes a larger and more tendentious claim on their behalf:

> The use of the potato . . . did, in fact, enable the workers to survive on the lowest possible wage. It may be that in this way the potato prolonged and encouraged, for another hundred years, the impoverishment and degradation of the English masses; but what was the alternative, surely nothing but bloody revolution. That England escaped such a violent upheaval in the early decades of the nineteenth century . . . must in large measure be placed to the credit of the potato.[23]

But, in popular belief at least, John Bull was a meat-eater, not a potato-eater. Again, the available statistics cannot show whether supplies of meat kept pace with the rapid increase in population between 1815 and 1850. Much of the selective breeding carried out by Bakewell and others in the eighteenth century, which produced the Hereford and the Aberdeen Angus, had the object of raising leaner animals brought earlier to slaughter, and yielding high quality, tender meat for the table.[24] But for the poorer – and larger – part of the nineteenth-century population, regular meat-eating was a luxury, the sure sign of a comfortable standard of living enjoyed only by artisans and other well-paid workers. As the eleventh child of a farm labourer, Alexander Somerville lamented that 'we never had butcher's meat',[25] while in 1880 the agricultural economist James Caird commented that 'thirty years ago not more than one-third of the people of this country consumed animal produce more than once a week'.[26]

Britain's 67,691 butchers of 1851 were still almost totally dependent on home supplies. There was a considerable movement of animals about the country, both on the hoof and, by the 1840s, on the railways, and Scottish or Irish cattle, sheep, and pigs were familiar sights in the markets of any large English town. But down to 1842 there was a prohibition on the import of livestock from foreign countries and, before the development of refrigeration, dead meat could not be transported any considerable distance except in preserved form. Several large American meat-packing houses were in existence by 1850 in Chicago, Buffalo, and Cincinnati, exporting mainly salt pork in barrels, a product which found some place in poorer, working-class diets as well as in sailors' rations. From the removal of the ban on live imports, numbers increased rapidly from 33,000 animals in 1845 to 309,000 by 1854,[27] when an English company undertook the construction of a railway across Denmark to facilitate shipment via Lowestoft.

In total, Professor Williams estimates that in 1850 the United Kingdom produced 900,000 tons of meat, equivalent to approximately 72 lb a head a

11

year; imports added around another 3 lb.[28] There are no comparable earlier statistics to indicate whether consumption had risen or fallen by this date. On the evidence of the Returns of Beasts Tolls at Smithfield market, Professor Hobsbawm argues that a *per capita* decline in London's meat consumption between the beginning of the century and the 1840s is 'almost certain':[29] while London's population index rose from 100 in 1801 to 202 in 1841, the number of beef cattle slaughtered increased only from 100 to 146 and sheep to 176 in the same period. But this is very partial evidence indeed. For one thing, it takes no account of increases in the weight of animals brought to market. For another, Smithfield did not deal in pigs, and pork in its various forms was the principal meat of the working classes. Equally important, no home- or country-killed meat came to Smithfield: it was sold mainly at Newgate, Leadenhall, Farringdon, and Whitechapel. Newgate market alone was reputed to sell three-quarters as many cattle and more calves than Smithfield in 1850.[30] The available meat statistics neither support 'optimists' or 'pessimists' in the standard-of-living debate, but they certainly do not prove a case for deterioration.

Strangely, the important place of fish in the English diet has been relatively neglected.[31] For those living on or near the coast fish was normally a cheap and plentiful source of nourishment, not so highly regarded as meat, but a tasty relish to add to bread or potatoes. It is reported, for example, that poor miners' families in Cornwall in the early nineteenth century would salt 1,000 pilchards to last them through the winter months.[32] The main disadvantage of fish was its high perishability, which limited inland supplies until the development of fast transport by rail. Although the abolition of the salt tax in 1825 encouraged preservation by salting and smoking (the traditional red herring began to give way to the milder kipper and bloater from the 1840s), the preference of most people was for fresh fish, brought to the fishmonger's slab daily.

For the high-priced market, fish was conveyed to inland towns by specially fast vans drawn by four or six horses – to London from the southeast coast, to Bristol and Bath from Brixham. In 1817 Billingsgate market already received 7,206 boxes of Scotch salmon, each weighing 100 lb, and packed in ice;[33] six years later, 12,000 tons of fish were sold there, equivalent to around 18 lb per year per head of London's population. The great expansion of fish supplies, however, took place in the 1830s and 1840s. New methods of fishing by trawling yielded larger catches, while longer voyages were made possible by the introduction of 'fleeting', whereby some boats stayed at sea for up to eight weeks but dispatched their catches daily by fast cutters.[34] For voyages as far as Iceland wellvessels were used, in which the fish were kept alive in tanks in the hold: on arrival at Grimsby they were rushed by rail to midland and northern towns. Of major importance to increasing supplies was the discovery between 1837 and 1843 of the Great Silver Pits, lying some sixty miles off the mouth of the Humber: they were immensely rich in cod, turbot, sole, and halibut, the 'inferior' haddock, plaice, and whiting being at first thrown back into the sea.[35]

By mid-century prodigious quantities of fish were arriving on the market. Henry Mayhew in 1851 gave a figure of 1,225 million herrings landed at Billingsgate, equal to 500 a head a year, assuming that they were all eaten locally: at four for a penny, Mayhew noted that 'the rooms of the very neediest of our needy metropolitan population always smell of fish, most frequently of herrings'.[36] Oysters, already on the way to becoming something of a luxury at two for a penny, were consumed at the rate of 124 million a year, about fifty per person. Mayhew also compiled a table of the estimated quantity of all fish sold at Billingsgate in a year (probably 1848 or 1849) from information supplied by 'the most eminent salesmen', showing a total weight of approximately 450 million lb, not counting shellfish. Herrings made up half the weight, followed by plaice, mackerel, and sole in that order.[37] What this meant in terms of *per capita* consumption can only be guessed, for Billingsgate served to some extent as a distributive as well as a local market, but even allowing only half the total to be eaten by Londoners this would still amount to around 90 lb a head a year – more, that is, than the estimated national average meat consumption of 75 lb. The large and apparently steeply rising level of fish consumption should not be ignored in the debate over the standard of living.

Imports of most foreign foods were discouraged throughout the earlier part of the century by tariff policies, designed partly to protect the English farmer and partly to raise revenue. Before the reintroduction of income tax in 1842, customs and excise duties on food made up almost half of total national revenue, an argument constantly employed by those who were hostile to a freer trade policy. Many of these were on articles of common consumption, and were therefore redistributive from the poorer to the richer. An informed witness before the Select Committee on Handloom Weavers' Petitions in 1834 calculated that a working man annually paid the following taxes – on malt £4 11s 3d, on sugar 17s 4d, on tea and coffee £1 4s 0d, and on other foods £3 – a total of £9 12s 7d out of his estimated annual wage of £22.[38]

The most notorious duty was, however, the Corn Law of 1815, and the numerous amendments through which it passed before its final repeal in 1846. The traditional view is that by forbidding the import of foreign wheat until English wheat stood at more than 80s per quarter, the Corn Laws deliberately kept the home market understocked, kept prices artificially high, and so were a major cause of the hunger and poverty of the period. This theory makes at least two assumptions which are by no means proven – that European grain producers such as Russia and Hungary had large surpluses of wheat which could have been available for Britain, and that such surpluses (had they existed) could have been sold here, even including the heavy freight charges by land and sea, at a price lower than that of home-grown corn. Both assumptions have been seriously questioned by recent writers, and it now seems likely that the Corn Laws were repealed precisely at the point when, for the first time in their history, they might have had any significant influence on price.

With commodities such as tea, sugar, and coffee, all of which had to be imported, the case was quite different. Here, the duty was a major factor in determining the ultimate price to the consumer, and changes in tariff rates often had marked and immediate effect on the level of consumption. From 1815–34 tea was charged an *ad valorem* duty of between 96 and 100 per cent; this was subsequently converted into a flat-rate duty, and from 1840 to 1853 all grades of tea paid 2s 2¼d per pound weight. The 1840s were, in fact, the period of heaviest taxation in the whole history of tea. The abolition in 1833 of the East India Company's monopoly of trade with China had brought down the prime cost of Bohea to 10d a pound, and of Congou (the quality generally drunk by the working classes) to 1s 2d; the duty consequently worked out at 350 and 280 per cent respectively. By comparison, the sugar duty, imposed for the benefit of our West Indian planters, was far less penal. Down to 1845, colonial sugar paid 25s 3d a hundredweight, foreign free-labour sugar 35s 9d. Peel's free trade budget of that year cut the amounts to 14s and 23s 4d at a loss to the Exchequer of £1,300,000 a year.[39] This was probably the most important fiscal concession affecting food to be made during the period, bringing down the retail price of sugar as it did from 8d a pound in 1830 to 5d by 1850. Coffee also benefited from the freer trade policy of the 1840s. In the earlier part of the century, the duty on British plantation coffee had varied at different times between 6d and 1s 6d a pound; in 1842 it was reduced to 4d a pound and that on foreign coffee first to 8d and then to 6d two years later.[40] By 1845 coffee consumption was approaching 2 lb per head a year, compared with a mere ounce at the opening of the century.

The duties on imported food had one good result for historians in that they produced statistics from which it is possible to calculate the *per capita* consumption with some confidence. It is worth looking at these, for remarkably different conclusions have been derived from them. Two 'optimistic' economic historians, Drs Chaloner and Henderson, have pointed to an increasing sugar consumption in the 1840s as 'an indication of rising living standards in these years'.[41] In 1801, the average consumption in Britain, not including Ireland, was 30 lb 10 oz a year, in 1811, 29 lb 4 oz, and in 1821, 19 lb 4 oz. The annual figures for 1830–50 are given in full in Table 1, where it will be seen that consumption remained below 20 lb a head until 1845, from which time it gradually climbed back to 30 lb by

Table 1 *Sugar consumption in Britain (excluding Ireland) 1801–50*[42]

Year	Average consumption of each person	Year	Average consumption of each person
1801	30.6 lb	1839	17.1 lb
1811	29.3	1840	15.3
1821	19.2	1841	17.7
1830	19.9	1842	16.8
1831	20.1	1843	17.1
1832	19.0	1844	17.6
1833	18.0	1845	20.3
1834	18.3	1846	21.6
1835	19.2	1847	23.6
1836	16.6	1848	24.9
1837	18.3	1849	24.1
1838	18.4		

1853. From 1839–45 sugar consumption was lower than at any time in the first half century: the increase was restricted to the later 1840s, and was due primarily to the lower tariff introduced in 1845 and the consequent fall in price. The case of sugar is a good example of the truth of G.R. Porter's remark, 'The consumption of this class of articles affords a very useful test of the comparative conditions at different periods of the labouring classes. If by reason of the cheapness of provisions, the wages of the labourer afford means for indulgence, sugar, tea, and coffee are the articles to which he earliest has recourse.'[43] The demand for sugar fluctuated in direct relation to price: 1840, the dearest year in the half century (73s 10d per hundredweight), corresponds with the lowest consumption (15.3 lb per head), and 1848, the cheapest year (36s 9d), with the highest consumption (24.9 lb) for thirty years.

The increase in coffee consumption during the first half of the century was also directly related to changes in the level of duty and, hence, ultimate cost. As Table 2 indicates, average consumption grew from 1 oz per head in 1801 to 1½ lb in 1841, following the tariff reduction of 1825 from 1s 0d to 6d a pound. A rise of such proportions is very significant, though it does not necessarily indicate an improvement in working-class standards. Coffee was primarily a middle-class drink, and rarely found a regular place in the wage-earner's budget.

A much truer indicator of standards is tea, which by 1850 was the drink of all classes. Tea consumption was remarkably stable throughout the period under discussion at around 1¼ lb per head a year; only in the

Table 2 *Coffee consumption in Britain (excluding Ireland) 1801–41* [44]

Year	Number of lb consumed	Average consumption
1801	750,861	0 lb 1.09 oz
1811	6,390,122	0 lb 8.12 oz
1821	7,327,283	0 lb 8.01 oz
1831	21,842,264	1 lb 5.49 oz
1841	27,298,322	1 lb 7.55 oz

decade 1841–50 did it reach 1½ lb after a slight fall in the 1820s and 1830s (Table 3). There was no change in duty between 1836 and 1853 to complicate matters, but the opening of the China trade to free competition in 1833 did produce a sharp fall in prices. The interesting fact is that consumption did not rise significantly for another dozen years and, as with sugar, the increase of the decade 1841–50 was confined to the last five years.

Table 3 *Tea consumption in the United Kingdom (including Ireland) 1801–50*

Period	Average number of lb of tea consumed per annum	Average consumption per head per annum
1801–10	23,717,882	1.41 (lb)
1811–20	24,753,808	1.28
1821–30	28,612,702	1.27
1831–40	34,441,766	1.36
1841–50	44,286,600	1.61

Of beer, the traditional drink of Englishmen, we cannot speak with such certainty. The difficulty is that official returns of beer production exist only for public and not for private brewing; the only way to arrive at total production is to calculate from the quantities of malt annually charged for duty. This method, carefully employed by Dr George Wilson, indicates a fall in beer consumption from the beginning of the century down to 1851, when it stood at 19.6 gallons per head a year; from this date the movement was upwards to 25 gallons in 1860, 28 in 1865, and 34.4 in 1876, the highest point in the century (Table 4). No increase in duty or price took place between 1830 and 1850 – on the contrary, the Beerhouse Act of 1830 introduced a much freer licensing system which resulted in 40,000 new public houses within five years. This, it would seem, accounts for the slight rise in consumption from 1834–6, which was very short-lived.

Table 4 *Beer consumption in the United Kingdom 1800–50*[45]

Year	Gross consumption (millions standard gallons)	Per head consumption (gallons)
1800–4	361 (average)	33.9
1805–9	371 (average)	32.8
1810–14	366 (average)	30.2 England and
1815–19	368 (average)	28.0 Wales only
1820–4	407 (average)	29.0
1825–9	426 (average)	28.4
1830	500	22.0 (United Kingdom)
1831	514	21.3
1832	509	20.8
1833	529	21.5
1834	576	23.1
1835	588	23.4
1836	613	24.1
1837	577	22.5
1838	578	22.3
1839	583	22.3
1840	568	21.4
1841	524	19.6
1842	512	19.0
1843	508	18.6
1844	527	19.1
1845	534	19.2
1846	582	20.7
1847	528	18.8
1848	529	19.0
1849	531	19.2
1850	540	19.6

Food consumption has naturally featured importantly in the debate between historians over the standard of living of the working classes in the first half of the nineteenth century. If it can be shown that consumption levels over a range of foods were rising, without corresponding falls in other foods, it would lend strong support to the 'optimists' who argue that industrialization was benefiting the majority of the population even in its early, formative period. The major items of food and drink which we have reviewed do not support such a conclusion. There is, for example, no convincing evidence that bread consumption rose over the period. Wheat prices were relatively stable between 1830 and 1850 at a time when prices generally were falling; bread was, therefore, relatively dearer at this time, and in particular years such as 1841, absolutely dearer. In Manchester in 1836 a 12 lb bag of flour cost 1s 8d or 1s 10d, but in 1841, a depression year, from 2s 4d to 2s 7d.[46] At such times – and there were cyclical depressions in 1831–2, 1839–42, and 1847–9 – it is highly likely that poor families had to reduce their bread consumption and transfer to cheaper foods. The increase in potato consumption was probably not an addition to total diet for most people, but an enforced substitution. A Select Committee on Agricultural Distress in 1836 was informed that 'two millions of persons who used to subsist on wheat flour now principally subsist on potatoes – a change which has been gradually coming on for twenty or twenty-five years'.[47] Whether such a change constituted a deterioration in standards is open to debate. In purely nutritional terms there was probably no loss, and possibly even some gain, but if people regarded potatoes as inferior food – which seems to be true at least in the south of England – the change should arguably weigh on the debit side of the scale. In the case of meat, the available statistics do not point to an increase in consumption. Here again, it is likely that consumption did fall during the 'bad years' of the late 1830s and early 1840s – an Anti-Corn Law League inquiry in 1842 reported a decrease of from 30 to 60 per cent[48] – but the case for a continuous decline throughout the first half of the century is not proven. The one food for which there appears to be a marked and sustained improvement in supply and distribution is fish, which for many inland inhabitants now found a regular place in their diet for the first time.

The conclusion must be that there does not seem to be any evidence of a general rise in consumption levels over the period 1815–50. The trend in sugar and beer was downwards until 1845, tea was practically stationary throughout the same period, while bread consumption probably rose only after 1847. Sugar and beer are perhaps the best indicators of working-class standards (tea was already a near-necessity, and its consumption highly inelastic), and on their evidence those standards were tending to fall rather than rise. However, it seems fairly certain that the trend for most foods turned quite sharply upwards after 1845 – the 1840s as a whole were not demonstrably 'hungrier' than earlier decades, although the early forties may have been. It appears that there might be more justification for the description 'the thirsty forties'.

This is perhaps as far as the national figures can take us. Statistics of *per capita* consumption at best establish a framework: they describe the 'average', and the average consumer no more existed in early Victorian England than he does today. To discover more about the food of the past we must turn to classes, groups, and actual people, their earnings and expenses, and, where possible, their budgets and household accounts. It is right to start with the occupation which in this period was still the largest of all, that of the agricultural labourer.

Notes

1 Mitchell, B.R. and Deane, Phyllis (1962) *Abstract of British Historical Statistics. Population and Vital Statistics* 8, 24 et seq.
2 Ashley, Sir William (1928) *The Bread of our Forefathers*, 1–8.
3 Fay, C.R. (1923–5) 'The miller and the baker: a note on commercial transition 1770–1837', *Cambridge Historical Journal* I, 89.
4 Eden, Sir Frederic (1797) *The State of the Poor* I, 496–7.
5 Clapham, J.H. (1939) *An Economic History of Modern Britain*, vol. 1, *The Early Railway Age (1820–1850)*, 158.
6 McCulloch, J.R. (1846) *A Dictionary, Practical, Theoretical and Historical, of Commerce and Commercial Navigation*, 182.
7 Cobbett, William (1823) *Cottage Economy*, no. III, para. 82.
8 Acton, Eliza (1857) *The English Bread Book*, 85.
9 Davies, Rev. David (1795) *The Case of Labourers in Husbandry*, 118.
10 Clapham, op. cit., 159, quoting from the Report of the Select Committee on Agriculture (1833), 9802.
11 Baxter, John (1944) *The Organization of the Brewing Industry*, unpublished University of London Ph.D. thesis.
12 Tuck, John (1822) *The Private Brewer's Guide*, 23.
13 Wilson, George B. (1940) *Alcohol and the Nation*, 55.
14 Blackman, Janet (1963) 'The food supply of an industrial town. A study of Sheffield's public markets, 1780–1900', *Business History* V (2 June), 83–97, to which I am much indebted in this section.
15 Dodd, George (1856) *The Food of London*, chap. III, 101 et seq.
16 Mingay, G.E. (1986) *The Transformation of Britain, 1830–1939*, 63–4.
17 Porter, G.R. (1847) *The Progress of the Nation* (new edn), 37–8.
18 Davies, op. cit., 21.
19 Oddy, D.J. (1977) Discussion of 'Changing patterns of food consumption in the United Kingdom' by T.C. Barker in John Yudkin (ed.) *Diet of Man: Needs and Wants*, 181.
20 Salaman, R.N. (1949) *The History and Social Influence of the Potato*. His figures were derived from Lord Ernle's dubious calculations of the acreage and annual yield of wheat in Britain. Translated into 'wheat availability' per head per day, and including imports, these give:

1825 1.6 lb   1835 1.5 lb   1840 1.5 lb   1843 1.3 lb   1846 1.25 lb
1847 1.5 lb   1851 1.6 lb   1860 1.7 lb   1870 1.9 lb   1879 2.0 lb

21 Porter, op. cit. (1851 edn), 538.
22 Salaman, op. cit., 613.
23 Salaman, op. cit., quoted in E.P. Thompson (1980) *The Making of the English Working Class* (Pelican edn), 348.
24 Williams, E.F. (1976) 'The development of the meat industry', in Derek J. Oddy and Derek S. Miller (eds), *The Making of the Modern British Diet*, 47.
25 Somerville, Alexander (1848) *The Autobiography of a Working Man, by One Who Has Whistled at the Plough*, 151.
26 Caird, James (1880) *The Landed Interest and the Supply of Food*, quoted in

Betty McNamee (1966) 'Trends in meat consumption', in T.C. Barker, J.C. McKenzie, and John Yudkin (eds) *Our Changing Fare. Two Hundred Years of British Food Habits*, 77.

27 Dodd, op. cit., 562.

28 Williams, op. cit., 50.

29 Hobsbawm, E.J. 'The British standard of living, 1790–1850', reprinted in Arthur J. Taylor (ed.) (1975) *The Standard of Living in Britain in the Industrial Revolution*, 78.

30 Hartwell, R.M. 'The rising standard of living in England, 1800–1850', in Taylor, ibid., 114.

31 The best accounts, on which I have drawn heavily here, are by W.H. Chaloner, 'Trends in fish consumption', in *Our Changing Fare*, op. cit., 94–114; T.C. Barker and John Yudkin (eds) (1971) *Fish in Britain: Trends in its Supply, Distribution and Consumption during the Past Two Centuries*, Department of Nutrition, Queen Elizabeth College, University of London; C.L. Cutting (1955) *Fish Saving*.

32 Chaloner, op. cit., 97.

33 Stern, Walter M. (1971) 'The fish supply to Billingsgate from the nineteenth century to the Second World War', in *Fish in Britain*, op. cit., 34.

34 Oddy, D.J. (1971) 'The changing techniques and structure of the fishing industry', in *Fish in Britain*, op. cit., 14.

35 Chaloner, op. cit., 106.

36 Mayhew, Henry (1851) *London Labour and the London Poor* I, 62.

37 ibid., 63.

38 Quoted in Thompson, op. cit., 336. The witness was R.M. Martin, author of *Taxation of the British Empire*, 1833.

39 Northcote, Stafford H. (1862) *Twenty Years of Financial Policy*, 65–6.

40 Porter, op. cit. (1847 edn), 559–60.

41 Chaloner, W.H. and Henderson, W.O. (1956) 'Friedrich Engels and the England of the 1840s', *History Today* (July), 456.

42 Porter, op. cit. (1851 edn), 541–3.

43 Porter, op. cit. (1851 edn), 562.

44 ibid., 549.

45 Wilson, op, cit., 331–3 (Appendix F, Table I).

46 'Comparative statement of the income and expenditure of certain families of the working classes in Manchester and Dukinfield in the years 1836 and 1841', *Journal of the Statistical Society* IV, 332.

47 Quoted in 'Consumption of food in the United Kingdom', *Quarterly Review* (April 1854), 589.

48 *Manchester Guardian*, 4 February 1843, 5.

2
The agricultural labourer

The standard of life from 1800 to 1834 sank to the lowest possible scale; in the south and west wages paid by employers fell to 3s to 4s per week, augmented by parochial relief from the pockets of those who had no need of labour; and insufficient food has left its mark in the physical degeneracy of the peasantry. Herded together in cottages which, by their imperfect arrangements, violated every sanitary law, generated all kinds of disease, and rendered modesty an unimaginable thing . . . compelled by insufficient wages to expose their wives to the degradation of field labour, and to send their children to work as soon as they could crawl . . . [the labourers] would have been more than human had they not risen in an insurrection which could only be quelled by force. They had already carried patience beyond the limit where it ceases to be a virtue.[1]

Such was the gloomy view of Rowland Prothero, Lord Ernle, the foremost agricultural historian of his day, a view which was fully endorsed by the first-hand evidence of contemporaries and the compilers of Parliamentary Blue Books, and which modern writers would wish to qualify, if at all, only in points of detail. The fact that Ernle's forecasts for the future of English farming proved to be wrong does not invalidate his judgement of the past.

The food of the agricultural labourer depended upon his general standard of living, and that standard depended, in turn, on the state of the agricultural economy of which he was a part. In good times, he might fare not too badly, in bad ones he was the first to suffer, and the difficulty was that agricultural prosperity was determined by a number of external factors – the demand for farm produce, the movement of prices, the extent of foreign competition – over which he had no influence. Uneducated and unenfranchised, immobilized by poverty and the Poor Laws, the labourer was peculiarly exposed to the vicissitudes of trade and the seasons, and in no real sense the master of his own destiny.

Since the outbreak of the French wars in 1793, farming had been chronically unstable. Increased demand for food from the growing population, inflation caused by the government's issue of paper currency, and Napoleon's attempted blockade of our shores between them produced a period of exceptionally high prices from which landed proprietors and farmers benefited more than wage-earners.[2] Open lands continued to be enclosed apace, heaths and uplands to be ploughed for arable which would just yield a profit at the unprecedented prices which wheat was now fetching.[3] Intensive farming for profit on the lines advocated by the 'improvers' was the order of the day on all estates large enough to take advantage of the new techniques.

These problems were compounded by a series of particularly poor harvests. Throughout the twenty-two years of war, harvests were of average yield in only six years, and there was a run of disastrous failures between 1809 and 1814.[4] In Kent, wartime scarcities and inflation pushed up the price of bread by 167 per cent between 1793 and 1812, well ahead of wage rises, forcing labourers to reallocate their expenditure away from relative luxuries such as meat, tea, and sugar. Dr T.L. Richardson has calculated that food and drink absorbed 67.7 per cent of the labourer's household expenditure at this time, but between 1793 and 1812 expenditure on bread and flour alone rose from 48 per cent of total food outlay to 74.2 per cent, while that on meat fell from 26.2 per cent to a mere 6 per cent.[5] The expansion of arable farming during the war years also resulted in greater irregularity of employment – a heavy demand for labour at harvest time but, for many day-labourers, underemployment or even unemployment for up to eight months in the year. Even in the 1790s, before many of the worst effects were felt, the Rev. David Davies had noted that in his Berkshire parish no labourer's family ate fresh meat, and few could afford more than 1 lb of bacon weekly; tea, at 1–1½ oz a week of the poorest quality, was the main drink, beer being quite out of reach 'except against a lying-in or a christening'. Since enclosure, no labourers kept cows, and milk, which had previously been a principal article of diet, was now virtually unobtainable. Almost all families, however careful, had a budget deficit, which was only made up by poaching, stealing, debt, or parish relief.[6]

Another development also produced an important change in the position of the labourer. In former times, large numbers of farm servants had lived in the farmhouse, boarded and lodged as part of their wage, and by all accounts boarded very well. In Hampshire, labourers 'living-in' with their employers generally fed on pork and pudding the greatest part of the year, 'except on Sundays, when a joint of meat is sometimes allowed'.[7] Well-fed labourers did not regard the pig as being in the same class as beef. In Middlesex, they had 'bread and cheese and pork for breakfast, coarse joints of beef boiled with cabbages and other vegetables, or meat pies or puddings for dinner, cold pork, bread and cheese, etc. for supper; and with every meal, small beer'.[8] But now the farmer produced for the market, and the less his household consumed, the more he had to sell. Increased wealth also engendered more polite manners and a desire for social segregation. Midday dinner in the farmhouse kitchen with the servants survived on some old-fashioned farms, especially in the north, though even here the trend was for the farmer and his family to eat at a separate, cloth-covered table while the labourers sat round a plain, scrubbed board at a distance. Beginning in the last decade of the eighteenth century, in the southern and midland counties, labourers were increasingly put on board wages and forced to live out, and although they received more money their standard of comfort unquestionably fell. The budgets of these 'free' labourers, collected by Davies and evaluated in present-day nutritional terms by Professor D.J. Oddy, indicate very inadequate levels of intake – only 1,900 kilocalories of energy value per person per day, 49 g of protein, 31 of fat, and 0.25 of calcium.[9]

Boarding-out was, then, the consequence of the high prices of the 'good years'. Even more disastrous for the labourer were the effects of the depression and the low prices which began in 1813 and lasted for more than twenty years. With the fall of Napoleon fell the best protection the English farmer had ever had, and not even the Corn Law could compensate him adequately. In 1813, wheat had still fetched 120s a quarter; in 1815 it stood at 76s and in 1822 only 53s. 'What we need is another war,' complained one farmer to Cobbett in that year.

In 1816 a melancholy Report on the Agricultural State of the Kingdom was issued by the Board of Agriculture, which chronicled the industry's rapid descent from prosperity to depression. For landowners and farmers it was a story of disastrous falls in profits, untenanted farms, and uncollected rents, for labourers of conditions of misery 'beyond all experience'. Of 273 letters received from all parts of the country in reply to the Board's questionnaire, 237 described lack of employment and evidence of labourers' distress. In Berkshire there was 'a great want of employ', in Buckinghamshire the labourers were 'very wretched from want of employment', in Cambridgeshire conditions were 'dreadful . . . healthy young men working for 4s a week', in Norfolk between one-quarter and one-third were out of work. Only in a minority of cases, where the labourer was allowed a little land to keep a cow or two, was he described as 'in a comfortable state, and . . . very generally equally sober, honest and industrious'.[10]

Falling prices, not only of wheat, but of meat and other foods, might, of course, have benefited the labourer had not his wages also fallen and become artificially determined by the extraordinary operation of the Poor Laws. Since the period of rapid inflation in the late eighteenth century a new problem of poverty had appeared in England, of labourers, who although fully employed, could not support themselves, their wives and families, out of their earnings. As early as 1795 the Rev. David Davies had concluded from his survey of the budgets of his parishioners in Berkshire that the earnings of a labourer and his wife were not sufficient to support a family of more than two children without parish relief, and the gap between wages and the prices of necessities was to widen in succeeding years. Less fortunate still were the growing numbers of those who could obtain work only from spring until harvest, and in winter would be utterly destitute. The old Elizabethan Poor Law was incapable of dealing with the new problems, and new remedies were proposed. First, in 1782, Gilbert's Act provided that work should be sought for the unemployed by the parish officers: wages would be paid directly to the parish, which would then reimburse the labourer with a sufficient maintenance. Next, in 1795, as a result of the decision of the Berkshire magistrates at Speenhamland, a similar system was extended to the employed poor whose wages were inadequate: they were to receive an 'allowance' from the parish calculated by reference to the prevailing price of bread and the number of children in the family.[11]

The effects of the new policies were fully manifested only in the years of depression after 1813. Widespread unemployment was inevitable as wheat prices tumbled and land went out of cultivation. However little the farmer paid, the labourer's wage was now made up to something approaching subsistence level by the 'bread and children' scale. Speenhamland now came in for strong criticism – that it had the positive effect of keeping wages artificially low, probably of favouring the lazy and shiftless because the unemployed labourer received exactly the same as the man who toiled for fourteen hours a day, possibly, as the Rev. Thomas Malthus claimed, of encouraging large families. By 1830, it had pauperized much of the agricultural south and east, and had reduced thousands of labourers into miserable dependence on parsimonious charity. Within one generation, high prices had first transformed the farm servant into a day labourer; low prices and the Poor Law had turned the day labourer into a pauper. The wave of incendiarism which spread over East Anglia and the home counties in the winter of 1830–1 was a modest demonstration by a population brought to breaking-point.[12]

A few years before this, in 1824, Parliament had made the first serious attempt to investigate the labourer's position by conducting a survey of agricultural wages.[13] That they had become miserably depressed there could be no doubt. In some southern counties they were as little as 3s a week for a single man and 4s 6d for a married man – no more, that is, than the scale permitted for a pauper – in some they were 5s, in others 8s or 9s. Astonishing variations were disclosed within small areas: in the district of Wingham in Kent, for example, wages in some parishes were 6d a day, and in others 1s 6d. Although bread prices had fallen by up to half by 1824 most wages had been reduced in line, and the labourer's purchasing power was no greater than in the years of high prices; in any case, his standard of life was now primarily determined by whether he could

24

obtain, and keep, regular employment. Over the country as a whole wages were lowest in the south and east, where the 'allowance' system was general, highest in the north and west, where it was not so universal and where there was often alternative industrial employment to be had. In Oldham, for example, a labourer could earn 12s a week, and in Cumberland up to 15s.

Wage figures indicate the fact of wide variations in the labourer's standard of life, but not much more. They do not tell us for how many weeks in the year wages were drawn, the extent of the wife's and children's contribution to the total earnings, the amount of the 'allowance', if any, or the value of 'extras'. We know that the price of many necessaries remained high, and it would also appear that house rent, an important item in the labourer's budget, soared in the 1820s:

> It is one of the chief causes of the agricultural labourers being in a worse state than they ever were [one witness told the 1824 Committee]. Before the War, the average rent of cottages with good gardens was 30s a year; it is now in our own neighbourhood commonly as high as five, seven, or even ten pounds per annum, and where cottages are in the hands of farmers, they always prohibit the labourers from keeping a pig, and claim the produce of the apple trees and of the vine which usually covers the house.[14]

The Committee was concerned with the amount of wages, and not with how they were expended, but one labourer, Thomas Smart, gave some description of his standard of life. He was then forty-six years old, having married at eighteen. He had had thirteen children, seven of whom were living, and the only parish relief he had ever had was for the burial of his children. By good luck and hard work he had always enjoyed steady employment. In 1812, just before the depression, he had earned 12s a week: now it was 8s. At harvest he made an extra 40s, and three of his children earned between them 6s a week. He lived almost entirely on bread and cheese, had often touched no meat for a month, got now and then a little bacon and sometimes a halfpennyworth of milk, but the farmers did not like selling it. His usual drink was tea. He had no pig, but he did have a garden where he grew potatoes. House rent and fuel cost £5 a year, shoes 15s for himself and £1 for the family. The fall in the price of salt had been a great help to him.

The eye-witness account can sometimes enliven the sober pages of Parliamentary reports. In his *Rural Rides*, compiled between 1822 and 1830, Willam Cobbett described the conditions of agriculture in southern England in a tone of passionate indignation. For all his prejudices, Cobbett was a countryman with a sharp eye and a sound judgement of land and men, and it was the decay and the miserable faces of the poor that everywhere most struck him. Derelict farms, farmhouses, and parsonages were everywhere to be seen, and churches large enough for a congregation of a thousand crumbled in deserted villages. But, by contrast, there were still grand houses and rich estates, the properties of absentee landlords, politicians, stockjobbers, and sinecurists from 'the great Wen' (London). Honest farmers were forced to sell out and emigrate, and the peasants were 'the worst used labouring people upon the face of the earth. Dogs and hogs and horses are treated with more civility, and as to food and lodging, how gladly would the labourers change with them!'[15] Cobbett estimated the needs of a family of five in bread, meat, and beer alone at £62 6s 8d a year: the labourer's wage in the wealthy parish of Milton was 9s a week, and the maximum parish 'allowance' would give another 7s 6d, so at best he could only earn half of the minumum necessary for what Cobbett, the traditionalist, regarded as 'basic foods'.[16] So it was throughout almost the whole area – starvation wages, and for the unemployed, an 'allowance' to support a family which was less than the pay of a single soldier. Near Warminster, the overseer had set thirty men to dig a twelve-acre field: at a wage of 9d a day it was as cheap as ploughing, though how the men could live on 4s a week was not disclosed:

> The labourers here look as if they were half-starved. . . . For my own part, I really am ashamed to ride a fat horse, to have a full belly, and to have a clean shirt upon my back when I look at these wretched countrymen of mine; while I actually see them reeling with weakness; when I see their poor faces present me nothing but skin and bone.

Only in Sussex did Cobbett find conditions which pleased him. Here the labourers' cottages had an appearance of comfort, with neat gardens full of vegetables – and not the cursed potato, 'Ireland's lazy root'. Near Eastdean, he talked to a young turnip-hoer who was sitting under a hedge at breakfast:

> He came running to me with his victuals in his hand; and I was glad to see that his food consisted of a good lump of household bread and not a very small piece of bacon. . . . In parting with him I said, 'You do get some bacon then?' 'Oh yes, Sir,' said he, with an emphasis and a swag of the head which seemed to say 'We must and will have that'. I saw, and with great delight, a pig at almost every labourer's house. . . . What sort of breakfast would this man have had in a mess of cold potatoes? Could he have worked, and worked in the wet too, with such food? Monstrous! No society ought to exist where the labourers live in a hog-like sort of way.[17]

Cobbett was, of course, a traditionalist, who roundly condemned the labourer for his new-fangled foods of tea and baker's bread, and exhorted him to return to the proper food of an Englishman. His greatest strictures were reserved for the potato, which he found was becoming the staple article of diet in many southern and south-western counties: it was not long since it had only been used to any great extent in Lancashire and Cheshire, but poverty and the potato, in Cobbett's eyes, went together. 'It is an undeniable fact that in proportion as this root is in use as a substitute for bread, the people are underfed.'[18] Certainly, Ireland was wretched enough in Cobbett's day, but the Irish peasant on his diet of potatoes, a little fat, and milk, was often better fed than the English labourer. Apparently what Cobbett particularly objected to was the fact that it was so easy to cultivate and cook, and therefore engendered 'slovenly and beastly habits amongst the labouring classes'.

Most contemporary writers who offered advice to the labourer in the form of cookery books and manuals of domestic economy followed Cobbett's line. Esther Copley, whose *Cottage Comforts* and *Cottage Cookery* circulated widely in the 1820s and 1830s, also condemned the beer-shop and the tea-kettle and suggested that the labourer might drink instead pure water or infusions of rue and strawberry leaves, 'which will give the flavour of green tea'. Possibly Miss Copley was right in saying that 'The want and misery of many families arise more from want of discretion in managing their resources than from the real scantiness of their income',[19] but to feed a family adequately on 4s or 5s a week would have required more than 'discretion'. The lady advised the poor that, when wheat was dear, good bread could be made out of mixtures of maize, barley, and rye, which was common practice anyway, and suggested that fuel could be saved by placing a lump of chalk under the coals, which would retain the heat for a long while. Her *Cottage Cookery* was a collection of economical recipes – potato-pie, stirabout, stewed ox-cheek, scrappie and so on – not all of which sound very appetizing; the directions for 'mutton chitterlings', for example, suggest that they should be obtained immediately the animal is killed, scoured many times in salt and water, and put to soak, the water being frequently changed for twenty-four hours: 'this must be repeated till they are quite white and free from smell'.[20]

Contemporary writers were unanimous in blaming the labourer for his extravagant diet, and tireless in demonstrating that by better management he might have more meat and more variety in his meals. None of them seemed to appreciate the obstacles to domestic baking and brewing which we have discussed earlier, or to recognize that white bread and tea were no longer luxuries, but the irreducible minimum below which was only starvation. These foods were not, in fact, extravagant. White bread, unlike the coarse, household bread, could be eaten without the addition of costly butter or cheese, and 2 oz of tea a week, costing 8d or 9d, made many a cold supper seem like a hot meal. In the margin of my copy of Cobbett's *Cottage Economy*, against the section on 'home baking', is the comment in a contemporary hand, 'Homes have ceased in England and that is why we emigrate'.

The radical reform of the Poor Law undertaken in 1834 seems to have had little immediate effect on the labourer's standard of life. The two most important principles of the new Act – the substitution of workhouse relief for the 'allowance' for the able-bodied, and the abrogation of the parish's responsibility of finding work for the unemployed – were designed, in part, to force him into independence and to dissipate the pools of labour which had kept wages low. Once wages were freed from the depressive effect of the 'allowance' it was hoped they would gradually climb back to a subsistence level. What the Amendment Act could not do, however, was to create employment in areas where there was still a surplus of labour, and in a period of renewed agricultural distress in the late thirties, it is scarcely surprising that the hopes of higher wages remained unfulfilled. A Parliamentary report in 1836 stated that 'wages still only suffice for the necessaries, I cannot say for the comforts',[21] while a similar report the next year showed that of fifty people relieved in one parish in 1834, only eighteen were in full work three years later; of the rest nineteen were in casual employment, four 'gone away', two transported, one in prison, one dead, five old and infirm.[22] Wage-levels seem, in fact, to have followed closely on changes in prices – a fall down to 1837 as prices fell, thereafter a slight increase as prices rose – and to have been largely independent of the new Act. A calculation by Purdy that the average wage rose from 9s 4d per week in 1824 to 10s 4d in 1837[23] means little because it does not take account of the increased price of corn or the fact that at the earlier date the labourer was probably receiving an 'allowance' in aid of wages.

The disappearance of the 'allowance' almost certainly meant that the labourer was compelled, to a much greater extent than formerly, to sell the labour of his wife and children in order to maintain his standard. This meant that the economic position of a man with a family of employable age (usually ten and upwards, though not uncommonly from seven or eight) tended to become considerably better than that of the single man – Dr Kay calculated that with four children in work, the family's earnings were more than doubled.[24] The expansion of the 'gang system' of employment of women and children was, therefore, an important though indirect effect of the New Poor Law.

Clearly, it is impossible to generalize about the standard of living of the labourer at this period. It varied with the size and age of his family, with different parts of the country and different times of the year, and, not least, with the degree of skill of the man himself, for it is wrong to suppose that all farmworkers were unskilled, and equally rated. The 'yearly men' with responsible positions, whom no farmer could afford to have underpaid or discontented, fared very much better than the day-labourers who, unfortunately, constituted the majority. The former were described as having 'the comfortable supper of Norfolk dumplings, potatoes, and, now and then, a little bacon or other meat', and living in cottages 'brightened with pictures, brass candlesticks, and perhaps a clock'.[25] Equally noticeable was the contrast betwen north and south, first mentioned by Sir Frederic Eden in the 1790s, but still true in the 1830s and later. A Scottish contributor to the *Quarterly Journal of Agriculture* in 1836 said that:

> In Scotland, milk and oatmeal make a plentiful house, and our ablest plough-men take nothing more. Potatoes, which the children of our gentry prefer to bread, are regarded with considerable scorn by labourers in the south of England. What an English labourer spends on his bacon, beer, and white bread is, in the hilly parts of Scotland, spent by the Scottish labourer on the education of his children.[26]

For 'Scotland' here may be read Cumberland, Westmorland, and the northernmost counties generally, but the strictures on the diet of the southern labourer were unjust. In the north, oatmeal was made palatable by the addition of milk, which was rarely available to the southern labourer who had no cow-pasture of his own and could not persuade farmers to go to the trouble of selling him a pint or two. More important, the conditions of service were quite different in the north. The yearly hiring of labour persisted much longer here, and it was still customary for the labourer to receive part of his wages in meal or grain, irrespective of the market prices, and to be given cow-pasture or accommodation for pig or poultry. For all these reasons the economic position of the northern labourer was more stable, and more conducive to thrift and frugality than it was in the south, where the only 'perquisite' many labourers ever received was a gallon of ale or cider in the harvest-field.[27]

A series of vivid and harrowing pictures of the life of this period was brought together in a volume published in 1904 by T. Fisher Unwin entitled *The Hungry Forties: Life Under the Bread Tax*. It was a collection of letters and other testimonies from contemporary witnesses, most of them agricultural labourers, and contained many references to the food which they had as children in the 1840s. This is, incidentally, apparently the first use of the term 'hungry forties', which was not a contemporary expression.[28] A Sussex woodman, Charles Robinson, told how in his 'younger days' (he was eighty-three at the time of the inquiry) the usual wage for field work was 9s a week, and a half-gallon loaf of bread (4 lb 5½ oz) cost 1s 2d, and so the family often lived on 'crammings':

> Made of what was left after the flour and the bran was taken away, and . . . mixed with a little bread flour, we called crammings; but more often we made a sort of pudding with it. You ask 'ow the people did get on? Well, they got into debt, and then again they lived on 'taters' and kept pigs, but butcher's meat we never 'eard of, never saw it except in the shops. Salt was 21s a bushel, and

when we killed a pig we 'ad to sell 'alf of it to buy the salt to salt down what was left.[29]

Charles Astridge of Midhurst also spoke of 'crammings', and testified:

We mostly lived on bread, but 'twasn't bread like 'ee get now; 'twas that heavy and doughy 'ee could pull long strings of it out of your mouth. They called it 'growy bread'. But 'twas fine compared with the porridge we made out of bruised beans; that made your inside feel as if 'twas on fire, and sort of choked 'ee. In those days we'd see children from Duck Lane come out in the streets of Midhurst an' pick up a bit of bread, and even potato peelings.[30]

Other witnesses spoke of the way that tea was eked out with burnt crusts of bread – at least it coloured the water and looked not unlike the real thing – of supper which consisted of a small pot of potatoes or a swede or turnip stolen from the fields, and of relieving the pangs of hunger with pig pease or horse beans. The melancholy picture which emerges is of a population which spent its life in semi-starvation, existing on a scanty and monotonous diet of bread, potatoes, root vegetables, and weak tea. Fresh meat was scarcely ever seen, unless the labourer dared to incur the severity of the game laws by poaching a rabbit or a hare; 'meat' meant salt pork or bacon, and a family was fortunate if it could afford these more than once a week. It is also clear that wheat flour was often of poor quality, and that rye bread and the even less attractive barley bread were still extensively used in the 1840s especially in the midlands and north. The one redeeming feature in the diet seems to have been the considerable quantities of vegetables – potatoes, beans, onions, turnips, cabbages, and so on – which the labourer unwillingly consumed.

As a picture of rural life in the 1840s, the accounts are probably substantially true. But they could be equally true as a description of the 1830s or the 1850s – indeed, some of them specifically refer to periods earlier or later than that which was supposedly the most 'hungry'. A Hertfordshire labourer spoke of the 1820s as his time of special distress, and at least two witnesses referred to the Crimean War (1854–6) as the worst in their memories. Again, for many the hungriest time was their early married life when they had families too young to be employed. Personal factors of this kind – the number and age of the children, the health of the chief bread-winner and his wife – were what mattered most, together with the state of the harvest and the demand for labour. During a period of good yields in the mid-1830s few complaints are heard, but scarcity and high prices in 1838–9, followed by a depression in industry which reduced the demand for agricultural produce, brought renewed troubles and discontent which found expression in a fresh outbreak of rick-burnings.

This time, however, a growing social conscience interested itself in the causes of the labourer's plight. Letters and articles appeared in *The Times* and in the local presses. Both Houses of Parliament debated the situation at length, and in 1843 an official report was issued which is of the highest importance for the revealing picture it gives of labouring life.[31] Although it was concerned primarily with the work and wages of women and children in agriculture, much evidence was given incidentally about diet, housing, and the standard of life generally, and again it is abundantly clear that this standard varied greatly with the circumstances of different families. The man's wage might be as little as 8s a week, but total family earnings as much as 18s – most incomes lay somewhere between the two extremes: Wiltshire, Dorset, and the south-western counties were still the poorest of all, East Anglia somewhat better, Yorkshire and Northumberland best of all; but all parts of the country had some grievances in common. Everywhere there were complaints about the high cost of house rents, the profiteering by village shopkeepers who often exploited their indebted customers, and the farmer's 'allowance' of beer or cider which both reduced wages and encouraged drunkenness.

Of Wiltshire, the report said:

> The food of the labourer and his family is wheaten bread, potatoes, a small quantity of beer, but only as a luxury, and a little butter and tea. To this may sometimes be added (but it is difficult to say how often or in what quantities) cheese, bacon, and in the neighbourhood of Calne, a portion of the entrails of the pig – a considerable trade being carried on at Calne in curing bacon. I am inclined to think that the use of bacon and these parts of the pig occurs where the earnings of the family are not limited to those of the husband. . . . Where from poverty bacon cannot be obtained, a little fat is used to give a flavour to the potatoes.[32]

A doctor of Calne testified that four out of every five women labourers who came to him for treatment suffered from complaints traceable to their food being 'insufficient in quantity and not good enough in quality' – he categorized diseases of the stomach, general debility, liability to fever, indigestion, and slow and difficult recovery from any illness. Among children scrofulous diseases were 'very common'. This witness went on to point out that in the Union Workhouse, where food was bought more cheaply by tender, the average cost of feeding each inmate was 1s 6d a week. How, he asked, could a labourer support even two children on 8s a week when, in addition to food, there was house rent, fuel, clothing, boots, medicine, and so on? 'When I reckon up these things in detail I am always more and more astonished how the labourers continue to live at all.'[33] The diet of a Calne stonemason, who earned almost twice as much as this (15s a week) was scarcely lavish. 'In the garden we raise plenty of potatoes. We have about a shilling's worth of meat a week; a pig's milt sometimes, a pound or three-quarters of a pound of suet, seven gallons of bread a week, sometimes a little pudding on a Sunday.' But this would have seemed like luxury to a poor widow and her eight-year-old son. When her husband was alive:

> We did very well, and lived very comfortable, for then we had four gallons of bread a week, 1 lb or 1½ lb of cheese, bacon, salt beef, butter, tea, sugar, candles, and soap, with beer on Saturday night. Since my husband's death, the Guardians allow 1s 6d a week for the child, and I earn 4s 6d a week. I pay:

	s	d	
For rent	1	6	a week
1½ gallons bread	1	6	
½ lb candles ⎫ ½ lb soap ⎭		4½	
¼ lb butter		2¾	
Tea		1½	
¼ lb sugar		2	
Rent of allotment		5¼	
	4s	4d	

> The 1s 8d that is left goes for firing, shoes, which cost a great deal, etc. My husband hired 54 lugs of land, and I continued it after his death; without it, I could not get on. It produces just potatoes enough for me and my child, also this last year, three bushels of wheat. I manage the ground entirely myself.[34]

The diet of East Anglia followed a similar pattern – bread and potatoes the great staples, small amounts of butter, cheese, tea and bacon, fresh meat rarely, if ever, flour dumplings and a red herring the occasional treats. From Lavenham, in Suffolk, comes a detailed account of earnings and expenditure from a woman 'whose family always appears clean and neat, and whose children are brought up to industrial [sic] habits'. In this family of two adults and five children, the husband's wage went entirely on bread; the earnings of his wife and three children, the youngest only eight, had to cover everything else:

Name	Age	Earnings		Expenditure		
		s	d		s	d
Robert Crick	42	9	0	Bread	9	0
				Potatoes	1	0
Wife	40		9	Rent	1	2
				Tea		2
Boy	12	2	0	Sugar		3½
				Soap		3

Name	Age	Earnings		Expenditure		
		s	d		s	d
ditto	11	1	0	Blue		$\frac{1}{2}$
				Thread etc.		2
ditto	8	1	0	Candles		3
				Salt		$\frac{1}{2}$
Girl	6	—		Coal and wood		9
				Butter		$4\frac{1}{2}$
Boy	4	—		Cheese		3
Total earnings		13s	9d	Total expenditure	13s	9d

But there are numbers of families who, although in the possession of the same amount of wages shown above, do not dispose of it with such frugality, but appear in the greatest state of destitution; many others, with the same number of children, do not get the wages this man's family have. The family I have given as an example is more to show you that with industry and frugality, their diet consists principally of bread and potatoes. There are, however, some who, when their families are grown up, by putting their earnings together, occasionally get a piece of meat at their supper-time, and their Sunday dinner.[35]

The vicar of Bexwell in Norfolk also testified that the food of his parishioners was principally bread, potatoes, and tea. 'The best and most careful labourers have bacon, and other meat twice or perhaps three times a week; but I have no hesitation in saying that no independent labourer can obtain the diet which is given in the Union Workhouse.' In mid-century, the amount of money spent each week by an adult worker in rural Norfolk was estimated at only 2s 0½d, the lowest amount in any agricultural county and only half that of a Northumbrian worker. Even so, Dr Anne Digby has noted that the Norfolk labourer's wife was renowned for her economical housekeeping and her ability to conjure a nutritious meal out of a few ingredients:

A typical cheap meal for a growing family was provided by a vegetable stew enlivened by a few scraps of meat or bacon and made more substantial by the addition of Norfolk dumplings. . . . Once a week there was butcher's meat, or bacon from a home-reared pig, while in coastal areas there might also be herrings. . . . Some tea or sugar, but very little milk or eggs were consumed, and butter, lard or cheese were almost luxuries.[36]

The best of the eastern counties was, it seeme, Lincolnshire. One witness said that 'labourers here are generally better fixed than in any county in England', which was almost certainly untrue, but at least there was more meat and more milk in the diet than in Norfolk and Suffolk. Bread and potatoes were still the great staples, but some labourers managed to get bacon every day, and vegetables, butter, cheese, and dumplings appear in the diet, as well as sugar and treacle. No doubt the lion's share of the meat went to the husband, and, as a butcher from Brigg testified, 'The women say they live on tea: they have tea three times a day, sop, bread, and treacle', yet there does seem to be less of the deadly monotony here than elsewhere. Probably this was because in some Lincolnshire parishes at least the labourer had a cottage and garden rent-free, a rood of land (a quarter acre) for potatoes, and the keep of a pig: some were even able to pasture a cow in return for some deduction in their wage. Such perquisites made a huge difference to the labourer's diet and general standard of life.[37]

In the last area to be investigated, the northern counties of Yorkshire and Northumberland, diet was still more varied and nutritious. In addition to the now universal bread, potatoes, and tea, there was milk and broth, oatmeal porridge and hasty pudding, pies and bacon much more frequently than in the south. The labourer was able to make significant contributions to his larder from the produce of his own garden or allotment, and the frequent mention of milk in the diet suggests that many had the use of a cow-pasture as well as a potato patch. In the East Riding a particularly high standard was ensured by the practice of feeding the labourer in the farmhouse and deducting 1s a day from his wage. Farmers apparently believed that they got more work out of their men by feeding them well: some labourers no doubt liked the system, but there must have been others who resented a 6s a week deduction from a wage of 13s, and were ashamed to take home to their families scarcely more than they had consumed in dinners.[38] From Bolton Percy, near York, came a budget which must have represented almost the pinnacle of a labourer's expectations. J. Allen earned the unusually high wage of 14s a week, while occasional earnings by his wife and one boy added another £14 7s 5d during the year 1841–2, bringing the total to £50 11s 9d. In this comfortable family of two adults and five children flour (this was home-baking territory) took £19 0s 5d – only two-fifths of the budget; £4 17s 1d went on butcher's meat, £3 10s 0d on sugar, tea, and coffee and £1 6s 4d on milk. Items such as treacle, rice, eggs, and apples appeared in this diet, while there was even 6s a year for the children's schooling and 17s 4d for contributions to a clothing club.[39]

In Northumberland, diet approached closely to the Scottish pattern with oatmeal porridge, bread made from barley and pea-meal mixed, milk, potatoes, and bacon. Eggs, butter, sugar, fruit pies, and treacle are also frequently mentioned, tea and coffee not so commonly as in the south. The improved standard of diet here was related to the system of employment by which the hind instead of receiving a weekly wage was hired for the year and received most of his wage in kind. In addition to a given number of bushels of wheat, oats, barley, rye, and peas, the labourer had a cottage and garden free, cow-pasture, and a potato-ground, coals, wood, and a few pounds in cash.[40] This, the so-called 'yearly bondage' system, although it was resented by some, probably produced a higher standard of living for the labourer than was found anywhere else in the country.

These, then, were the real conditions of rural life in the 'hungry forties'. To try to estimate whether they had deteriorated or not seems a somewhat unprofitable exercise when, by present-day standards, the whole of the first half of the nineteenth century was miserably hungry for many labourers. Several contributors to T. Fisher Unwin's volume said that in their young days they could scarcely ever remember not feeling hungry, and this must have been the experience of all but a fortunate minority. This was a population existing on the edge of starvation. Many died in the first few weeks and months of life, fundamentally of under-nourishment, and those who survived to go out to long hours of field-work at nine or ten years old had inherited their strength from sturdier ancestors. Moreover, it was a stock continually degenerating as thousands of the most ambitious and enterprising left the country which could not offer them a tolerable maintenance for America and the colonies. Ironically, it was the abundant produce of the new lands overseas which ultimately rescued the English labourer from his wretchedness.

But in the first half of the century, before education, trade unions, and the franchise had begun to bring power and articulation to the labourer, his resentment at the conditions of his life could often be expressed only in outbreaks of violence. Although the numerous labourers' riots of the period included a variety of grievances and demands – a minimum wage of 2s a day, improved poor relief, and the withdrawal of the threshing machines which were taking away winter employment – food was often at the basis of the discontent, as it had been in the bread riots of the eighteenth century. In 1816, when much of Norfolk, Suffolk, and Cambridgeshire was in turmoil, the cry was for 'Bread or Blood'.[41] The Swing Riots which spread over much of southern and eastern England in 1830–1 concerned low wages, seasonal unemployment, and the high cost of food. In 1836 and 1837 Norfolk labourers plundered flour from the carts of Poor Law Relieving Officers, while in Kent in 1838 'Sir' William Courtenay led his band of followers under the emblem of a loaf of bread on a pole.[42] Hunger and anger were fused in these risings, and in the rick-burnings that lit the night skies in many counties during the 1830s and 1840s. One terse comment in the sober *Report on the Agricultural State of the Kingdom in 1816* sums up the plight of the labourers throughout almost all this period: 'They suffer.'[43]

Notes

1 Prothero, Rowland E. (1888) *The Pioneers and Progress of English Farming*, 224–5.

2 Easton, Josiah, *Reports Respecting Grain and the Corn Laws, 1814–1815* V, 12. The author calculates from farm records that comparing the ten-yearly period 1773–82 with 1803–12, the bushel of wheat increased from 5s 11d to 12s 6d, meat from 2¾d to 8¾d per lb, butter from 6¼d to 1s 4d per lb, wages from 1s 2d to 2s 4d a day.

3 From 1805–13 wheat averaged 100s 4d per quarter, compared with 49s between 1774 and 1790: W. Hasbach (1920) *A History of the English Agricultural Labourer*, 176.

4 Fussell, G.E. and Fussell, K.R. (1981) *The English Countryman, His Life and Work from Tudor Times to the Victorian Age*, 128.

5 Richardson, T.L. (1976) 'The agricultural labourer's standard of living in Kent, 1790–1840', in Derek J. Oddy and Derek S. Miller, *The Making of the Modern British Diet*, 105 (Tables I and II).

6 Davies, David (1795) *The Case of Labourers in Husbandry, Stated and Considered*, 8–24.

7 Driver, A. and Driver, W. (1794) *Agriculture of Hampshire*; Marshall, William (1817) *A Review of the Reports to the Board of Agriculture from the Southern and Peninsular Departments of England*, 293.

8 Middleton, John (1795) *Agriculture of Middlesex*; Marshall, op. cit., 131.

9 Oddy, D.J. (1981) 'Diet in Britain during industrialization', paper at Leyden Colloquium, *The Standard of Living in Western Europe* (September), 15.

10 Board of Agriculture (1816) *The Agricultural State of the Kingdom, in February, March and April, 1816*. Republished, with an Introduction by Gordon E. Mingay (1970), 7 *passim*.

11 The 'Bread Scale', or Speenhamland System, was graduated to cover changes in the price of the gallon loaf from 1s to 2s and the variations in the size of the family up to seven children. It was headed 'This shows at one view what should be the weekly income of the industrious poor'. Some representative figures only are given below:

Cost of gallon loaf	Income for single man	Married man
s d	s d	s d
1 0	3 0	4 6
1 6	4 3	6 3
2 0	5 0	7 6

Married man with 2 children	Married man with 7 children
s d	s d
7 6	15 0
10 3	20 3
12 6	25 0

12 For detailed and vivid descriptions of the 'last labourers' revolt' see J.L. Hammond and Barbara Hammond (1911) *The Village Labourer, 1760–1832*;

E.J. Hobsbawn and G. Rudé (1973) *Captain Swing* (2nd edn).

13 *Labourers' Wages*: Report from the Select Committee on the Rate of Agricultural Wages, and on the Condition and Morals of Labourers in that Employment, SP (1824) (392).
14 ibid., 47.
15 Cobbett, William (1830) *Rural Rides*, 390.
16 ibid., 372.
17 ibid., 75.
18 Cobbett, William (1830) *Cottage Economy*, paras 78 and 99.
19 *The Family Economist: a Penny Monthly Magazine directed to the Moral, Physical and Domestic Improvement of the Industrious Classes* (1848), 66.
20 Copley, Esther (1849) *Cottage Cookery*, 92.
21 Reports from the Select Committee on the State of Agriculture, First Report, SP (1836) (79), Q. 8.198.
22 Poor Law Amendment Act: Minutes of Evidence taken before the Select Committee of the House of Lords, Parts I and II, SP (1837–8) (719), 270.
23 *Journal of the Statistical Society* XXIV (1861).
24 ibid., I (1838), 181.
25 Springall, L. Marion (1936) *Labouring Life in Norfolk Villages, 1834–1914*, 23.
26 *Quarterly Journal of Agriculture* (1836), 19.
27 Garnier, Russell M. (1895) *Annals of the British Peasantry* 306 et seq.
28 For a full discussion of the derivation of the phrase, see W.H. Chaloner (1957) *The Hungry Forties: a Re-Examination* (The Historical Association Aids for Teachers Series), no. 1.
29 Unwin, T. Fisher (ed.) (1904) *The Hungry Forties: Life under the Bread Tax. Descriptive letters and other testimonies from contemporary witnesses*, 22.
30 ibid., 28–9.
31 Reports of Special Assistant Poor Law Commissioners on the Employment of Women and Children in Agriculture (1843) (510), XII.
32 ibid., 18–19.
33 ibid., 58–9.
34 ibid., 69–70.
35 Reports, 1843, op. cit., 233.
36 Digby, Anne (1978) *Pauper Palaces*, 23.
37 Reports, 1843, op. cit., 254–5.
38 ibid., 295.
39 ibid., 302–6. Calculated by Pamela Horn (1980) *The Rural World, 1780–1850. Social Change in the English Countryside*, 266–7 (Appendix 4).
40 ibid., 297.
41 Peacock, A.J. (1965) *Bread or Blood. The Agrarian Riots in East Anglia, 1816*.
42 Rogers, P.G. (1961) *The Battle in Bossenden Wood. The Strange Story of Sir William Courtenay*. (This was probably the assumed name of J.N. Tom, who was killed in the battle with eleven or twelve of his followers.)
43 *The Agricultural State of the Kingdom, 1816*, op. cit., 33. The comment was specifically applied to the parish of Chatteris, Cambridgeshire.

✵ 3 ✵

The town worker

[Before the Industrial Revolution] the workers enjoyed a comfortable and
peaceful existence. . . . Their standard of life was much better than that of the
factory worker today.

F. Engels, *The Condition of the Working Class in England* (1845)[1]

The most revolutionary social change which took place during the first
half of the nineteenth century – a change creating problems which have
not yet been solved – was the rapid growth of towns, and particularly of
the industrial towns of the midlands and north of England.

The cause of this change was, of course, the development of manufacturing industry associated with the Industrial Revolution which had begun
in the latter part of the preceding century. Its origins were certainly earlier
than 1750, and it can be argued that its completion is not yet, but there can
be no doubt that the pace of change was very rapid, and very evident,
between about 1780 and 1850 when, as a result of the invention of
machines for spinning and weaving, and the development of the steam
engine, the textile trades were transformed into factory industries centred
in Lancashire and Yorkshire. Coal-mining and the iron industry were also
growing rapidly in response to the new demands, while improved
communications by canals, railways, and steamships were distributing the
ever-increasing products of industrialism at home and overseas. Our
period fitly ends with the Great Exhibition of 1851, which demonstrated in
a spectacular way the industrial predominance of 'the workshop of the
world'.

But although industry was making such rapid strides, it is wrong to
suppose that even at the end of this period England had become a mainly
industrial society. Of 6,700,000 occupied persons classified in the census
of 1841, only 2,619,000 derived their livings from commerce, trade, and
manufacture: there were still a million and a quarter in agriculture, and
very nearly a million in domestic service. Manufacture was moving up into
first place, but industrialization was still far from being a completed
process. Textiles was the largest industry in 1841 with 619,000 employees
(just over half in factory employment, the rest in domestic spinning and
weaving); the metal trades involved 303,000 and mining 173,000.[2]

38

Was this growing population of industrial workers better or worse off than their rural predecessors? Was the standard of life of the town worker higher than that of the agricultural labourer? Ever since the Industrial Revolution itself controversy has raged as to whether industrialization came as a boon or a curse to the English working classes, and an answer to the question seems little nearer today than it was a century ago. For one thing, complete and reliable statistics by which the standard may be measured – wages, prices, consumption of goods, and so on – are not available for the period under discussion. For another, the 'standard-of-living controversy' has been a favourite arena for opposing political beliefs. Most of the early writers of English economic and social history were socialists, imbued with the express or implied purpose of showing the development of capitalist industry as a calamity for the working classes: excessive and unhygienic factory labour, the exploitation of women and children, overcrowding in insanitary slums – these and many other evils have all been laid at the door of the factory system.[3] Only in more recent years has the pessimistic account of emergent industrialism been repainted by a school of historians who see the factory system as the saviour of the masses, who point to the higher earnings of town workers compared to agricultural labourers, the advantages of separating work from the home, and the beneficial effects of factory employment on labour organization and on the status of women.[4]

Some of the recent writers have recognized that changes in diet may be a valid indicator of changes in the standard of living and have attempted to trace from the available statistics the course of *per capita* consumption in a number of basic foods. The consumption statistics for a number of foods have previously been cited (pp. 15–17); useful as they are in indicating national trends, however, they tell us little about the actual diets of groups and individuals who rarely, if ever, conform to the average. In reality there were very wide differences between the earnings – and hence, consumption habits – of skilled and unskilled workers, of factory operatives and unmechanized, domestic workers. To discuss 'average' consumption is to ignore the important economic results which industrialization did produce – improvement for some categories of labour and deterioration for others. Moreover, it neglects the fact that the first half of the nineteenth century saw the rise to importance of a virtually new social class whose consumption habits, in food at least, approached those of the landed gentry. Though still numerically small, the middle class of 1850, with its large families and armies of domestic servants, accounted for a much greater proportion of total food consumption than its numbers would suggest.

Even among wage-earners, the range of earnings in the early nineteenth century was so large that it is misleading to speak of a single 'working class'. At the top stood groups of workers in skilled trades unaffected by recent industrialization and forming an élite of labour – compositors, who at the beginning of our period could earn 40s a week and more,[5] London tailors with 36s,[6] and carpenters with 30s. Other examples of high earnings, all around 30s a week, include shipwrights, bricklayers, masons, and plasterers. Next to the 'labour aristocracy' came the 'new' skilled trades associated with the factory system and its demands. A Manchester cotton spinner in 1833 made 27s a week, a Durham miner 2s 9d a day; the railways also created remunerative occupations for some hundreds of thousands, a railway mason earning 21s a week in 1843 and a navvy 16s 6d, rising to 33s and 24s respectively in the 'boom' year of 1846. Skilled workers in the new metal trades – engineering, boilermaking, and so on – were also sharing in the prosperity of the times with wages of 23s and upwards. In sharp contrast to these two moderately well-paid groups, however, were the large numbers of workers in old hand-trades now in competition with factory production. The handloom-weaver who, at the end of the eighteenth century, stood among the aristocrats of labour with earnings of up to 30s a week, was gradually reduced to a starvation wage of 1d an hour as the power-loom took over:[7]

Wages of a Bolton handloom-weaver

1797	1800	1805	1810	1816	1820	1824	1830
30s	25s	25s	19s	12s	9s	8s 6d	5s 6d

In 1830 there were still 200,000 handloom-weavers in the cotton industry, and more than that in wool: between them, they probably outnumbered all workers in factories at that date. When we add to them the large numbers employed in other depressed hand-trades – the framework-knitters of Nottinghamshire and Leicestershire, earning an average of 5s 3d per week in 1833, the silk-workers of Spitalfields, the Coventry ribbon-makers, the Birmingham nail-makers, the lace-workers, shoe-makers, and seamstresses – we have a vast army of low-paid workers for whom there was as yet no place in factory employments. It was in these still unrevolutionized trades, and in the occupations which were by nature casual and seasonal, such as general labouring and portering, that the greatest poverty lay, and in the period under discussion, these groups greatly outnumbered the factory workers. In the census of 1851, the ten largest occupational groups were in order, agriculture, domestic service, cotton, building, labourers (unspecified), milliners and seamstresses, wool, shoe-making, coal-miners, and tailors, and only two of these (cotton and wool) were partly factory trades. For a minority of the working classes early industrialization brought unexpected wealth, for some it meant little change either way, for many it brought a poverty heightened by the memory of past prosperity. As the century advanced, the wealthy minority grew and the poor majority dwindled, but in the years before the Great Exhibition there were probably at least as many who lost by industrialism as gained by it.

Clearly, then, it is impossible to discuss the diet of town workers as a whole when their earnings ranged from 5s to 40s a week. It is also important to remember that their economic position was affected by other factors which made that position unstable, even precarious. Employment, even for skilled workers, tended to be highly irregular in the early stages of industrialization, so that the same man might alternate between periods of prosperity and poverty in a matter of months or even weeks. Commercial crises and cyclical depressions, which occurred every eight to ten years in the first half of the century, produced widespread unemployment, especially in export trades such as textiles, and half-time working or the complete closure of mills for a few months could bring sudden disaster to Bolton, Bury, Leeds, or Bradford, which were virtually dependent on one industry.

Trade cycles resulted in great swings in the purchasing power of the worker between good years and bad. Depressions in the basic industries centred on 1816, 1826–7, 1841–3, and 1848–9, with that of the early 1840s almost certainly the worst of the whole century. John Bright described a procession of 2,000 women and girls through the streets of Rochdale in 1842: 'They are dreadfully hungry – a loaf is devoured with greediness indescribable, and if the bread is nearly covered with mud it is eagerly devoured.'[8] Professor Hobsbawn has noted that while at this time approximately 10 per cent of the whole population were officially classified as paupers, in Bolton in 1842 60 per cent of millworkers were unemployed, 87 per cent of bricklayers, 84 per cent of carpenters, and 36 per cent of ironworkers. Two-thirds of London tailors were out of work and three-quarters of Liverpool plasterers; one in every three of Clitheroe's population of 6,700 were receiving poor relief, as were one in five of Nottingham's population, while between 15 and 20 per cent of Leeds inhabitants had an income of less than 1s per head per week.[9] At such times the problem was to keep body and soul together. For John Castle, an unemployed silk weaver of Colchester, dinner for three was 'a pennyworth of skimmed milk thickened with flour',[10] while Charles Shaw in the Potteries remembered with bitterness the bread provided for the destitute by the parish, which seemed to be made out of straw, plaster of Paris, and alum:

The crowd in the market-place on such a day formed a ghastly sight. Pinched faces of men, with a stern, cold silence of manner. Moaning women, with crying children in their arms, loudly proclaiming their sufferings and wrongs. Men and women with loaves or coals, rapidly departing on all sides to carry some relief to their wretched homes – homes, well, called such. . . . The

41

silence froze your heart, as the despair and want suffered had frozen the hearts of those who formed this pale crowd.[11]

Better than this was the soup provided by Alexis Soyer, the famous chef of the Reform Club, who, after his return from relieving the starving Irish in 1847, opened model soup-kitchens for the destitute weavers of Spitalfields: his recipe costed a quart of soup and a portion of bread at $1\frac{5}{8}$ d.[12]

The movement of prices was an additional cause of instability to the town worker. Although the general direction of prices after 1815 was downwards, food remained dear, and the price of bread in particular fluctuated widely within short periods. At a time when up to half the earnings of some working-class families went on bread alone, this was a matter of vital importance. Assuming six 4-lb loaves to be the weekly ration for a family of two adults and three children, which seems to have been typical, the cost of this in London varied as follows:

1830	1835	1840	1845	1850	1855
5s 3d	3s 6d	5s	3s 9d	3s 5d	5s 5d

So the man in full employment at 30s a week, and with bread at $1\frac{3}{4}$d a pound, might be affluent, while the same man on half-pay with bread costing $2\frac{1}{2}$d a pound could be practically a pauper. Other food prices varied less than bread, but remained high at a time when prices generally, and wages, were falling, so that food was in effect relatively dearer in these years. And at particular times, as between 1836 and 1841, food prices could turn sharply upwards, without any corresponding advance of wages (see Table 5). Tea and house rent were the only items to show a fall during these years, the latter end of which coincided with the worst of the cyclical depressions, with mass unemployment and wage-cuts in the factory districts.

Towns also had important effects on food habits. As we have seen, urban life necessarily meant a greater dependence on the professional services of bakers, brewers, and food retailers generally, partly because living conditions were overcrowded and often ill-equipped for the practice of culinary arts, partly because many women worked at factory or domestic trades and had little time or energy left for cooking. Tenemented houses, occupied by many of the poorer working classes in London and other cities, were rarely supplied with anything more than an open fire for cooking: few weekly tenants could afford the iron cooking-stove with boiler recommended by Francatelli and other food reformers[13] which, in any case, became a landlord's fixture. In this respect, the back-to-back house typical of many northern and midland towns had a distinct advantage: here, a simple cooking-range with oven and water-boiler was usual by the 1830s, and helped to keep alive the tradition of home cooking. Else-

Table 5 *Retail prices in Manchester of the following articles of household expenditure in the year 1841, compared with 1836* [14]

Articles	1836	1841	Percentage alteration in price since 1836	
			Rise	Fall
Rent, cottage property	5s 0d	4s 0d		20
Flour, per doz. lb	1s 8d–1s 10d	2s 4d–2s 7d	27	
Meat, per lb	$4\frac{1}{2}$d–5d	8d–$8\frac{1}{2}$d	54	
Bacon, per lb	$4\frac{1}{2}$d–5d	7d	40	
Oatmeal, per peck of 10 lb	1s 0d	1s 4d	33	
Butter, per lb	9d–10d	1s 0d–1s 1d	33	
Eggs		No variation		
Milk, per pint	$1\frac{1}{2}$d	$1\frac{1}{2}$d		
Potatoes, per 20 lb	7d–8d	11d–1s 0d	50	
Tea, per lb	6s 0d	5s 0d		17
Coffee, per lb	1s 8d–2s 0d	2s 0d		
Sugar, per lb	$5\frac{1}{2}$d–6d	8d–$9\frac{1}{2}$d	45	
Treacle, per lb	$2\frac{1}{4}$d	$3\frac{1}{2}$d	50	
Soap, per lb	5d	5d		
Candles, per lb	$6\frac{1}{2}$d	$6\frac{1}{2}$d		
Salt, per 4 lb	1d	1d		
Coals, per cwt	7d	7d		

where, however, the kind of food which most commended itself was that which needed least preparation, was tasty, and, if possible, hot, and for these reasons bought bread, potatoes boiled or roasted in their jackets, and bacon, which could be fried in a matter of minutes, became mainstays of urban diet. Tea was also essential, because it gave warmth and comfort to cold, monotonous food. But roasts and broths, stews and puddings became for many inhabitants of the new towns the Sunday feast, for only on the day of rest were long preparation and cooking possible. The recipe books and manuals of domestic economy written for the poor probably had little influence for this reason: the working classes were not interested, as the *Family Economist* thought they should be, in how to make a shilling's worth of meat do for three family dinners by making economical soups and stews, and various dishes made with rice and Indian corn. One recipe 'for a Good Breakfast, Dinner or Supper' suggested: 'Put one pound of rice and one pound of Scotch barley into two gallons of water, and boil them gently for four hours over a slow fire; then add four ounces of treacle and one ounce of salt, and let the whole simmer for half-an-hour. It will produce *sixteen pounds* of good food.'[15] The poor rightly thought little

43

more of this sort of stuff than they did of Count Rumford's famous soup. Women and children preferred the monotony of bread, potatoes, and weak tea, with occasionally a little butter, cheese, and bacon, to these washy messes which savoured of the workhouse 'skillee'. What little meat there was was often reserved for the husband's evening meal, and he might also have a slice of pie, meat, or sausages for his dinner at a coffee stall if he could not get home. It is hard to imagine how men could have borne the long hours which they worked without a diet considerably higher in energy value than that received by the rest of the family.

Many contemporary writers were pessimistic about the effects of the developing factory system on the home life of the working classes, especially where girls and married women were employed and taken away from their domestic duties. For Engels, 'Family life for the worker is almost impossible under the existing social system.' A girl who has worked in a factory since the age of nine has never had the chance of acquiring any skill in household duties, he claimed. 'Consequently, all the factory girls are wholly ignorant of housewifery, and are quite unfitted to become wives and mothers. They do not know how to sew, knit, cook or wash.'[16] Such a view seems at odds with the reputation for good home cooking and baking which survived in many of the Lancashire and Yorkshire textile districts. In any case, it is clear that the largest proportion of women employed in textile factories were between the ages of sixteen and twenty-one; after that there was a rapid reduction, and the number of wives at work was quite small, varying between about 10 and 25 per cent of the adult women.[17] It should also be remembered that where there were several earners in a family the total income compared favourably with that of the very best-paid workers, allowing a quite sufficient expenditure on food, clothing, and domestic comforts generally. Leonard Horner, the factory inspector responsible for the Lancashire district, wrote in his *Report* for 1837: 'No unprejudiced observer could come to any other conclusion that in no occupation could there possibly exist among the working people a larger proportion of well-fed, well-clothed, healthy and cheerful-looking people.'[18]

Another advantage of life in the town was that food could be bought in small quantities (tea and sugar by the ounce, for example) from the shop on the corner. Possibly the most important 'amenity' of the early industrial town was the ubiquitous chandler's shop, willing to tide its regular customers over a crisis by advancing bread and groceries on credit. Of course, the system had its disadvantages. The easy availability of credit meant that many working people went through their lives in debt, their earnings perpetually mortgaged in advance. It also tended to put them at the mercy of unscrupulous shopkeepers, who could overcharge, give short weight, and adulterate the goods of customers who were bound to them by ties of indebtedness. This kind of petty tyranny was the price which many had to pay for a degree of security; people who had no savings and few possessions could scarcely have survived without the chandler's slate.

A rapid growth in the numbers of shops seems to have kept at least in step with the growth of town populations and, in some cases, to have moved well ahead. In Manchester and Salford, for example, shops selling non-perishable foods increased from 1,000 in 1834 to 4,000 by the early 1870s, while the population scarcely more than doubled.[19] Fixed shops were now generally used by the working classes for day-to-day purchases, with markets increasingly reserved for larger, weekend shopping of meat and vegetables. Even here, however, by the 1850s butchers were concentrating their activities into fixed shops. Keen competition was characteristic of food retailing in the towns, where, it was estimated in 1843, prices were between 10 and 25 per cent lower than in rural areas.[20] In particular, the middle years of the century saw the emergence of the general store, or corner shop, serving all the food needs of a locality except for fresh meat. The corner shop was especially characteristic of the poorer parts of towns, where it might be the only local shop: in the main shopping streets there was more specialization – between the grocer selling tea, coffee, sugar, dried fruits, spices, and condiments, and the provision dealer in butter, cheese, bacon, ham and eggs.[21] Flour was sold by the general grocer, bread by the baker, either over the shop counter or, in better-class districts, by delivery. Grocers and general stores were the most numerous category of all shops by mid-century, closely followed by bakers.[22]

The practice of employers paying part of the wage in 'truck' was an evil which survived well into this period. In view of the high proportion of wage-earners employed by small masters, it seems likely that Huskisson's estimate – that truck accounted for one-quarter of all earnings – was exaggerated, but we know that it invaded a wide range of employments and was particularly common in some of the heavy industries. A good deal of truck was in the form of food, or of tickets exchangeable for food at the 'tommy shop', especially in coal-mining and railway building, where the employer could claim that he was providing a service in areas ill-supplied with shops. Obviously, there existed here a golden opportunity for fraud of all kinds, and the complaints of the Barnsley miners in 1842 that they were forced to take 'provisions of the worst quality and at prices far above the market' are echoed throughout contemporary literature. In the areas where it was widespread, truck had important effects in reducing real wages by non-competitive pricing, and the frequency with which the practice was investigated by Parliament, and legislation passed against it, suggests that it continued to cause much concern to what was supposedly a 'free economy'. As late as 1871 the Commission on the Truck System found it to be still common in colliery districts, iron works, railway building, and some workshop industries such as nail-making.[23]

Once the day's work had begun in factory or foundry, mine or workshop, there was little pause for food or rest in what seem to us unbelievably long hours of labour. The saddest case of all in a sad history of industrial feeding was that of the pauper children who were, in the early part of the century, 'apprenticed' by parish authorities to mill-owners in the north and became slaves in all but name for seven or fourteen years. Robert Blincoe, who wrote a personal memoir on life as a parish apprentice, spoke of the diet as 'the scantiest share of coarsest food capable of supporting animal life':

> The store pigs and the apprentices used to fare very much alike; but when the swine were hungry, they used to grunt so loud they obtained the wash first to quiet them. The apprentices could be intimidated and made to keep still. The fatting pigs fared luxuriously compared with the apprentices. They were often regaled with meal balls, made into dough, and given in the shape of dumplings.

He went on to say that he and others who worked in a part of the factory near the pigsties used to keep a sharp eye on the fatting pigs and their meal balls, and as soon as the swineherd withdrew Blincoe would stealthily slip down, plunge his hand in at the loop-holes, and steal as many dumplings as he could grasp:

> The pigs, usually esteemed the most stupid of animals, learned from experience to guard their food by various expedients; made wise by repeated losses, they kept a keen look-out, and the moment they ascertained the approach of the half-famished apprentices, they set up so loud a chorus of snorts and grunts, it was heard in the kitchen, when out rushed the swineherd armed with a whip, from which means of protection for the swine this accidental source of obtaining a good dinner was soon lost! Such was the contest carried on for some time at Litton Mill between the half-famished apprentices and the well-fed swine.[24]

A woman who knew at first hand the conditions in an 'apprentice house' where the children were boarded testified that they

> were fed chiefly on porridge, which was seasoned with beef and pork *brine*, bought at the Government stores, or those of contractors – the 'bottoms' of casks supplied to the Navy. This nauseous mixture was sometimes so repulsive even to the hungry stomachs that it was rejected. . . . They were fed out of troughs, much resembling those used by pigs.[25]

Pauper 'apprentices' were, fortunately, a very small proportion of the factory population, and the practice did not continue after the reform of the Poor Law in 1834. Ordinary factory workers, adults and children, provided their own food, which they ate during the permitted breaks. These, it is true, were often much too short before the Factory Act of 1833 laid down some statutory minima. A witness before Michael Sadler's Committee on Factory Children's Labour of 1831 said that he was seven when he started work: the hours of labour were 5 a.m. to 8 p.m. with half an hour allowed at noon. 'There was no time for rest or refreshment in the afternoon; we had to eat our meals as we could, standing or otherwise. I had $14\frac{1}{2}$ hours actual labour when seven years of age: the wage I then received was two shillings and ninepence per week.' This witness explained that the dust in the atmosphere often got into the food and spoiled it. 'You cannot take food out of your basket or handkerchief but what it is covered with dust directly. . . . The children are frequently sick because of the dust and dirt they eat with their meal.'[26] This was probably the extreme case. At 'good' mills there was an hour for dinner at noon, half an hour for breakfast, and another half-hour for 'drinking' in a day starting at 6 a.m. and ending at 8 p.m., but in a great many factories up to half the total mealtimes might be taken up in cleaning the spindles.[27] 'The child snatches its meal in a hurried manner in the midst of work, and in a place of dust – in a foul atmosphere and in a temperature equal to a hothouse.' Conditions in the coal-mines were even worse. The Royal Commission of 1842 revealed that:

> Of all the coal districts in Great Britain there are only two (South Staffordshire and the Forest of Dean) in which any regular time is usually set apart for the rest and refreshment of the workpeople during the day. . . . In the great majority of the coal districts of England, Scotland and Wales no regular time whatever is even nominally allowed for meals, but the people have to take what little food they eat during their long hours of labour when they best can snatch a moment to swallow it.[28]

There were, even in the early nineteenth century, some 'model employers' who recognized the importance of adequate diet for their employees and were pioneers of industrial welfare generally. Samuel Oldknow at Mellor Mill, although working his apprentices for long hours, fed them almost lavishly with porridge and bacon for breakfast, meat every day for dinner, puddings or pies on alternate days, and, when pigs were killed, pies which were full of meat and had a short crust. All the fruit in the orchard was eaten by the children. He also organized supplies of necessary foods for his adult workpeople, rearing bullocks, keeping a herd of dairy cows and a market garden of three acres to supply fresh vegetables.[29] When factories or mines were established in rural areas, remote from shops and ill-served by communications, some provision of this kind was essential, but Oldknow and others were exceptional in regarding such services as a duty, dissociated from any idea of profit. The London Coal

Company, for example, provided its workers on Tyneside with wheat, rye, and other grain at cost price, and in fact put itself considerably out of pocket by paying the heavy transport charges. At one point it bought an old lead mill at Tynebottom, and refitted it as a corn mill to supply the whole district, so breaking the exorbitant charges of the local millers.[30] The most outstanding example of an enlightened employer was, of course, Robert Owen during his management of the New Lanark cotton mills from 1799 to 1824. Dr Henry MacNab, visiting this model community numbering over 2,000 in 1819, described the spacious kitchens, bake-house, and store-rooms, the dining-room, 110 ft by 40 ft, in which employees could, if they wished, take all their meals at very moderate cost, and the vegetable garden which was granted to every householder. Owen also provided a shop selling provisions and clothing of the best quality at little more than cost price. 'In one of our walks we met a woman with a choice piece of beef purchased at the establishment. She told us that she had paid only 7d per pound, and that she could not have bought it under 10d in Glasgow market.'[31]

Owen's great underlying purpose was to improve human character, to change the labour-force which he inherited at New Lanark – poor, ignorant, given to vice and drunkenness – into an efficient, honest, and happy community. Few employers in the early nineteenth century had any such moral concern, though one of the most widely held attitudes about working people was that they were extravagant and improvident, that their incomes would be quite adequate for their needs if only they were laid out economically and not squandered on expensive foods and drink. Dr Andrew Ure, writing in 1835 on the condition of cotton operatives, ascribed the gastralgia from which many of them suffered to their preference for highly flavoured food, and in particular their fondness for 'rusty' bacon. 'In this piquant state it suits vitiated palates accustomed to the fiery impressions of tobacco and gin. . . . Hypochondriasis, from indulging too much the corrupt desires of the flesh and the spirit, is in fact, the prevalent disease of the highest-paid operatives.'[32] As well as condemning alcohol, the doctor deprecated the use of tea and milk because of their impurity: it is not clear from his account what factory workers should drink, if anything. At a somewhat earlier period Hannah and Martha More had expressed similar disgust at the luxurious way of life of glassworkers in the Mendips, especially those living in the village known locally as 'Little Hell'.

> Both sexes and all ages herding together; voluptuous beyond belief . . . the body scarcely covered, but fed with dainties of a shameful description. The high buildings of the glass-houses ranged before the doors of the cottages – the great furnaces roaring – the swearing, eating and drinking of

48

these half-dressed, black-looking beings, gave it a most infernal and horrible appearance. One, if not two joints of the finest meat were roasting in each of these little hot kitchens, pots of ale standing about, and plenty of early, delicate-looking vegetables.[33]

A somewhat more sympathetic account of occasional indulgence at work is given by Charles Shaw, who had worked as a potter's boy in Staffordshire in the 1840s. At ten years old he worked from four or five in the morning until nine or ten at night on the most meagre fare: 'Bread and butter was made up in a handkerchief, with a sprinkling of tea and sugar. Sometimes there was a little potato pie, whith a few pieces of fat bacon on it to represent beef. The dinner-time was from one till two o'clock and from then until nine or ten the weary workers got no more food.' It is scarcely surprising that, working in a temperature approaching that of the ovens, the potters brought in ale to their work, and occasionally stayed on drinking through the night. 'It was easy to cook, with a stove in each shop. A sheep's pluck and onions was a favourite dish. Sometimes ropes of sausages would be sent for.'[34] The potters seem moderate compared with the glassworkers and their 'delicate-looking vegetables'.

Possibly there was something in the industrial environment which predisposed workers to indulgence when the opportunity presented itself, but there was nothing new in the alternation of feasting with fasting. This had been the rural pattern for centuries, and like much else was merely carried over into life in the new towns. Probably the extent of drinking did not increase either, although it became more evident, and more exposed to public criticism, in the town. The surprising fact is that *per capita* beer consumption fell continuously throughout the first half of the nineteenth century (see Table 4, page 17), at a time when drinking can hardly have been more attractive and despite the Beerhouse Act of 1830 which greatly increased its availability. The estimated national drink bill was high enough by any standard:[35]

Year	Total cost (thousands of pounds)	Cost per head £ s d		
1820	50,441	2	8	6
1825	67,027	2	19	5
1830	67,292	2	16	5
1835	80,528	3	3	0
1840	77,606	2	18	10
1845	71,632	2	12	11
1850	80,718	2	18	10

An expenditure on drink of nearly £3 a year for every man, woman, and child in the country – £15 or so for every houshould – was certainly enough to keep many families poor, and to make some destitute. Again, average statistics are misleading. With the growth of the Temperance Movement after 1830, some families gave up drink completely, but others continued to spend one-third or one-half of all their earnings on it. It is easy to condemn the waste, poverty, crime, and disease which were unquestionably caused by alcohol; it is also important to remember its attractiveness at this period. The public house was warmer, more comfortable and more cheerful than the home usually was, and it provided quick escape for men and women who were too tired and too uneducated for intellectual pursuits and were not given the time or the facilities for constructive leisure activities. Many work customs traditionally involved drinking – the 'footings' of apprentices, the celebrations when a man had served his time, got married, or had a child, the annual 'weighgoose' and other holiday festivities. But the fatigue and heat of some occupations such as mining, iron-moulding, dock labouring or pottery work required large quantities of body fluid to be replaced by liquid of some kind, and given the relative cheapness of beer and the scarcity of pure water in many areas, it is not surprising that beer was often preferred.[36] The harrowing scenes described by Charles Shaw in the Potteries in the 1840s – of wages not paid out until Saturday night in a public house, of wives desperately trying to coax their husbands home before all was spent, and of men who, despite their entreaties, continued drinking until the following Tuesday[37] – were reproduced on a lesser scale in many English industrial towns.

Actual budgets and biographical accounts of meals left by working people are, unfortunately, all too few. The worker or his wife rarely kept household accounts, and we have to rely to some extent for a picture of urban diet on calculations which were made for specific purposes – by the worker in order to demonstrate his need for higher wages, by middle-class writers on domestic economy in order to show him how he ought to lay out his earnings. Some of the following budgets may, therefore, be nearer the 'ideal' than the 'actual', although the close agreement between many of them suggests that they are probably very near to reality. They are arranged chronologically, and illustrate all levels of earnings.

In 1810, the London compositors, probably the highest paid of all artisans, submitted a claim to their employers for an increase in view of the rising cost of living. Their wages at that time varied, according to whether they were engaged on reprint or manuscript work, from £1 17s 6d to £2 0s 9d a week. In order to substantiate their claim for higher wages, they compiled a typical weekly budget for a compositor, his wife and (small) family of two children:[38]

	s	d
Rent, per week	6	0
Bread and flour, 5 quarterns	6	$9\frac{1}{4}$
Meat, 14 lb at 9d per lb	10	6
Butter, 2 lb at 1s 4d per lb	2	8
Cheese, 1 lb		11
Porter, 3 pints per day	4	$4\frac{1}{2}$
Candles, $1\frac{1}{2}$ lb	1	$7\frac{1}{2}$
Coals (average price), 1 bushel	1	9
Soap, starch and blue		9
Tea, $\frac{1}{4}$ lb at 7s per lb	1	9
Sugar, 2 lb at 9d per lb	1	6
Vegetables	1	6
Milk		7
Pepper, salt, vinegar, etc.		6
Clothing, shoes, and mending	4	0
Schooling, books, etc.	1	6
Benefit Society		10
	£2 7s	$6\frac{1}{4}$d
Average earnings	£1 19s	$2\frac{1}{2}$d

This was affluence approaching middle-class standards. The heavy expenditure on meat, rent, and clothes, and the inclusion of items for education and insurance are particularly interesting.

This budget makes a startling comparison with that prepared nine years later by the Nottinghamshire framework-knitters during their negotiations for higher rates of pay. In the preceding years, especially during the Luddite rising of 1811–12, there had been frequent hunger riots and attacks on the shops of bakers, butchers, and greengrocers. In 1819 a petition was presented to the Lord Lieutenant of the County which recited:

> From the various and low prices given by our employers, we have not, after working from sixteen to eighteen hours per day, been able to earn more than from four to seven shillings per week to maintain our wives and families upon, to pay taxes, house rent, etc. . . . and though we have substituted meal and water, or potatoes and salt for that more wholesome food an Englishman's table used to abound with, we have repeatedly retired after a hard day's labour, and been under the necessity of putting our children supperless to bed to stifle their cries of hunger; nor think that we give this picture too high a colouring when we can most solemnly declare that for the last eighteen months we have scarcely known what is to be free from the pangs of hunger.[39]

This was the poverty-line diet, the irreducible minimum which was as bad as anything that the poorest agricultural labourer experienced. It could apply as well to 1819 as to 1850, perhaps the only difference being that at the earlier date the diet of oatmeal or potatoes was still resented as a recent

51

and unusual innovation, whereas, by 1850, it had become accepted by many as normal. Geography, of course, played an important part in determining the diet of the poorest. When William Lovett was living with his grandmother in Cornwall on 5s a week, 'our food consisted of barley-bread, fish and potatoes, with a bit of pork on Sundays'.[40] The Lovetts were lucky to live on the sea-coast, where cheap fish abounded. In an inland town like Nottingham, a red herring was an occasional luxury to add flavour to the dinner.

Between these two extremes of wealth and poverty, the compositors and the framework-knitters, lay the middle stratum of skilled workers and factory operatives, with earnings of £1 a week and upwards. Mrs Rundell, whose *System of Practical Domestic Economy* was the best-selling cookery book of the first half of the nineteenth century, gave two suggested budgets for incomes of 33s and 21s a week respectively (Table 6). Both are for a family of husband, wife, and three children – still small by contemporary standards. Mrs Rundell notes that:

> We have, in this Estimate, taken the expense of each child at one shilling and ninepence per week; and though a child in arms will not cost so much, yet the expense of lying-in will be fully equivalent. After the third child, the wife will naturally cause the oldest to attend to the youngest, and by that means gain time for other purposes. . . . Besides, in manufacturing neighbourhoods children are taught at an early age to earn something towards their own support. These and similar circumstances will tend to counter-balance such dilemmas as may arise, that would otherwise be disheartening.

Both are 'ideal' budgets for skilled workers in regular employment and with less than average-size families. It is interesting that even on 21s a week the family is supposed to dispense with tea and 'incidents', and to make do with cheap cuts of meat. This lower budget can be compared with that of a Northumberland miner in the next year, 1825, given in an anonymous pamphlet, *A Voice from the Coal Mines*. The man's earnings average £2 a fortnight, but deductions for fines, rent, and candles bring it down to 30s or 15s a week. Again the family is of three children:

	s	d
Bread, $2\frac{1}{2}$ stone at 2s 6d per stone	6	3
1 lb butcher's meat a day at 7d a lb	4	1
2 pecks potatoes at 1s per peck	2	0
Oatmeal and milk for 7 breakfasts at $4\frac{1}{2}$d each morning	2	8
	15s	0d

The family need as well to produce comfort:

Table 6 *Mrs Rundell's budgets for a husband, wife, and three children, 1824*[41]

	Earnings 33s per week			Earnings 21s per week	
	s	d		s	d
Bread and flour for					
5 persons, 24 lb	3	9		3	6
Butter, 2 lb at 9d	1	6	⎫		
Cheese, $\frac{1}{2}$ lb at 10d		5	⎬	1	9
Milk		8	⎭		
Tea, $\frac{1}{4}$ lb at 5s 4d	1	4		—	
Sugar, $2\frac{3}{4}$ lb at 6d	1	$4\frac{1}{2}$			9
Grocery		$9\frac{1}{2}$			6
Meat, 7 lb at 6d	3	6	(6 lb at $4\frac{1}{2}$d)	2	3
Vegetables (including			(including		
35 lb potatoes)	1	4	28 lb pots)	1	2
Beer, or Table Ale	2	3		1	2
Coals ($1\frac{1}{2}$ bushels at					
1s 4d per bushel)	2	1	($1\frac{1}{4}$ bushels)	1	9
Candles		$4\frac{1}{2}$			$3\frac{1}{2}$
Soap, etc., for washing		$4\frac{1}{2}$			$3\frac{1}{2}$
Sundries for cleaning, etc.		3			1
	£1 0s 0d			13s 6d	
Clothes, haberdashery, etc.	5	6		3	6
Rent	3	6		2	3
Incidents	1	3		nil	
Total expenses	£1 10s 3d			19s 3d	
Saving $\frac{1}{12}$	2s 9d		Saving $\frac{1}{12}$	1s 3d	

	s	d
2 oz tea	1	0
2 lb sugar at 8d per lb	1	4
1 lb salt butter	1	2
1 lb cheese		9
Pepper, salt, mustard, vinegar		4
Soap, starch, blue, etc.	1	6
Tobacco, $1\frac{1}{2}$ oz		$5\frac{1}{4}$
1 pint of ale a day	1	9
Clothing for 5 persons	3	0
	£1 6s	$3\frac{1}{4}$d

Is this too much, asks the writer? He replies that colliers would die if they did not take their children to work fourteen hours a day as soon as they could walk.[42]

Even so, it is doubtful whether he could have made good the 11s deficit, and in all probability he had to sacrifice a good deal of his pound of meat a day. The factory worker on a comparable wage, according to Dr James Kay, received little or no fresh meat. Describing the daily life of a Manchester operative in 1832, Kay says that he rose at five o'clock in the morning, worked at the mill from six till eight, and then returned home for half an hour or forty minutes to breakfast. This consisted of tea or coffee with a little bread. He then went back to work until noon. At dinner-time, the meal for the inferior workmen consisted of boiled potatoes, with melted lard or butter poured over them and sometimes a few pieces of fried fat bacon. Those with higher earnings could afford a greater proportion of animal food, though the quantity was still small. Work then resumed from one o'clock until seven or later, and the last meal of the day was tea and bread, sometimes mingled with spirits.[43]

A few years later, in 1841, S. R. Bosanquet quoted Dr Kay as saying 'England is the most pauperized country in Europe'. Bosanquet was writing a frankly propagandist work on *The Rights of the Poor*, but his examples, harrowing as they are, were fully authenticated. After citing a number of recent deaths in London caused by starvation – men and women who had died in the streets or shortly after admission to a workhouse – he quotes extensively from Dr Howard's essay on *The Morbid Effects of Deficiency of Food*, written after some years as a surgeon at the Royal Infirmary and the Poor-House at Manchester:

> The public generally have a very inadequate idea of the number of persons who perish annually from deficiency of food. . . . Although death directly produced by hunger may be rare, there can be no doubt that a very large proportion of the mortality amongst the labouring classes is attributable to deficiency of food as a main cause, aided by too long continued toil and exertion without adequate repose, insufficient clothing, exposure to cold and other privations to which the poor are subjected.[44]

Bosanquet himself quotes a number of weekly budgets of London families where the man is in full work, saying, 'They will furnish a standard from which to estimate the condition of larger families, or of families where, from illness, or other causes, the expenses are increased or the employment is irregular.' With earnings of 30s a week and upwards, a skilled London workman could live in reasonable comfort:

The town worker

Richard Goodwin, 45 Great Wild Street: a wife and five children:

	s	d
2 oz tea		8
7 oz coffee		$10\frac{1}{2}$
3 lb sugar	1	9
1 cwt coals, $\frac{1}{2}$ bushel coke, wood	2	3
12 loaves at 8d	8	0
18 lb potatoes		9
$1\frac{1}{2}$ lb butter	1	6
1 lb soap, $\frac{1}{2}$ lb soda		7
Blue and starch		2
Candles		7
Bacon	2	6
Greens or turnips, onions, etc.		6
Pepper, salt, and mustard		3
Herrings		9
Snuff		6
Rent	4	0
Butcher's meat, 6d a day	3	6
	£1 9s	$1\frac{1}{2}$d

With earnings of 21s a week, nearly all the above items had to be drastically reduced – bread to seven loaves, bacon to 1s, and so on – and at 15s a week, the wage of a labourer in regular employment, Bosanquet thought it just possible for a man, wife, and three children to exist. This probably represents a fairly typical semi-skilled worker's budget of the period:[45]

	s	d
5 4-lb loaves at $8\frac{1}{2}$d	3	$6\frac{1}{2}$
5 lb meat at 5d	2	1
7 pints of porter at 2d	1	2
$\frac{1}{2}$ cwt coals		$9\frac{1}{2}$
40 lb potatoes	1	4
3 oz tea, 1 lb sugar	1	6
1 lb butter		9
$\frac{1}{2}$ lb soap, $\frac{1}{2}$ lb candles		$6\frac{1}{2}$
Rent	2	6
Schooling		4
Sundries		$5\frac{1}{2}$
	15s	0d

The pint of porter a day is hardly extravagant, nor the cheap meat at 5d a pound; 2s 6d rent would provide one room, or at best two, and there is nothing here for vegetables – other than potatoes – for milk, clothing, or medicine. But sickness or widowhood could easily shatter even this frail standard of life. Elizabeth Whiting, a forty-year-old widow, had four young children to provide for:[46]

> 6 Cottage Place, Kenton Street – Pays 3s a week rent, owes £1 13s. Does charing and brushmaking; earned nothing this week; last week 3s; the week before 5s 8d.

Expenditure

	s	d
Dec. 15, 1839		
Sunday: Bought on Saturday night, Potatoes $1\frac{1}{2}$d, bacon 2d, candle $\frac{1}{2}$d, tea and sugar 2d, soap $1\frac{1}{2}$d, coals 2d, loaf $8\frac{1}{2}$d	1	6
Monday: Tea and sugar 2d, butter $1\frac{1}{2}$d, candle $\frac{1}{2}$d		4
Tuesday: Coals		2
Wednesday: Tea and sugar 2d, candle $\frac{1}{2}$d, wood $\frac{1}{2}$d, potatoes 1d		4
Thursday: Coals		1
Friday and Saturday		–
	2s	5d

> Had five 4-lb loaves this week from the parish.

In the same year, 1841, a detailed survey of the earnings and expenditure of nineteen working-class families in Manchester and Dukinfield was made on behalf of the Mayor, William Neild, for the Statistical Society. This was a particularly valuable record, because it gave in complete detail and from the personal statements of the people concerned a precise account of the condition of workers in the cotton industry. The first twelve cases were Manchester families 'selected because they were of sober and industrious habits. Their employment, also, during the general depression which has for some time existed in the trade of this district, has been almost uninterrupted, and their weekly wages have remained the same.' These were exceptionally fortunate families. The remaining seven cases were of Dukinfield families, who, like the majority of cotton workers at this time, had suffered reductions in their earnings, and were, therefore, more typical of the general state of Lancashire. We give four of the nineteen cases – nos 4 and 6 as examples of moderately comfortable families from Manchester, nos 14 and 19 as more representative Dukinfield families. All are skilled workers. No. 4 is a storeman, with eight in the family and a high total income of £2 17s or 7s $11\frac{1}{2}$d per head: no. 6 is an overlooker, six in family, with an income of £1 14s or 5s 8d each: no. 14 is a dresser with the same size of family, an income of £1 4s or 4s each, and no. 19 a mechanic's assistant with 16s or only 2s 3d each for the family of seven.

The last family was accumulating debt at the rate of 4s a week, despite its very modest expenditure on such things as meat and tea: indeed, six out of

56

The town worker

Table 7 *William Neild's budgets of Lancashire cotton workers, 1841*

	No. 4		No. 6		No. 14		No. 19	
	s	d	s	d	s	d	s	d
Rent	4	0	5	0	3	0	2	8
Flour or bread	10	0	5	10	5	0	5	3
Meat	10	0	4	8	2	9	1	6
Bacon	1	0		4	—		1	0
Oatmeal	—		—			5		10
Butter	4	0	2	0	2	0	1	3
Eggs	—		1	0	—		—	
Milk	—			10		$10\frac{1}{2}$	1	6
Potatoes	3	0	1	8	1	0		10
Cheese	1	0		9	—			8
Tea	1	3	1	0		$7\frac{1}{2}$		6
Coffee	1	2		6		6		3
Sugar	2	6	2	0	1	9	1	3
Treacle	—		—			$4\frac{1}{2}$		6
Tobacco		9	—		—		—	
Soap		9		6		9		10
Candles		6		6		3		2
Salt		2		$\frac{1}{2}$		1		1
Coals	—		1	2	1	6		10
Yeast	—		—			3		$3\frac{1}{2}$
Totals	£2	0s 1d	£1	7s 10d	£1	1s $1\frac{1}{2}$d	£1	0 $4\frac{1}{2}$d

the seven Dukinfield families were in debt to local shopkeepers. Apart from this, the most interesting point in the budgets is the increased proportion of earnings spent on bread, and the decreased proportion on butcher's meat, as the income falls. The amounts, expressed as percentages of total income, are as follows:

	On bread	On meat
Case no. 4	17.5	17.5
Case no. 6	16.9	13.8
Case no. 14	20.8	11.4
Case no. 19	32.8	9.4

This was the observation accurately made by Engels in his *Condition of the Working Class in England* in 1844:

The better-paid workers, especially those in whose families every member is able to earn something, have good food as long as this state of things lasts; meat daily, and bacon and cheese for supper. Where wages are less, meat is used only two or three times a week, and the proportion of bread and potatoes increases. Descending gradually, we find the animal food reduced to a small piece of bacon cut up with the potatoes; lower still, even this disappears, and there remains only bread, cheese, porridge and potatoes until, on the lowest round of the ladder, among the Irish, potatoes form the sole food.[47]

On the evidence of the Manchester survey, the amount spent on oatmeal increased similarly and that on butter, cheese, sugar, and tea fell. The poorer the family, the greater the dependence on cheap, carbohydrate foods, and the smaller the intake of proteins. There is only one redeeming feature in no. 19's budget – the very sensible expenditure of 1s 6d a week on milk.[48]

The Neild budgets have been analysed by J.C. McKenzie and evaluated in present-day nutritional terms (see Table 8). It will be seen that only the best paid of the regularly employed workers achieved a diet which would now be regarded as adequate for health in calories and protein; all but one of the Dukinfield families were seriously below the recommended allowances, the inference being that the male wage-earner, who would have needed some 2,800–3,000 calories a day for moderate work, took a larger share of the available food at the expense of his wife and children. The effects of such low diets would tend to be restricted physical growth and rickets in children, susceptibility to certain diseases such as tuberculosis and gastro-intestinal fevers, anaemia in women and, at times of crisis, epidemic diseases such as typhus, the so-called 'famine fever'.

All the families in the Statistical Society's survey were of skilled workers, and all were in employment. For budgets of poorer workers we have to turn to an inquiry made by Alexander Somerville, who spent the spring and summer of 1842 touring the manufacturing areas of the north in an effort to show that the depressed state of agriculture was due to the lack of purchasing power of the industrial population. Accrington, for example, was engaged almost exclusively in the cotton trade: of the 3,738 workers in the town, only 1,389 were fully employed in 1842 at an average wage of 8s 8d per week; 1,622 were partly employed at 4s 10d each and 727 were totally unemployed and destitute. An employer told him that in 1836 he paid his block printers 17s a week, now not quite 6s. 'Need you be told', asked Somerville, 'that with 17s there would be loaf-bread and butcher-meat and cheese and butter used, while with 6s there can be little more than oatmeal gruel, potatoes and salt.'[49] In the course of his survey he collected a large number of budgets from families, each consisting of the parents and four children, and these were then averaged to represent weekly incomes of 5s 6d, 10s, 15s 6d, and 25s 6d. The two lowest are given since the higher ones correspond closely to those in the Statistical Society's survey (see Table 9).

Only in the two higher categories was anything available for meat or butter, cheese or beer, and it is interesting to find that even tea has been

The town worker

Table 8 *William Neild's Manchester and Dukinfield budgets, 1841*[50]

	Protein (g)		Calories		Iron (mgs)		Vitamin C	
	1841	NRC rec'd	1841	NRC rec'd	1841	BMA rec'd	1841	BMA rec'd
Average for all families	65	64	2,300	2,400	15	12	50	20
Average for Manchester families	71	65	2,600	2,500	16	12	57	20
Average for Dukinfield families	51	62	1,900	2,400	12	12	36	20
Family 1	83	65	2,800	2,300	16	12	56	20
2	76	70	2,400	2,500	16	12	41	20
3	82	60	2,900	2,500	18	12	68	20
4	79	70	2,600	2,500	17	12	75	20
5	72	60	2,600	2,500	17	12	49	20
6	65	60	2,100	2,300	13	12	58	20
7	69	65	2,600	2,500	18	12	58	20
8	74	65	2,400	2,500	14	12	24	20
9	67	70	2,600	2,500	16	12	60	20
10	72	65	2,700	2,500	18	12	90	20
11	55	65	2,200	2,500	14	12	42	20
12	63	65	2,300	2,300	15	12	67	20
14	44	60	1,700	2,300	11	12	33	20
15	65	60	2,300	2,300	15	12	52	20
16	50	55	1,800	2,200	11	12	33	20
17	50	65	1,900	2,500	12	12	31	20
18	52	65	1,900	2,500	13	12	44	20
19	45	65	1,600	2,500	11	12	25	20

Note:
1 Family 13 is not used due to insufficient information.
2 'Appropriate allowances are made in the calculations for the differing nutritional needs of men, women, and children.
3 NRC = National Research Council of the US, recommended daily allowances.
  BMA = British Medical Association, recommended daily allowances.

squeezed out in the lower budgets. Again, the considerable expenditure on milk, long before its nutritional properties were known scientifically, is the saving feature of the 5s 6d budget.

The real question is, of course, how many families fell into the 5s 6d and 10s categories and how many were in the comparatively comfortable

Plenty and Want

Table 9 *Alexander Somerville's budgets of northern industrial workers' families, 1842*

| | Weekly earnings per family | | | |
	5s	6d	10s	0d
Bread and flour	1	9	2	6
Oatmeal	1	0	1	10
Potatoes		10	1	8
Milk		11		6
Bacon		2		8
Soap and candles		4		6
Coals		6		9
Sugar and treacle	—			5
Tobacco and snuff	—			2
Clothing	—			6
Rent	—			6
Total	5s	6d	10s	0d

circumstances of the Manchester families? There can be no exact answer to this, because, for the reasons previously given, the fortunes of a family could fluctuate greatly from one year to another. As Somerville said, 'When trade was in a thriving condition, by far the greatest proportion of families belonged to this fourth class (26s 6d a week), a smaller proportion to the third (15s 6d), and comparatively few to the second or first. Now in 1842, when trade is prostrate, the greatest proportion of families belong to the first and second classes, and comparatively few to the third and fourth.' It must also be remembered that in this period of incomplete industrialization, there were as many unskilled as skilled workers whose earnings were permanently in Somerville's first and second categories.

1842 was, admittedly, a 'bad' year, but in the decade of the forties there were as many 'bad' years as good. Prosperity returned briefly from 1843 to 1845, but 1846 saw a railway crisis, the great Irish potato famine and renewed depression in a number of major industries. In 1847, when provincial banks failed and alarm was even felt for the Bank of England, Alexis Soyer headed a public subscription for soup-kitchens for the starving during yet another cyclical depression. Only after 1848 were there signs of that settled and expanding prosperity which, in retrospect, has been called 'The Golden Age': a period when, for the first time, all grades of industrial workers began to share significantly in the fruits of industrialization; 1848 rather than 1850 marks the end of the hungry half-

60

century, the period when the diet of the majority of town-dwellers was at best stodgy and monotonous, at worst hopelessly deficient in quantity and nutriment. Almost half the children born in towns died before they reached the age of five, and a high proportion of those who did survive grew up ricketty, deformed, and undernourished. The long-term effects of this physical degeneration were only demonstrated many years later in the Boer War and the First World War, when medical examinations revealed the mass unfitness of urban recruits. The 'C3 nation' which so disturbed the public conscience in 1918 had its origins in the dietary inadequacy of the early nineteenth century.

By 1850 a distinctive urban, working-class dietary pattern was in the process of emerging. In earlier decades of the century it had not been markedly different from the rural pattern, with the same dependence on basic foods such as bread, potatoes, bacon, cheese, and butter, all of which were either processed foods or foods which had a lengthy marketing and storage period. Perishable foods like fresh vegetables, fruit, milk, fish, and meat were severely limited by transport difficulties before the railway age, and were therefore expensive. As previously demonstrated, income had a direct and major influence on choice, the poorer working classes being restricted to a narrow range of mainly starchy foods providing cheap sources of energy. Town workers were necessarily more dependent on commercially made products (bread was the first, and most important, 'convenience food') bought at shops and markets, and rarely had the opportunity of supplementing their diet from home-grown sources. But, for the better-off worker, towns by mid-century offered a greater variety of foods, both fresh and prepared, than was available in the countryside, and the opportunity to indulge in what had formerly been regarded as luxuries: in particular, the average consumption of meat, fats, sugar, and milk by the sort of people represented by the Neild budgets was greater than that of rural workers half a century earlier,[51] as was that of fish, tea, and coffee. A trend towards increased consumption of fats and sugar, and an increased use of mildly stimulating beverages, was already becoming apparent by mid-century, and indicative of the kinds of food choices more people would make as resources became available.

Notes

1   Translated by W.O. Henderson and W.H. Chaloner (1958), 10.
2   Porter, G.R. *The Progress of the Nation* (1847 edn), 78.
3   See, for example, the writings of A. Toynbee, S. and B. Webb, J.L. and Barbara Hammond, and G.D.H. Cole.
4   See, for example, the writings of J.H. Clapham, I. Pinchbeck, T.S. Ashton, and W.H. Chaloner.

5 Howe, Ellic (ed.) (1947) *The London Compositor. Documents relating to Wages, Working Conditions and Customs of the London Printing Trade, 1785–1900*, 163.

6 Wood, George H. (1900) *A Glance at Wages and Prices since the Industrial Revolution*.

7 Porter, op. cit., 457.

8 Quoted by Norman McCord (1958) *The Anti-Corn Law League*, 127.

9 Hobsbawm, E.J. (1975) 'The British standard of living, 1790–1850', in Arthur J. Taylor (ed.), *The Standard of Living in Britain in the Industrial Revolution*, 69–71.

10 *The Autobiography of John Castle (1819–1889)*, quoted in John Burnett (ed.) (1982) *Destiny Obscure. Autobiographies of Childhood, Education and Family from the 1820s to the 1920s*, 57, 262–9.

11 Shaw, Charles (1903) *When I Was a Child*, repub. 1977, 42–3.

12 Volant, F. and Warren, J.R. (eds) (1859) *Memoirs of Alexis Soyer*, repub. 1985, 110–28.

13 Francatelli, Charles Elme (1852) *A Plain Cookery Book for the Working Classes*, repub. 1977, 9–10. Francatelli was formerly maître d'hôtel and chief chef to the Queen.

14 Neild, W. (1841) 'Comparative statement of the income and expenditure of certain families of the working classes in Manchester and Dukinfield, in the years 1836 and 1841', *Journal of the Statistical Society of London* IV, 322.

15 *The Family Economist. A Penny Monthly Magazine devoted to the Moral, Physical and Domestic Improvement of the Industrious Classes* I (1848) 147.

16 Engels, Friedrich (1845) *The Condition of the Working Class in England*, trans. W.O. Henderson and W.H. Chaloner (1958), 145, 165–6.

17 Pinchbeck, Ivy (1930/1985) *Women Workers and the Industrial Revolution, 1750–1850*, 197.

18 Quoted in Pinchbeck, ibid., 311.

19 Scola, R. (1975) 'Food markets and shops in Manchester, 1770–1870', *Journal of Historical Geography* 1, 153–68.

20 Barker, T.C. (1966) 'Nineteenth century diet: some twentieth century questions', in T.C. Barker, J.C. McKenzie, and John Yudkin (eds) *Our Changing Fare. Two Hundred Years of British Food Habits*, 21.

21 Blackman, Janet (1976) 'The corner shop: the development of the grocery and general provisions trade', in Derek J. Oddy and Derek S. Miller (eds) *The Making of the Modern British Diet*, 148–61.

22 Alexander, D. (1970) *Retailing in England during the Industrial Revolution*, 18–25.

23 Hilton, G.W. (1960) *The Truck System*.

24 Brown, John (1832) *A Memoir of Robert Blincoe, an Orphan Boy*.

25 'Alfred' (Samuel Kydd) (1857) *The History of the Factory Movement, from the year 1802 to the enactment of the Ten Hours' Bill in 1847* I, 25.

26 Reports from the Select Committee on the Bill for the Regulation of Factory Children's Labour (Sadler's Committee), 1831–1832, XV: Evidence of Joseph Haberjam.

27 *A Sketch of the Hours of Labour, Mealtimes, etc. etc. in Manchester and Its Neighbourhood* (1825).

28 Children's Employment (Mines), Royal Commission, First Report (1842) (380), XV.

29 Unwin, George (1924) Samuel Oldknow and the Arkwrights, 173 et seq.

30 Raistrick, Arthur (1938) *Two Centuries of Industrial Welfare* (Supplement No. 19 to the *Journal of the Friends' Historical Society*).

31 Quoted in Sir Noel Curtis-Bennett (1949) *The Food of the People: being the History of Industrial Feeding*, 153. et seq.

32 Ure, Andrew (1861) *The Philosophy of Manufactures, or an Exposition of the Scientific, Moral and Commercial Economy of the Factory System* (3rd edn), 385–7.

33 Roberts, Arthur (ed.) (1859) *Mendip Annals; or a Narrative of the Charitable Labours of Hannah and Martha More* (3rd edn), 61–2.

34 Shaw, op. cit., 52–5.

35 Calculated from William Hoyle (1871) *Our National Resources, and How They are Wasted. An omitted chapter in Political Economy*, series continued in *Hoyle and Economy* (1887).

36 Harrison, B. (1971) *Drink and the Victorians. The Temperance Question in England, 1815–1872*.

37 Shaw, op. cit., chap. VIII, 67 et seq.

38 Howe, op. cit., 163.

39 *Modern Nottingham in the Making*, quoted by J.D. Chambers (1945), 32.

40 *The Life and Struggles of William Lovett in his pursuit of Bread, Knowledge and Freedom* (1876), 13.

41 Rundell, Mrs (1824) *A System of Practical Domestic Economy* (new edn).

42 Anon (1825) *A Voice from the Coal Mines*, quoted in J.L. Hammond and Barbara Hammond (1917) *The Town Labourer, 1760–1832*, 34–5.

43 Kay, James Phillips (1832) *The Moral and Physical Condition of the Working Classes Employed in the Cotton Manufacture in Manchester*.

44 Bosanquet, S.R. (1841) *The Rights of the Poor and Christian Almsgiving Vindicated*, 51–2.

45 ibid., 91 et seq.

46 ibid., 101–2.

47 *Karl Marx and Frederick Engels on Britain* (1953), 107.

48 Neild, op. cit., 323 et seq.

49 Somerville, Alexander (1843) *A Letter to the Farmers of England on the Relationship of Manufactures and Agriculture by One who has Whistled at the Plough*, 4.

50 Adapted, by kind permission, from J.C. McKenzie (1962) 'The composition and nutritional value of diets in Manchester and Dukinfield in 1841', *Transactions of Lancashire and Cheshire Antiquarian Society* 72, 123–40.

51 Oddy, D.J. (1983) 'Diet in Britain during industrialization', paper presented at Leyden Colloquium, *The Standard of Living in Western Europe* (September), II (Table 2).

⇉ 4 ⇇
The food of the rich

On May Day 1845, nearly at the close of the half-century of hunger, Benjamin Disraeli's political novel *Sybil*, was published with the famous sub-title *The Two Nations*. The theme was boldly stated – a gilded society, light-minded politicians, and a young queen called to reign over

> Two nations; between whom there is no intercourse and no sympathy; who are as ignorant of each other's habits, thoughts and feelings as if they were dwellers in different zones, or inhabitants of different planets; who are formed by a different breeding, are fed by a different food, are ordered by different manners, and are not governed by the same laws.
> 'You speak of . . . ' said Egremont, hesitatingly, 'THE RICH AND THE POOR.'

As a comment on the new social relationships created by the Industrial Revolution, Disraeli's view was naïve and inadequate. Certainly since the Norman Conquest, and probably since a good deal further back, English society had consisted of the two sharply divided 'nations' of which he wrote – of prosperous landowners on the one hand and poor, propertyless peasants on the other. There was more in common, it has been said, between the medieval English serf and his counterpart in France or Germany than between the serf and his own lord. Disraeli's comment was, in fact, more true of feudal than of industrial society, where the new feature was the multiplication of social classes and sub-classes and the blurring of the formerly sharp lines between 'the rich and the poor'. We have already discussed the impossibility of treating the town worker as a homogeneous class at a time when the economic and social differences between a craftsman and an unskilled worker were much greater than they are today, and the barriers more difficult to surmount. The differences within the ranks of 'the rich' were greater still. Between the great landed magnate with an income of £10,000 a year and the little, back-street shop-keeper with £150, between the small tenant-farmer who employed two labourers and the manufacturer who employed 2,000, there was, outwardly at least, next to nothing in common. We treat them together in this chapter for only one reason – that they all enjoyed some margin of income

64

over necessary expenditure and were all able to make some choice in their selection of food.

At the pinnacle of the rich in the years before 1850 still stood the landed aristocracy, the body of hereditarily titled peers and baronets who drew their revenues from estates and lived, for at least part of the year, in their country mansions. Some, it is true, had discovered coal or other mineral deposits beneath their wide acres and were not slow to exploit them; some, less endowed, had permitted their daughters to marry wealthy Indian nabobs, bankers, or even ironmasters; but, on the whole, the class was still a tightly closed, self-generating circle. Farming, especially the new farming of the 'improving' landowners, recovered its profitability after the immediate post–1815 depression. The aristocracy were still regarded as the natural leaders of fashion and society and, despite the widening of the franchise in 1832, still wielded an influence over both Houses of Parliament that was near-monopolistic.

Immediately below them in seniority, if not always in wealth, stood the wider group of county families, the knights of the shires, the squires, the untitled, though wealthy, freehold farmers. Many of them had enhanced their fortunes during the scarcities of the Napoleonic Wars and, despite their complaints, were still living handsomely after 1815 on the sale of corn and meat to the growing town populations. The gentry provided the lesser leaders of local society and, through their appointment to the magistracy, largely controlled county administration.

It is not easy, from the inadequate census returns of the period, to estimate the size of these two groups which together constituted the 'upper class'. The census of 1841 gives, for England, 119,000 adult males of independent means, and 141,000 occupiers of land employing labourers[1] out of a total population of 15,000,000. Probably the majority of both these groups could be regarded as 'gentry', and we have to add to the figures wives, children, and a circle of dependent relatives. In 1867, when Dudley Baxter published his well-known study of the distribution of the national income, he estimated that only 49,500 persons were in receipt of incomes of over £1,000 per annum, which did not, of course, include dependants or servants.

So far, the pattern was traditional and largely unchanged. What was new and striking about the social structure of early Victorian England was the rapid growth in the size and power of the middle classes who, before the nineteenth century, were a relatively minor section of society. Their origins, it is true, can be traced as far back as the Middle Ages in the professions of law, medicine, and the Church, and in the merchants whose business lay, as Lewis and Maude have said, 'in the use and the abuse of money'.[2] Industrialization added a third and highly important element – the capitalist manufacturer, using his own or others' capital to

65

employ workmen to spin cotton, mine coal, or build ships, while the growth of manufacturing industry in turn gave rise to new professional needs – to bankers and brokers, insurers and shippers, engineers and designers. A whole new range of managerial and clerical occupations which demanded literacy as a minimum and offered substantial rewards to men of enterprise and imagination was coming into being. Added to this, the enormous growth of towns called for more architects and survey-ors, doctors, and local government officers, more teachers and clergy, and more shopkeepers than ever before. Out of this amalgam was gradually rising by 1850 not a single middle class, but a tier of middle classes: at its top the greatest manufacturers and merchants, as rich as and richer than the gentry, with whom they were already intermingling through the agencies of marriage and the reformed public schools; in the middle, the members of the professions, both the 'learned' and the new and, as yet, unrecognized; at its base the petty tradesmen and employers, the clerks, the Nonconformist clergy and the apothecaries – men whose incomes might be little more than those of artisans, but whose habits of thought and dress, aspirations and ideals, were very different.

Again, the census returns are inadequate as a guide to the size of the middle classes. Using them to the best advantage, G.D.H. Cole has sug-gested that, in 1851, teaching occupied about 100,000, the other profes-sions 150,000, and the services of government and local government 75,000. Those engaged in merchanting, shopkeeping, and financial occupations numbered about 130,000, clerks and commercial travellers 60,000.[3] To these have to be added the small but highly important group of 'manufacturers employing capital in all branches', numbering 86,000 in 1851. With their wives and families, the English middle classes at the time of the Great Exhibition perhaps numbered some 3,000,000: they were still small, though growing rapidly, and in 1867 Dudley Baxter assigned them and the upper classes together 5,500,000 (23 per cent) out of a total popula-tion for Great Britain of 24,000,000.

For both classes these were years of unparalleled opportunity, wealth and display. With incomes as yet largely untaxed, quick fortunes to be made from enterprising speculation, and an ever-growing range of products on which money could be spent, early Victorian England became a period of conspicuous expenditure and social imitation such as had never been seen before. The landed gentry, formerly the sole exemplars of taste and fashion, now found that position being challenged by the 'new rich', anxious to demonstrate that humble origins did not imply a lack of culture and refinement. Already by the 1840s and 1850s it seems that the hard work, thrift, and abstemiousness on which many of the middle classes had founded their fortunes were coming to be replaced by competi-tive expenditure. The new values were demonstrated in terms of houses and furnishings, horses and carriages, the lavish employment of domestic servants, dress, and – not least – in terms of food.

The first half of the nineteenth century was in this, as in many other respects, a period of social transition when new dietary habits, which subsequently became the accepted pattern, were being formed. In these years the choice of foods, their manner of preparation, order of service, and even the times of eating, all became matters of high social importance and class demarcation: in particular, the dinner-party became a prestige symbol which at once announced the taste, discrimination, and bank balance of the donor. In eighteenth-century leisured society the practice had been for a large late breakfast, a light cold luncheon, and an early dinner at about 5 or 6 p.m. Breakfast, especially in the country, had been a substantial meal of cold meats and game, cheese and ale, fish, eggs, often chops and steaks. For a man who was going out hunting or shooting or about the business of the estate, and would not return until dinner-time, this was a necessary start to the day; he might take a sandwich in his pocket, and at home his wife might take a snack and some wine at noon, but there were, in effect, only two main meals a day. By the 1830s this pattern was changing. In great houses, where an important party was being entertained, breakfast might still be an elaborate meal at ten o'clock, for which ladies and gentlemen dressed formally, but generally it had become earlier, lighter, and unpunctual, with a variety of grilled dishes kept hot and served from about eight o'clock onwards. Ale had been superseded by tea and coffee, and although cold meats on the sideboard were still common, and a plentiful supply of boiled eggs, more attention was now paid to the hot toast and fancy breads, the butter and preserves which were gradually transforming the meal. A Holland House breakfast of the period consisted of 'very good coffee, very good tea, very good eggs, butter kept in the midst of ice, and hot rolls', and this kind of fashionable simplicity no doubt commended itself to Victorian businessmen who were under the necessity of ordering an early coach or catching an early train to the city.

The time and composition of the luncheon depended largely on whether 'the master' returned home for it or not, but generally it became a much more substantial meal than formerly. It might almost be said that the early Victorian age invented luncheon as a third meal of the day, as breakfast became earlier and dinner later. Indeed, the word itself had an uncertain history, developing from the eighteenth-century 'nunchin', defined by Dr Johnson in 1757 as 'a piece of victuals eaten between meals', to Jane Austen's 'noonshine' (1808), and with 'luncheon' apparently still common usage in rural Wiltshire as late as the 1890s.[4] As the middle classes tended to live farther and farther out in the suburbs, travelling home for luncheon often became impossible: the husband ate at his club or a chop house, his wife had a light, cooked meal of meat or fish, often using up the remains of the previous night's dinner. It became common practice at this time to permit the children, who were usually condemned to the nursery and schoolroom, to take luncheon with mother, at least when she did not have guests. In upper-class households luncheon developed between 1830 and 1860 from a cold collation to which everyone helped themselves, into a more or less elaborate hot meal, served between one and two o'clock. Coffee was not generally offered after luncheon until the 1870s. Luncheon was, therefore, partly the innovation of ladies of leisure, partly the response of professional and businessmen to earlier starts and longer journeys to work. But not all men approved of the interruption, or required more than a glass of wine and a biscuit or two in their offices, Macaulay complaining bitterly in 1853 of the detested necessity of breaking the labours of the day by luncheon.[5]

In the afternoon ladies took 'carriage exercise', calling or leaving cards at their friends' or acquaintances'; if they were offered refreshment, it was still usually cake and wine, or, in the country, home-made cordials. Although tea had been a fashionable drink for a century and more, it was not generally taken at 'tea-time'. Fanny Kemble, the actress, writes that when she was staying at Belvoir (the seat of the Duke of Rutland), a co-guest, the Duchess of Bedford, used to invite her to private tea-drinkings in the afternoon. It was the Duchess who introduced afternoon tea at her country house, Woburn, and at her town house in Belgrave Square,[6] and it seems that the fashion was spreading in polite society from the 1840s onwards. Lower down the social scale, middle-class ladies also found it pleasant occasionally to appear at nursery tea, the last meal of the day for children.

Refreshment at tea-time became more necessary as the dinner-hour became more postponed. There were probably a number of practical reasons for this – the lengthening of Parliamentary sittings for politicians and of office hours for businessmen, the longer journey home, and the extension of the day by gaslight – but social imitation was again an important factor. Queen Victoria, when she came to the throne, dined as late as eight o'clock (eight-thirty at Windsor), and this helped to establish a pattern of later dining in fashionable circles: seven-thirty was the favourite time by mid-century, though some great families, like the Hollands and the Russells, dined at seven o'clock, and the Carlyles, following the middle-class pattern, at six. Coffee was by now served at dinner, immediately after the dessert and before the ladies left the gentlemen to their port, and there would also be a tea-table set out in the drawing-room between nine and ten o'clock for those who felt the need of a refreshing and digestive drink. A cold punch and cakes might also be provided but a formal supper of hot or cold dishes, served at ten or eleven o'clock, was no

The food of the rich

longer required except at late evening parties and supper-balls.

It is tempting to argue that all that had happened was a change of names – that, as De Quincey pointed out in 1839, 'the two o'clock meal used to be called dinner, whereas at present it is called luncheon; the seven o'clock meal used to be called supper, whereas at present it is called dinner'.[7] This, of course, disguises the important social change that the principal meal of the day, the meal of hospitality and the meal at which the most prestigious dishes of meat, fish, and game were served had, in fashionable urban society, become postponed by five or six hours. In the provinces, and especially in the country houses of squires and large farmers, the older pattern survived well into our period and was, indeed, recommended by many of the writers who were beginning to take an interest in what was known as 'regimen'. Dr Kitchiner, whose books on diet and cookery enjoyed a wide popularity until the 1840s, advised early rising and exercise before breakfast, which should consist of 'good milk gruel, or beef tea, or portable beef tea', followed by more exercise before luncheon at noon. This should be 'a bit of roasted poultry, a basin of good beef tea, eggs poached . . . fish plainly dressed or a sandwich – stale bread – and half a pint of good home-brewed beer'. Dinner at five – 'which should be confined to one dish of roasted beef or mutton five days in the week – boiled meat one, and roasted poultry one – with a portion of sufficiently boiled ripe vegetables – mashed potatoes are preferred'.[8] The advice on 'Beauty Training for Ladies' given in *The Family Oracle of Health* for 1824 is similar though somewhat less spartan:

> Before breakfast you must walk . . . from half a mile to three miles . . . and if you botanize by the way it will be of immense advantage. The . . . breakfast itself – not later than eight o'clock ought, in rigid training, to consist of plain biscuit (not bread), broiled beef steaks or mutton chops, under-done without any fat, and half a pint of bottled ale – the genuine Scots ale is the best. . . . Should it be found too strong fare at the commencement, we permit instead of the ale, one small breakfast cup – not more – of good strong black tea or of coffee – weak tea or coffee is always bad for the nerves as well as the complexion. [After more walking, dinner at two] the same as breakfast, no vegetables, boiled meat, nor made-dishes being permitted, much less fruit, sweet things or pastry. Those who are very delicate may begin with a bit of broiled chicken or turkey, but the steaks and chops must always be the chief part of your food.

Vegetables other than potatoes, butter, cream, milk, cheese, and fish are all 'prohibited'.[9] Whether ladies, even for the sake of their complexions, ever submitted to such a diet is not known, but something like this kind of traditional English fare continued to be the stock-in-trade of numerous recipe books having a wide circulation in this period.

Among country squires and parsons, doctors and attorneys, there was the utmost suspicion of the 'fancy French dishes' which were appearing on the tables of the rich: a good dinner was still one, like that of Squire Higgins, where all the dishes were placed at once on the table – 'six or seven ribs of roast beef . . . a boiled turkey . . . and an enormous ham . . . two assaults on the first only seemed to be provocative of further displays of vigour with reference to the second and third';[10] or the city merchant's dinner-party described in *Phineas Quiddy* which consisted of 'a tureen of pea-soup, a fine cod's head and shoulders, a roast sirloin of beef, a stewed rumpsteak and an apple-pie. There were no impertinent and miserable attempts at foreign cooking . . . not a single dish appeared upon the table under false pretences.' For those who favoured this kind of traditional fare numerous essentially 'English' recipe books continued to appear, and to circulate in several editions, throughout the period. In the 1820s and 1830s, Dr Kitchiner[11] and Mrs Rundell[12] were the accepted authorities on 'plain cookery', Kitchiner being particularly critical of 'the multiplicity of dishes which luxury has made fashionable at the tables of the Great, the Wealthy – and the Ostentatious'. It is more surprising to find the *Epicure's Almanac* for 1841, which gives 365 recipes, one for each day of the year, containing fewer than a dozen continental dishes,[13] and the *Complete Art of Cookery* of 1848 which will have none of French cuisine but contains recipes for cooking neats' tongues, boiled haunch of venison, roasted pig whole, and so on.[14] Again, Eliza Acton's *Modern Cookery*, which was the best-selling recipe book in the generation before Mrs Beeton, devoted only fifteen of its 650 pages to 'Foreign and Jewish Cookery'.[15]

In fashionable circles, however, French cookery and service had become *de rigueur* by the 1830s and 1840s, and this was, perhaps, the other most outstanding dietary change of the period. In food, as in dress and manners, France's leadership had been recognized in the late eighteenth century, but the Revolution and the Napoleonic Wars had produced an anti-Gallic feeling which to some extent delayed the adoption of French fashions here. The essential difference lay in the fact that whereas the English dinner was served with all the dishes together, the French was served with a series of dishes in succession, divided into two great courses. These were generally sub-divided still further by *entrées*, or side-dishes, in the first course, and *entremets* in the second. More emphasis was placed on the sweet dishes and dessert at the end of the meal, and, of course, in the preparation of all foods much more importance was attached to flavouring, sauces, and appearance. The multiplication of separate dishes also demanded a considerable variety of wines to accompany the different parts of the meal.

The way in which the French pattern was gradually introduced is described by Captain Gronow, a famous London socialite and member of the Prince Regent's set in the years immediately after 1815. This is the grand dinner in transition:

The food of the rich

Mulligatawny and turtle soups were the first dishes placed before you; a little lower the eye met with the familiar salmon at one end of the table and the turbot surrounded by smelts at the other. The first course was sure to be followed by a saddle of mutton or a piece of roast beef; and then you could take your oath that fowls, tongue and ham would as assuredly succeed as darkness after day. Whilst these never-ending 'pièces de résistances' were occupying the table, what were called French dishes were, for custom's sake, added to the solid abundance. The French, or side-dishes, consisted of very mild but very abortive attempts at Continental cooking; and I have always observed that they met with the neglect and contempt that they merited. The dessert, generally ordered at Grange's, or at Owen's in Bond Street, if for a dozen people, would cost at least as many pounds. The wines were chiefly port, sherry and hock; claret and even Burgundy being then designated 'poor, thin, washy, stuff'.

French dishes first appeared 'on the side', and for some time the unhappy compromise between French and English continued. A writer in 1824 says, 'It is a bad dinner when there are not at least five varieties – a substanial dish of fish, one of meat, one of game, one of poultry, and above all, a ragoût with truffles. . . . They form the absolute minimum and *sine qua non* of a dinner for one person.'[16] The dinner described by Prince Pückler-Muskau, a German visitor to England in 1829, is also of the inter-mediate type.

After the soup is removed, all the covers are taken off, every man helps the dish before him, and offers some of it to his neighbour. . . . If he wishes for anything else, he must ask across the table, or send a servant for it – a very troublesome custom in place of which some of the most elegant travelled gentlemen have adopted the more convenient German [and French] fashion of sending ser-vants round with the dishes. . . . At the conclusion of the second course comes a sort of intermediate dessert of cheese, butter, salad, raw celery, and the like; after which ale, sometimes thirty or forty years old, and so strong that when thrown on the fire it blazes like spirit, is handed about. The table-cloth is then removed: under it, at the best tables, is a finer, upon which the dessert is set. . . . Three decanters are usually placed before the master of the house, generally containing claret, port and sherry, or madeira. The host pushes these in stands, or in a little silver wagon on wheels, to his neighbour on the left.[17]

Already by the 1820s the fashionable thing was to follow French practice: Sturgeon, in his remarkably modern *Essays on Good Living*, advises the gourmet never to accept invitations to dinner unless a second course is to be served, and suggests that 'if you wish to appear particularly well-informed, endeavour to collect the names and ingredients of a few rare dishes, such as Côtelettes à la purée de bécasses, Rognons au vin de Cham-pagne, Dindes aux truffes, etc.'[18]

The first cookery book which was avowedly of the new type, containing nearly 2,000 previously unpublished recipes, was apparently Richard

71

Dolby's *Cook's Dictionary*, which appeared in 1830.[19] It received a highly enthusiastic press and became an immediate success, running through several editions in the next few years. Dolby had been chef at the famous Thatched House Tavern in St James's Street, where, according to the *Weekly Journal*, 'The author has superintended the preparation of feasts partaken of by the most dignified personages of the land (his late Majesty included). . . . At one of the late City banquets peremptory directions were given that every dish in the dinner and the dessert should be prepared from [his] receipts.' Dolby was also probably the first writer to include specimen menus in his book, with diagrams illustrating how the dishes should be disposed on the table around the central decorative *plateau* or *pièce montée*. His dinner for eighteen persons is a typical example of the 'new' cookery which would have been enjoyed at fashionable London parties in the 1830s:

Bill of Fare for Eighteen Persons

January

FIRST COURSE

Purée de Gibier	*Purée of Game*
Potage à l'Allemande	*Consommée with Nouilles*
Tranches de Cabilleau, etc.	*Slices of Crimped Cod and Smelts*
Matelote de Carpes	*Matelote of Carp*

RELEVÉS	REMOVES
Tête de Veau a la béchamelle	*Calf's Head, bechamel sauce*
Boeuf rôti	*Roast Beef*
Dindon à la financière	*Turkey with financier sauce*
Langue de Boeuf en chartreuse	*Tongue in chartreuse*

ENTRÉES	ENTRÉES
Vol au Vent d'Homard	*Patty with ragout of Lobster*
Perdrix aux Choux	*Partridges with Cabbage, etc.*
Files de Volaille piqués	*Fillets of Fowl larded*
Turban Filets de Lapereau, etc.	*Turban of Fillets of Rabbit Espagnole sauce*
Cassolettes d'un Salpicon, etc.	*Cassolettes of Salpicon of Beef Palates*
Côtelettes de Mouton à la Soubise	*Mutton Cutlets, Soubise sauce*
Tendrons de Veau, etc.	*Tendrons of Veal, purée of Endive*
Pâté d'Alouettes aux Truffes	*Lark Patty with Truffles*

SECOND COURSE

Quatre Bécasses	*Four Woodcocks roast*
Deux Faisants	*Two Pheasants*

Un Chapon au cresson	*Capon garnished with cresses*
Perdreaux rôtis	*Partridges roast*
Petits Pâtés garnis de conserves	*Fancy Pastry garnished with conserves*
Salsifis à l'Espagnole	*Salsify Espagnole sauce*
Champignons à la poulette	*Mushrooms poulette sauce*
Gelée de Ponche	*Punch Jelly*
Suédoise de Pommes	*Suedois of Apples*
Œufs Pochés aux épinards	*Poached Eggs on dressed Spinach*
Friture d'Huîtres	*Friture of Oysters*
Crème d'orange	*Orange Cream*

RELEVÉS	REMOVES
Petits Ramaquins de Fromage	*Small Ramaquins of Cheese*
Vanille Soufflée	*Vanilla Soufflée*
Boudin de Citron	*Lemon Pudding*
Tourte de conserves de Prune	*Tart of preserved greengages*

The Soups and Fish to be served first, the Entrées and Removes next, and after the Second Course the four Removes in place of the Roasts.

The growth of French cuisine in England owed much to the large numbers of immigrant French chefs who settled here in the late eighteenth and early nineteenth centuries, some of whom came as political refugees during the French Revolution when the great households were broken up, some who were attracted by the high salaries which the English nobility and moneyed classes could offer for illustrious ornaments to their establishments. One of the greatest was Felix, chef first to Lord Seaford and later to the Duke of Wellington, whom he ultimately abandoned because of the Duke's lack of gastronomic interest. 'I serve him a dinner that would make Ude or Francatelli burst with envy, and he says nothing; I serve him a dinner dressed, and badly dressed, by the cook-maid, and he says nothing. I cannot live with such a master, if he was a hundred times a hero.'[20]

Antonin Carême, the author of *Maître d'Hôtel Français* and *L'Art de la Cuisine Française*, was chef to the Regent at a salary of £2,000 a year, and one of his pupils, Francatelli, who was also a writer and an artist, was in turn chef at Chesterfield House, at Crockford's famous gambling club, and finally *maître d'hôtel* to Queen Victoria and the Prince Consort. Louis Eustache Ude had previously made Crockford's outstanding for its cuisine, after acting as *maître d'hôtel* to Madame Letitia Bonaparte, whose service he left over some arithmetical difference. Writing in the *Quarterly Review* in 1835, a noted gourmet, Abraham Hayward, said:

The most eminent cooks of the present time in England are Pierre Moret of the Royal Household; Aberlin, chef to the Duke of Devonshire; Crépin of the Duchess of Sutherland's household; Durand, Paraire, Gérin, Mesmer;

Labalme, cook to the Duke of Beaufort; Bory, cook to the Duke of Buccleuch; Auguste Halinger, cook to Baron de Rothschild; the brothers Mailliez; Brûnet, cook to the Duke of Montrose; Lambert, to Mr Charles Townley; Valentine, to Lord Poltimore; Hopwood, to Lord Foley; George Perkins, to the Marquis of Bristol; Louis Besnard, to Mr Maxse; Frottier, to the Duke of Cambridge; Perren, to the Marquis of Londonderry; Bernard to Lord Willoughby d'Eresby; Guerault, to Mr H.T. Hope; Chaudeau, to the Marquis of Lansdowne; Rotival, to Lord Wilton; Douetil, to the Duke of Cleveland; Palanque, to the Carlton Club; and Comte, to Brookes's.[21]

The impressive list omits the man who, through his writings, was to be the most influential of all chefs in mid-Victorian England – Alexis Soyer, the only chef to be honoured by mention in the *Dictionary of National Biography*. Leaving France during the Revolution of 1830, he served in several great houses until 1837, when he became chef to the Reform Club, a position which he held for thirteen years. During this time he turned out a stream of delicacies such as London had never known: he was continually inventing new and ever more elaborate dishes which quickly made the reputation of the Reform. Several of his banquets have become legendary – his coronation breakfast for 2,000 members and friends, the dinner to Ibrahim Pasha in 1846, where the dessert, called *Crème d'Égypte à l'Ibrahim* consisted of:

a pyramid about two and a half feet high, made of light meringue cake, in imitation of solid stones, surrounded with grapes and other fruits, but representing only the four angles of the pyramid through sheets of waved sugar to show to the greatest advantage an elegant cream à l'ananas, on the top of which was resting a highly finished portrait of the illustrious stranger's father, Mehemet Ali.

The *Morning Post* paid as much attention to the menu as to the speeches. On another occasion he prepared a dish for a banquet at York, attended by the Queen and Consort, which included five turtle heads, twenty-four capons (the two small *noix* from each side of the middle of the back only used), eighteen turkeys, eighteen fatted pullets, sixteen fowls, twenty pheasants, forty-five partridges, a hundred snipes, forty woodcocks, thirty-six pigeons (*noix* only in each case), ten grouse, six plovers, thirty-six quail, and seventy-two larks stuffed.[22] From such extravagances Soyer went on to establish soup-kitchens during the Irish famine of 1847 and later organized the victualling and dietary of hospitals in the Crimea, both of which he did with outstanding success. His published works, which became culinary classics, include *The Gastronomic Regenerator* (1846), *Charitable Cookery, or The Poor Man's Regenerator* (1847), *The Modern Housewife, or Ménagère* (1849), and *A Shilling Cookery for the People* (1855). His biographers commented: 'He benefited the middle class with his *Modern Housewife*, the tradesman with his *Shilling Cookery* and the labourer with *The Poor Man's Regenerator*. Such instructions never were published before in so comprehensive a manner, and the enormous sale of his works has no parallel in the annals of cookery.'[23]

But to look only at the menus for banquets and dinner-parties would be to give a very false impression of the normal daily food of the rich during this period. A society hostess gave a dinner-party once or perhaps twice a week, a middle-class family probably once a month. In either case it was a major operation which required at least a whole day's preparation, often involving the services of outside caterers and a prodigious outlay of time, energy, and money. (Disraeli is credited with setting the fashion of employing outside caterers to provide dinner at a fixed price.) It is doubtful whether even ample Victorian appetites could have coped with a daily dinner-party, despite the prevalence of 'peristaltic persuaders'. The daily fare, even of the most wealthy, was necessarily much less elaborate.

It has never been easy for sociologists to define exactly where the 'middle classes' start or end. Mrs Rundell, in her *New System of Domestic Economy*, made the distinction rest entirely on income, and after discussing budgets for the poor in Part I of her book, she commences the budgets of 'gentlemen' in Part II with an income of £150 per annum. Small shopkeepers, schoolmasters, and clerks were certainly earning as little, or less, than this in 1824 and for a good many years to come, but it is unlikely that they would have received the title. At £250 per annum a man was fairly and squarely in the middle class, his wife employed at least one domestic servant and had been promoted to a 'lady'. The lavish employment of domestic staff was, of course, a distinguishing feature of the life of the rich: at £250 per annum, according to Mrs Rundell, a man employed one maidservant (at £16 per annum); at £400 per annum, two maids, a horse, and a groom; at £1,000, three maids, a coachman, and a footman; and at £5,000 per annum, thirteen male and nine female servants. In the census of 1851 domestic servants were, at 1,039,000, the second largest occupational group in the country, and they continued to grow in numbers to 1,500,000 in 1911.

We give (in Table 10) Mrs Rundell's budget for an income of £250 per annum. The heavy consumption of meat – half a pound every day for each member of the household – plus a fair quantity of fish is interesting, as is the small consumption of milk (3d each per week could give only two pints). The high cost of tea and sugar before the tariff reduction of the 1840s and 1850s is also noticeable. But the budget, imaginary as it is, was probably quite near to reality because it corresponds very closely with independent estimates of the same period. The *Family Oracle of Health*, for example, gives a budget of £300 per annum for a man with a wife and

75

Table 10 *Income – £250 per annum. Family – a gentleman, his lady, three children and a maidservant. Provisions and other articles of household expense*

	Weekly			Annually		
	£	s	d	£	s	d
Bread and flour, 1s each		6	0			
Butter, $3\frac{1}{2}$ lb at average 1s a lb		3	6			
Cheese, $\frac{1}{4}$ lb each, $1\frac{1}{2}$ lb at 10d		1	3			
Milk, 3d each		1	6			
Tea, 5 oz at 8s a lb		2	6			
Sugar, $4\frac{1}{2}$ lb at 8d a lb		3	0			
Grocery, including spices, condiments, etc. 6d each		3	0			
Butcher's meat, 18 lb at 7d a lb		10	6			
Fish, 6d per day		3	6			
Vegetables and fruits, 6d each		3	0			
Beer and other liquors 1s a day		7	0			
Coals and wood		3	9			
Candles, oil, etc., 2 lb a week		1	2			
Soap, starch, etc., 2 lb a week		1	2			
Sundries, for cleaning, scouring, etc.			9			
	£2	11s	7d	£134	2s	4d
Extra for entertainments, medicine, and other incidents				7	11s	0d
				£141	13s	4d
Clothes (gent. £14, lady £12, children £10)				36	0	0
Rent, taxes, etc.				25	0	0
Education, extra and private expenses				10	10	0
Maidservant				16	0	0
Total expenses				£229	3s	4d
Reserve, $\frac{1}{12}$				20	16	8
Amount of income				£250	0s	0d

only one child, and two maids, where the amount spent on meat and fish corresponds almost exactly.[24]

For a slightly higher income bracket, where the annual expenditure on food amounts to £270, Dr Kitchiner puts meat at £65 – again a proportion of between one-fifth and one-quarter of the whole; milk costs only £7 a year. This household is described as one 'where there is plenty of good

76

provisions, but no affectation of profusion'. Allowance is made for two maids and a manservant, and a dinner-party once a month. The weekly *Economist and General Adviser* for 1825 also gives a closely similar budget for £250 per annum with a wife, three children, and one maid, which allows 14s a week for meat and fish, only 1s 6d for milk, and 3s for vegetables and fruits.[25] This pattern seems to have remained typical throughout the period under discussion. Variations in the price of bread mattered little to families who spent proportionately little on it, and meat, which was such a major item of expenditure, had fallen by 1d or 2d a pound by 1850 to 7½d–8½d for good quality beef and mutton. More significant were the reductions in the prices of tea and sugar, following the tariff reforms of Peel and Gladstone in mid-century: by 1859 a fair tea could be bought for 4s a pound (against 8s twenty-five years earlier), a cheap one for 3s, and sugar could be had for 7d instead of 8d or 9d. A dozen oysters, the best natives, also cost 7d, though butter at 1s 2d a pound was still relatively expensive. The significant thing about the movement of prices in these years is that luxuries fell more than necessities, a fact which contributed importantly to the high, and rising, standards of the wealthier classes.

Income – £300 a year
4 Adults, 1 Child

	s	d	
Bread	5	0	weekly
Meat	9	0	
Cheese, butter, ham	4	6	
Milk and cream	2	0	
Vegetables and fruit	4	0	
Fish	5	0	
Groceries	11	0	
Beer	9	0	
£2	9s	6d	

Household budgets in themselves do not give much indication of the actual composition of meals. For this, our best guide is Alexis Soyer, whose *Modern Housewife or Ménagère* of 1849 gives hundreds of recipes and menus designed for the middle-class housewife; its widespread use is evidenced by the fact that within two weeks of publication it went into a second edition, and by 1851 sales had reached 21,000. Particularly revealing are the imaginary letters and conversations which are inserted throughout the text. A 'Mrs B', for example, traces the growth of her husband's fortunes from small shopkeeper to prosperous merchant in a series of bills of fare:[26]

Plenty and Want

When I was first married and commencing business, and our means were limited, the following was our system of living:

SUNDAY'S DINNER *Roast Beef, Potatoes, Greens and Yorkshire Pudding*
MONDAY *Hashed Beef and Potatoes*
TUESDAY *Broiled Beef and Bones, Vegetables and Spotted Dick Pudding*
WEDNESDAY *Fish, if cheap, Chops and Vegetables*
THURSDAY *Boiled Pork, Peas, Pudding and Greens*
FRIDAY *Pea Soup, Remains of Pork*
SATURDAY *Stewed Steak with Suet Dumpling*

After two years business had increased, and there were now three clerks who dined with the family. Also, Mrs B had been with her husband on a visit to France, 'where my culinary ideas received a great improvement'. Her weekly menus now looked very different:

SUNDAY *Pot-au-feu, Fish, Haunch of Mutton or a quarter of lamb or other good joint – two Vegetables – Pastry and a Fruit Pudding – a little Dessert*
MONDAY *Vermicelli Soup made from the Pot-au-Feu of the day previous – the Bouilli of the Pot-au-Feu – Remains of the Mutton – Two Vegetables – Fruit Tart*
TUESDAY *Fish – Shoulder of Veal Stuffed – Roast Pigeons or Leveret or Curry – Two Vegetables – Apple with Rice, and light Pastry*
WEDNESDAY *Spring Soup – Roast Fowls, Remains of Veal minced, and Poached Eggs – Two Vegetables – Rowley Powley Pudding*
THURSDAY *Roast Beef – Remains of Fowl – Two Vegetables – Sweet Omelet*
FRIDAY *Fish – Shoulder of Lamb – Mirotan of Beef – Two Vegetables – Baked Pudding*
SATURDAY *Mutton Broth – Broiled Neck Mutton – Liver and Bacon – Two Vegetables – Currant Pudding*

Mr B. continued to prosper and later menus became more elaborate still:

Now . . . our daily bill of fare consists of something like the following:
One Soup or Fish, generally alternate – One Remove either Joint or Poultry – One Entrée – Two Vegetables – Pudding or Tart – A Little Dessert.
  This may seem a great deal for two persons, but when you remember that we almost invariably have one or two to dine with us, and the remains are required for the breakfast, lunch, nursery, and servants' dinners, you will perceive that the dinner is the principal expense of the establishment.

The guests here were merely Mr B.'s assistants. When a real dinner-party was given, Mrs B. now adopted a completely French service, and provided:

The food of the rich

First Course

*One Soup, say Purée of Artichokes – One Fish, Cod Slices
in Oyster Sauce – Remove with Smelts or White Bait
Removes – Saddle of Mutton – Turkey in Celery Sauce
Two Entrées – Cutlets à la Provençale – Sweetbreads
larded in any White Sauce
Two Vegetables – Greens, Kale, Potatoes on the Sideboard*

Second Course

*Two Roasts – Partridges – Wild Ducks
Jelly of Fruit – Cheesecakes – Meringue à la Crème
Vegetables – French Salad on the Sideboard
Removes – Ice Pudding – Beignet Soufflé
Dessert of eleven dishes*

By this time, Mrs B. must have been graduating from Soyer's *Modern Housewife* to his *Gastronomic Regenerator*, a collection of 2,000 elaborate dishes based on the Reform Club's recipes and aimed at the 'Kitchens of the Wealthy'. According to *The Times* review, he accomplished this feat in the remarkably short space of ten months, while at the same time 'he furnished 25,000 dinners, 38 banquets of importance, comprising above 70,000 dishes, besides providing daily for sixty servants and receiving the visits of fifteen thousand strangers, all too eager to inspect the renowned altar of a great apician temple'. The *Regenerator*, although costing a guinea, reached its sixth edition within three years, and became the acknowledged classic of *haute cuisine*.

Mrs Rundell gives a budget for an income of £1,000 a year in 1824, 'The family consisting of a Gentleman, his Wife and three Children; with an establishment of three Female Servants, a Coachman and a Footman – in all ten Persons; a Chariot or Coach, Phaeton or other four-wheel Carriage, and a Pair of Horses.' The household consumes $52\frac{1}{2}$ lb of meat a week – an allowance of $\frac{3}{4}$ lb for each person each day – in addition to fish and poultry, $\frac{3}{4}$ lb of butter each per week is allowed, and a guinea a week is set aside for beer and other liquors. The smallest items are still vegetables and fruit (9d each per week) and eggs and milk ($4\frac{1}{2}$d each per week). The coachman receives £24 per annum, the footman £22, the cook £16, the housemaid £14 14s, and the nurserymaid £10 10s, while the two horses cost between them £65 17s a year. The horse was considerably more expensive to keep than the man – and G. R. Porter, the statistician, put the number used exclusively for riding or drawing carriages in 1844 at 146,000.[27]

Again, it is necessary to distinguish between the everyday, family dinners and those served at dinner-parties: the menu would also depend on the degree of conversion to French cooking. At £1,000 a year, the

family dinner of the now old-fashioned English pattern would probably be
something like that given by Reynolds:[28]

Spitchcock Eels
Remove – Chine of Lamb Cresses
Potatoes   Damson Pudding   Stewed Carrots
Cold Beef
Scrag of Veal smothered with onions
Remove – a Fruit Pie
Mashed Potatoes trimmed with small slices of Bacon
Broccoli
Peas Soup
Hashed Hare

There seems an odd lack of design about such a meal, the main object
presumably being to place a number of substantial dishes on the table
from which the family could make a selection. Thomas Walker, who
through his weekly journal *The Original* was an early advocate of
simple – though good – living, gave as his ideal menu, 'Turtle, followed
by no other fish but whitebait; which is to be followed by no other meat but
grouse, which are to be succeeded by apple fritters and jelly.'[29] Something
between the two was probably the daily fare of the rich in the middle of the
century.

It would be quite otherwise when a dinner-party was to be given. For
one of half a dozen or more guests professional caterers would almost
certainly be employed, the best silver, china, and glass brought out, and
the meal served *à la française*. At larger parties it was not uncommon for
guests to bring their own footmen to assist at table: a meal could easily last
for two or three hours, and without an adequate number of waiters there
could be annoying delays as the innumerable dishes were brought round.
Too many waiters, on the other hand, only added to the confusion. The
meal itself followed a fairly formal pattern – soups, fish, entrées (by the
1850s 'flying dishes' of oyster or other pâtés were sometimes inserted
before these), and various roasted meats to close the first course; game and
poultry to begin the second course, elaborate sweets, savoury dishes, ices,
and dessert to follow. The usual wines were sherry, Madeira, and champagne, which grew in popularity as the century progressed, and the meal
ended with coffee and liqueurs. This was the irreducible minimum: for
larger parties, the number of *entrées* was increased – for six or eight
guests, four *entrées*; for twelve, six; for eighteen, eight; and so on.

Appetites were evidently larger then than today but, even so, one
wonders how the Victorian stomach coped with such quantity and variety.
Ladies, and some gentlemen, refused some of the courses, or took a
perfunctory helping, and the length of the meal certainly aided digestion.
But the waste at dinner-parties and banquets must have been enormous,

even allowing for what the servants could consume. A dinner served by Francatelli to Queen Victoria about 1840 includes four soups, four fish, four *hors d'oeuvres*, four *relevés*, sixteen *entrées*: there were three joints on the sideboard, including a haunch of venison, and the second service comprised six roasts, six *relevés*, two *flancs*, four *countre-flancs*, sixteen *entremets* – a grand total of seventy dishes.[30] The Queen herself preferred plain food.

The growth of entertaining was a marked feature of early Victorian social life. For politicians, as for professional and businessmen, it was a necessary part of 'public relations', and for their wives and daughters it gave a unique opportunity to display their finest clothes and latest acquisitions. The increasing ease of communication by road and rail was also an important factor in facilitating social intercourse between more distant friends and relatives. The family and the home were central institutions in Victorian middle-class life. Formerly, social relationships had been a good deal more mono-sexual: gentlemen had met for talk and business in the coffee-houses, but ladies had been little seen in public. By this time, the few famous coffee-houses that remained – Garraway's, the Rainbow, and one or two more – were pale imitations of their former splendours, no longer places of fashion, and little used by 'the quality'.[31] To a considerable extent their place had been taken by clubs, both the 'public' kind, such as the Carlton, the Travellers', the Country, Brooks's, and the Reform, where an excellent meal could be had for 3s or 4s, and the numerous 'private' clubs formed by friends sharing some common interest or calling. Of these, probably the best known was the Sublime Society of Beefsteaks, which lasted from its foundation by John Rich in 1732 down to 1869. The main function of the club – apart from a good deal of mock ceremonial and practical joking – was to eat beefsteaks of the finest quality, of which the Duke of Norfolk regularly consumed three or four pounds at a sitting. The club numbered among its members at various times the Prince of Wales, the Earl of Sandwich, John Wilkes, the Duke of Sussex, and Lord Brougham, besides actors, painters, and authors. But the clubs of Pall Mall were also much more patronized at this period and many new ones were formed. Not all of them could provide a cuisine like that of the Reform, but they had a high standard of catering at moderate prices, and were increasingly used by city men for lunch and for entertaining (exclusively male) guests to dinner: In 1832 the Athenaeum (established 1830) served 17,323 dinners at 2s 9d, 3s 0d, and 4s 6d each, with a modest average consumption of wine of half a pint per person. The subscription was six guineas a year. Apart from the Reform, the clubs having the highest gastronomic reputations were apparently the Garrick, Boodle's ('the country gentleman's club'), and the Royal Thames Yacht Club.

The inns, eating-houses, and hotels of this period had a generally poor reputation, and were used from necessity rather than for pleasure:

> I have dined at eating-houses [complains the author of *Memoirs of a Stomach*] the effluvia of which, steaming up through the iron grating, made me qualmish before eating, and ill all the day after. I have enjoyed myself at some of the finest clubs in town; I have luxuriated at some of the best restaurants in Europe; I have groped my way down hypocausts in Fleet Street, and dined in cavern-like taverns, wishing myself a thousand miles away the moment the eternal joint was uncovered.[32]

Apart from one or two first-class but expensive hotels in the West End, like the Clarendon, the Bedford, Clunn's, and Mivart's, and a few new railway hotels, there was a serious shortage of comfortable accommodation, and outside the great cities the traveller was usually condemned to put up at one of the old country inns of coaching days, 'miserable, comfortless, the four-poster bed occupying almost all the bedroom, wax candles (to be paid for extra) and a menu consisting invariably of "Chop, sir, steak, broiled fowl". It was a blessed thing when the stage coaches were run off the roads by the winged engine of the rail.'[33] Unfortunately, the coaching inns had to be used for want of any alternative, and could abuse their monopoly by charging 15s to £1 a day for inferior food and accommodation. Some of the leading provincial hotels seem to have overcharged and traded on their reputations:

> I went one evening in the autumn of 1850 into a leading hotel at Scarborough with my brother, and we ordered a plate of sandwiches and a bottle of Pale Ale. On my word in print, I was charged for this, and I paid seven shillings (it was put down in the bill as two luncheons at three shillings each, and the 'Bass' at its usual price). The sandwich was not near so excellent as you get with a glass of ale for fourpence in London, and as regards the beer, had it been furnished at my club, I should have 'backed my bill'.[34]

The restaurant had hardly arrived in 1850. Outside the London clubs there was a serious gap between the dear hotel or inn and the cheap chop house, where the steaks and pies might be well cooked, but where the shilling 'ordinary' consisted all too often of 'parboiled oxflesh, with sodden dumplings floating in a saline, greasy mixture, surrounded by carrots looking red with disgust and turnips pale with dismay'.[35] A few chop houses, however, retained a good reputation for first-class roasts and steaks cooked and served in the traditional way – Simpson's in the Strand, The Ship and Turtle in Leadenhall Street, and Dolly's Chop House in St Paul's Churchyard. What was probably the first 'good food guide' to London eating-houses – *London at Table: How, When and Where to Dine and Order a Dinner, and Where to Avoid Dining* – appeared in 1851, at a time when millions of visitors to the Great Exhibition were experiencing the great dearth of places of refreshment. A few restaurants, mostly

French, were given the seal of approval – Rouget's, Grillon's, Howchin's, Ellis's, and Fenton's; however, the anonymous author complained:

> One evil of long standing still exists in London – and that is the difficulty of finding an Hotel or Restaurant where strangers of the gentler sex may be taken to dine. It is true that since our intercourse with the Continent, some coffee-rooms have been opened where gentlemen may take their wives and daughters, but it has not yet become a recognized custom. . . . To give a private dinner with ladies it is necessary to go to the 'Albion' or 'London Taverns', where nothing can exceed the magnificence of the rooms . . . wine exquisite, price in accordance.[36]

It may have been true – and we have the testimony of Ude for it – that 'cookery in England, when well done, is superior to that of any country in the world', and Hayward himself believed that gastronomy had emigrated to England in the days after Waterloo. English beef and mutton, salmon and trout, pheasant and venison were certainly unrivalled for quality, and the development of speedy communications meant that they could now be brought to table in perfect condition: the Carlton Club, for example, made a point of serving Severn salmon, caught that morning, at seven o'clock dinner, and it was no longer necessary to travel to Devonshire to enjoy John Dory, or to Worcester to taste lampreys in perfection. But delicacies like these were, as yet, restricted to the very few. The greatest chefs of the day, like the greatest singers and dancers, had been attracted to England by the wealth of the richest country in the world, brought to serve as ornaments to the acquisitive society which industrialism had fostered. In the process the Victorian upper classes, who denounced gluttony almost as vehemently as they did immorality, had their palates educated, and came to be as fond of good food as they were of other sins of the flesh. Probably no civilization since the Roman ate as well as they did. The whole resources of culinary art were at their command, and combined with the achievements of modern science to place the delicacies of the world on the tables of the rich. In nothing was the contrast between wealth and poverty more obvious than in food. House, dress, or manners might be a misleading test of income in 1850, but a man's dinner-table instantly announced his taste and his standard of living to the world at large. 'Tell me what you eat,' said Brillat-Savarin, 'and I will tell you what you are.'

Notes

1 Porter, G.R. (1847) *The Progress of the Nation*, 56 et seq.
2 Lewis, R. and Maude, J. (1949) *The English Middle Classes*, 27.
3 Cole, G.D.H. (1951) 'The social structure of England' (Part 1: 'The working classes'), *History Today* (February), 60.

4 Palmer, Arnold (1952) *Movable Feasts. A Reconnaissance of the Origins and Consequences of Fluctuations in Meal Times*, 30–1.

5 ibid., 59.

6 Peel, Mrs C.S. (1934) 'Homes and habits', in G.M. Young (ed.) *Early Victorian England, 1830–1865* I, 97.

7 Quincey, T. de, *The Casuistry of Roman Meals*, quoted in Palmer, op. cit., 63.

8 Kitchiner, William (1824) *The Art of Invigorating and Prolonging Life, and Peptic Precepts. To which is added, The Pleasure of Making a Will*, 21 et seq.

9 *The Family Oracle of Health* (1824) II.

10 Burgon, Dean, *Lives of Twelve Good Men*, quoted in Charles Cooper (nd) *The English Table in History and Literature*, 197.

11 Kitchiner, William (1817 etc.) *The Cook's Oracle, containing Receipts for Plain Cookery on the most Economical Plan for Private Families*.

12 A Lady (Mrs Rundell) *A New System of Domestic Economy, formed upon Principles of Economy, and adapted to the Use of Private Families*.

13 Hill, Benson E. (1841) *The Epicure's Almanac, or Diary of Good Living*.

14 Reynolds, M.E. (1848) *The Complete Art of Cookery*.

15 Acton, Eliza (1856) *Modern Cookery for Private Families* (new edn).

16 *The Family Oracle of Health* II, op. cit.

17 Pückler-Muskau, Prince, *Tour in England, Ireland and France in the Years 1828–1829*.

18 Sturgeon, Launcelot (1822) *Essays, Moral, Philosophical and Stomachical on the Important Science of Good Living*, 42.

19 Dolby, Richard (1830) *The Cook's Dictionary and Housekeeper's Directory: a New Family Manual of Cooking and Confectionery on a Plan of Ready Reference never hitherto attempted*.

20 Hayward, Abraham (1852) *The Art of Dining, or Gastronomy and Gastronomers*, 17.

21 ibid., 77.

22 Dodds, John W. (1953) *The Age of Paradox: A Biography of England 1841–1851*, 297.

23 Volant, F. and Warren, J.R. (eds) (1859) *Memoirs of Alexis Soyer*, Introduction, VII.

24 op. cit.

25 *The Economist and General Adviser*, No. 36 (Saturday, 22 January 1825), 57.

26 Soyer, Alexis (1849) *The Modern Housewife or Ménagère*, 406 et seq.

27 Porter, op. cit., 163.

28 Reynolds, op. cit., 303.

29 Hayward, op. cit., 92.

30 Cooper, op, cit., 175.

31 *Doings in London; or Day and Night Scenes of the Frauds, Frolics, Manners and Depravities of the Metropolis* (14th edn, 1850), 354.

32 *Memoirs of a Stomach, Written by Himself, that All who Eat may Read* edited by a 'Minister of the Interior' (nd, *c.* 1850).

33 Smith, Albert (1855) *The English Hotel Nuisance*, 24 et seq.

34 ibid., 26.
35 *Memoirs of a Stomach*, op. cit.
36 Anon (1858) *London at Dinner; or, Where to Dine*, 11. Originally published in 1851 as *London at Table; or How, When and Where to Dine and Order a Dinner, and Where to Avoid Dining.*

❧ 5 ❧
Food adulteration

In any discussion of changes in the standard of diet in the nineteenth century, it is necessary to look at the quality as well as the quantity of food which English people consumed. So far we have spoken of the foods of the period as though they were constant and stable factors, as though the bread, the tea, or the beer of 1850 were essentially the same commodities as today. In fact, this was very far from the case. Adulteration of food prevailed in the first half of the nineteenth century to an unprecedented and unsupposed extent, and had far-reaching social, economic, and medical consequences which must not be overlooked in the debate about standards of life in early Victorian England.

In primitive and agrarian societies there was, no doubt, trickery, substitution of bad for good, petty dishonesty of many kinds but systematic adulteration ·would not have been possible. Food adulteration is essentially a phenomenon of urban life, and its historical origins cannot be traced back earlier than the city states of the classical world. As soon as there emerged a consuming public, distinct and separated from the producers of food, opportunities for organized commercial fraud arose: cheaper and nutritionally inferior substitutes might be used to replace the proper constituents of a food, essential ingredients might be removed, or foreign substances added to impart fictitious flavour, appearance, or strength.

The earliest mention of adulteration comes from Athens, where frequent complaints about the quality of wine eventually compelled the appointment of inspectors to watch over this essential of life; the name of one Canthare, who was particularly skilful in artificially maturing new wines, has come down to us. Similarly in Rome, according to Pliny, it was impossible to obtain the natural wines of Falerno, and certain wines from Gaul were notoriously sophisticated with aloes and other drugs. Roman bakers were accused of adding 'white earth' (possibly carbonate of magnesia) to their bread, which they obtained from a hill outside Naples.

There is little evidence of such practices in England before the Middle Ages. In an agricultural society, living directly on and off the land, each village – and each household within each village – was to a large extent self-sufficient, and every housewife was her own baker, butcher, and brewer. Only with the emergence of a distinct town-life in the centuries after the Norman Conquest, and a growing number of merchants, artisans, and shopkeepers who were necessarily dependent on others for the supply of their food, do we find the first examples of deliberate adulteration. Dr Frederick A. Filby has traced the history of food frauds in these early centuries from the viewpoint of a chemist primarily interested in adulteration as 'one of the factors that lay behind analytical chemistry', drawing his evidence from City Letter Books and guild ordinances.[1] He unearthed some picturesque instances of early sophistications – the piece of iron inserted into an underweight loaf of bread, sugar in ale used to disguise dilution, and 'foreign' wines manufactured from native English fruits – but on the whole, the bakers, brewers, and garblers emerge with remarkably clean records. Dr Filby concludes that 'until the nineteenth century there was but little, and very slow, development in either adulteration or its detection', and there seems no reason to quarrel with his verdict. Certainly there was no widespread organized trade in deception: the cases that occurred were isolated in extent and generally crude in their execution, and were almost always detected by vigilant local authorities.

Before the rapid growth and urbanization of the population in the nineteenth century, the conditions of widespread adulteration did not exist. Outside London and the few other great cities, food producer and food consumer were still not widely separated; they generally lived in the same small market-town or village, probably in the same street, and a fraudulent grocer or brewer would quickly lose his reputation and his custom. Moreover, central governments and local municipalities regarded themselves as having a duty to protect the public against false dealings, and to punish transgressors severely. It was for this reason that for more than five hundred years, from 1266 onwards, the price and quality of bread and ale were nationally controlled by the system of Assizes,[2] while local inspectors, often acting in conjunction with the guilds, kept watch over other foods. Offenders might find themselves pilloried, imprisoned, dragged on hurdles through the streets, and if still recalcitrant, finally banished from the town.

By the closing decades of the eighteenth century, however, the quality of many foods was rapidly deteriorating, and it is certain that during the next hundred years adulteration became an exceedingly widespread and highly remunerative commercial fraud. Public complaints against millers, bakers, and brewers had been raised during periods of scarcity and high prices in the 1750s[3] and again in the 1790s,[4] but little credence was given to reports which were apparently prejudiced and exaggerated. It was only in 1820, when Frederick Accum published his *Treatise on Adulterations of*

Food and Culinary Poisons, that the subject was ventilated for the first time in a thoroughly dispassionate and scientific manner. Accum had acquired a high reputation as an analytical chemist, first in the Brande Pharmacy, then as an assistant to Davy at the Royal Institution, and later as Professor of Chemistry at the Surrey Institution, and his work as a consultant to manufacturers of many kinds placed him in a unique position to investigate the frauds of the day. As long ago as 1798 he had begun to contribute articles to the *Journal of Natural Philosophy* on the purity of drugs and medicines, in the course of which he had drawn attention to the great skill misdirected to adulteration; he then continued analytical work on food for the next twenty years, publishing, among other works, technical treatises on baking, brewing, wine-making, and 'Culinary Chemistry'.[5]

Accum's researches disclosed that almost all the foods and drinks of his day were more or less heavily adulterated, and he fearlessly exposed the methods used and the names of convicted persons. His *Treatise* dealt in detail with the frauds practised on some two dozen articles in common use, ranging from bread, beer, and tea to wines and spirits, condiments and confectionery. In baking their bread, he found that the London bakers invariably used alum as an adulterant for whitening the inferior grades of flour known as 'seconds': 'without this salt it is impossible to make bread from the kind of flour usually employed by the London bakers as white as that which is commonly sold'. The finest white flour went to the confectioners and pastry-cooks, and the 'baker's flour is very often made of the worst kinds of damaged foreign wheat, and other cereal grains mixed with it. . . . Common garden beans and pease, are frequently ground up among the London bread flour.'[6] By the addition of a small quantity of alum (about 4 oz to the sack of 240 lb was the usual amount in Accum's day), the baker was able to pass off a cheap loaf as being made from the more expensive 'firsts' flour, and, of course, to charge for it at the higher price. He also occasionally added potatoes for cheapness, and sub-carbonate of ammonia to produce a light loaf from spoiled or 'sour' flour.

The offence here was perhaps not too heinous, for the use of alum was a fraud on the pocket rather than a danger to health. The adulterations of ale and porter which Accum disclosed were far more serious. In the single year of 1819 there were nearly a hundred convictions of brewers and brewers' druggists under the Excise laws for using *cocculus indicus* (a dangerous poison containing picrotoxin), multum, capsicum, copperas, quassia, mixed drugs, harts-horn shavings, orange powder, caraway seeds, ginger, and coriander: these were all employed as cheap substitutes for malt or hops, allowing beer to be diluted by giving it a false appearance of 'strength' and flavour. Accum found that the average alcoholic strength of many samples of London porter purchased at Barclay's, Hanbury's, and other leading firms, was 5.25 per cent, but when the same beers were bought at the public house they averaged only 4.5 per cent. The public taste at this time was for 'hard, old beer' which had been matured in the brewers' vats for twelve or eighteen months. But long storage was an expensive business, and Accum revealed that some brewers and publicans resorted to sulphuric acid to 'harden' new beer: on the other hand, if storage had continued too long and the beer had turned sour, preparations of oyster shells were available to 'recover' it.[7] Those who preferred to drink tea were hardly more fortunate. Large quantities were manufactured from native English hedgerows, the leaves of ash, sloe, and elder being curled and coloured on copper plates: an official report a few years earlier estimated that 4,000,000 lb of this rubbish were annually faked and sold, compared with only 6,000,000 lb of genuine tea imported by the East India Company. There were eleven convictions for this offence between March and July 1818. In one case, the *Attorney-General* v. *Palmer*, the defendant, a grocer, had carried on the regular manufacture of fictitious tea at premises in Goldstone Street. He employed agents to collect black- and white-thorn leaves from hedges round London, paying them at the rate of 2d a pound. Those destined for 'black tea' were boiled, baked on iron plates, and when dry, rubbed by hand to produce the necessary curl; the colour was given by adding logwood. 'Green tea' was made by pressing and drying the leaves on sheets of copper, and then colouring with Dutch pink and poisonous verdigris to impart the fine green bloom. The teas were then sold at 3s or 4s a pound for mixing with genuine tea. Palmer was convicted, and fined £840.[8]

It is not possible to do more than mention a few more of Accum's revelations – the poisonous pickles which owed their green colour to copper, the 'nutty' flavour in wines produced by bitter almonds, the rind of Gloucester cheese coloured with vermilion and red lead, and the pepper adulterated with the sweepings of the warehouse floors – commodities known in the trade as 'DP' (pepper dust) or, more inferior still, 'DPD' (dust of pepper dust). 'Does anything pure or unpoisoned come to our tables, except butchers' meat?' asked the *Literary Gazette* after reading Accum. 'We must answer, hardly anything. . . . Bread turns out to be a crutch to help us onwards to the grave, instead of the staff of life; in porter there is no support, in cordials no consolation, in almost everything poison, and in scarcely any medicine cure.'

There is no doubt that Accum's *Treatise*, appearing at a time when a series of Excise convictions of brewers had already aroused public interest, created a deep and immediate impression which, for the first time, directed attention to the urgent need for reform. The book itself was a tremendous success, with its arresting title and emblem of skull and cross-bones with the quotation, 'There is Death in the Pot' (2 Kings iv, 40): the first edition of a thousand copies sold out in less than a month, and a fourth edition had appeared within two years. It has been suggested that it was the most widely reviewed chemistry book ever written, and it seems that there was scarcely a newspaper or periodical published in 1820 which did not contain a lengthy notice – occasionally critical, though much more often enthusiastic. Yet the book had no immediate effect in reducing adulteration – indeed, it is possible that in exposing the techniques of fraud Accum instructed others in the very art he wished to suppress. In any case, within a few months of the book's publication, Accum's career in England came to a sudden end. In April 1821 he was indicted by the managers of the Royal Institution for mutilating books in their library (some thirty end-pages were found in his possession, which he had probably taken for making notes), and he chose to leave the country rather than face public trial and disgrace. *Adulterations of Food* had raised up many powerful enemies who were only too pleased to make capital out of the situation; the press and public opinion swung sharply against the man who had been for a time London's most popular scientist, friends deserted and his publishers refused to handle any more of his work. Thereafter, contemporary writers studiously avoided mentioning his name, and even Accum himself, from the safety of a Berlin professorship, usually wrote under the pseudonym 'Mucca'. Although all the facts in the case are by no means clear, there is a strong suspicion that there existed a deliberate conspiracy of vested interests determined to discredit and silence Accum, which succeeded in its object by driving him out of the country.

The circumstances of Accum's disappearance unquestionably caused some people to doubt the truth of his findings, but although public interest and concern about adulteration waned after 1820, it never wholly disappeared. Economists, doctors, and others had at last been compelled to take notice of a great and growing evil, and reference to adulteration now came to be made in such respectable works as Dr Ure's *Dictionary of Chemistry*,[9] McCulloch's *Dictionary of Commerce*,[10] and the medical writings of Paris[11] and Pereira.[12] For most people, however, the next milestone came in 1830, when there appeared an anonymous tract entitled *Deadly Adulteration and Slow Poisoning Unmasked: or Disease and Death in the Pot and Bottle*.[13] It was far less authoritative than its predecessor, and evidently not the product of independent research. It aimed, in an earlier tradition, at sensational disclosures – oil of vitriol and white arsenic in gin, *nux vomica* and opium in beer, pulverized gypsum, whiting, and burnt bones in bread, to name only a few – yet many of its claims were not exaggerated. *Nux vomica*, another narcotic like *cocculus indicus*, was discovered by Excise seizures, gypsum and whiting were found in subsequent analyses of bread, and there is proof that large quantities of ground Derbyshire stone were also used in place of flour. A witness before a House of Commons Committee in 1818 stated that when crushed and rolled into a fine powder, it was impossible to detect it in bread – 'the magistrates there [Sheepshead in Leicestershire] had some baked on purpose, and it could not be discovered; there is, I believe, two or three hundredweight lying in Leicestershire. There is not a baker in that neighbourhood who was not detected in using it'.[14] *Deadly Adulteration* was at least important in reviving interest in the subject, and in showing that new and dangerous frauds were still being devised.

Bad as this was, all the evidence of Parliamentary reports, trade guides, and scientific investigations indicates that adulteration increased in the following years to reach a peak in the middle of the nineteenth century. The next major contribution to knowledge was a work entitled *A Treatise on the Falsifications of Food*,[15] written in 1848 by an analytical chemist who had been investigating adulteration for the past twelve years, and it set a new standard by its original analyses and detached expression. The book leaves no doubt that adulteration had greatly increased since Accum's day, and had now reached terrifying proportions, Mitchell reported, for example, that he had never examined a single sample of baker's bread that did not contain alum; the amount used was generally about a hundred grains to the 4-lb loaf, but he had occasionally found whole crystals of alum the size of a pea. Boiled potatoes were frequently used in bread, and sometimes carbonates of magnesium and ammonia. In samples of flour he had found chalk, potato-flour, pipe-clay, and powdered flints, and one small bun which he analysed contained three grains of alum and ten of chalk. A very common adulteration of beer was with sulphate of iron, or 'heading', which made it possible for publicans who diluted their porter to serve it with a frothing head – regarded by the customer as a sign of strength. Again, the manufacture of 'British tea' which Accum had described was still carried on, and had, indeed, grown in extent. There existed at least eight factories in London in the 1840s expressly for the purpose of drying used tea-leaves and reselling them to fraudulent dealers: according to George Phillips, the head of the Chemical Department of the Inland Revenue, the practice was as follows: 'Persons were employed to buy up the exhausted leaves at hotels, coffee-houses and other places at $2\frac{1}{2}$d and 3d per pound. These were taken to the factories, mixed with a solution of gum, and re-dried. After this the dried leaves, if for black tea, were mixed with rose-pink and black lead to "face" them, as it is termed by the trade.'[16] Henry Mayhew also describes how the purchase of spent leaves was a regular street-trade in the 1840s and 1850s, being collected from servants in the larger houses, and particularly from charwomen, who apparently regarded them as a legitimate perquisite.[17] There can be no doubt about the truth of these reports for, apart from the Excise convictions, Mitchell's analyses disclosed a wide variety of colouring matters including black lead, Prussian blue, indigo, Dutch pink, turmeric, and the poisonous copper carbonate and lead chromate.[18]

To quote only one more example of Mitchell's revelations, he found that it was now practically impossible to buy pure coffee. It almost always had large proportions of chicory, roasted corn, the roots of various vegetables, and colouring matters such as red ochre. He had also found in coffee a substance which appeared to be baked horses' liver, from which it would seem that even the knacker's yard had been pressed into the service of adulteration.

The testimony of chemists like Accum and Mitchell is fully endorsed by evidence from Parliamentary papers, from trade guides published for the instruction of bakers and brewers, and from numerous other reliable sources. Although there was no government inquiry into adulteration in this period, several Parliamentary committees touched on the subject incidentally. In 1815, for example, one witness before a Committee of the House of Commons which was investigating the assize of bread, himself a baker, stated that 'the use of alum is indispensable'.[19] Another said, 'Potatoes are used very much, that I believe is generally known; these improve the bread wonderfully, better than alum or anything else, it makes it rise and saves yeast.'[20] The anonymous author of *The Guide to Trade*, published in 1841, recommends his readers to add a peck of potatoes – somewhat ambiguously referred to as 'fruit' – to a sack of 'seconds' flour, together with eight ounces of 'stuff' (a mixture of salt and alum).[21] For the brewer and publican there was a whole library of 'Guides', 'Friends', and 'Vade Mecums' containing the latest information on adulteration, substitutes, and remedies. Probably the best known and most influential was Samuel Child's *Every Man his own Brewer*, which appeared first in 1790, but went through twelve editions during the first half of the nineteenth century. This remarkable work purported to be written 'for the general benefit of society, and particularly for the lower classes', and to divulge methods of brewing 'which have been long kept an impenetrable secret'. He prefaces his recipe for porter with the following comment:

> However much they may surprise, however pernicious and disagreeable they may appear, I have always found them requisite in the brewing. . . .

One Quarter of Malt	2 oz Spanish liquorice
8 lb hops	1 oz cocculus indicus
6 lb treacle	2 drachms Salt of Tartar
8 lb liquorice root	$\frac{1}{4}$ oz heading
8 lb essentia bina	3 oz ginger
8 lb colour	1 oz linseed
4 oz lime	2 drachms cinnamon.[22]
$\frac{1}{2}$ oz capsicum	

Oddly enough, Child omits coriander seed – which other brewers included – as 'pernicious, not to say poisonous in the highest degree', while he recommends the deadly *cocculus indicus* as 'indispensable'. The reason he gives for the use of all these substances is that 'malt, to produce intoxication, must be used in such large quantities as would very much diminish, if not totally exclude, the brewer's profits'.

In addition to the trade guides, which, despite the fact that they advocated the use of illegal substances, were sold quite openly, the would-be adulterator could seek the advice of the numerous druggists who specialized in the preparation of these nostrums. Many posed openly as 'bread doctors' or 'brewers' druggists', while others carried on the trade more discreetly as an adjunct to their legitimate business: most seem to have been itinerant, although there were evidently brewers' druggists with shops in London, twenty-seven of whom were prosecuted and convicted between 1812 and 1819. As late as 1850, Dr Normandy reported that he had seen 'a cart bearing the inscription in staring paint of "Brewers' Druggist" . . . standing in broad daylight, at midday, before a publican's shop',[23] although it appears that by this time it was becoming a dangerous business to operate openly in towns, and most did their trade in the country, advising small brewers and bakers that they must keep up with the London practice if they wished to make profits.

The growth of adulteration to such alarming proportions had no single cause. It cannot simply be ascribed to greed and the desire for unlawful profit – 'the eager and insatiable thirst for gain' which Accum believed characterized the traders of his time. There is no good reason to suppose that the Victorians, ambivalent as they may have been, were conspicuously more immoral than earlier generations; indeed, a new awareness of social evils of all kinds was one of their more redeeming features. The root causes of adulteration are to be found in the changes which took place in this period of rapid industrialization and urbanization, a period when an ever-increasing proportion of the population was becoming dependent on commercial services for the supply of its food and, as capitalism and specialization advanced, further and further removed from the ultimate food-producers. At the same time, the medieval control over food standards by national and local regulation came to be abandoned – partly because of administrative difficulties but, more fundamentally, because of a changed conception of the role of the state and a doctrinaire belief in the efficacy of free competition to ensure the best interests of the consumer. These changes, coinciding with unparalleled inflation and shortages during the French wars, combined to produce a situation in which it was, for the first time, easy, safe, and profitable to adulterate.

The organization of the food trades themselves went through

far-reaching changes in these years. Until the eighteenth century many bakers had been their own millers, and most publicans their own brewers; by 1850 both were increasingly dealing with remote, highly capitalized, and mechanized producers, to whom they were frequently bound by ties of debt. In other trades such as grocery, the wholesaler or agent had become interposed between retailer and purchaser, and had often acquired a dominating position.[24] In these new, impersonal conditions, the old local relationships and sanctions, which had done much to maintain high quality, largely broke down.

The abandonment of the policy of food control was an even more important stimulus to adulteration. It is true that, by the later eighteenth century, the system was becoming increasingly difficult to administer, and to have enforced the ancient Assizes of Bread and Ale over the new towns and suburbs would have required an executive force which it was quite beyond the powers of decayed guilds and corrupt municipalities to command. But, more fundamentally, the policy was discontinued because of the changed climate of economic opinion. By 1815 enlightened legislators of all parties had come to accept without reservation the doctrine of free trade according to Adam Smith, and to believe that society as a whole would be most benefited when its economic affairs were regulated by the inexorable – and necessarily just – laws of supply and demand. The generation which abolished the East India Company's monopoly, permitted workmen to combine and to emigrate, and began to tackle the tariff jungle, could clearly not countenance the perpetuation of archaic restrictions on the internal economy. It was precisely in this spirit that the Assize of Bread was repealed in 1815 after a perfunctory Committee had pronounced a classical exposition on the futility of economic regulation: 'Your Committee are distinctly of opinion that more benefit is likely to result from the effects of a free competition . . . than can be expected to result from any regulations or restrictions under which [the bakers] could possibly be placed.'[25]

From this time onwards there was no general attempt by government to intervene between producer, retailer, and consumer in order to regulate the price or quality of food. The Customs and Excise Department was, of course, concerned to see that duty was paid on beer, spirits, and on imported foods such as sugar, tea, and coffee, and to this end it attempted to enforce a number of eighteenth-century statutes which classified adulteration, like smuggling, as a fraud on the revenue. We have already seen how singularly unsuccessful they were. Despite an elaborate organization and a staff of nearly five thousand officers, the Excise was utterly incapable of suppressing adulteration even in the limited range of dutiable commodities over which it had authority. In any case, the Excise

94

was interested only in those adulterations which touched the public purse: about the public health it was supremely indifferent.

It was in accord with the prevailing belief in free competition that some contemporaries regarded monopoly as one of the principal causes of adulteration. Undoubtedly, monopoly affected some trades adversely, but it does not seem to have been a factor of general importance. The example most frequently cited in the early part of the century was that of the eleven great brewers of London,[26] who, it is known, regularly met together to fix a common price and strength for porter, and adopted practically uniform methods of manufacture. But the fact is that only one conviction for adulteration was ever obtained against the great houses, and that not for a dangerous ingredient: Barclay's, Meux's, and the rest employed methods of economy which could possibly be criticized, but compared with the small brewers, they were justly renowned for the good quality of their beers. Monopoly exerted a far more prejudicial effect on the retail of beer than on its manufacture. The practice of 'tying' public houses to a particular brewer had begun in the eighteenth century, and by 1850 the majority were held in this way. There is good evidence that when brewers had these assured outlets for their beer they often dealt on unfavourable terms with their tenants, and so, in effect, forced them to adulterate in order to make a living. In country districts, where one brewer often enjoyed a perfect monopoly by virtue of owning the only inn, he could sometimes supply it with the most offensive liquor which he was unable to get rid of elsewhere.

The other food industry to be characterized by a degree of mono-polization was flour-milling. We know that local monopolies existed in the later eighteenth century, for some of the earliest attempts at co-operation were directed towards establishing corn mills in order to break the hold of the miller who supplied inferior and adulterated flour at high prices. Later, many millers followed the example of the brewers by taking over bakers' shops and placing journeymen in them as their agents: this was particularly common in the 'underselling' branch of the trade, where adulteration was greatest.[27] It seems that where a miller had a guaranteed outlet through a 'tied' baker, he was often tempted to deteriorate the quality of flour, and also to connive at adulteration by the baker so long as a large turnover was maintained.

By and large, however, competition was much more characteristic of the food trades in the nineteenth century than monopoly, and it is to the excessive degree of this competition that we must look for the principal cause of adulteration. In the case of the baker, the publican, and the grocer, it existed in such acute form that they were constantly driven to quasi-legitimate means of earning a livelihood, and it is no coincidence that it was in these trades that adulteration was at its height. The bakers are the most obvious case in point. Under the Assize system there could be no competition in price, only in quality. The trade was reckoned a good one, for the 'allowance' guaranteed security and reasonable profits without excessive labour. But the abolition of price-fixing in 1815 brought a revolution which transformed baking into one of the most depressed, overcrowded, and unremunerative trades of the day. By 1850, fifty thousand bakers were struggling to exist in conditions of intense competition: three-quarters of them were 'undersellers', selling below the regular price, and there had even appeared a class of 'cutting bakers' who undersold the undersellers.[28] In London the price of the quartern loaf now varied by as much as 3d. In such circumstances it was all but impossible for bakers to remain honest men. When bread was sold at or below the cost of flour, as frequently happened, the baker had to devise means of making it go further or replacing it by other materials, and once the process had started, competition acted as a vicious spiral, driving him to deteriorate quality to the limit consistent with producing a saleable loaf. As a witness before the Committee on Journeymen Bakers put it, 'They only exist now by first defrauding the public, and next getting eighteen hours work out of the men for twelve hours' wages.'[29]

Excessive competition was similarly created by legislative action in the retail of beer. In reaction against the severity of earlier licensing policy, the Beerhouse Act of 1830 permitted anyone to sell beer on payment of a two-guinea Excise fee: the result was that ordinary houses, chandlers' shops, and mere country shacks were rapidly turned into beer houses. In Liverpool alone fifty new beer-shops opened every day for several weeks, and over the whole country 45,000 were established within eight years. Goulborn, the Chancellor of the Exchequer, had said in moving the bill, 'This measure . . . would work well. It would conduce at once to the comfort of the people in affording them cheap and ready accommodation; to their health in procuring them a better and more wholesome beverage.' His optimism was ill-founded. Intense competition for custom soon developed between the beer-shops, and between the beer-shops as a whole and the fully licensed inns and taverns which could also sell wines and spirits and were prepared to make little or no profit on the sale of beer in order to ruin the beer-shops.

The result was a fierce 'price war', and by the middle of the century thousands of beer-shops were selling porter at 3d a quart instead of the standard 4d by diluting with water and making up for lack of strength by adding *cocculus indicus* or other drugs. Although it was frequently stated by expert witnesses before Parliamentary committees that no publican could make an honest living by selling at 3d a pot, nothing was done for many years to reverse the disastrous policy of 1830: despite all evidence to

96

the contrary, the blind belief of Victorian legislators in the efficacy o. unrestricted competition remained unchanged and practically unchallenged.

Competition was probably seen in its ugliest aspect in the contract system for the supply of groceries. Public institutions – hospitals, prisons, workhouses, barracks, schools, and so on – were normally supplied by tender, the lowest often being accepted in the interests of economy. Boards of Guardians, responsible for the administration of workhouses, not uncommonly accepted contracts under market price, caring little about the quality of the foods supplied. There is good reason to suppose that such institutions suffered from adulteration to an enormous extent. When Dr Hassall analysed samples of arrowroot supplied to London workhouses, he found three-quarters of them adulterated with potato flour, tapioca starch, and sago powder.[30] The large number of deaths at Drouitt's Institution for pauper children in 1850 was ascribed by Dr Wakley, the coroner, to the adulteration of the oatmeal with barleymeal; the latter was less nutritious and more aperient, and diarrhoea and vomiting had been prominent symptoms of the outbreak. This was one of the commonest of all adulterations, and did not end here despite the publicity given to the Drouitt's case. In 1852, several London vestries advertised for oatmeal, and accepted a tender which was 3s a load below the next lowest: a competitor, who did not see how it could be done at the price, suggested an inquiry, when it was found that a large proportion of the 'oatmeal' consisted of inferior barleymeal.[31] Many instances also came to light of adulterated butter, tea, coffee, pepper, and other articles supplied by contract to public institutions, and we must conclude that this kind of fraud was extremely common in the middle of the last century.

The high price of many foods and drinks, due in large measure to the heavy taxation which they were made to bear, was a minor though significant cause of adulteration. A connection can undoubtedly be traced between the extensive adulteration of tea, coffee, beer, sugar, spirits, wine, and pepper and the severe duties which were levied on them: in 1853, immediately before Gladstone's free trade budget, tea was still charged at 1s 10d a pound, pepper at 6d, coffee at 3d, brandy at 15s a gallon, rum at 8s 2d, and British spirits at 7s 10d, while sugar, butter, and cheese paid variable, though appreciable, amounts. Many of these were articles of heavy working-class consumption, and it is hardly surprising that public houses and grocers' shops, struggling to exist in conditions of intense competition, sought to lower the cost to their customers by illicit means. The dilution of beer and spirits with water, which was the commonest of all frauds throughout the century, is the most obvious example of the use of an untaxed adulterant in order to lower cost.

We have now looked at some of the causes – economic, legislative, and

nce of adulteration in the middle of the century. The
why did the public allow themselves to be cheated and
way? The answer is, of course, that the majority did not
a small minority of educated people had heard of the
s of Accum and the other chemists, and these tended to be the
who could afford to pay more for their food and obtain it pure at
-priced shops. It was well known that the heaviest adulteration was
und in the 'low neighbourhoods' of cut-price shops. But for the poor,
who had to prefer cheapness, there was no real choice, especially when, as
was often the case, they were in debt to a local tradesman and had to take
what he offered. Ignorance and poverty between them condemned the
mass of the population to an adulterated diet. Nevertheless, it has also to
be admitted that even when people became aware of the existence of
adulteration, and were financially able to exercise a choice, some
continued to prefer the impure to the genuine. Eating habits are highly
conservative, and people had for so long been conditioned to impure
bread, tea, pickles, and the rest that they did not always immediately like
the flavour or appearance of unadulterated foods. Early pioneers of pure
food sometimes encountered strong consumer resistance – co-operative
societies, for example, experienced such difficulty in selling uncoloured
teas that at least one went to the trouble of employing a lecturer to tell
people what good tea should look like.[32] For all these reasons, any great
improvement in the quality of food had to wait until effective legislation
against adulteration was introduced in the 1870s.

When we turn from the causes of adulteration to consider its effects, it is
necessary to keep in mind several distinct aspects – commercial, fiscal,
medical, and moral. Adulteration was a deliberate fraud for the sake of
gain, and its most direct effect was financial loss to the consumer. Those
who gained were sometimes the manufacturers, who because of their
command of plant or machinery were often able to adulterate on a large
scale and in comparative secrecy; millers, brewers, coffee and cocoa
grinders, and the preparers of drugs fall into this category. More often,
however, it was the retailer who benefited most from adulteration, and,
indeed, depended on it for his existence. We have seen how large sections
of the baking and beer-selling trades were maintained by these means,
and the same is true of the retail of coffee, milk, and other things. The
wholesale price of coffee in mid-century was 9d a pound, of chicory 3d; by
mixing equal proportions an article costing 6d or 7d was retailed at
anything from 1s to 1s 6d a pound. Milk was generally bought wholesale at
3d a quart and retailed at 4d, but the addition of only 10 per cent of water
increased the profit by 40 per cent: such an adulteration was very difficult
to detect, and was one of the most persistent until modern times. At a
meeting of the Society of Public Analysts in 1893 a member recalled the

case of a wholesale dealer who made £1,200 a year simply by adulterating pepper. Examples might be multiplied, but it is sufficiently evident that adulteration had come to be regarded as a normal and almost legitimate method of carrying on trade. The gain of the seller in all these cases was, of course, the loss of the buyer, a loss which affected the whole community in some degree, but which fell particularly heavily on the poorer classes, who were unable to afford the luxury of pure food. Although it would be impossible to express this loss arithmetically, there can be no doubt that adulteration was one of the factors which helped to make the poor poor in the middle of last century.

It follows that as well as involving loss to the individual, adulteration caused a serious reduction in the public revenue. Duties on articles of consumption accounted for at least half the total national revenue in the middle of last century, and many of the items so taxed – malt, spirits, tea, sugar, coffee, and so on – were among those most heavily adulterated. Again, it is impossible to calculate this loss exactly, because the precise extent of adulteration cannot be gauged, but P.L. Simmons, the contemporary authority on commercial products, put it at between two and three million pounds a year, and Dr Hassall thought that it must be as much as seven millions.[33] A loss of this size represented one-tenth of total revenue: it was more than the stamp duty and half the receipts from income tax.

To prevent these losses, the Excise Department maintained a staff of nearly five thousand officers scattered about the country, and sixty or seventy analytical chemists centred in London. The inefficiency – some said corruption – of this department was notorious, even at a time when the civil service as a whole was not conspicuous for probity. George Phillips, the Chief Chemical Officer of the Board, stated before a Parliamentary committee in 1855 that during the last twelve years his department had examined forty samples of hops (thirty-five of which were adulterated with *cocculus indicus*, grains of paradise, and tobacco), 105 of spirits, and 142 of tea. Of the samples of coffee analysed, only 13 per cent had been found adulterated, but a Treasury minute of 1851 had permitted the sale of mixtures of coffee and chicory, provided the product was labelled as a 'Mixture': consequently a compound of 5 per cent coffee with 95 per cent chicory could, provided it was labelled, pass as genuine.[34] In general, the attitude of the Excise Department towards the adulterator seems to have been most accommodating: it had not even objected when in 1851 Messrs Duckworth of Liverpool took out a patent for a machine which compressed chicory into the shape of coffee-beans, the whole object of which was to defraud.[35]

Much more important than purely financial or fiscal considerations, however, were the effects of adulteration on health. Adulteration operated here in two main ways. First, as we have seen, many frauds consisted of replacing the proper constituents of a food with cheaper and possibly worthless substances – water in milk or beer, chicory in coffee, barleymeal in oatmeal, and so on. At first sight, these might be dismissed merely as frauds on the pocket, but in fact, by lowering the nutritional value of the foods concerned, several of them basic articles of diet, public health could be seriously affected. A spectacular instance of the effects of adulterated oatmeal was the mortality at Drouitt's Institution, referred to on p. 97. More often, however, the effects of undernourishment were only to be seen indirectly in the prevalence of disease and the short expectation of life which characterized the earlier nineteenth century. In particular, children reared on a diet of adulterated bread and diluted milk were ill-equipped to resist the infectious diseases and gastric complaints which took such a heavy toll of infant life. Although alum in bread was not poisonous, there is good evidence that it inhibited digestion and so lowered the nutritional value of the food; together with impoverished milk it could well be one of the reasons for the physical degeneracy of the Victorian poor.

Second, numerous adulterations were quite directly and immediately harmful to health. In the 1850s Dr Hassall compiled a list of more than thirty injurious substances which he had discovered in foods and drinks: it included *cocculus indicus* in beer and rum, sulphate of copper in pickles, bottled fruits, and preserves, lead chromate in mustard and snuff, sulphate of iron in tea and beer, copper carbonate, lead carbonate, bisulphate of mercury and various other mineral colouring matters in sugar confectionery. Several of these were deadly poisons if taken in sufficient quantity, and numerous cases are on record of death caused by *cocculus indicus* in rum, paralysis due to lead in cayenne pepper and snuff, and the poisoning of children by mineral dyes in sugar confectionery. Scarcely a year passed when deaths were not reported from this last cause. In one instance, fifteen people died after eating lozenges bought in Bradford market – the sweet manufacturer had asked a chemist for plaster of Paris but had been given white arsenic by mistake – and on another occasion twenty guests at a public banquet in Nottingham were taken ill after eating green blancmange, which had been coloured by arsenite of copper. Only one died.[36] Much more often the quantity of poisons used was not sufficient to produce immediate symptoms, but many of them were cumulative, and would leave trace elements of lead, copper, mercury, and arsenic to build up in the system over the course of time. Here again, we may well have a cause of the chronic gastritis which was one of the commonest diseases of urban populations in the early nineteenth century.[37]

Finally, in the widespread extent of adulteration there clearly lay moral implications for a nation which prided itself on its high standards of morality, public as well as private. The man who deliberately cheats and poisons his neighbour for the sake of gain would be regarded by most civilized nations in much the same way as the thief or the murderer, yet, little more than a century ago, an important section of the English middle class – the class which had taken upon itself the moral leadership of society, and the task of reforming the vices alike of the aristocracy and the lower orders – not only practised adulteration but accepted it as a normal agency of commerce. Business morality was never lower than at the time when Christian observance was at its most ostentatious, and in this, as in contemporary sexual attitudes, we have a striking illustration of the ambivalence of which the Victorian character was capable.

No member of the group betrayed the conspiracy of silence, no word of criticism or self-reproach ever issued from those who stood to gain by adulteration. On the contrary, when faced with irrefutable evidence of their offence, adulterating traders put forward a number of justifications designed to prove that they were, in fact, performing a public service – that adulterations were only practised in response to public taste, that they constituted 'improvements' and lowered the price of foods which would otherwise have been too expensive for the poor to buy. Needless to say, it was not mentioned that adulteration was always for the profit of the seller and at the expense of the buyer, and that, quite apart from the possible dangers to health, adulterated goods were dearest in the end. The strange double morality of the day ignored these, as it did other inconvenient facts, and for many years after the end of the present period shopkeepers continued to conduct their business on the maxim of the common law, '*Caveat emptor*' ('Let the buyer beware!').

Notes

1 Filby, Frederick A. (1934) *A History of Food Adulteration and Analysis.*
2 Webb, Sidney and Webb, Beatrice (1904) 'The assize of bread', *Economic Journal*, 14.
3 My Friend, a Physician (1757), *Poison Detected*; Emanuel Collins (1758) *Lying Detected*; Henry Jackson (1758) *An Essay on Bread . . . to which is added an appendix explaining the vile practices committed in adulterating wines, cider, etc.*; Sampson Syllogism, a Baker (1757) *A Modest Apology in Defence of the Bakers.*
4 *The Crying Frauds of London Markets, proving their Deadly Influence upon the Two Pillars of Life, Bread and Porter* by the Author of the *Cutting Butchers Appeal* (1795).
5 Browne, C.A. (1925) 'The life and chemical services of Fredrick Accum', *Journal of Chemical Education* (New York) (October, November, and December).

6   Accum, Fredrick (1820) *A Treatise on Adulterations of Food, and Culinary Poisons*, 132 et seq.
7   ibid., 173 et seq.
8   *The Times*, 18 May 1818.
9   Ure, Andrew (1835) *A Dictionary of Chemistry and Mineralogy* (4th edn).
10 McCulloch, J.R. (1834) *A Dictionary, Practical, Theoretical and Historical of Commerce and Commercial Navigation*.
11 Paris, J.A. (1826) *A Treatise on Diet*.
12 Pereira, J. (1843) *A Treatise on Food and Diet*.
13 *Deadly Adulteration and Slow Poisoning Unmasked; or Disease and Death in the Pot and Bottle* by an enemy to Fraud and Villany (nd, 1830–1).
14 Committee of the House of Commons on Petitions of the Country Bakers 1818: Minutes of Evidence, 20–1 (evidence of Francis Crisp).
15 Mitchell, John (1848) *A Treatise on the Falsifications of Food, and the Chemical Means Employed to Detect Them*.
16 Hassall, A.H. (1855) *Food and Its Adulterations: Comprising the Reports of the Analytical Sanitary Commission of 'The Lancet'*, 278.
17 Mayhew, Henry (1861) *London Labour and the London Poor* II, 149–50.
18 Mitchell, op. cit., 167–8.
19 Report from the Committee of the House of Commons on the Laws relating to the Manufacture, Sale and Assize of Bread (1815): Minutes of Evidence, 79.
20 ibid., 69.
21 *The Guide to Trade: The Baker* (1841), 33 et seq.
22 Child, Samuel (Brewer) (1820) *Every Man his own Brewer: a Practical Treatise explaining the Art and Mystery of Brewing Porter, Ale, Twopenny and Table Beer, etc.*
23 Normandy, A. (1850) *The Commercial Handbook of Chemical Analysis*, 61.
24 Fay, C.R. (1923–5) 'The miller and the baker: a note on commercial transition, 1770–1837', *Cambridge Historical Journal* I, 89.
25 Report, op. cit., reprinted in *The Pamphleteer* VI (1815), 162.
26 Barclay, Perkins & Co., Truman, Hanbury & Co., Reid & Co., Whitbread & Co., Combe, Delafield & Co., Henry Meux & Co., Calvert & Co., Elliot & Co., Taylor & Co., and Cox and Camble & Co.,
27 Report addressed to Her Majesty's Principal Secretary of State for the Home Department Relative to the Grievances complained of by the Journeymen Bakers (1862).
28 Read, George (1848) *The History of the Baking Trade*.
29 Report, op. cit., 107.
30 Hassall, op. cit., 349.
31 Burn, J.D. (1855) *The Language of the Walls, and a Voice from the Shop Windows, or the Mirror of Commercial Roguery* by 'One who Thinks Aloud', 335.
32 Select Committee on Adulteration of Food, etc.: Third Report (1856), 270–3. Also J. Woodin (1852) *The System of Adulteration and Fraud now Prevailing in Trade*.
33 Hassall, Arthur Hill (1857) *Adulterations Detected: or Plain Instructions for the Discovery of Frauds in Food and Medicine*, 694.

34 Select Committee on Adulteration of Food, etc.: Second Report (1855), Q. 2142 et seq.

35 ibid., Qs. 2135–41.

36 Anon (1856) *The Tricks of the Trade in the Adulteration of Food and Physic*, 45.

37 Greg, W.R. (1831) *An Inquiry into the State of the Manufacturing Population, and the Causes and Cures of the Evils therein existing*, 7 et seq.

Part Two

1850–1914

⇒ 6 ⇐
Feeding the nation

The standard of living

For historians of diet the second half of the nineteenth century presents something of a puzzle. Most economic and social historians are agreed that from some date around the Great Exhibition onwards the wealth derived from Britain's predominant industrial and commercial position began to be shared to a growing extent by all sections of the community, and that perhaps for the first time the majority of the working classes began to enjoy a taste of the prosperity which was making us the richest nation the world had ever seen. Industrialization was still far from a completed process in 1850, but the extensions of the revolution which were now taking place were proceeding under more adequate safeguards with respect to the health and comfort of the worker, his wife and children. Factory Acts and trade unions were beginning to give him a new protection and a new status; industrial towns were ceasing to be the unorganized barracks of slum populations; above all, a brisk demand for labour was providing employment, a rising standard of life, and – what was new for the majority of wage-earners – some margin of income over necessary expenditure. Yet, even at the end of the period, there is massive evidence of poverty and ill-health, overcrowding, insanitary housing, and alarmingly low levels of nutrition among large sections of the population.

The years 1850–1914 in reality comprise not one but three periods with distinct economic characteristics. The first, lasting from 1850 until 1873, has often been selected as 'The Golden Age' of Victorian prosperity, a period of boom and rising prices under the impact of new gold discoveries in California and Australia, but also a time when average wage-increases more than kept pace with the rise in prices. Another favourable circumstance was that food prices rose less than most others, resulting in marked increases in the use of tea, sugar, and other 'luxuries'. Beer consumption reached an all-time peak in 1876 at thirty-four gallons per head a year, though it is also noticeable that investments in savings banks and friendly societies, as well as subscriptions to trade unions, were mounting appreciably. Other classes, it is true, shared quite as much, and possibly more, in this prosperity. It has been calculated that profits grew faster than the total wages-bill at this time, and it is in these years that the solid foundations of many middle-class fortunes were being laid in commerce and wise speculation: how unequally the national income was still divided was startlingly demonstrated by Dudley Baxter in 1867.[1] Some of the rich were getting richer, but the important feature of this period was that, contrary to Karl Marx's prognostication, many of the working classes were taking the first great stride out of that poverty which had been their lot for a century past. Professor Bowley calculated that over this period there was a rise in real wages of 32 per cent, the main advance occurring from around 1860 onwards, but such estimates tend to under-represent the effects of irregular and casual earnings and periods of unemployment which many less skilled workers still experienced. In a recent study of living standards in the Black Country Dr Barnsby found sustained full employment only in the years 1845–55 and 1870–4, and concluded that there was no substantial rise in real wages until the 1890s.[2]

Improvement continued for most workers, however, between 1873 and 1896, a period of very different character which contemporaries designated the 'Great Depression'. Newly industrialized nations like Germany and the United States were now seriously challenging Britain's predominance, and we never again enjoyed the 40 per cent of world trade in manufactured goods which we had had in 1876. This was a time of falling prices and a lowering in the rate of growth of total industrial production: profits slumped badly in such staple industries as shipbuilding and iron and steel, and most of all in agriculture when free trade Britain became flooded with cheap imported corn and meat. But the 'Great Depression' was primarily a depression for landowners and capitalists rather than for wage-earners. For those who could keep their jobs – and unemployment probably reached a maximum of 10 per cent in the mid-1880s – falling prices brought increased purchasing power, and the lower cost of basic foods in particular left a bigger margin which could go towards providing a better and more varied diet. Real wages increased over the period by around 35 per cent, and there is a good case for selecting the 1880s as one of the decisive periods in the improvement of the standard of living of the working classes. Paradoxically, the period of the 'Great Depression' brought for some of the poor a significant advance in comfort, an enlargement of the social amenities of life, and the formation of new hopes and realizable ambitions.

From 1896 down to the outbreak of the First World War forms a third, and distinct, economic period. To the outward eye Edwardian England had recovered from the effects of the depression, and was never more affluent or more powerful. With income tax usually under a shilling in the pound, a luxury Mayfair flat for £150 a year, and a 'general' maid-housekeeper for £20 a year, the better-off classes could afford to live lavishly and often extravagantly: for many of them these were years of conspicuous expenditure and abandonment of the frugality of earlier decades in favour of amusement and indulgence. Despite the development of social services such as education and housing and the beginnings of National Insurance and old age pensions, all of which involved some redistribution of wealth from the richer to the poorer sections of the community, the national income was still divided in much the same unequal way described by Dudley Baxter. In 1911 another economic statistician calculated that one-third of it was received by an 'upper class' of 1,400,000 persons, while the working class of 39,000,000 had to be content with the same fraction.[3] Moreover, the standard of life of many wage-earners was suffering some deterioration at this time due to a rise in the cost of living which was not accompanied by a corresponding increase in wages: the result was that the purchasing power of the pound fell from 20s in 1896 to 16s 3d in 1912. This came as a serious check to the steady growth of real wages which had been continuing since mid-century, and partly accounts for the widespread social unrest, the militant labour movements and revolutionary politics which marked the years immediately before the outbreak of war.

Although some progress had been made in the condition of the working classes since the middle of the century, it is important to remember that destitution was still an outstanding characteristic of industrial society up to the First World War. Between a quarter and a third of the whole population still lived in 'poverty', carefully defined by Rowntree as 'earnings . . . insufficient to obtain the minimum necessaries for the maintenance of mere physical efficiency'. Rowntree had found in his survey of York, carried out in 1899, that 27.84 per cent of its citizens were living in poverty so defined, while a few years earlier Charles Booth's investigation of London had given the closely similar figure of 30.7 per cent. In 1900 one in five of the whole population could still expect a pauper's funeral from the workhouse in which they would end their days, and more than half the children of the working class would still grow up in poverty, under-nourished and underweight, the target for epidemic and deficiency diseases which were still prevalent in English towns and villages. One in six babies of working-class parents died before reaching the age of twelve months, while in 1913 the President of the Board of Education admitted, on the evidence of the recently introduced medical inspection of elementary school children, that 10 per cent suffered from defective nutrition.[4] The reports of Booth, Rowntree, and other social investigators at the turn of the century made it clear beyond dispute that poverty could not be shrugged off as the just reward of the specially idle or the specially improvident, but that it was a normal condition of industrial society; that although factors such as ill-health, old age, widowhood, and excessive expenditure on drink no doubt contributed to its extent, its primary and fundamental cause was simply inadequate earnings.

The money wages received by the working classes illustrate the trends previously described – some improvement from 1850 up to the late 1890s, followed by a levelling off from then until 1914. When Professor Levi drew up his Report on the Wages and Earnings of the Working Classes in 1885, he was in no doubt about the gains which had been made since the middle of the century:

> With the enormous increase of wealth in the United Kingdom, the position of the working classes has likewise greatly improved. In a large number of instances working men of 1857 have become middle-class men of 1884. . . . Cases of rising from the ranks are by no means so rare as we might imagine. But working men of the present day are much better off than they were twenty-seven years ago, for all wages are higher. In 1857 the wages of common labourers were 15s to 17s a week; now they are from 20s to 22s showing an increase of thirty per cent. In 1857 a joiner got 27s; now he gets 33s 6d or 36s with piecework. . . . Agricultural wages have risen more than thirty per cent, from 8s and 10s to 13s and 15s and even 18s a week. Domestic servants, formerly satisfied with £9 and £10 per annum, now easily get £14 and £16.[5]

Levi's optimistic conclusion was that, 'Now, unless wasted, wages equal, if not exceed, what is required for legitimate wants, and, if well thrifted, leave a surplus.'

Ten years later, in 1896, W. H. Mallock was still optimistic in his account of *Classes and Masses.* The tendency of the modern industrial system, he believed, was to make the poor richer, the rich, on average, poorer, and, above all, to increase the size of the middle class. Like the political economist Giffen, he considered that the working classes had increased in wealth more rapidly than any other section of the community, and that nearly the whole of the advantages gained during the past half-century had gone to them.[6] From 1896 onwards, however, the wage-earner in general ceased to make further gains. The agricultural labourer, still the poorest-paid of all workers, had added 5s a week to his wage since mid-century, but in 1900 he received, on average, only 14s 6d a week; the London compositor, once the aristocrat of labour, now had his 39s equalled by skilled fitters and exceeded by the iron-founder who could make up to 42s a week. Somewhere between the two extremes stood the great majority of workers in skilled and semi-skilled occupations – the carpenters with 10½d an hour, the bricklayer's labourers with 7d, and the London dockers who, a few years earlier, had almost starved in a strike to win as much as 6d an hour. An experienced male shop assistant received 28s or 30s for eighty hours' work a week, and a police constable up to 35s. In 1906 the wage census discovered that, 'The weekly rates of wages (exclusive of bonus, if any) of over one-fourth of the adult workmen fell below 20s, and those of nearly two-thirds below 25s, while rather less than a fifth were rated at 30s or more.' On the eve of the First World War the typical wage-earner was still far from affluence, though one stage further removed from poverty than he had been for several generations past. Compared with his grandparents, however, he did have the advantage of cheap food – the result of free trade in imports, more intensive farming for the market, and lower costs of distribution. A weekly wage below 21s would still imply poverty for a family of two adults and three children, as Booth and Rowntree argued, but with flour at 1s a stone, potatoes ½d a pound, cheese at 8d a pound, eggs 1d each, frozen beef and mutton at 4½–5½d, tea at 1s 6d, and sugar at 2d a pound[7] there were clear gains for the majority of working people who lived above the 'poverty line'.

Food consumption and expenditure

Food continued to be the major item of working-class expenditure throughout this period and a large part of the wage-increases gained was appropriated to it. It was noticeable, however, that as incomes grew the proportion devoted to food declined: it was calculated in 1885 that whereas the working classes spent 71 per cent of their earnings on food and drink, the middle classes only spent 44 per cent.[8] Examining this phenomenon in greater detail, the Board of Trade in 1889 estimated that those with incomes of between £28 and £40 a year devoted 87.42 per cent to food, while at an income of £150 a year only 34.81 per cent was spent in this way.[9] The neglected subject of food consumption and expenditure was beginning to attract considerable interest from economists and statisticians towards the end of the century, and from their calculations it is possible to construct a picture of the changing food habits of the English people in these years.

The first of all attempts to measure the consumption of a considerable section of the population was made by Dr Edward Smith in a Report to the Privy Council on the Food of the Poorer Labouring Classes, published in 1863. Smith had collected the weekly budgets of several hundred agricultural labourers and poorly paid domestic industrial workers such as shoemakers, needlewomen and stocking-weavers: see Table 11, p. 112 below. 'The average quantity of food supplied', concluded Smith, 'is too little for health and strength.'[10]

It seems clear that the diet of these numerically large classes was as bad in 1863 as it had been earlier in the century, and that they were not yet sharing in the gains being made by other sections of labour. Yet, a few years after this, the economist Stephen Bourne was in no doubt that as a nation we were consuming much more food than we had even twenty

Plenty and Want

Table 11 *Dr Edward Smith's survey, 1863 (quantities per adult)*

	Agricultural labourers	Indoor workers
Bread	$12\frac{1}{3}$ lb	$9\frac{1}{2}$ lb
Sugar and treacle	$7\frac{1}{3}$ oz	8 oz
Butter, dripping, suet	$5\frac{1}{2}$ oz	5 oz
Bacon and meat	1 lb	$13\frac{1}{2}$ oz
Milk	$1\frac{1}{2}$ pints	1 pint
Cheese	$5\frac{1}{2}$ oz	—
Tea	$\frac{1}{2}$ oz	$\frac{3}{4}$ oz

years before. He was most impressed by the greatly increased quantity of imported foods now consumed:

> an increase totally out of keeping with that which has taken place in the population. The estimated number of inhabitants to be fed in 1854 was 27,800,000: in 1874, 32,400,000 – a difference of 4,600,000 or 16 per cent; whereas the supplies of food from abroad, after making due allowance for those re-exported, cannot be taken at less than 150 per cent more than they were twenty years ago. The reason for this is . . . that with increasing means of purchasing food, the quantity consumed by the mass of the people is greater.[11]

In 1881 a Committee appointed by the British Association for the Advancement of Science considered for the first time how much the population spent per head on food and other items. Since no official statistics existed for the home production of wheat, meat, and other foods, the Committee had to rely on estimates of yield made by agricultural economists such as James Caird, which cannot be regarded as much more than informed guesses. Even so, the figures arrived at probably indicate accurately enough the directions in which consumption habits were moving, and the timing of the Report is particularly useful for showing the changes which were beginning to be evident in the critical 1880s. It is interesting to find, for example, that more money was now spent on meat than on bread, and that the estimated consumption of 1¾ lb of meat per head a week compares closely with that of the present day. Potatoes were easily the most important vegetable food, with a consumption of approximately 6 lb a week, but more money now went on milk and eggs than on potatoes, and such 'luxury' foods as sugar, tea, and butter were taking high proportions of total expenditure. Beer and spirits, however, still accounted for more than 2d of the 9½d which was the average daily expenditure on all articles of food and drink. The complete calculation was as follows:[12]

Feeding the nation

Table 12 *Total food and drink*

	Total expenditure	Expenditure per head per day
Bread	£77,500,000	1.41d
Potatoes	33,200,000	0.64d
Vegetables	17,000,000	0.32d
Meat	99,800,000	1.87d
Fish	14,500,000	0.26d
Butter and cheese	36,000,000	0.67d
Milk and eggs	42,000,000	0.78d
Fruit, etc.	11,100,000	0.19d
Sugar	27,000,000	0.50d
Tea	15,300,000	0.29d
Coffee, etc.	3,000,000	0.05d
Beer	75,000,000	1.4d
Spirits	40,000,000	0.75d
Wines	9,000,000	0.16d
	£500,400,000	9.60d

Average food consumption immediately before the outbreak of the First World War was calculated by Sir Alfred Flux as follows:[13]

Table 13 *Estimated annual consumption per head of certain foods in the United Kingdom, 1903–13*

		lb
Fruit		61
Vegetables (other than potatoes)		60
Butter		16
Eggs	(number)	104
Cheese		7
Margarine		6
Sugar		79
Meat		135
Potatoes		208
Wheat flour		211

Professor D.J. Oddy has examined changes in food consumption between 1886 and 1914 in greater detail.[14] It is clear that up to the First World War bread retained its place as the staple of English diet, total flour

113

consumption increasing from 200 lb to around 220 lb per head per annum: it is likely, however, that this does not imply that more bread was being eaten, but rather more cakes, biscuits, puddings, and pastry. In their growing capacity to choose, people were not yet eating less of the cheap, filling foods, Professor Oddy's calculation of potato consumption also indicating a small rise from 176 lb a head in 1889–93 to 189 lb in 1904–8:[15] this may have been associated with more home cooking, given the increased availability of gas cookers by the turn of the century, and with the widespread popularity of fish and chips by this time. Average fish consumption increased from 25 lb to 30 lb a year over these years. But perhaps the best indicator of improvement in the standard of living was meat, the tasty, protein-rich food to which people always turned when resources allowed: Professor Oddy's estimate of a rise from 96 lb a year in the mid-1880s to 111 lb in 1909–13 is somewhat lower than that of Flux, though still suggestive of a substantial gain. Increased purchasing power also went on dairy produce, milk consumption growing from 15 gallons to 22 gallons a year and butter from 11 lb to 16 lb, well ahead of the new product margarine, which from its first appearance in the 1870s rose to 6.5 lb a year by 1914. Sugar consumption leapt after the abolition of duty in 1874 from 41 lb a year in 1861 to 87 lb in 1914.

In the consumption of drink there was a noticeable trend towards non-alcoholic beverages. Tea saw a spectacular rise from a mere 1.6 lb per year in the decade 1841–50 to 5.7 lb in 1891–1900 (Table 14). Coffee consumption more than doubled between 1850 and 1880, but subsequently fell as tea asserted its position as the national drink. The most rapid rise among the beverages was, however, in cocoa (virtually a new product in the nineteenth century), the imports of which grew from an insignificant 523,000 lb in 1822 to 22,440,000 lb in 1894, and *per capita* consumption from a mere 0.2 lb a year in 1870 to 1.18 lb by 1910. Most of this was for drinking, at home and in the several thousand 'coffee public-

Table 14 *Tea consumption in the United Kingdom (including Ireland), 1850–1900*

Period	Average number of lb of tea consumed per annum	Average consumption per head per annum in lb
1851–60	65,160,456	2.31
1861–70	97,775,548	3.26
1871–80	144,462,622	4.37
1881–90	178,130,836	4.92
1891–1900	224,176,800	5.70

houses' which flourished briefly in the 1880s and 1890s, but by this time substantial amounts were being used by the rapidly growing chocolate and confectionery industries which were beginning to rival the Swiss and Dutch imports.[16] But the temperance movement, which had been active since the 1830s, does not seem to have had a major effect on the consumption of alcohol, which reached a peak in 1875–6 at 34 gallons of beer and almost 1.5 gallons of spirits per head per year. Thereafter there was a fall to between 28 and 30 gallons of beer to the end of the century, a rise to 32 gallons in 1900, and then a continued fall to 1914.[17] In 1871 Leone Levi had estimated that 56 per cent of the whole population drank alcohol in some form, and at the end of the century Joseph Rowntree and Arthur Sherwell believed that men drank twice as much as women, giving an annual consumption of 73 gallons of beer and 2.4 gallons of spirits for every adult male.[18] It seems that one of the most immediate effects of rising standards had been to increase the consumption of alcohol, but that this was gradually replaced by more varied and nutritious food and an increased expenditure on other comforts, and leisure pursuits.

Lower food prices were the major cause of the increased consumption of this period, and another reason for selecting the 1880s as a crucial decade in the improvement of English diet is the fact that the largest falls occurred then. Estimates drawn from a wide range of items show that the retail price of food in a typical workman's budget fell by 30 per cent in the ten years from 1877 to 1887 – by far the most significant price change of the century. The immediate reason for this was the large-scale import of cheap wheat and meat, but a longer-term cause was the gradual lowering of taxes on food, wihch had been continuing since Peel's free trade budgets of the 1840s. One of the biggest subsequent reductions was in the tea duty – from 1s 10d per pound in 1853 to 6d in 1865 and 4d in 1890. Altogether between 1841 and 1882 taxes on tea, sugar, coffee, and corn were lowered from £15,800,000 to £4,800,000, while those on beer, spirits, wine and tobacco were raised from £18,100,000 to £37,300,000, a fact which tempted Leone Levi to believe that, 'The financial administration of late years has been altogether in favour of our labouring classes.'[19]

Food supplies

Between 1851 and 1911 the population of England and Wales, which had already doubled during the first half of the century, doubled again from 17,900,000 to 36,000,000. This continued rapid growth in total numbers, coupled with an increasing consumption of foods of foreign origin, meant that Britain necessarily became much more dependent than formerly on imports for the supply of her food. Already in 1850 the day was passing when we could hope to supply ourselves even with the basic articles of wheat and meat, although it was not until the 1870s that imports of these became really sizeable: in the intervening 'Golden Age' English farmers had utilized the new agricultural machinery, rotational systems, artificial fertilizers, and other techniques of 'high farming' to go a long way towards self-sufficiency. The decisive change was the opening-up of the North American interior by railways, a process not completed until after the end of the Civil War in 1866. Only then could the vast quantities of wheat grown in the mid-western states be moved to the Atlantic ports for shipment to Europe, wheat so cheap that it could sell here, including transport costs, for half the price of home-grown grain. Most American wheat found its way into free trade Britain, which, since the abolition of the Corn Laws in 1846, had no restrictions on imported grain; continental countries, still protecting their farmers, kept it out by high tariff barriers. The result was that wheat prices in England tumbled from 58s 8d a quarter in 1873 to 26s 4d in 1893, bringing down the price of the 4-lb loaf to as little as 6d for the first time in the century. In the meantime, the volume of wheat imports had risen from 17.23 million hundredweights in 1857 to 50.97 twenty years later,[20] and by 1880 English bread was made almost equally of home and foreign grain. This was not the end of the story. The decline of English wheat production continued with the emergence of Canada and India as large-scale producers towards the end of the century, so that by 1914 we imported more than 100 million hundredweight and British farmers contributed less than one-quarter of our needs. Nearly four million acres of arable land had passed out of cultivation in the process.

Many wheat farmers had turned over in the 1870s to meat production, and for a time the collapse of British agriculture was staved off. Meat imports, whether in the form of live cattle or preserved (usually salted) meat, presented serious transportation problems, and even in 1880 they accounted for only about one-sixth of total consumption.[21] Preserved meats were generally very poor in quality and eaten only because of their cheapness – considerable quantities of dried beef known as 'Hamburg beef' came from Germany,[22] and from the early 1860s onwards tinned boiled mutton and beef from Australia began to appear on the English market. The huge meat-canning firms of Chicago and Cincinnati came into the field about ten years later, starting with P.D. Armour in 1868. Tinned meat was regarded with a good deal of suspicion on medical grounds and certainly most of it seems to have been very unappetizing: it came in big, thick, clumsy red tins which, on opening, disclosed a large lump of coarse-grained lean meat, fibrous in texture, with a large piece of unpleasant-looking fat on one side of it. Its only advantage was its cheapness – from 5d to 7d a pound, which was approximately half that of fresh meat. Improvements in processing and canning gradually raised the quality, and corned beef, which first appeared in 1876 and met initial

116

resistance, soon became popular with the working classes because of the convenience of purchase by the slice. A much superior alternative from the United States which also appeared in the 1870s was, however, chilled beef, which commanded a price comparable with the best English and Scottish joints: packed in ice at a temperature of 29–30°F, it arrived in a soft state, its only disadvantage being its short life of 15–20 days from slaughter to the butcher's shop.[23] The import of meat on a large scale had to wait until the development of steamships with refrigerated holds which could bring whole carcasses across the oceans in perfect condition, and it took more than thirty years of experimentation in Australia and the Argentine before the first really successful cargo of frozen beef and mutton was brought from Melbourne to London in the S.S. *Strathleven* in 1880. Meat which had sold for 1½d a pound in Australia now fetched 5½d at Smithfield. Within a few years pork from the USA, beef from the Argentine, and lamb from New Zealand were flooding the English market. By 1902 the value of imported meat, either frozen or chilled, had reached nearly £50,000,000 and more than 56 lb a year was consumed per head of the population. Cheap and good imported meat had a major impact on the diet of the working classes, and although a market still existed among the better-off for the prime cuts of home-produced meat, the English farmer on the eve of the First World War contributed less than half our total requirements.

On a smaller scale, the growing supplies of fish in the second half of the century provided another important adjunct to diet. In the 1860s and 1870s the development of the steam trawler and the use of ice for preservation enabled the rich grounds of the North Sea to be tapped for the first time. Fish packed in ice could now be landed in excellent condition and dispatched by rail to inland towns the same day, and at the end of the century the introduction of the fast deep-sea trawler again extended the area of operations as far as Iceland, the Faroes, and the White Sea. The landed weights of British catches of wet fish doubled from 553,000 tons in 1887 to 1,140,000 tons in 1911:[24] by this time the fishing industry was increasingly concentrated in the east coast ports, with Hull and Grimsby landing almost 40 per cent of the total English catch. The rise in popularity of the fried fish-and-chip shop seems to have coincided with the new supplies of cheap cod (and, possibly, of vegetable fats and oils) which became available in the closing decades of the century. Its origins are obscure, but it seems likely that it grew out of the hot-pie shop, which was well known in early Victorian England: fish was first added as a side-line, but ultimately triumphed over its competitor. Mayhew reported in 1851 that fried fish was hawked around the London pubs in the form of sandwiches, but when the French chip was added is not recorded. Lancashire claims to be the birthplace of the combination, and it was in

Oldham that the engineering firm of Faulkner and Co. began manufacturing ranges for chip frying between 1870 and 1875. At all events, the fish-and-chip shop had become socially and dietetically significant well before 1900; it was the outstanding example in England of a gastronomic institution designed principally for the working classes, and there can be no doubt that it made an important contribution to the protein content of the urban diet.

By the early years of the twentieth century, mass imports from the New World and Australasia had almost halved the cost of bread and meat to the English consumer. It followed that many families now had more income available for dairy products, for fruit, vegetables, eggs, and other foods which had previously been eaten in only small quantities. The British farmer was not slow to respond to the new situation, and one of the principal ways in which agriculture recovered from the depression of the 1880s was by abandoning the attempt to share in the world's grain markets and specializing in those things not so exposed to com-petition – dairy farming, market gardening, poultry rearing, and fruit growing. The acreage of land under small fruit, for example, increased from 15,949 in 1871 to 76,331 by 1914,[25] one important result of which was the rapid growth of the jam and preserve industry from the 1890s onwards. Imports of fruit grew rapidly in the closing decades of the century, reaching a total of 11.3 million hundredweights by 1913; more than 7 million hundredweights of this were of citrus fruits, predominantly oranges, the average consumption of which stood at 14.7 lb a year. West Indian bananas, scarcely known until the late nineteenth century, were being consumed at the rate of twenty a year by 1914, and were credited with being more popular among the poor than apples.[26] Again, the British farmer could by no means satisfy the increased demand for dairy products. By 1902, imports of these had reached the remarkable figure of £41,700,000, the principal items being Danish butter (£9.3m), Canadian cheese (£4.3 m), North American lard (£3.8m), and Dutch margarine (£2.4m).

The new methods of communication by railways and steamships were now bringing tropical and sub-tropical agriculture to the service of the English consumer in this period. The 'new colonial policy' which developed in the later decades of the century placed particular emphasis on the transplanting of cash crops to parts of the Empire, and although some of the attempts were unsuccessful, others opened up vast new sources of food supply for the mother country. Up to 1870, for example, more than 90 per cent of Britain's tea still came from China, which, it had been assumed, alone possessed the necessary climate, soil, and technical skill for successful tea growing; after several false starts, commercial cultivation began in India in the 1830s and in Ceylon (after the failure of a coffee-planting experiment) in the 1870s. The success of Indian cultivation, in particular, was enormous, exports growing from 1,000,000 lb in 1860 to 100,000,000 lb by the end of the century. By 1900 India supplied 50 per cent of our requirements, Ceylon 36 per cent, and China a mere 10 per cent. In the same period sugar plantations from the West Indies were successfully introduced as far afield as Queensland, while the cocoa bean became an important export from the Gold Coast and Nigeria following the opening up of their interiors by railways. Products of tropical agriculture that were wholly new in the nineteenth century include West African palm oil, ground nuts from Gambia, and West Indian bananas.

The market for these and other transoceanic fruits – pineapples, peaches, and so on – developed as rapidly as the means of conveyance, whether in the refrigerated hold or the sealed can, could be contrived. The effect was greatly to enrich the nutritional value and the variety of English diet. Britain's dependence on overseas sources for the supply of her food was, therefore, firmly established between 1870 and 1910, during which time the total value of all imported items rose from £77,000,000 to £219,000,000.[27] Free trade had greatly reduced the cost of living of the consumer, and there were few before the First World War who dared oppose the almost axiomatic principle that Britain should export her manufactures and import her daily bread – Joseph Chamberlain and the Conservative party discovered in 1906 that to advocate the return of tariffs, even for the noble cause of Empire unity, was political suicide. The strategic implication of the policy of dependence was only realized in 1916 when German submarines threatened to starve the British people into surrender.

The food industries

In 1850 the food industries, if such they can be called – 'trades' was the contemporary term – were still generally small-scale and unrevolutionized, supplying narrow, local markets in much the same way as they had done for centuries past. Improved communications, technological changes, and the easier availability of capital were, by the end of our period, to transform many of them into large-scale, highly mechanized industries, concentrated into fewer units with wide distribution networks. The manufacture of food was, strangely enough, the last major industry to experience an 'industrial revolution'.

The single exception to this generalization was brewing, which even at the beginning of the nineteenth century was coming to be carried out on mass-production lines in London and other leading centres. Significantly, London brewers had been among the first customers for James Watt's steam engine, and already by 1815 the eleven leading firms were turning out two million barrels a year – perhaps one-fifth of national production.

Three years later Parliament was astonished to learn that 'they meet together like partners in one concern, and fix the price of porter'[28] for it was common knowledge to a nation which had learnt its Adam Smith that any such meeting must 'end in a conspiracy against the public, or in some contrivance to raise prices'. By mid-century the London brewers had entrenched themselves still further, and when George Dodd visited them in 1856 he was bound to admit, with some reluctance one feels, that they were 'among the most complete manufacturing concerns in the metropolis'.[29] He illustrated the vast size of their operations by a few statistics relating to Barclay and Perkins in Southwark – that the brewery covered an area of twelve acres, used 100,000 gallons of water a day, had a porter brewhouse as large as Westminster Hall and 200 store-vats with a capacity of 30,000 gallons each; 200 of the finest carthorses finally dragged the butts to the publicans. Outside London, however, the large brewer had not yet achieved a dominating position. In 1851, 2,200 Common Brewers accounted for 53.5 per cent of total production, but the remaining half was supplied by nearly 40,000 small publican brewers and beer-retailer brewers:[30] centres of capitalist brewing like Burton, Norwich, and Liverpool were growing rapidly, but the small man was still important for supplying local markets with beers of various types and strengths. Shortly after this, however, he was almost to disappear. The growth of the 'tied-house' system meant that the large brewers were able to control assured outlets for their beer, while the development of a railway network gave them the ability to command national markets. Later nineteenth-century brewing history is characterized by the rise of large firms outside London and a marked trend towards amalgamation and concentration of production in public limited companies. Brewing was now by far the largest of the food trades with, even in 1870, an estimated capital of £41,000,000 and some 840,000 people engaged in manufacturing and retailing.[31] Between 1880 and 1914 the decline of the small brewers was particularly rapid; by the later date only 3,593 remained, and forty-seven firms accounted for 45 per cent of all the beer brewed. The ten largest still produced a quarter of the total – a somewhat remarkable perpetuation of the position in 1815.

By contrast, milling only became a large-scale industry in the closing years of the century. From time immemorial the wheat grain had been ground between stones, first in the quern, later in the windmill or watermill, and finally in the steam-mill; in 1879 there were no fewer than 10,450 mills in the UK.[32] With stone-milling it was very difficult to obtain more than one quality of flour from the same wheat – the practical separation was simply between flour and bran. Some advances had been made in the middle of the century which partly remedied this disadvantage. 'High milling' was introduced, in which the mill-stones

120

were placed wide apart and some of the wheat was ground twice, and it was thus possible to produce a superior 'Patents' flour; also the use of silk gauze for 'bolting' instead of woollen or linen cloth allowed a finer separation of the bran than formerly. Already the time had passed when the English loaf was made from English wheat. By 1886 only 36 per cent of wheat milled in Britain was home-grown; millers generally preferred the 'hard' American wheat, both because of its cheapness and because it gave a higher yield of flour with 'strong' baking qualities. Its disadvantage was that it did not grind well between stones, producing a somewhat brown flour.[33] The revolutionary innovation which gave the miller a far greater degree of control over the grinding process, and which was at the same time quicker and cheaper, was the introduction of roller-milling in the 1880s. The idea of crushing the grain between rollers was at least a century old, but no real advance was made until the invention of porcelain rollers in about 1870. Thereafter the process spread rapidly in Austria, Hungary, and America, and the first roller-mill was established in Glasgow about 1872. By 1878 Radford of Liverpool was operating one with a capacity of 3,000 sacks a week, and within a few years huge new roller-mills, concentrated mainly on the ports, had almost superseded the old method. Typical of the new miller-industrialists was Joseph Rank, who came from a line of millers in Hull. He first automated his windmill, then in 1885 borrowed capital to establish a roller-mill: around 1904 he expanded to London and South Wales, and by 1914 was milling two million sacks of flour a year.[34] By this time more than 80 per cent of flour was roller-milled, and the trade was beginning to be dominated by a handful of large producers – Ranks, Spillers, Vernons, and the Co-operative Wholesale Society. Roller-milling at last made possible the production of flour of any desired degree of fineness. By the end of the century grain was being passed through some fifty machines involving eighteen pairs of rollers and eighteen purifiers before it emerged, usually in six grades of flour. Despite this, it was whiter and lighter than stone-milled flour, its baking qualities were improved, and 'it had not had the life crushed out of it'.[35] Moreover, the public's demand for ever-whiter bread could now be satisfied legitimately, because in the rolling process the dark wheat-germ was flattened into a tiny flake which could be sifted off with the bran; previously it had been ground up with the flour and had darkened it. No one at the time realized that the wheat-germ was the principal source of the valuable mineral salts, fats, and vitamins of the wheat berry, and that it also contained a high proportion of protein.

The baking trade itself began to undergo some far-reaching and overdue changes in the closing years of the century. Until then, the oldest and most basic food industry had remained in an astonishingly backward state, as the factory inspector H.S. Tremenheere discovered in his report on the trade in 1862: 'There is probably no branch of trade supplying a vast and constant demand which has so completely remained in the primitive condition of ministering to that demand from a multitude of small and isolated sources as the baking trade.'[36] At this time there were more than 50,000 bakers and confectioners in Britain, almost all in a very small way of business; ten sacks of flour a week, which was an average in 1815, was still considered a fair trade in 1862, and only one firm, Nevill's, did as much as a hundred. Again, technological changes had hardly begun to affect the trade, despite the fact that breadmaking machinery was now well past the experimental stage. Stevens, who had patented a cheap and efficient dough-kneader in 1858, found 'very few [bakers] who were disposed to free themselves from the prejudice which often interposes when something new is suggested'. The dough continued to be kneaded by hand by overworked, underpaid journeymen who spent up to eighteen hours a day in cellar bakeries infested with vermin and with no proper arrangements for ventilation or sanitation. The outraged authoress of *The English Bread Book* was disgusted to find the exertions of the half-naked journeymen were such as 'to cause streams of perspiration to flow and mingle with the alimentary substance'.[37]

Improvements began in the 1880s, partly as a result of legislation[38] but mainly in consequence of greater capital investment following the Companies Act, so that by 1890 William Jago, the great exponent of scientific baking, was able to report to the Royal Society of Arts that 'The system of making bread in large factories rather than small bakehouses has of late made steady progress'.[39] By the end of the century all but the smallest bakehouses had a dough-kneader, and other machinery was being employed for a variety of purposes unimagined a generation earlier – flour sifting and mixing, dough rolling and moulding, and so on. Equally important, the output of the average bakery had grown to fifty sacks a week. Increased mechanization, technical knowledge, and capital were at last coming to the aid of the baker, though growth in scale was still a slow process. By 1910 there were still only 21 multiple-shop bakeries, owning between them 451 branches.[40] Some, like E. H. Nevill and J. and B. Stevenson, were becoming household names in London, while others also operated restaurants or cafés selling bread and confectionery as part of their catering trade: the Aerated Bread Co., established in 1862, was the first to do so, growing to 100 branches by 1900 but rivalled after 1894 by J. Lyons and Co. Even so, on the eve of the First World War the multiples probably only produced 1½–2½ per cent of all bread, the co-operative societies 6½–7½ per cent: the remaining 90 or more per cent was still baked by some 33,000 master-bakers.[41] There can be little doubt that the public had also benefited in the process. The bread of 1914 was not only cheaper, but purer and better baked than it had been for a century past.

Of the new food industries which developed during these years, one of the most important was margarine, which first appeared on English tables in the 1870s. The invention of this cheap butter substitute was made by a French food technologist, Mège-Mouriés, in 1869, and considerably developed by American stockyard interests shortly afterwards, the original raw material being the softer part of the caul fat of oxen. The progress of the industry in America and Holland was remarkably rapid, and as early as 1876 England was importing over a million pounds of what was euphemistically known as 'butterine'; production was only started here on a sizeable scale by the Danish manufacturer Monsted in Cheshire in 1889. Besides Monsted, who supplied the Maypole Dairy Company, the principal manufacturers were the two Dutch firms of Ven den Bergh and Jurgens: strong competition for outlets developed between all three, Van den Bergh eventually contracting with Liptons and Jurgens with the Home and Colonial Stores.[42] In the 1890s, it was found possible to blend certain vegetable oils, particularly ground-nut oil, with the beef fat, and before 1914 some margarine was being made entirely of vegetable-oil mixtures. Great advances in the purity, taste, and appearance were made by pioneers like Storch, and the new product rapidly found an important place in working-class diet. Its nutritional disadvantage was that whereas beef-fat margarine had contained appreciable amounts of vitamins, vegetable-oil margarine contained practically none. The diet of the poorest classes in 1914, which often consisted essentially of bread made from roller-milled flour, margarine, and condensed skimmed milk was, therefore, a terribly impoverished one. This particular deficiency was not remedied until the introducion of 'vitaminized' margarines in the 1930s.

Other food industries which grew rapidly from the 1880s onwards include biscuit, jam, and chocolate manufacture. The first two had been produced domestically for centuries past, but their development to factory industries was a result of the rising living standards of the later nineteenth century and of the new technologies which made mass-production possible. It is significant that biscuit manufacture on a commercial scale, pioneered by Huntley and Palmer at Reading, grew to importance at the time when bread consumption was beginning to fall, and so provided a new outlet for the flour of the roller-mills.[43] The use of machinery to produce reliable standard quantities and qualities of flour and other ingredients was essential to the biscuit maker, whose reputation depended on maintaining a uniform product of high purity. By 1900 Huntley and Palmer were employing 6,000 workers and producing 400 varieties of biscuits compared with Peak Frean's 200 varieties, though both were now experiencing strong competition from Scotland (McVitie and Price and MacFarlane Lang) and from Jacobs of Dublin.[44] Machinery also played an essential part in the rise of the cocoa and chocolate industries: by the 1890s it was being employed for removing the shell of the bean, extracting the fat, powdering the cocoa, and moulding the chocolate, and the industry was already coming to be dominated by a trio of giant firms. Imports of cocoa retained for home consumption mounted from 4,006,000 lb in 1865 to 22,440,000 lb in 1894. Jam-making was possibly the least advanced technology in the years before 1914. The agricultural depression of the 1870s and 1880s was the event which compelled English farmers to search for new markets: before the discovery of means of storing fruit pulp to make jam out of season, the manufacturers added orange marmalade and other products in order to maintain a continuous output. It seems that the methods employed were purely empirical, for the jam-makers knew nothing of pectin and until about 1900 did not even use a jam-boiling thermometer.[45] Nevertheless, commercial jam production expanded rapidly after the abolition of the sugar duty in 1874, when W.P. Hartley and Stephen Chivers entered the field and soon rivalled the earlier Dundee firm of James Keiller and Sons. Lipton began jam manufacturer at Bermondsey in 1892 and the CWS in 1897. Sales of jam by this time were enormous, especially in industrial areas where a sweet, highly flavoured spread that was cheaper than butter and made margarine more palatable quickly became popular.

Similarly, the manufacture of dairy products was little affected by new techniques until almost the end of the century. George Dodd had written enthusiastically in 1855 of the growing quantities of milk brought to the capital by rail, but outside London the best milk was still that produced by town and suburban cow keepers up to the time of the great cattle plague ten years later: after that dairymen were compelled to organize the train-borne supply more carefully and extensively. The development of milk-trains was helped by the use of water-coolers at or near the farm, and large churns of tinned steel plate were introduced for conveyance between it and the roundsman's cart. Milk bottles were beginning to appear by 1900, but only for milk that had been 'pasteurized' against tuberculosis by Pasteur's method of heat-sterilization. Methods of preserving milk also date from the latter half of the century – dried-milk powder was being made by 1855, but the more important form was tinned condensed milk, which was pioneered by the American Gail Borden. As Margaret Hewitt has pointed out, the working classes were only able to afford the cheapest varieties of this, and although when the tin was opened it was probably purer than the cow's milk they could purchase, it was devoid of vitamins A and D and of fats, and was made from evaporated skimmed milk; hence the prevalence of rickets among children to whom it was fed.[46] Ian Buchanan has more recently argued that condensed milk was a major, indirect cause of the diarrhoea, gastritis, and enteritis which were responsible for up to one-third of infant mortality before 1914: the opened cans of this sugary fluid attracted the common house-fly which was the main infective agent of these diseases.[47] In this instance – as in that of roller-milled flour – technology scarcely benefited the consumer. Butter-making, however, was revolutionized by the invention of the centrifugal cream-separator in 1877, which enabled the larger dairies to economize both in the labour of skimming and in the space that had previously been occupied by the large shallow pans in which the cream had risen. Again, factory processes were advantageously applied to cheese-making following the work of bacteriologists on the enzyme-ripening agent; before the end of the century, factory-made 'cheddar' was being exported from the United States, Canada, and Australia and sold here for less than the home-made product. The application of science and technology to the food industries, both in methods of manufacture and in processes of preservation by refrigeration and canning,[48] had made significant advances in the decades immediately before the outbreak of war and, with the exceptions previously mentioned, was having important effects in lowering the cost and widening the variety of the English diet.

The retailing revolution

The later nineteenth century also saw the beginnings of important changes in the retailing and distributive branches of the food industries. Of these, one of the most far-reaching in its effects was the growth of co-operative retail societies, which concentrated on supplying their members with foods pure in quality and moderate in price, and on the principle of distribution of profits as dividend to purchasers. The first societies of which records exist, dating back to the 1760s, were small corn-mills and baking establishments formed in response to the frauds and extortions of local traders, but the modern form of co-operative society began with the Equitable Pioneers of Rochdale, a group of twenty-eight poor weavers who opened their little store in Toad Lane in 1844. They had been inspired the previous year by listening to George Jacob Holyoake, who had told them:

> Anybody can see that the little money you get is half-wasted, because you cannot spend it to advantage. The worst food comes to the poor, which their poverty makes them buy and their necessity makes them eat. Their stomachs are the waste-baskets of the State. It is their lot to swallow all the adulterations on the market.[49]

The principles of the Pioneers were simple and businesslike – to buy wholesale, sell, only for cash, at local retail prices, and to divide the profits among members as dividend at the end of a year's trading. They began by selling flour, oatmeal, butter, and sugar, later tea and other groceries, later still coal, clothing, and furniture. To cut out the profits of middle-men, and so reduce the price to the member, was an important though subsidiary aim: the fundamental purpose was 'to improve the moral character of trade rather than make large profits'. After the first few precarious years, the success of Rochdale gave a great impetus to the spirit of co-operation throughout the country, and in the years after 1850 scores of societies embodying the same principles sprang up, particularly in the north and midlands: in 1862 a Wholesale Society was established to supply societies with some of the goods they sold. But membership, on the strict basis of cash transactions, was not immediately open to the majority of the English working class, still tied by indebtedness to local tradesmen who, in the face of competition by the 'Stores', were now often more accommodating than before. As late as 1880 the total membership of all societies was only 600,000. The big advance came in the last two decades of the century, with the rise in real wages and the fall in price of foodstuffs. By 1914 there were 3,800,000 members and the societies had a combined annual turnover of more than £100,000,000. Co-operation was already playing a highly significant part in food retailing, and, with dividends of 2s 6d and more in the pound, in working-class savings.

Most consumers, however, both in town and country, continued to rely on the local shopkeeper for their groceries and other provisions. A new problem arose after the middle of the century owing to the rapid growth of suburbs round London and other cities, and was at first met partly by the extensive hawking of provisions by itinerant dealers. Henry Mayhew estimated that in addition to 30,000 coster-mongers, who generally worked the streets close to the markets, there were well over a thousand itinerant traders in 1861 in London alone, the largest group being the tally-men, who hawked tea and other groceries round the suburbs, selling the goods on credit and collecting weekly payments in satisfaction of the debts run up. Alternatively, larger dealers would advertise goods by handbills, and then send ready-made-up parcels all over London by van.[50] This latter method seems to have played a large part in the rise of multiple- or chain-grocers, who depended primarily on their sales of packet-tea. The idea of retailing tea in sealed packets under a proprietary name had first occurred to the Quaker, John Horniman, in 1826, partly as a means of ensuring that his tea reached the consumer in a pure state at a time when adulteration was rife. His sealed, lead-lined packets acquired a high reputation, and by the 1870s his was easily the largest firm in the trade, with a sale of five million packets a year.[51] In 1884 packeting was first put on a mass-production basis when the Mazawattee Tea Co. offered a high-priced, extensively advertised pure Ceylon tea. By the end of the century, the packet teas of such firms as Horniman's, Mazawattee, Lipton's, Lyons', and the Maypole Dairy Co. had acquired a dominating position in the retail trade.

126

The prototype of the modern multiple-grocer was Thomas Lipton, who opened his first shop in Glasgow in 1871: ten years later he began his first branch in Leeds, and through the 1880s opened shops in most principal English cities.[52] The principles of his success were to offer only a limited range of goods strongly in demand by working-class customers, bulk purchases, quick turnover, and low profit margins, and, like the co-operative societies, insistence on cash purchases. Lipton did not deal in tea until 1889, when be began his campaign by offering it at 1s 7d a pound – 'The Finest the World can Produce'; until then no tea had sold under 2s 6d a pound. His success was spectacular. By 1914 he had a grocery empire of 500 shops, and a score or more of imitators and rivals.[53] John James Sainsbury's expansion was of a rather different kind, remaining largely London-based before 1914. From his first dairy in Drury Lane in 1869 he gradually opened branches in the suburbs (Croydon in 1882, the first purpose-designed Sainsbury shop) and in middle-class southern towns (Guildford in 1906), appealing in their decor and wider range of products to a higher-income clientele. By 1914 he had 115 branches.[54] More akin to the Lipton pattern of national multiples were the Home and Colonial Stores, established in 1888 and with 400 branches in many towns by 1914, and the Maypole Dairy Co., established in 1898, which carried specialization further than any by only selling butter, margarine, tea, and condensed milk until 1922.[55] By the outbreak of the First World War the shopping habits of the working classes were being transformed by the rise of the multiples, offering goods of reliable quality at the lowest prices and at convenient times (often from 7 a.m. until 10 or 11 p.m.), and already threatening the existence of the traditional corner shop and open market. In 1910 114 grocery firms owned 2,870 branches and a mere 23 meat companies controlled 3,828 butchers' shops.[56]

Intense competition was a leading characteristic of the food trades in the second half of the century, and it was partly a desire to reduce this as far as possible which led to the growth in size of units, concentration and amalgamation in both the productive and distributive sides of the industry. The policy of selling through assured outlets not available to competitive producers was seen most clearly of all in the 'tied-house' system of beer retail, which developed very rapidly at this time, although its origins can be traced back much earlier. A complaint appeared, for example, in the *Monthly Review* in 1773 that brewers 'not content with such trade and gain as might fairly and spontaneously arise' were buying up public houses in order to sell their own beers exclusively.[57] Already by 1815, 14,000 of the 48,000 licensed houses in the country belonged to brewers, and in London nearly half the total. With the only outlets for their product severely restricted under a monopoly granted by the magistrates, it was perhaps inevitable that the great brewers should compete with each other to control them. Parliamentary committees complained in vain that the practice was 'very prejudicial to the interests of the community at large'[58] by raising prices and reducing quality, but nothing could be done to arrest its continued growth. When the new class of 'beerhouses' was introduced in 1830 in response to demands for a freer licensing policy, a high proportion of the 123,000 established quickly became the property of brewers, or were tied to them by advances, while, in the closing decades of the century, the policy of reducing the total number of licences in the interests of temperance only led to a greater scramble for the few remaining 'free' houses. The *Country Brewers' Gazette* complained in 1897 that 'Brewers are competing one against another in such a ridiculous fashion that prices have been run up 200 or 300 per cent on the actual value of the houses', while next year a Royal Commission reported that 'tied houses' now numbered 75 per cent of all the licences in the country, and that in many towns monopoly was all but complete.[59]

Although the public house remained the principal leisure centre of a high proportion of working people down to 1914, eating outside the home was still exceptional. The public house might offer bread, cheese, and pickles to encourage the consumption of liquor, and hawkers might bring round hot pies, sausages, and saveloys to tempt the drinker, but only with rising standards of living in the late nineteenth century did catering for the working classes develop on a commercial scale. One form, the fried fish-and-chip shop, grew rapidly to an estimated 25,000 by 1914,[60] and clearly met a demand for tasty, cheap, and convenient food available until late in the evening. Like the corner shop, these were generally very small-scale businesses, their proprietors barely removed from the customers they served. More closely related to the retailing revolution were the new chains of cafés and teashops which appeared towards the close of the century, catering for a respectable, though not affluent, clientele of clerks, female 'typewriters', and shoppers up from the suburbs. Modest chains of between twenty and sixty such shops, offering a cheap, limited luncheon menu, had already been established by the Aerated Bread Co., Lockharts, and Pearce and Plenty (steak pudding and potatoes 5d, tea 1d), but the out-standingly successful venture was that of Joseph Lyons in 1894, financially backed by the tobacco business of Salmon and Gluckstein. Lyons' principles of respectability, quality, cheapness, speed, and cleanli-ness ensured quick success – to the extent of 250 teashops all over the country by the 1920s.[61] In the years before 1914 the food trades as a whole, last of all the major industries to be 'revolutionized', were already becoming dominated by large-scale producers with highly mechanized plants and extensive distribution networks. Man's most basic need was at last becoming big business.

Feeding the nation

Notes

1 Dudley Baxter's estimate of the distribution of the national income covered approximately ten million persons in England and Wales in receipt of independent incomes:

Class	Income per annum	Number of recipients	
Upper class	Over £5,000	7,500 ⎫	49,500
Upper class	£1,000–£5,000	42,000 ⎭	
Middle class	£300–£1,000	150,000	150,000
Lower middle class	£100–£300	850,500 ⎫	1,853,500
Lower middle class	Under £100	1,003,000 ⎭	
Skilled labour class	Under £100	1,123,000 ⎫	
Less skilled labour class	Under £100	3,819,000 ⎪	7,785,000
Agricultural workers and unskilled labour class	Under £100	2,843,000 ⎭	

2 Barnsby, G. (1971) 'The standard of living in the Black Country during the nineteenth century', *Economic History Review* XXIV, 220–39.
3 Money, L.C. (1911) *Riches and Poverty*.

Income per annum	Number of recipients (including families)
Over £700	1,400,000
£160–£700	4,100,000
Under £160	39,000,000

4 Oddy, D.J. (1982) 'The health of the people', in Theo Barker and Michael Drake (eds) *Population and Society in Britain, 1850–1980*, 127.
5 Levi, Leone (1885) *Wages and Earnings of the Working Classes*, Report to Sir Arthur Bass, MP, 30.
6 Mallock, W.H. (1896) *Classes and Masses, or Wealth, Wages and Welfare in the United Kingdom*, 31.
7 Mingay, G.E. (1986) *The Transformation of Britain, 1850–1939*, 155.
8 Levi, op. cit., 65.
9 Board of Trade, Labour Statistics (1889) *Returns of Expenditure by Working Men*, PP LXXXIV.
10 Smith, Edward (1864) *Practical Dietary for Families, Schools and the Labouring Classes*, 202–3.
11 Bourne, Stephen (1880) *Trade, Population and Food, A Series of Papers on Economic Statistics*, 46.
12 Report of the 51st Meeting of the British Association for the Advancement of Science (1881) *Report of the Committee . . . on the Present Appropriation of Wages, etc.*, 276 et seq.
13 *Journal of the Royal Statistical Society* (1930), 93, 538.
14 Oddy, D.J. (1970) *The Working Class Diet, 1886–1914*, unpublished University of London Ph.D. thesis.
15 ibid., 30.
16 Othick, J. (1976) 'The cocoa and chocolate industry in the nineteenth

century', in Derek Oddy and Derek Miller (eds) *The Making of the Modern British Diet*, 78 et seq.

17 Dingle, A.E. (1976) 'Drink and working-class living standards in Britain, 1870–1914', in *The Making of the Modern British Diet*, ibid., 118.

18 Rowntree, Joseph and Sherwell, Arthur (1900) *The Temperance Problem and Social Reform*, pp. 5–6.

19 Levi, op. cit., 56.

20 Bourne, op. cit., 84.

21 ibid., 92.

22 Smith, Edward (1874) *Foods* (3rd edn).

23 McNamee, Betty (1966) 'Trends in meat consumption', in T. C. Barker, J.C. McKenzie, and John Yudkin, (eds) *Our Changing Fare*, 82–3.

24 Oddy, D.J. (1971) 'The changing techniques and structure of the fishing industry', in T.C. Barker and John Yudkin (eds) *Fish in Britain. Trends in its Supply, Distribution and Consumption during the Past Two Centuries*, 17 (Table 1).

25 Ernle, Lord *English Farming Past and Present* (new (6th) edn), with introductions by G.E. Fussell and O.R. McGregor (1961): Appendix VIII, 'Agricultural statistics, 1866–1935', 512.

26 Torode, Angeliki (1966) 'Trends in fruit consumption', in *Our Changing Fare*, op. cit., 115–28.

27 *English Farming Past and Present*, op. cit., Appendix VII, 'Annual values of imports, 1866–1935', 510.

28 *Hansard*, 1 May 1818.

29 Dodd, George (1856) *The Food of London*, 463 et seq.

30 Baxter, John (1944) 'The organization of the brewing industry', unpublished University of London Ph.D. thesis.

31 Levi, Leone (1871) *The Liquor Trades*.

32 Hunt, Sandra *'The changing place of bread in the British diet in the twentieth century'*, series of unpublished research papers sponsored by the Rank Prize Funds (Brunel University), 'The structure and economics of the baking and milling trades, 1880–1914', 1.

33 ibid.

34 Burnett, R.G. (1945) *Through the Mill. The Life of Joseph Rank*; Joseph Rank Ltd. (1956) *The Master Millers, The Story of the House of Rank*.

35 Ashton, John (1904) *The History of Bread*, chap. 8.

36 Report addressed to Her Majesty's Principal Secretary of State for the Home Department relative to the Grievances complained of by the Journeymen Bakers (1862), XIII.

37 Acton, Eliza (1857) *The English Bread Book*, 31.

38 On the recommendation of the 1862 Report, Acts were passed prohibiting nightwork by juveniles and compelling the inspection of bake-houses. For fuller details, see the author's articles in the *Bakers' Review*, 4 May 1962, 765 et seq., and 15 June 1962, 1011 et seq.; also, the author's 'The baking industry in the nineteenth century' in *Business History*, June 1963, 98 et seq.

39 Jago, William (1890) The Cantor Lectures on 'Modern developments of bread making', *Journal of the Royal Society of Arts*, 38.

40 Jefferys, James B. (1954) *Retail Trading in Britain, 1850–1950*, 213–14.
41 Hunt, op. cit., 11–16.
42 Fraser, W. Hamish (1981) *The Coming of the Mass Market, 1850–1914*, 159.
43 Huntley & Palmers Ltd was founded by Thomas Huntley in 1826 and by 1851 was already employing 300 workpeople. Carr's of Carlisle owe their origin to Jonathan Dodgson Carr in 1831, and Peek, Frean & Co. Ltd was started by James Peek at Dockhead in 1857. ('A saga of biscuit-making', *Grocer*, Monthly Supplement, August 1956.)
44 Corley, T.A.B. (1976) 'Nutrition, technology and the growth of the British biscuit industry, 1820–1900', in *The Making of the Modern British Diet*, op. cit., 21.
45 Derry, T.K. and Williams, Trevor I. (1960) *A Short History of Technology*, 694.
46 Hewitt, Margaret (1958) *Wives and Mothers in Victorian Industry*, 137.
47 Buchanan, Ian (1985) 'Infant feeding, sanitation and diarrhoea in colliery communities, 1880–1911', in Derek J. Oddy and Derek S. Miller (eds) *Diet and Health in Modern Britain*, 148–78.
48 For details of the history of canning of foods see J.C. Drummond and Anne Wilbraham (1939) *The Englishman's Food. A History of Five Centuries of English Diet*, chap. XVIII, 'Preservation of food'; *Historic Tinned Foods*, International Tin Research and Development Council, publication no. 85 (1939).
49 Holyoake, G.J. (1908) *The History of Co-operation*, 270–1.
50 Mayhew, Henry (1861) *London Labour and the London Poor*, I, *London Street-Folk*, 509–11.
51 Day, Samuel Phillips (1878) *Tea: Its Mystery and History*, 58.
52 Mathias, P. (1967) *Retailing Revolution*, 98. (The classic work on the rise of the multiples.)
53 Waugh, A. (1951) *The Lipton Story*.
54 Boswell, James (ed.) (1969) *JS 100. The Story of Sainsbury's*.
55 Fraser, op. cit., 114.
56 ibid., 116 (Table 9.1).
57 *Monthly Review* XLVIII (January 1773), 20.
58 Report of the Committee Appointed to Enquire into the State of the Police of the Metropolis and . . . upon the execution of the laws relating to the Licensing of Victuallers, etc., 1817.
59 Royal Commission on the Liquor Licensing Laws, IX: Précis of Minutes of Evidence (1898), Q.22.242.
60 Cutting, C.L. (1955) *Fish Saving: A History of Fish Processing from Ancient to Modern Times*, 241.
61 Richardson, D.J. (1976) 'J. Lyons and Co. Ltd: caterers and food manufacturers, 1894–1939', in *The Making of the Modern British Diet*, op. cit., 163–6.

7

Rural England: romance and reality

He used to tramp off to his work while town folk were abed,
With nothing in his belly but a slice or two of bread;
He dined upon potatoes, and he never dreamed of meat
Except a lump of bacon fat sometimes by way of treat.

Agricultural Labourers' Union Ballad[1]

The cottage homes of England,
  By thousands on her plains,
They are smiling o'er the silvery brook
  And round the hamlet fanes.

From glowing orchards forth they peep,
  Each from its nook of leaves.
And fearless there the lowly sleep
  As the birds beneath the eaves.

From a poem by Felicia Hemans

Francis George Heath, writing on *British Rural Life and Labour* in 1911, entitled one of the chapters of his book 'Romance and reality'. Nearly forty years before, in 1873, he had tramped the west country 'pencil and notebook in hand' to investigate the condition of the rural labourer, and he recalled an episode when one day he stumbled by chance on an idyllic scene:

> Away from the main road, a lane led up to the right, and a peep over the hedge revealed just a glimpse of the whitewashed walls and the low thatched roof of a cottage. . . . Down one side of the lane gurgled a limpid stream of water. . . . Another turning, this time round to the left after a few steps up the lane, and a pretty sight met my view. Straight in front a narrow path led up under a kind of vista. On the right of this path there was a line of creeper-bound cottages, eighteen in all. . . . Facing the cottages was a row of little gardens overshadowed by fruit trees. Here and there rustic beehives were scattered over these gardens which contained flowers and shrubs in addition to their little crops of vegetables. The walls of some of the cottages were almost hidden by the creepers which trailed upon them. The little 'nook' was shut in on almost every side by orchards.

But unlike Mrs Hemans, Heath penetrated inside one of 'the cottage homes of England'. At No. 1 lived a carter, his wife, his bedridden mother, and his family of five children, only one of whom, at nine-and-a-half, was old enough to work. The carter earned 10s a week, less £3 5s 0d a year for the rent of a tiny potato ground, less 10s a year for rates – which included a gas rate for the adjoining parish. The oldest boy earned 5d a day and a pint of cider. The family existed in abject poverty and misery. The roof leaked and there were broken panes in the windows. In the two bedrooms, heaps of rags served as bedclothes. Some of the children had no shoes.[2]

Throughout Victorian times, and later, romantic myths about the countryside and countrymen persisted. Writers eulogized the beauty of country mansions and the pleasures of rural recreation[3] while making no reference to the work and wages of the labourer who made English agriculture the profitable plaything of the rich, as well as the tidiest in Europe: others proclaimed the benefits of a feudal relationship, the kindness and concern of landlords towards an ungrateful peasantry whose only return was a sullen deference. 'Never once in all my observation,' wrote Richard Jefferies to *The Times* in 1872, 'have I heard a labouring man or woman make a grateful remark, and yet I can confidently say that there is no class of persons in England who receive so many attentions and benefits from their superiors as the agricultural labourers.'[4] A romantic nostalgia for the past clouded the judgement of such writers, who claimed to have the interests of the countryside at heart, as well as the memories of some labourers when attempting to recall the stories of their own lives. An old Hampshire woman told W. H. Hudson in 1902 that

> Nothing's good enough now unless you buys it in a public house or a shop. It wasn't so when I was a girl. We did everything for ourselves, and it were better, I tell 'e. We kep' a pig then – so did everyone; and the pork and brawn it were good, not like what we buy now. We put it mostly in brine, and let it be for months; and when we took it out and boiled it, it were red as a cherry and white as milk, and it melted just like butter in your mouth. . . . And we didn't drink no tea then. . . . We had beer for breakfast then, and it did us good. It were better than all these nasty cocoa stuffs we drinks now. . . . And we had a brick oven then and could put a pie in and a loaf and whatever we wanted and it were proper vittals.[5]

If memory did not play her false, she was an unusually fortunate young girl. This was not the experience of most agricultural labourers in the middle of last century.

The general state of the rural labourer between 1850 and 1914 was one of chronic poverty and want, acute at the beginning of the period, slightly alleviated towards the end of it. His real position was summed up accurately enough by Sidney Godolphin Osborne when he remarked, 'The constant wonder is that the labourer can live at all,' and even more succinctly by Canon Girdlestone's comment that labourers 'did not live in the proper sense of the word, they merely didn't die'. The condition of the labourer was strangely independent of the fortunes of agriculture as a whole – or rather, it varied inversely with such fluctuations; when farming was at its most prosperous in the middle decades of the century the labourer was at his poorest, and only in the period of agricultural depression after 1874 was a dawning improvement discernible. In such conditions the labourer could feel little concern or sympathy for the fate of his employer. Nor, last of all workers to be enfranchised, in 1884, could he expect Parliament to be very conscious of his interests. Speaking of the agricultural legislation of the period in its effects on labour, Dr W. Hasbach wrote, 'Such reforms as were effected were more or less accidental and unintentional. Not till towards its end do we come upon direct, purposeful and effective action definitely concerned with the problem of the agricultural labourer.'[6] Although, in the long view, the new Poor Law of 1834, the repeal of the Corn Laws in 1846, and the Education Acts of 1870–6 may all have been necessary conditions of the labourer's progress, their immediate effect in each case was adverse, while the legislative campaigns in favour of allotments and against the gang system were either failures or not directly beneficial to the adult worker. To a considerable extent the labourer was the instrument of his own ultimate improvement, both by leaving the land which would not yield him a reasonable livelihood, and by forming effective trade unions for those who stayed behind. A rural exodus of considerable proportions was one consistent feature of this period, the total number of agricultural workers falling from 965,514 in 1851 to 643,117 in 1911 (see Table 15). For the last thirty years of the century, 100,000 workers left the land in each decade to swell the populations of towns, colonies, and the United States.

The period of agricultural history from 1850 to 1874 has been variously described as 'The Golden Age' or that of 'High Farming'.[7] The gloomy prognostications about the effects of the repeal of the Corn Laws were not fulfilled in these years; England was not swamped with foreign corn, but in expectation of fierce competition landlords introduced improvements which, for a time, made English farming the model for Europe and the world. Improvements in seeds, manures, tools, machinery, and breeds of cattle, the introducion of methods of land drainage and the application of new means of communication and new knowledge of science all contributed to the intensity and efficiency of farming practice. 'The traveller who passes today through almost derelict districts,' wrote Hasbach in a famous passage, 'must find himself wishing that he had seen these same places in the days when drain-pipes lay heaped upon the fields, great sacks of guano stood in serried ranks, the newest machines were busily at work in field or meadow, and the beasts, in clean and airy

Table 15 *The agricultural population. Census returns of those who were engaged on farms in England and Wales in 1851, 1861, 1871, 1881, 1891, 1901, 1911*

Occupations	1851	1861	1871	1881	1891	1901	1911
Farmers and graziers	249,431	249,735	249,735	223,943	223,610	224,299	208,761
Relatives of farmers and graziers assisting on farms	111,604	92,321	76,466	75,197	67,287	107,783	97,689
Farm bailiffs or foremen	10,561	15,698	16,476	19,377	18,205	22,662	22,141
Agricultural workers of all classes on farms	965,514	983,824	962,348	870,798	780,707	620,986	643,117
Totals	1,337,110	1,341,578	1,305,025	1,189,315	1,089,809	975,730	971,708

Table 16 *The rate of agricultural wages in 1850–51*

	Northern counties			
Midland and western counties	*Weekly wages*		*East and south coast counties*	*Weekly wages*	
	s	d		s	d
Cumberland	13	0	Northumberland	11	0
Lancashire	13	6	Durham	11	0
West Riding	14	0	North Riding	11	0
Cheshire	12	0	East Riding	12	0
Derby	11	0	Lincoln	10	0
Nottingham	10	0			
Stafford	9	6			
	Southern counties				
Warwick	8	6	Norfolk	8	6
Northampton	9	0	Suffolk	7	0
Bucks	8	6	Huntingdon	8	6
Oxford	9	0	Cambridge	7	6
Gloucester	7	0	Bedford	9	0
North Wilts	7	6	Hertford	9	0
Devon	8	6	Essex	8	0
			Berks	7	6
			Surrey	9	6
			Sussex	10	6
			Hants	9	0
			South Wilts	7	0
			Dorset	7	6
Average of west	10	0	Average of east	9	1

	s	d
Average of all *northern counties*	11	6
Average of all *southern counties*	8	5
Average over the whole	9	6

stables, were fattened on foods hitherto unknown.'[8]

The beasts were more fortunate than the men who tended them. When James Caird made his detailed survey of English agriculture for *The Times* in 1850–1, he found that the wages of adult labourers varied from 7s a week in south Wiltshire to 15s a week in parts of Lancashire: the average for the whole country was 9s 6d, but for the northern counties it was 11s 6d against 8s 5d for the southern.[9] This disparity between the earnings of those in the corn counties and those in the mixed husbandry counties of the north was due, he believed, to the proximity there of manufacturing and mining industry, which offered competing and better paid employment for the labourer. When Arthur Young calculated wages in 1770, they had been slightly higher in the south than in the north (7s 6d as against 6s 9d): in Berkshire and Wiltshire they were therefore precisely the same in 1851 as they had been eighty years earlier, and in Suffolk absolutely less. Caird concluded that 'in some of the southern counties . . . wages are insufficient for healthy sustenance', and, in consequence, more labourers were still dependent on the Union for poor relief sixteen years after the Poor Law Amendment Act. Wiltshire had the highest proportion of paupers to the total population with 16.1 per cent; Dorset had 15.7 per cent and Oxford 15.1 per cent, but the average for the northern counties was only 6.2 per cent. Caird also found that the poverty of the southern labourer was clearly evidenced by the character of his diet. A Dorset labourer earning 6s a week and paying 1s for his cottage, described a day's food:

After doing up his horses, he takes breakfast, which is made of flour with a little butter and water 'from the tea-kettle' poured over it. He takes with him to the field a piece of bread and (if he has not a growing family, and can afford it) cheese to eat at midday. He returns home in the afternoon to a few potatoes, and possibly a little bacon, though only those who are better off can afford this. The supper very commonly consists of bread and water. . . . Beer is given by the master in haytime and harvest.[10]

On large estates wages were generally a shilling higher, and in addition to a beer allowance of a gallon a day in the harvest-field the labourer received turf and brushwood for fuel and often a small potato-ground. In Suffolk – another poor county – a week's budget for man and wife (no children in this case) consisted of the items shown below.[11] 'Sundries' would have to include clothing, shoes, soap and candles, yeast and salt, household replacements and medicine, besides any additional food which such a scanty diet required.

	s	d
1 stone of flour	1	10
$\frac{1}{2}$ lb of butter		6
1 lb of cheese		$7\frac{1}{2}$
$1\frac{1}{2}$ oz of tea		$4\frac{1}{2}$
$\frac{1}{2}$ lb of sugar		2
	3	6
Rent of cottage	2	0
	5	6
Weekly wages	8	0
Balance for sundries	2s	6d

The contemporary evidence suggests that only slight improvements in the labourer's position occurred during the decade which opened with the Great Exhibition. Prices of necessaries continued high – especially during the shortage years of the Crimean War, when wheat reached 72s 5d (1854) and 74s 8d (1855), and the combination of this with low wages made things as bad as they had been in the 1840s or earlier. Alexander Somerville reported of Somerset labourers in 1852 that:

> For years past their daily diet is potatoes for breakfast, dinner and supper, and potatoes only. This year they are not living on potatoes because they have none (the crop failed) and the wretched farm labourers are now existing on half diet, made of barley, wheat, turnips, cabbages and such small allowance of bread as small wages will procure.[12]

Joseph Arch remembered eating barley bread during his boyhood in Warwickshire about this time:

> and even barley loaves were all too scarce . . . The food we could get was of very poor quality, and there was far too little of it. Meat was rarely, if ever, to be seen on the labourer's table. . . . In many a household even a morsel of bacon was considered a luxury.

But Arch's father grew carrots and turnips in his garden, and the family never stole, or begged for food at the rectory as many villagers had to do.[13] Diet in Norfolk at this time seems to have been a little better and rather more varied, though still largely meatless:

> Wheaten bread of the best quality was the principal food; it appeared at every meal with, or without, a little butter or cheese, and an onion or apple. If there was time and inclination for cooking, the principal meal came at the end of the day. There was the traditional Norfolk dumpling, made like bread with yeast, and dropped into boiling water after it had risen before the fire; potatoes or cabbage, if they were grown in the garden, completed the dish, unless earnings were sufficient for a little bacon or meat perhaps once a week. Herrings made a variation, and meat and fruit pies appeared on special occasions like harvest time. This diet [says Miss Springall]iseems to have changed very little between 1834 and 1876.[14]

The labourer's dietary position was, of course, influenced by factors other than wages. The wide extent of truck (payment in kind), which employers claimed was a hidden advantage to their workers, in many cases merely forced them to take inferior goods at inflated prices or limited the way in which they could spend their earnings. The Rev. Lord Sidney Godolphin Osborne described the practice in his native Dorset, where on some estates labourers were paid 'almost entirely on the truck system'. For best wheat they were charged 7s a bushel or 56s the quarter, and for the inferior 'tailings' 6s – 'at least 1s a bushel too much'. This, with cottage

138

rent at 1s, would absorb the whole of a labourer's wage. But often the
farmer would require his men to take inferior qualities of butter and
cheese, which could not be sold in the market, or beef and mutton from
diseased animals. 'Many of us must even get in debt to them,' one labourer
told Osborne, 'and then you see, Sir, we must go on.'[15] The diseased
mutton was the only 'fresh' meat which many labourers tasted, unless
they dared to defy the Game Laws by snaring a rabbit or knocking a hare
over the head. Many must have done this, either because they had a
craving for meat which could not otherwise be satisfied, or because they
had a natural love of sport with the added spice of beating the gamekeeper,
but they took a terrible risk. The penalty for poaching was still
transportation until 1857, and thereafter imprisonment or a heavy fine;
and by a new law of 1862 a labourer who was seen after dark carrying any
suspicious-looking bundle could be compulsorily searched by a police
officer. It had been the custom for women cleaning turnips in the field to
take two or three home with them as a perquisite, and farmers had tacitly
recognized the custom, but after the new Act several women in
Warwickshire were searched, charged with stealing turnips, and fined. On
another occasion in 1873 a labourer was fined £1 9s 6d for picking a little
liverwort for his sick wife. In these conditions it is probable that no more
than a very small proportion of labourers were systematic poachers: only
those who did not have a regular job to lose, who lived in 'open' parishes
or on the edges of commons or woods, might make a regular practice of it.
The old labourer who told John Halsham that as a boy he had lived with
his father in the woods, 'and most days we'd a hare . . . or a pheasant he'd
pick up a day or two after a shoot, and we'd wild duck sometimes, and I got
trout out of the brook',[16] was exceptionally lucky and quite untypical.

Personal evidence of this kind is useful, though a great deal must be
accumulated before any general picture emerges. Fortunately, it can be
supplemented by evidence from the first national food inquiry ever undertaken in Britain, conducted in 1863 by Dr Edward Smith on behalf of the
Medical Officer of the Privy Council (Sir John Simon) and published as an
appendix to the Sixth Report. This was a remarkable pioneering survey
which opened up an entirely new sphere of sanitary inquiry. Smith had
previously investigated the physical condition and state of nourishment of
Lancashire workers during the Cotton Famine, in the course of which he
had estimated the weekly minimum of food necessary for subsistence and
sufficient to prevent diseases bred by starvation: thus thirty years or more
before the surveys of Booth and Rowntree he had invented the concept of
a 'minimum subsistence level' below which civilized life was not possible,
and based not merely on crude earnings but on the nutritional value of
food. As then calculated, his estimate of minimum subsistence for an adult
was 28,600 grains of carbonaceous and 1,330 grains of nitrogenous foods

weekly, roughly equivalent to about 2,760 kilocalories and 70 g of protein a day.[17]

His inquiry of 1863 covered the food of 'the poorer labouring classes', in which category he included farm labourers and certain badly paid domestic workers such as silk-weavers, shoemakers, stocking and glove-weavers, and needlewomen. The families of 370 English labourers from every county except Herefordshire were examined, either by Smith personally or by other 'competent persons', who included doctors and boards of guardians, and there seems no reason to doubt that the findings were reasonably representative. Although it was shown that the labourer's diet was on the whole superior to that of the indoor workers, one surprising conclusion was that Welsh, Scottish, and Irish farm labourers were all better fed than the English, and in particular consumed more milk. On average, however, the English labourer's diet was considerably above the minimum subsistence level:

	Carbonaceous foods	Nitrogenous foods
England	40,673 grains	1,594 grains
Wales	48,354 grains	2,031 grains
Scotland	48,980 grains	2,348 grains
Ireland	43,366 grains	2,434 grains

Even in the lowest-fed counties, Somerset, Wiltshire, and Norfolk, the carbonaceous content was more than 31,000 grains, but in ten (Berkshire, Rutland, Oxfordshire, Hampshire, Staffordshire, Somerset, Cornwall, Wiltshire, Cheshire, and Essex) the nitrogenous content was below the minimum. Again, Smith's inquiry demonstrated very clearly the difference in standard between north and south, Northumberland, Durham, and Cumberland having a particularly good and Wiltshire, Dorset, and Somerset a particularly bad nutritional record. Other significant conclusions were that, although agricultural labourers as a class were not badly fed, their wives and children frequently were, as the lion's share of food went to the bread-winner; that his position was particularly unfavourable when there were several children under ten years of age, or where his wife could find no by-employment, where the house rent was high, or where vegetables could not be grown.

Turning to the consumption of particular foods, Smith found, as may be expected, that bread was the principal article of subsistence, being eaten at the average rate of 12¼ lb per adult weekly, or 55¾ lb per family: the lowest consumption (less than 10 lb) was in Cornwall, the highest (more than 15 lb) in Northumberland. The extent to which domestic baking had declined by this time was shown by the fact that 30 per cent of families bought bakers' bread exclusively, and another 50 per cent used it as an adjunct: it appears that it had practically died out in the poor south-western and southern counties and only survived strongly in the more prosperous north. Where flour was bought for baking it was almost everywhere the white wheaten flour known as 'seconds', and in only one of the 370 cases investigated was it whole brown meal; white bread was preferred because it was more palatable with little or no butter or other addition, and because it was less purgative, and it is interesting to find that Smith defended its use as 'based upon principles of sound economy, both as regards the cost of food and the nutriment which the young and old members of a family can derive from it'.[18] The only other meal of any importance was oatmeal, purchased occasionally by 20 per cent of families mainly for making gruel, but used for making cake only in Cumberland, Westmorland, and Northumberland. It was now as expensive as wheat flour, and consequently had been given up in Derbyshire and other areas where it was formerly popular. Small quantities of dried peas and rice found their way into the majority of households, mainly in the wintertime in place of fresh vegetables.

It is clear from Smith's report that the second food of the English labourer was potatoes, not meat. They were consumed at the rate of 6 lb per adult weekly, or 27 lb per family, and 87 per cent of households used them. The average consumption figure is perhaps rather meaningless as the use of potatoes depended largely on the availability of allotments at a reasonable rental, and where a quarter- or half-acre potato-ground could be had for £1 or £2 a year, the consumption was very much heavier. In such cases 56 lb per family weekly was not uncommon. Again, Smith approved of their general adoption, chiefly on the ground that cooked potatoes made a hot dinner or supper when added to the morsel of meat available, which 'otherwise would be a dry, cold and uninviting meal'. Meat was, in fact, a luxury in the labourer's diet. Each adult consumed on average only 16 oz each week, and Smith included both fresh meat and bacon in the category since he found that they were regarded as inter-changeable. Thirty per cent of all families never ate butcher's meat. Again, the variation from the average consumption was very great – in Salop, Essex, Somerset, Wiltshire and Norfolk less than 7 oz were consumed by adults weekly, while in Durham, Lancashire, Northampton, Surrey, and Yorkshire it was more than 24 oz, and in Northumberland as much as 35 oz. When fresh meat was eaten it was generally beef or mutton, although Smith found that sheep's head and pluck were frequently used by poorer families, or half a cow's head would provide Sunday dinner and broth for the children throughout the week as well as dripping. Pickled pork was almost the only meat available in Dorset, Somerset, and the eastern counties, but this, like bacon, had the great advantage that it did not shrink when cooked and could be cut up easily into small pieces for flavouring potatoes and vegetables. Whenever possible, meat was eaten at the Sunday dinner, which was often the only occasion in the week when the whole family dined together; what was left was reserved for the husband, who took a little with him for dinner in the fields or ate it for supper at night, his wife and children existing mainly on bread, potatoes, and weak tea. Smith remarked that 'This is not only acquiesced in by the wife, but felt by her to be right, and even necessary for the maintenance of the family. . . . The important practical fact is, however, well established, that the labourer eats meat or bacon almost daily, whilst his wife and children may eat it but once a week.'[19]

Of other foods the most widely used was sugar, at 7½ oz for adults weekly and 33¾ oz per family. Much of it went to sweeten tea, though in the poorest counties this was drunk without either sugar or milk, and an increasing amount was in the form of treacle, which at 4d a pound was a cheap substitute for butter. Sugar in 1863 was still in a transitional stage, regarded by better-off families as a necessity but by the poorer as a luxury. Tea was by now a necessity, 99 per cent of all the families consuming it at the average rate of ½ oz per adult weekly, 2¼ oz per family. Coffee was much less popular, partly because it needed more preparation and partly because it was less palatable without the addition of sugar or milk, but tea had become the staple drink of wife and children, often being taken (very weak) two or three times a day. The husband drank his beer or cider 'allowance' in the field, and tried to keep some back to bring home with him for supper. A surprising discovery was the small quantity of dairy produce which labourers were able to obtain, often, it seems, because farmers would not take the trouble to sell it in the small amounts which could be afforded, preferring to dispose of the milk and butter off the farm in bulk to nearby towns. Consequently the average quantity of milk consumed was only 1.6 pints per adult weekly, of butter, dripping, and suet combined 5½ oz, and of cheese 5½ oz: only in comparatively few families was butter eaten every day, 'since', said Smith, 'the poorer for the most part had two days a week in which the children ate dry bread'. They and their mothers were the chief casualties of the labourer's low standard of living.

Translated into modern nutritional terms, the average quantities of food in the labourer's family budget produced 2,760 kilocalories per person per day, 70 g of protein, 54 g of fat, 0.48 g of calcium, and 15.9 mg of iron. Smith's diets did not record the ages of children, and the calculations are therefore derived from a straight division of the total family food by the number in the family. We know that the husband received the 'lion's share' of some foods – particularly meat – and, indeed, 2,760 kilocalories would not have provided enough energy for a man in heavy agricultural work by at least 1,000 kilocalories a day. It follows that his wife and children were receiving less than the calculated averages by unknown, but possibly large, amounts. Professor John Yudkin has commented on this: 'The figures for calorie intake suggest that they were low enough both to affect growth and to restrict physical output. Quite apart from long hours and poor working conditions, the small intake of food must have contributed to a state of chronic exhaustion of the workers.'[20] Added to this, the protein intake was almost certainly inadequate for pregnant and lactating women and for growing children and adolescents, while the amount of calcium was very low by modern standards.

The bare statistics of consumption do not indicate much about the kind of meals which labourers actually ate. Smith made careful inquiry into this, too, and the following are typical examples of daily fare from different parts of the country:

DEVON (Case No. 135). *Breakfast and supper* – tea-kettle broth (bread, hot water, salt, and $\frac{1}{3}$ pint of milk), bread and treacle. *Dinner* – pudding (flour, salt and water), vegetables, and fresh meat; no bread.

(Case No. 163). *Breakfast* – wife has tea, bread and butter; husband, tea-kettle broth with dripping or butter added, and with or without milk, also bread, treacle or cheese. *Dinner* – fried bacon and vegetables or bacon pie with potatoes and bread. *Supper* – tea, or milk and water, with bread, cheese and butter.

DORSET (Case No. 191). *Breakfast* – water broth, bread, butter, tea with milk. *Dinner* – husband has bread and cheese: family take tea besides. *Supper* – hot fried bacon and cabbage, or bread and cheese.

WILTSHIRE (Case No. 211). *Breakfast* – water broth, bread and butter. *Dinner* – husband and children have bacon (sometimes), cabbage, bread and butter. Wife has tea. *Supper* – potatoes or rice.

(Case No. 212). *Breakfast* – sop, bread, and sometimes butter. *Dinner* – bread and cheese. *Supper* – onions, bread, butter or cheese.

LINCOLNSHIRE (Case No. 248). *Breakfast* – milk gruel, or bread and water, or tea and bread. *Dinner* – meat for husband only; others vegetables only. *Tea and supper* – bread or potatoes.

NOTTINGHAMSHIRE (Case No. 255). *Breakfast* – children – thickened milk; others – tea or coffee, and bread and butter with cheese sometimes. *Dinner* – little meat, and potatoes. *Supper* – bacon or tea.

DERBYSHIRE (Case No. 281). *Breakfast* – coffee, bread and butter. *Dinner* – hot meat, vegetables and pudding daily. *Tea* – tea, bread and butter. *Supper* – hot, when not hot dinner.

CUMBERLAND (Case No. 301). *Breakfast* – husband – oatmeal and milk porridge: the others – tea, bread, butter and cheese. *Dinner* – meat and potatoes daily, bread, cheese and milk. *Supper* – boiled milk, followed by tea, bread, butter and cheese.

LANCASHIRE (Case No. 304). *Breakfast* – milk porridge, coffee, bread and butter. *Dinner* – meat and potatoes, or meat pie, rice pudding or a baked pudding; the husband takes ale, bread and cheese. *Supper* – tea, toasted cheese, and bacon instead of butter.

YORKSHIRE (Case No. 471). *Breakfast* – husband – milk and bread: family – tea, bread and butter. *Dinner* – husband – bacon daily: others – three days weekly, potatoes or bread, tea. *Tea* – tea, bread and butter.[21]

Dr Smith's report indicates that labourers' wages had moved up somewhat since Caird's survey a dozen years before – by a mere 4 per cent in what was already a high-wage county like Lancashire, but by as much as 52 per cent in Surrey and 58 per cent in Gloucestershire. The average rise over all counties was 28 per cent, and it is noticeable that the gap between north and south had closed somewhat. But although the trend was upward, it was from a miserably low base.

In 1867, as in 1843, a Royal Commission inquired into the employment of women and children in agriculture[22] and the reports of the numerous commissioners are a terrible indictment of the conditions of crushing poverty still prevailing in an era of agricultural prosperity. Of the eastern and south-eastern counties, the Rev. J. Fraser said that 'the dominant fact over the whole district was the insufficiency of wages, which varied between ten and thirteen shillings a week': the inevitable result was the extensive employment of women, often in organized gangs, and of children from the age of six or seven upwards. Again, conditions in the northern counties were in sharp contrast, and Northumberland, where the yearly hiring and yearly payment still persisted, stood out as a bright spot. Here children were only employed in summer, and not under eleven years of age; regular work began at about fourteen, so that many had an opportunity of acquiring some education, which was rare in the south. As far south as Derbyshire the labourer could still earn his 15s a week, but in Dorset and Devonshire he fell back into penury and debt with 8s. It seems likely, however, that shortly after this time wages again took a slight upward turn, partly, it was reported, as a result of agitation by the newly formed Agricultural Labourers' Unions: an official inquiry of 1872 showed a range of day labourers' wages from 10s 4d (Dorset) to 20s 6d (Durham), the mean for England and Wales being 14s 8d.[23] The reliability of such estimates is doubtful, and in any case the relevant statistic is not so much the labourer's wage as the family earnings. When wife and children also worked in the fields, as was often the case, or at domestic industries such as the stocking frame, seaming, glove-stitching or straw-plaiting, T.E. Kebbel believed that 'the average weekly cash earnings . . . may be set down probably at 18s a week, exclusive of "allowances", and, if harvest money is added, at £1'.[24] A case was mentioned in the 1867 Report of a labourer near Market Harborough whose total earnings for the year were

£103 9s 0d: he was exceptionally fortunate in having three sons between the ages of fourteen and nineteen who could all contribute usefully to the family budget. But, as the author of *The Seven Ages of a Village Pauper* explained, the worst times in a labourer's life were, first, when he was raising a growing family, his wife unable to work and often incurring medical expenses and, second, when in old age he could only work casually, or not at all. In this Oxfordshire village, although only one in every ten of the inhabitants were in receipt of poor relief at any given time, between one-half and three-quarters of all were forced to live 'on the rates' at some period in their lives.[25]

Although the labourer's position at this period could perhaps nowhere be described as comfortable, there were clearly important variations in the degrees of his discomfort. As we have seen, his position depended partly on region, on the size and age of his family, and on the extent to which they could contribute to the household budget. But, equally important, was the skill of the housewife in adapting a limited range of simple foodstuffs into nourishing and palatable meals, even when income and cooking facilities were very restricted. At Harpenden in Hertfordshire in the 1860s and 1870s, for example, the labourer's wage was 11s to 13s a week, supplemented by some straw-plaiting by his family. The cottages here rarely had an oven or range, so the bulk of food was prepared by boiling in a large iron pot over the open fire, or by frying: potatoes, greens, flour dumplings, and whatever meat was available were all cooked together, though usually in separate nets which allowed the cooking time of different items to be controlled. The dumplings, with a filling of streaky bacon, pickled pork or liver, mixed with onion and potato, were particularly important for the man's dinner-basket in the field, where they were either eaten cold or heated over a gypsy fire; the basket also contained some large 'door-steps' of bread, one or two raw onions, a horn of salt, and a can of cold tea. Some of the rows of cottages had a communal bakehouse at the rear, and some home-baked their own bread, usually fortnightly. Most of the men had allotments of ten or twenty poles, rented at 3d a pole a year, and many kept a pig, or occasionally two: pickled pork was a great favourite, and accounted for around two-thirds of all the meat eaten. Most of the farmers allowed gleaning after harvest, and the women and children could gather enough wheat to produce from two to seven bushels of flour, depending on the number in the family.[26]

Budgets of the 1870s show no great change from the earlier period, except that the region of most wretched conditions seems to have shifted a little farther into the south-west. Up until now Dorset had had the reputation of greatest poverty, but Francis George Heath discovered even worse conditions in Somerset when he made his investigation in 1874. Here, a typical young married labourer earned at day-work and extra piece-work an annual total of £31 16s 6d. His expenses for his family of four children were:[27]

Per annum	£	s	d
Rent (2s per week)	5	4	0
Poor rates		7	6
Tithes		1	6
Coal (1 cwt per week)	2	12	0
Shoes and mending	2	5	0
Bread (4s 6d per week)	11	14	0
Potato-ground ($\frac{1}{4}$ acre)	2	0	0
Seed potatoes	1	0	0
Club pay		12	0
Soap		10	10
Tea (3d per week)		13	0
Candles		7	6
Butter ($\frac{1}{4}$ lb per week)		17	14
Treacle ($\frac{1}{2}$ lb per week)		6	6
Matches, thread and tape		3	6
Broom and salt		2	0
Cups, saucers, plates		1	8
Children's schooling (1d per week each)		17	4
Tools and repairs	1	18	1
Total	£31	13s	9d
Balance		2s	9d

In this household, as in many described by Heath, there was no meat from one year's end to another. Few could afford to pay 1s a pound for it at the village shop, and those who did manage to get any generally did so by fattening their own pig, which Heath described as 'the live savings bank'; by the time the pig was fattened and ready for killing half often had to be sacrificed to pay the tradesman who had supplied its meal, but usually there was some pork and bacon left for the family besides enough cash to buy another 'suckling'.

Keeping a pig was a sure sign of a standard of living somewhat above the poverty line. Flora Thompson described how in her north Oxfordshire village all the family would sacrifice for the sake of the pig, and much time and trouble would be spent saving scraps and foraging for it:

The family pig was everybody's pride and everybody's business. Mother spent hours boiling up the 'little taturs' to mash and mix with the pot-liquor . . . and help out the expensive barley meal. The children, on their way home from school, would fill their arms with sow thistle, dandelion and choice long grass, or roam along the hedgerows on wet evenings collecting snails in a pail for the pig's supper. These piggy crunched up with great relish.[28]

All the labour of feeding, killing, and preparing the various joints and products was well worth while, however: when the remains of the pig were hung up on a wooden rack across the kitchen ceiling 'that was a better picture than an oil painting'.[29]

But at Athelney in Somerset Edwin H. earned 9s a week to provide for himself, his wife, and eight young children: they had not tasted meat for six months, and at 7d the quartern loaf, baker's bread was a luxury they could not afford. Here the wife bought meal and made a coarse bread at home.[30] And in North Devon, Canon Girdlestone, who was urging migration to the higher earnings of the north as the only solution for the labourer, described conditions as follows:

Wages are for labourers 8s or 9s a week, with two or one and a half quarts of cider daily, valued at 2s per week, but much over-valued. Carters and shepherds get 1s a week more, or else a cottage rent free. The labourer has no privileges whatever. He rents his potato-ground at a high rate. Though fuel is said to be given to him he really pays its full value by grubbing up for it in old hedges in after-hours. In wet weather or in sickness his wages entirely cease so that he seldom makes a full week. The cottages, as a rule, are not fit to house pigs in. The labourer breakfasts on tea-kettle broth, hot water poured on bread and flavoured with onions; dines on bread and hard cheese at 2d a pound, with cider very washy and sour, and sups on potatoes or cabbage greased with a tiny bit of fat bacon. He seldom more than sees or smells butcher's meat. He is long lived, but in the prime of life 'crippled up', i.e. disabled by rheumatism, the result of wet clothes with no fire to dry them by for use next morning, poor living and sour cider. Then he has to work for 4s or 5s per week, supplemented scantily from the rates, and, at last, to come for the rest of his life on the rates entirely. Such is, I will not call it the life, but the existence or vegetation of the Devon peasant.[31]

The prosperity of the 'Golden Age' came to a sudden end in 1874 when, for the first time, free trade exposed English agriculture to the competition of the world's grain and meat producers, and from this time until 1896 there followed a period of almost uninterrupted depression, deepened at times by domestic catastrophes such as bad harvests and cattle plagues. With great stretches of land going out of cultivation and much more under-cultivated, the immediate effect of the agricultural crisis on the worker was to reduce the demand for labour and to lower wages, sometimes by 1s, occasionally by 2s, a week; not surprisingly, the rural exodus continued at an increased pace, and farmers complained that with the departure of their best labourers they now had to pay more to get the same quantity of work done. Nor was the labourer yet helped by falling prices which, on average, remained the same between 1871 and 1880 as in the previous decade – meat prices, in fact, were rising until the late 1870s. A witness before the Royal Commission on Agricultural Depression of 1882 summed up the effects: 'I should say that the landlord suffers least . . . that the farmer suffers most, but that he feels his suffering less than the labourer. To the labourer it is a question really of less food, to the farmer it is not absolutely a question of bread, it is comforts or no comforts.'[32]

Francis Heath entitled the final chapter of his book *The English Peasantry*, written in 1874, 'The future of the English peasantry', and prognosticated that, 'A happier condition of life for the immediate future of our peasants may be anticipated without indulgence in any visionary ideas.' Revisiting the four western counties of Wiltshire, Dorset, Somerset, and Devon in 1880 he was already able to report on 'dawning improvement'. Although 10s or 11s a week was still the average wage in this part of England, 'privileges' were beginning to disappear, or, where they survived, were no longer regarded as part-payment of the wage, and some improvement in cottage accommodation was noticeable. The character of diet was also on the turn. From Dorset it was reported:

the labourer decidedly lives better than he did, for he 'sees', 'smells' and 'tastes' meat regularly, instead of once a week as formerly. A slice of fat bacon no longer satisfies.

In Devonshire the usual fare was:

for breakfast, 'broth' made of fat, bread and water; for the mid-day meal perhaps a little bread and cheese or potatoes and pork – sometimes, for a change, a little dried fish instead of pork; for the evening meal a cup of tea with dried bread. Pies and pasties are the great feature of the Cornish diet. The ordinary pasty of the Cornish labourer is clean, wholesome and nutritious.

And from Somerset a correspondent reported that the labourer's fare consisted of:

Breakfast (before seven a.m.) of bread and bacon or dripping, with fried potatoes; a lunch at about ten or eleven of bread and cheese and cider; dinner, if taken in the fields, of bread and cold bacon or other cold meat, washed down with cider, or, if near enough to home, a dish of hot vegetables with a little meat. Further, the peasant has a slight meal of bread and cheese at about four o'clock and a substantial supper soon after leaving work, of hot vegetables with meat or fish of some kind, boiled or fried, and tea and bread and butter – the whole making a grand total of no inconsiderable amount, and which only fairly hard work and fresh air enable him to digest.[33]

In these and other budgets of the 1880s there is both more quantity and more variety, and the increasingly regular use of meat and fish is particularly significant. Although Canon Tuckwell's estimated budget for a family of six which allowed 6 lb of meat weekly at 8d a pound may well be optimistic, it seems that some meat every day was now general, at any rate for the husband: the interesting thing about Tuckwell's budget of 1885 is the fall in price of other foods – bread which could now be bought for 4d to $4\frac{1}{2}$d the quartern loaf, sugar at 3d a pound, and tea at 2s a pound. This supposedly typical family spent more on meat than on bread, and consumed half a pound of tea, two pounds of sugar, and a shilling's worth of milk each week.[34]

While the agricultural industry continued to stagnate in the 1890s, the condition of the labourer continued to improve. The seven voluminous Reports of the Royal Commission on Labour which were published in 1893 can be summarized as follows: in the south of England the labourer's position had improved compared with twenty-five years earlier, though in many parts it was still far from satisfactory; in the north, no change of any importance had taken place; money wages had been on the increase, and, generally speaking, employment had become more regular; women's and children's labour had greatly diminished; the exodus from the land had continued in almost every county. Actual wages still only averaged 13s $5\frac{1}{2}$d a week, ranging from 10s in Wiltshire and Dorset to 18s in Lancashire and Cumberland, but the important point was that their purchasing power had increased because of the low price of provisions; moreover, shorter hours meant that the labourer had more leisure-time to devote to his allotment and so could raise more potatoes and vegetables than formerly.

The allotments movement had made considerable progress in most parts of the country, sometimes against the wishes of farmers who did not want their labourers to over-tire themselves when working on their own account, and even, as at Tysoe in Warwickshire, where the vicar thought that one-sixteenth of an acre was the right amount.[35]

Village co-operative societies, and vans sent round by nearby town societies, were also beginning to make a useful contribution to the food of the farm worker. 'His standard of life is higher,' said the Report: 'He dresses better, he eats more butcher's meat, he travels more, he reads more, and he drinks less.'[36] But still there was the big gap in conditions between the purely agricultural counties of the south and east and those of the midlands and north, where nearness to industry and mining forced up wages to a competitive level. Commissioner Bear, who reported on Bedford, Hampshire, Huntingdon, and Sussex, said: 'The agricultural labourers were never so well off as they have been during the last few years, [but] I am far from saying that the condition of the labourers, and especially that of the day-labourers, is satisfactory'; while the reporter on Berkshire, Oxfordshire, Shropshire, Cornwall, and Devon wrote that: 'The large majority of labourers earn but a bare subsistence. . . . An immense number of them live in a chronic state of debt and anxiety, and depend to a lamentable extent upon charity.'[37]

149

The 2 oz of tea per family a week which Smith had found in 1863 had grown to $\frac{1}{2}$ lb thirty years later, and many families now spent 1s 6d or more on tea and sugar weekly. This, the increased consumption of meat, butter and cheese, and the not infrequent mention of tinned salmon and sardines – even of labourers' wives buying a bottle of port wine – is all evidence of a generally increased standard of comfort and a trend towards a more standardized dietary among farmworkers. By the early 1890s Argentine beef and New Zealand lamb were appearing on labourers' tables at Sunday dinner. But the improvement was not universal, and where wages were still low and there were many mouths to feed, little had changed. In three Berkshire labourers' budgets collected by the Royal Commission, bread took at least 6s a week, almost half the total earnings, and there was no fresh meat, only bacon.

Some of the Commission's reporters even found signs of a deterioration in physique in parts of the country where traditional local foods were being abandoned. This was particularly noticeable in Northumberland, where the hinds and shepherds, formerly reared on a nutritious diet of milk, fat bacon, porridge, wholemeal bread, and butter, had been described in 1867 as a 'splendid race'. In 1893 Arthur Fox wrote:

Owing to change of diet, especially since payment in kind was given up, there has been a falling off in strength and stamina. . . . The children are being brought up on tea instead of milk and, without it, porridge is disliked and given up. . . . There is probably a good deal of truth in what one old man, William Stenhouse of Wark, said to me on this subject – 'A man should eat the food of the country in which he is born. This foreign stuff, such as tea, is no forage for a man. Bannocks made of barley and peas made a man as hard as a brick. Men would take a lump of bannock out for the day, and drink water, but now they eat white bread and drink tea, and ain't half so hard.'[38]

More, of course, were surviving.

By 1900 the indications were that the fortunes of the labourer were at last on the turn. So many had left the land that when Rider Haggard made his tour of *Rural England* in 1901 he found widespread depopulation and a scarcity of labour which had forced up wages even in a depressed county like Dorset:

I am told that at the annual hiring-fair just past the old positions were absolutely reversed, the farmers walking about and importuning the labourers to come and be hired instead of, as formerly, the labourers anxiously entreating the stolid farmers to take them on at any pittance. Their present life is almost without exception one of comfort, if the most ordinary thrift be observed. I could take you to the cottage of a shepherd, not many miles from here, that has brass rods and carpeting to the staircase, and from the open door of which you hear a piano strumming within. Of course, bicycles stand by the doorway. . . . The son of another labourer I know takes dancing lessons at a quadrille class in the neighbouring town.[39]

In 1902, Wilson Fox received detailed evidence from 114 investigators as to the wages and expenditure of labourers, which he published in a Board of Trade Report:[40] the statistics were supplied by Local Government Board inspectors, members of local authorities, the clergy and tradesmen, as well as by agricultural labourers themselves. Of an average weekly wage, including all extra earnings, of 18s 6d, 73 per cent was spent on food in the way shown in Table 17.

Table 17 *Average consumption and cost of food by agricultural labourers' families in England in 1902*

Articles	Northern counties		Midland counties		Eastern counties		Southern and south-western counties		General average for England	
	lb	oz	lb	oz	lb	oz	lb	oz	lb	oz
Beef or mutton	4	10	3	12	1	12	3	5	3	$5\frac{3}{4}$
Pork	0	3	1	5	2	1	0	14	1	$1\frac{3}{4}$
Bacon	3	7	3	0	2	0	2	6	2	$11\frac{1}{4}$
Cheese	0	12	1	5	1	2	1	10	1	$3\frac{1}{4}$
Bread	5	0	27	0	17	0	29	0	19	8
Flour	23	0	7	0	20	8	9	0	14	14
Oatmeal and rice	1	4	1	8	1	0	1	4	1	4
Potatoes	26	0	22	0	24	0	31	0	25	12
Tea	0	8	0	7	0	$6\frac{1}{2}$	0	9	0	$7\frac{1}{2}$
Coffee or cocoa	0	1	0	5	0	1	0	$3\frac{1}{2}$	0	$2\frac{1}{2}$
Butter	1	6	0	15	0	$14\frac{1}{2}$	0	15	1	$0\frac{3}{4}$
Lard, margarine, or dripping	1	13	0	10	0	15	0	12	1	$0\frac{1}{2}$
Sugar	4	12	4	12	4	0	3	12	4	5
Syrup, treacle, or jam	1	12	1	8	1	0	2	4	1	10
Milk { new or skimmed	$6\frac{1}{2}$ pints		4 pints or 9 pints		$3\frac{1}{2}$ pints or $7\frac{3}{4}$ pints		4 pints or $9\frac{1}{2}$ pints		$4\frac{1}{2}$ pints or $8\frac{3}{4}$ pints	
Average total value	14s	$10\frac{1}{2}$d	13s	$6\frac{1}{2}$d	12s	$4\frac{1}{2}$d	13s	$4\frac{3}{4}$d	13s	$6\frac{1}{2}$d

Note:
The average family was taken to be the labourer, his wife and four children.

Table 18

Articles	High-wage counties		Low-wage counties		
	Northern counties	Midland counties	Eastern counties	Southern and south-western counties	General average for England
	s d	s d	s d	s d	s d
Bread and flour	2 $10\frac{3}{4}$	3 $0\frac{3}{4}$	3 10	3 $10\frac{1}{4}$	3 5
Meat (including beef, mutton, pork and bacon)	5 $2\frac{1}{2}$	4 $9\frac{3}{4}$	3 2	3 $5\frac{1}{2}$	4 2
Total	8s $1\frac{1}{4}$d	7s $10\frac{1}{2}$d	7s 0d	7s $3\frac{3}{4}$d	7s 7d
Percentage of total value of food consumed	54.5	58.2	56.6	54.6	56.0

The table is revealing in a number of respects – for showing the increased consumption of fresh beef and mutton, which was now as large as that of pork and bacon, the ½ lb of tea, the 4¼ lb of sugar, the 1 lb of butter, and the 1¼ lb of cheese. Milk, too, had increased noticeably, while new items in the labourer's diet included jam, syrup, margarine, and cocoa. The most striking fact, however, was that expenditure on meat was now, on average, greater than that on bread, and even in the low-wage counties of the south and east the two figures approached closely (see Table 18).

Table 17 does not include items 'sometimes purchased', for instance eggs and fish, tinned meats, currants, raisins, and pickles, nor does it take account of the vegetables and fruit grown on allotments. In all, there can be little doubt that substantial gains had been made in the labourer's position, which were clearly reflected in the sample menus which the report contained:

CAMBRIDGESHIRE. *Breakfast* – bread, butter, cheese, tea. *Dinner* – meat, puddings, pork or bacon, potatoes and vegetables, cheese, perhaps beer (on Sundays, beef or mutton, puddings). *Tea* – bread, butter, cheese, tea; perhaps herrings or a little cold pork. *Supper* – bread, cheese, perhaps a glass of beer.

DERBYSHIRE. Weekdays – *Breakfast* – bread, butter, bacon, cheese, tea. *Dinner* – beef, pork or bacon, potatoes, tea or beer. *Tea and supper* – bread, butter, syrup, jam, tea; perhaps fish (fresh or tinned). Sundays – *Breakfast* – bread, butter, bacon, tea. *Dinner* – beef or pork, occasionally a fowl, potatoes, tea, beer. *Tea* – bread, butter, jam, tinned fish, tea; perhaps some fancy bread. *Supper* – the same sort of diet as tea, perhaps some beer.

DORSET. *Breakfast* – bread, butter, cheese, cold bacon, tea (Sundays, fried bacon). *Dinner* – boiled bacon, potatoes and other vegetables (Sundays, mutton or beef, with pudding); or salt pork, vegetables, dumplings (Sundays, a little fresh meat or pork). *Tea* – bread, butter or jam, cheese, tea (Sundays, cake). *Supper* – very rarely any, or if any, vegetables and salt pork.

Variations on this standard pattern included tarts and 'toad-in-a-hole' (a small loaf with a piece of bacon or other meat in the middle) in Devonshire, oatmeal porridge in the more northerly counties, onion and potato pudding in Huntingdonshire, stews in Staffordshire and Norfolk, fruit pies in Yorkshire. Nearly everywhere dumplings were eaten, and puddings of rice or tapioca; least frequently mentioned were milk and eggs, which were included only in Devonshire, and apparently only eaten there when they could be bought at eighteen for a shilling.

Francis Heath's last volume on *British Rural Life and Labour*, published in 1911, painted an optimistic picture of the progress and prospects of the farm labourer which was in sharp contrast to his earlier surveys of 1880 and 1874. But the evidence on which Heath drew was the 1903 Report previously quoted, and there is reason to doubt whether the details there given as to earnings and expenditure, accurate or not at the time, were correct a few years later. In the years immediately before the First World War a number of social investigators, inspired by the pioneering work of Charles Booth and Seebohm Rowntree, were conducting detailed surveys of the labourer's standard of life from personal investigation rather than the second-hand (and possibly biased) reports of farmers and boards of guardians, and with reference to every family in a particular village or area rather than a supposedly 'typical' statistical sample. Investigating every household in the single village of Ridgmount in Bedfordshire, H.H. Mann discovered that the average wage of a labourer, at full rates and including extras, was 14s 4d, not 16s 2d as given by the Board of Trade; he went on to state that 34.3 per cent of the older population of the village was without the means of sustaining life in a state of mere physical efficiency according to Rowntree's standard.[41] The Board of Trade, he argued, had not allowed enough when working out their averages for the far greater number of lower-grade labourers over foremen and other higher paid categories. An article by C.R. Buxton in the *Contemporary Review* for August 1912 showed that in Oxfordshire villages the average wage was between 10s and 12s a week, and that because of lost time in wet weather 'hundreds of them have gone home at the week-end during the winter months with only 8s for the week': in a family of two adults and three children, the average amount of money available for each person for each meal was

¾d. In circumstances like this, where so little was available for food, it seems that the art of cooking had made little progress either: in her study of Corsley in Wiltshire Maude Davies found many families in which 'the wife cooks only once or twice a week in the winter. She cooks oftener in summer when potatoes are more plentiful.'[42] Finally, in the year before the outbreak of war, Seebohm Rowntree himself investigated in extreme detail the earnings and budgets of forty-two labourers from all parts of the country.[43] Taking the weekly wage of 20s 6d, which Professor Atwater had calculated as the minimum necessary to maintain a family of two adults and three children (the dietary was more austere than that in the workhouse, containing no butcher's meat, only a little bacon and tea, and no butter or eggs), he found that only in five northern counties (Northumberland, Durham, Westmorland, Lancashire, and Derbyshire) was 'the wage paid by farmers sufficient to maintain a family of average size in a state of merely physical efficiency'. In many cases, of course, the labourer's wage was supplemented by the earnings of other members of the family and by what he could raise on his allotment, but even allowing for all these additions, and for what was gained by charity, Rowntree discovered that in almost every case the nutritional value of the food consumed was less than that deemed necessary for a man engaged in only 'moderate' labour. In only one of the forty-two cases – a Yorkshire family having a combined income of 23s $2\frac{1}{2}$d – was the minimum protein requirement of 125 g a day reached, and in only ten was the energy value minimum of 3,500 kilocalories attained. On average, there was a deficiency of 24 per cent of protein and 10 per cent of calories in the forty-two families.[44]

Underfeeding was still the lot of the majority of English labourers in 1914, and the Essex family who told Rowntree that they never felt 'completely satisfied like', except after Sunday dinner, was probably not untypical. The advances of the 1880s and 1890s were not, it seems, maintained subsequently, principally because price levels turned upwards after 1900, while wages remained practically stationary.[45] If the labourer's diet was less scanty and monotonous than it was in 1850, it was still nutritionally inadequate, especially in protein-rich foods such as meat, milk, eggs, and butter. In many of the households investigated by Rowntree, fresh meat was 'for the man only', in twenty of the forty-two no butter at all was eaten, and in the twenty-six which obtained fresh milk the consumption was only $5\frac{1}{2}$ pints per family per week.[46]

The gains and losses over the previous half-century are not easy to assess. An Oxfordshire labourer with four young children and a wage of 8s a week represented the poorest of Rowntree's case studies: he was able to buy 5 lb of frozen brisket a week for 2s 0d, and 28 lb of bread for 3s $2\frac{1}{2}$d – prices well below those of mid-century – while advances in food technology were evidenced by the pound of Quaker Oats (3d) and, less desirably, two pounds of margarine (1s) and condensed milk ($3\frac{1}{2}$d). The allotment movement had certainly contributed something to the labourer's diet – Rowntree estimated that approximately one-twelfth of the food consumed was self-produced – although other attempts to ameliorate his position, such as the smallholdings campaign, had proved illusory. Perhaps the most helpful sign was that the plight of the agricultural labourer was at long last attracting widespread public interest and anxiety. The nation had recently been alarmed by reports of physical deterioration among town-dwellers. Now it discovered that its supposedly healthy country stock, the 'backbone of England' which could always be relied on to buttress the national stamina in times of need, was itself under-nourished and economically inefficient. Was not a healthy peasant population socially desirable? Ought not the continued drift from the land be stopped, and, if so, how? A new awareness of the social problems of the countryside was dawning when the events of August 1914 blotted out any possibility of rural reform.

Notes

1 Quoted in Joseph Arch (1898) *The Story of His Life, told by Himself*, edited with a Preface by the Countess of Warwick, 98.
2 Heath, Francis George (1911), *British Rural Life and Labour* 181 et seq.
3 e.g. Howitt, William (1862) *The Rural Life of England* (3rd edn).
4 *Village Politics: Addresses and Sermons on the Labour Question* (1878), 85.
5 Hudson, W.H. *Hampshire Days* in G.E. Fussell (1949) *The English Rural Labourer, His Home, Furniture, Clothing and Food from Tudor to Victorian Times*, 128.
6 Hasbach, W. (1920) *A History of the English Agricultural Labourer*, trans. Ruth Kenyon, 217 et seq.
7 For a standard description of this period see Lord Ernle, *English Farming Past and Present* (new (6th) edition with Introductions by G.E. Fussell and O.R. McGregor, 1961), chap. XVII. More recent studies are in G.E. Mingay (ed.) (1981) *The Victorian Countryside*, 2 vols.
8 Hasbach, op. cit., 246.
9 Caird, James (1852) *English Agriculture in 1850–51*.
10 ibid., 84–5.
11 ibid., 147.
12 Somerville, Alexander (1852) *The Whistler at the Plough*.
13 Joseph Arch, op. cit., 10–15.
14 Springall, L. Marion (1936) *Labouring Life in Norfolk Villages 1834–1914*, 56–7.
15 White, Arnold (ed.) (nd) *The Letters of S.G.O.* 2 vols, I, 16–18.
16 Halsham, John (1897) *Idlehurst*.
17 Sixth Report of the Medical Officer of the Privy Council (1863). Appendix No.

6: Report by Dr Edward Smith on the Food of the Poorer Labouring Classes in England, 232.

18 ibid., 239.

19 ibid., 249.

20 Barker, T.C., Oddy, D.J., and Yudkin, John (1970) *The Dietary Surveys of Dr Edward Smith, 1862–3. A New Assessment*, 46.

21 Sixth Report (1863), op. cit., 256 et seq.

22 Reports of the Commissioners on Children's, Young Persons' and Women's Employment in Agriculture, 1867–70. For an excellent summary of the Reports, see Hasbach, op. cit., Appendix VI, 404 et seq.

23 Earnings of Agricultural Labourers. Returns of the average rate of weekly earnings of agricultural labourers in the unions of England and Wales, SP 1873, (358) LIII.

24 Kebbel, T.E. (1870) *The Agricultural Labourer: A Short Summary of His Position*, 29.

25 Bartley, George C.T. (1874) *The Seven Ages of a Village Pauper. Dedicated to One Million of Her Majesty's Subjects whose Names are now unhappily and almost hopelessly inscribed as Paupers on the Parish Rolls of England.*

26 Grey, Edwin (1934) *Cottage Life in a Hertfordshire Village*, repub. 1977, chap. 3, 96–127.

27 Heath, Francis George (1874) *The English Peasantry*, 41–2.

28 Thompson, Flora (1973) *Lark Rise to Candleford* (Penguin edn), 24.

29 Samuel, Raphael (ed.) (1975) *Village Life and Labour*, History Workshop Series, 200.

30 Heath (1874), op. cit., 79.

31 ibid., 99–100.

32 Quoted in Hasbach, op. cit., 295.

33 Heath (1911), op. cit., 286 et seq.

34 Tuckwell, Rev. Canon (1895) *Reminiscences of a Radical Parson*.

35 Ashby, M.K. (1974) *Joseph Ashby of Tysoe, 1859–1919*, 126.

36 Report of Royal Commission on Labour: *The Agricultural Labourer*, vol. I (England), C. 6894, I–XIII (1893), pt II, 44.

37 ibid., 46.

38 ibid.: Report by Arthur Wilson Fox (Assistant Commissioner) upon Poor Law Union of Glendale (Northumberland), 110.

39 Haggard, H. Rider (1902) *Rural England. Being an account of agricultural and social researches arrived at in the year 1901 and 1902* 2 vols, I, 282–3.

40 British and Foreign Trade and Industry; Memoranda, Statistical Tables and Charts prepared in the Board of Trade with Reference to various matters bearing on British and Foreign Trade and Industrial Conditions, Cd. 1761 (1903), XVIII: *Consumption of Food and Cost of Living of Working Classes in the UK and certain Foreign Countries*, 209 et seq.

41 Mann, H.H. (1904) 'Life in an agricultural village', *Sociological Papers*, quoted in F.E. Green (1913) *The Tyranny of the Countryside*, 228 et seq.

42 Davies, Maud F. (1909) *Life in an English Village*, 211.

43 Rowntree, B. Seebohm and Kendall, May (1913) *How the Labourer Lives. A Study of the Rural Labour Problem.*

44   ibid., 'Adequacy of diet', 299 et seq.
45   Rowntree calculated that the labourer's cost of living increased 15 per cent between 1898 and 1912, while his wages rose only 3 per cent (ibid., 26–7).
46   ibid., 308–9.

※ 8 ※

Urban England: poverty and progress

Most observers of the social scene in the middle of the last century were still uncertain whether the rapidly developing industrialization of Britain was benefiting or deteriorating the lot of the worker. In the depressed years of the early 1840s few were in doubt. Samuel Laing, whose essay on *National Distress* was awarded first prize in a competition in 1844, believed that:

> Society has been startled by the discovery of a fearful fact, that as wealth increases, poverty increases in a faster ratio, and that in almost exact proportion to the advance of one portion of society in opulence, intelligence and civilization, has been the retrogression of another and more numerous class towards misery, degradation and barbarism.[1]

It was not difficult to support his gloomy contention by a mass of statistical information recently made available by Parliamentary Blue Books and the researches of private social investigators. In 1841 more than 8 per cent of the population of England and Wales were officially classed as paupers, and this at a time when the New Poor Law had determined to reduce pauperism by attaching the most unpalatable conditions to relief. In Manchester more than half of the inhabitants required the assistance of public charity in bringing their offspring into the world; in Leeds more than one-third of the whole adult population had no regular employment, while over large areas of the industrial north and midlands wages in the old craft industries were depressed to an impossibly low level. By the 1840s Lancashire handloom-weavers could earn no more than 4s 11½d per family per week, and their lot was paralleled by that of the Coventry ribbon-weavers, the Yorkshire linen-weavers, and the Nottinghamshire framework-knitters. These were the multitudes who inhabited back-to-back slums in narrow courts and alleys or, less fortunate still, shared rooms and even cellars in overcrowded tenements, the squalor of which was only now being exposed by the sanitary reports of Edwin Chadwick.[2] Those who had employment in the new factories and mines were certainly better off, but they were as yet a minority of the labouring population – of those employed in cotton factories, for example, only a quarter were males

158

over eighteen years of age, the rest being women and children whose earnings were pitifully small. Laing in 1844 summarized the effects so far of the introduction of machinery on the worker:

> About one-third plunged in extreme misery, and hovering on the verge of actual starvation; another third, or more, earning an income something better than that of the common agricultural labourer, but under circumstances very prejudicial to health, morality, and domestic comfort – viz. by the labour of the young children, girls, and mothers of families in crowded factories; and finally, a third earning high wages, amply sufficient to support them in respectability and comfort.[3]

Generalized assessments of this kind can be enriched by first-hand evidence of the lives of working people.[4] One such autobiography describes the early life of Thomas Wood, who was born at Bingley in Yorkshire in 1822, the eldest of a family of five of a respectable, hard-working handloom-weaver.[5] Thomas was evidently an intelligent boy who, after learning to read the first chapter of St John's Gospel at a little private school, went at the age of six to Bingley Grammar School, through the influence of his grandfather with the vicar, Dr Hartley. Here he learnt Latin grammar and writing free, though his parents paid 1s 6d a quarter to the school for fire and cleaning. After only two years he had to leave to wind bobbins at home for his father, and, thereafter, Sunday school was the only formal education Thomas received; after the School Feast in 1831, when the children had marched round the town for two-and-a-half hours, they were regaled with half a gill of beer and half a teacake. Shortly after this he went to work at the mill from 6 a.m. to 7.30 p.m., with forty minutes allowed for dinner, at a wage of 1s 6d per week: 'Small as it was, it was a sensible and much needed acquisition for the family store.' Here he stayed for five years, until, at thirteen, his father resolved that Thomas should be taught a trade, and he was apprenticed to a local mechanic. To do this was a great sacrifice for the family; by the time he had worked out his apprenticeship at twenty-one he was still earning only 8s a week, and was now the eldest of ten children in the family, all still at home. 'Our food was of the plainest, the quantity seldom sufficient. I seldom satisfied my appetite unless I called at Aunt Nancy's after dinner to pick up what she had to spare. As to the luxury of pocket money, it was unknown.' To pay his 1½d a week subscription to the Mechanics' Institute library, Thomas collected and sold bundles of firewood, mushrooms, and fruit in season.

> In due course I was 21. I was called upon by the master of the shop to provide a supper for the men to celebrate the occasion. In consideration of my poverty they agreed to have the supper in the shop instead of a public house. The master . . . cooked it in his house hard by. It was a quiet, economical affair, but I had to borrow the money to defray the expense. Trade was bad in the extreme [1843].

Thomas stayed with his master for two more years at a wage rising to £1 a week; then he moved to a bigger engineering works at Oldham, where a wage of 28s a week seemed a fortune. Here, at Platts Bros, he had the experience of working with the new Whitworth machines, but found his workmates

> wicked and reckless. Most of them gambled freely on horse or dog races. . . . Flesh meat, as they called it, must be on the table twice or thrice a day. A rough and rude plenty alone satisfied them, the least pinching, such as I had seen scores of times without murmur, and they were loud in their complainings about 'clamming'.

After fourteen months here Thomas was dismissed along with fifty others. He walked to Huddersfield in search of work, then to Leeds, and eventually found employment in a small engine shop at Stockton at 23s a week. Here he boarded with a butcher and grocer, where 'there was an abundance to eat. Though potatoes were 2s a stone we had them twice a day. I often wished father and mother could have my supper instead of me.' The last entry in the autobiography, written in 1846, records a visit to his parents, now ill and in debt:

> I found father and mother suffering great want from the scarcity of work and the high price of the absolute necessities of life. [Potatoes] . . . were 2s per stone. Flour was usually 4s 6d and upwards. . . . Father would have died and seen his children die before he would have paraded his wants, or, I believe, asked for help.

Here the account ends, though we know that Thomas later became a textile engineer and, when his health failed, a school attendance officer at Keighley. He died in 1881.

Wood's autobiography makes it clear that life in the early 1840s was, even for the skilled engineer, uncertain, and for the practitioners of a dying craft like handloom-weaving, precarious in the extreme. But with the passing of this decade, a spirit of buoyancy and optimism is almost immediately discernible, of which the Great Exhibition was at once the evidence and the symbol. In 1851 W.R. Greg pointed, from his own great experience of working-class life, to the advances which the masses had made in recent years, stressing particularly the benefits which had derived from the reduced taxes on food.[6] Between 1830 and 1851 the duties on imported wheat and meat were abolished, those on sugar, coffee and tea substantially reduced:

> In fact, with the single exception of soap, no tax is now levied on any one of the necessities of life; and if a working man chooses to confine himself to these, he may escape taxation altogether. Whatever he contributes to the revenue is a purely voluntary contribution. If he confines himself to a strictly wholesome

160

and nutritious diet, and to an ample supply of neat and comfortable clothing – if he is content, as so many of the best, and wisest, and strongest, and longest-lived men have been before him, to live on bread and meat and milk and butter, and to drink only water; to forego the pleasant luxuries of sugar, coffee, and tea, and to eschew the noxious ones of wine, beer, spirits, and tobacco – he may pass through life without ever paying one shilling of taxation, except for the soap he requires for washing – an exception which is not likely to remain long upon the statute-book. Of what other country in the world can the same be said?

The fact that the working classes annually spent £53,000,000 on beer, spirits, and tobacco – a sum greater than the total annual revenue of the kingdom – was, Greg believed, sufficient evidence of their material advance.

Again, biographical records can help to illuminate the story. In 1947 a labourer who was feeding the furnace of the Clitheroe destructor picked off a heap of rubbish a manuscript cash book which proved to be the diary of John Ward, a weaver at Low Moor Mill, Clitheroe. It covers the years 1860–4, describing in some detail the everyday things of life as well as Ward's important part in the local trade union movement and the effects of the Cotton Famine on the Lancashire cotton trade.[7] Before that calamity overtook the industry, Ward was living not uncomfortably, though the dearness of food was a frequent entry in the diary: 'June 23rd, 1860. It has been fine today. I went up to Clitheroe to meet the Committee. . . . I then had a look through the Market, and saw new potatoes selling at 2½d per pound and butcher's meat 9d and 10d per pound, so I got none.' He bought when potatoes fell in July to 5 lb for sixpence. On Christmas morning he got 'a good breakfast of currant loaf, tea and whiskey', possibly traditional fare for he had the same again a year later, but there is no mention of anything special for dinner. Another memorable breakfast was on Easter Sunday: 'I got a good Cumberland breakfast of ham and eggs, which I cannot afford to get above once in a year.' All this seems spartan enough, but the important thing is that Ward thought – and thought correctly – that he was better off than he had been earlier in life. Reviewing the past year, on New Year's Eve 1860, he wrote:

As this year has closed I can say that I am no worse off than at the beginning. If I am anything changed it is for the better. I have better clothes, better furniture, and better bedding, and my daughter has more clothes now than ever she had in her life; and as long as we have good health and plenty of work we will do well enough.

Here was the rub. Shortly after this John Ward, like thousands of others in the cotton industry, had to endure three years of half-time work or no work at all when the American Civil War interrupted cotton imports to

161

Lancashire. But, in general, the second half of the century saw industrial employment becoming more plentiful, more regular, and more remunerative, with wages advancing more rapidly than prices and, consequently, marked increases in the standard of comfort of the worker. More specifically, the third whom Laing had categorized in 1844 as 'earning high wages, amply sufficient to support them in respectability and comfort' grew in size as the century progressed, while the third 'hovering on the verge of actual starvation' tended to diminish.

Industrialization ultimately demanded more skilled workers, less manual and unskilled labour, and though it killed old crafts like handloom-weaving, framework-knitting and lacemaking – painfully enough in many cases – it created new ones like that of the engineer, the coal-miner, and the foundry man as well as a host of ancillary industrial and commercial occupations. A comparison of the occupations of the people in 1851 and 1901 shows by how much the poorly paid employments like agriculture, linen, lace, and silk had contracted, and the relatively well-paid ones like iron and steel, machine-making and ship-building had increased during the half-century of continued industrial-ization (Table 19).

The diet of urban workers in the latter half of the century had certain well-defined characteristics which distinguished it from that of country workers. Earlier in the century there had been less difference between the two, but as urban life developed into a distinctive environment it produced marked effects on the food habits of the town-dweller. This was already apparent in the early 1860s when Dr Edward Smith carried out his pioneer investigations into diet on behalf of the Privy Council. The working class in towns could, he believed, be divided into four groups for dietary purposes: infants, young children, the wife, and the husband,[8] the diet of the first being particularly bad.

> Many mothers are ignorant of the fact that milk is still as necessary for the nutrition of the child after it is weaned as it was before, and they feed it with whatever food they or the older children take. Others, however desirous they may be, are unable to obtain milk; and others still, being obliged to work away from home, leave the babe to the care of a young child or to the want of care of a neighbour; or if she be always or generally away from home, pays a fixed sum for the maintenance and care of the child to someone who has an interest in feeding it on the least expensive food. Hence, speaking generally, the infant is fed both before and after it is weaned upon a sop made with crumbs of bread, warm water and sugar, and in some cases a little milk is added. Bits of bread and butter, or of meat, or any other kind of food which the mother may have in her hand are added, and not infrequently drops of gin or Godfrey's Cordial, or some other narcotic are administered to allay the fretfulness which the want of proper food causes.

Table 19 *Total number of persons in England and Wales occupied in the under-mentioned groups of industries (compiled from the census reports, 1851–1901)*

Groups of industries	Year					
	1851	1861	1871	1881	1891	1901
Agriculture	1,904,687	1,803,049	1,423,854	1,199,827	1,099,572	988,340
Building	398,756	472,222	583,019	686,999	701,284	945,875
Coal-mining	193,111	270,604	315,398	383,570	519,144	648,944
Cotton	414,998	492,196	508,715	551,746	605,755	582,119
Lace	61,726	54,617	49,370	44,144	34,948	36,439
Woollen and worsted	255,750	230,029	246,645	240,006	258,356	236,106
Linen	27,421	22,718	18,680	12,871	8,531	4,956
Silk	130,723	116,320	82,963	64,835	52,027	39,035
Iron and steel[1]	95,350	129,507	191,291	200,677	202,406	216,022
Machine-making and shipbuilding[2]	80,528	123,812	172,948	217,096	292,239	—[3]
Tailoring	139,219	142,955	149,864	160,648	208,720	259,292
Boot and shoe	243,935	255,791	224,559	224,059	248,789	251,143
Printing and book-binding	32,995	46,576	64,226	88,108	121,913	149,793
Furniture	47,958	64,148	75,202	84,131	101,345	121,531
Earthenware	46,524	53,611	65,478	68,226	82,760	92,556

Note:
1 Including ironfounders.
2 Excluding blacksmiths and ironfounders.
3 In 1901 a different classification was adopted from that of previous censuses, which makes it impossible to give a comparative figure.

The horrors of infant feeding and 'baby-farming' in Victorian times have been documented by Dr Margaret Hewitt.[9] The ignorance of even the most elementary principles of diet and hygiene which she discloses is appalling, but it has to be remembered that the 'germ theory' of infection was still new knowledge in the 1870s, and that the first patent baby food was only introduced by Liebig in 1867. Although by 1914 many of the present-day foods had appeared on the market – Allenbury's, Nestlé's, Benger's and so on – they were still scarcely available to the working classes on grounds of cost. Nor was fresh milk always obtainable in the towns, especially during the earlier part of the period. Smith believed that the 'proper quantity' of milk for infants was two to three pints per day: in his surveys he found that the average amount consumed per person was less than one pint a week.

Turning to young children, he found that:

> In very poor families the children are fed at breakfast and supper chiefly upon bread, bread and treacle, or bread and butter, with so-called tea; whilst at dinner they have the same food, or boiled potato or cabbage smeared over with a little fat from the bacon with which it was boiled, or in which it was fried, or have a little bacon fat or other dripping spread upon the bread, and drink water or join the mother at her tea. On Sundays they usually have a better dinner, and on week days, when a hot supper is provided instead of the dinner, they join in eating it.

The amount of milk, meat, and vegetables was, Smith noted, particularly deficient for growing children. But probably it was the wife who fared worst of all:

> On Sundays she generally obtains a moderately good dinner, but on other days the food consists mainly of bread with a little butter or dripping, a plain pudding, and vegetables for dinner or supper, and weak tea. She may obtain a little bacon at dinner once, twice, or thrice a week; but more commonly she does not obtain it.

When meat or fish was obtained, it was often in the form of sheep's trotters, sausages, black puddings, herrings, fried fish, 'or similar savoury but not very nutritious food'. The husband was by far the best-fed member of the family, receiving the lion's share of whatever meat was available and having at least one hot meal a day – dinner or supper depending on whether he could get home at midday – with potatoes and other vegetables. Tea was not yet generally drunk by men, who preferred beer or coffee.

The disadvantages of town life from a dietary point of view were considerable. From contemporary accounts it seems that the poorer classes were generally very ill-supplied with cooking equipment, with the result that their methods of preparing food were limited. Coupled with this was, in most parts of the country at least, the dearness of fuel, which could mean that only two or three hot meals were prepared in a week. The domestic gas oven dates from about 1855, when Smith and Phillips offered one to the public at the price of £25, and it was not until the 1890s that much cheaper forms came into common use. Before that housewives roasted the joint before an open fire or baked in a brick oven in the scullery or outhouse. The alternative method of cooking, developed from the 1820s onwards, was the iron range, of which two main versions existed – the cottage or 'Yorkshire' range, with an openable, barred firebox, an oven to one side and a hot water boiler on the other; and the much larger and more elaborate closed 'kitchener' with a series of ovens, boilers, and hot-plates, and designed for use in middle-class houses.[10] Even small ranges cost from £7 upwards, and since they had to be built in and properly flued, they were regarded as landlords' fixtures: their progress in working-class homes was slow, and versions of these were still being installed in council houses in the 1920s. For convenience, especially in the summer months when space heating was not needed, the clear advantage lay with the gas cooker. Improvements were made in the 1860s and 1870s with the introduction of bunsen-type burners and independent gas rings, but their availability to the working classes dated from the 1890s when the renting of stoves from gas companies and payment by penny-in-the-slot meters were developed.[11] London led the way in this, with 77 per cent of those served by the Gas, Light, and Coke Company having a cooker by 1914; progress was much slower in those northern towns where coal could be had cheaply.[12]

Other difficulties which the housewife had to face were the small outlay which she could make for food at any given time, the absence of an adequate water supply, and the fact that she had little time or opportunity to cultivate culinary skills when, as was often the case, she had to contribute to family earnings by paid employment inside or outside the home.

To accuse the urban housewife in such conditions of extravagance and bad management – as so many would-be philanthropists did – was to misunderstand her problems. That she was all too often ignorant of domestic affairs was unfortunately true, for she had never had the opportunity to learn: those who had had the experience of domestic service in middle-class households soon discovered that the methods practised there were inappropriate for their own slender means, nor were cookery lessons at the parsonage of much value for the same reasons. Formal instruction in domestic economy for girls in board schools was introduced by the new Education Code of 1876, but, not untypically, no financial provision for practical training in any branch of the subject was made, and an inspector subsequently reported that 'the girls stumble through a mixture of learned nonsense concerning carbonaceous and nitrogenous products, but they cannot tell you how to boil a potato or cook a roast of meat'. The same criticism applies to the cookery classes introduced in the 1890s by the technical education committees, where the accent was placed on elaborate dishes suitable for an upper-class cuisine. Dr Hewitt remarks justly, 'Nothing perhaps so clearly indicates the profound ignorance of the middle-and upper-class Victorian of the domestic needs and conditions of the working classes than the unreality with which they attempted to improve the level of housewifery of their social inferiors.'[13]

In the meantime the woman who wished to improve her domestic skill was left to battle with a variety of recipe books ostensibly written for the enlightenment of the ignorant poor. The authors of these works included such gastronomic giants as Soyer (*A Shilling Cookery for the People*, 1855) and Francatelli (*A Plain Cookery Book for the Working Classes*, published in 1852 at 6d), as well as dieticians like Dr Edward Smith (*Practical Dietary*, 1864) and Sir Henry Thompson (*Food and Feeding*, 1884). All contained numerous well-intentioned recipes for cheap and economical dishes ranging from stirabout and oatmeal broth to risotto and pilaff. Smith worked out detailed specimen menus, costed on the basis of 1½d for breakfast, 2d for dinner, and 1d for supper each day, to provide the necessary minimum amount of carbon and nitrogen: his meals included a great deal of porridge, suet pudding, and skimmed milk, the meat being restricted to a little bacon and an occasional liver pudding or faggot.[14] Most of the writers advocated some particular food or dish which they thought to be specially commendable to the poor on grounds of economy – in Smith's case this was American bacon and in Thompson's the more sophisticated haricot bean, *pot-au-feu*, and *bouillabaisse*. There is little evidence that the English working man was dissuaded of his antipathy towards soups and 'messes' by such recipes. In any case, what were cheap peasant dishes in the south of France or Turkey were not necessarily so in Manchester or Birmingham, where to obtain three or four pounds of fish (whiting, sole, haddock, red mullet, and conger eel), onions, carrots, tomatoes, bay leaves, garlic, cloves, thyme, parsley, capsicums, pimento, and slices of orange and lemon would have exhausted the patience as well as the budget of most busy housewives.[15] Probably her husband would not have eaten it anyway. The advice to the poor of Charles Elmé Francatelli, former maître d'hôtel and chief chef to Queen Victoria, was equally inappropriate: 'To those of my readers who, from sickness or other hindrance, have not money in store I would, say, strive to lay by a little of your weekly wages . . . that your families may be well fed and your homes made comfortable.'[16]

Against these obvious difficulties of urban diet can be set a few advantages. Compared with the country village, the town had far more shops, and hence a wider choice of food. Moreover, because of keen competition between grocers and bakers, town food prices were almost always lower than those of the village shop which could exact monopoly prices. The greater specialization possible in towns also produced such useful institutions as the tripe shop and the pork butcher where, besides bacon, ham, pies, and sausages, there could be had such regional delicacies as faggots, black puddings, brawn, and haslet. The fish-and-chip shop has previously been discussed. It is possibly true, as H.D. Renner claims, that English towns were not so well served with food shops as Paris or Vienna, where one block of flats contained enough inhabitants to give butchers, grocers, greengrocers, and bakers a livelihood. The practice therefore developed in some continental cities of using the ground floor for shops, and the cellars for such purposes as baking and storing meat. The fact that food – and bread in particular – could always be obtained fresh obviated the necessity in England of having regard to its keeping quality. Toast, Renner believes, was essentially an English invention for masking staleness.[17] Even so, shopping for essentials in the English industrial town rarely involved walking much further than the shop on the corner, and this easy access often meant that food was bought in dribs and drabs daily, even meal by meal. Even at the end of the century, the poor still bought tea by the half- or quarter-ounce, a farthing's worth of milk and a pennyworth of bits of meat. John A. Hobson wrote, in *Problems of Poverty*:

> A single family has been known to make seventy-two distinct purchases of tea within seven weeks, and the average purchases of a number of poor families for the same period amount to twenty-seven. Their groceries are bought largely by the ounce, their meat or fish by the halfpennyworth, their coal by the hundredweight or even by the pound.[18]

In addition to the shops, the food requirements of the large industrial towns were in part supplied by street-traders, who purveyed an astonishing volume and variety of comestibles. As described by Henry Mayhew in London, these street-sellers were by no means restricted to the coster-mongers dealing in fruit and vegetables, but included soup and eel traders (500), whelk-sellers (300), tea and coffee stall-keepers (300), sellers of sheep's trotters (300), muffins (500), ginger-beer (1,500), besides smaller numbers dealing in pies, hot potatoes, ham sandwiches, and confectionery.[19] Many of these street-trades were quite new, or had grown greatly in recent years – the ice-cream trade had only started in 1850 and patrons were still very uncertain how they should eat this novelty, while fried fish (no chips yet) was also a recent introduction. A piece of plaice or sole, battered and fried in oil, was sold with a slice of bread for 1d; oysters, at four for 1d, were already becoming something of a delicacy and not eaten by the poorest classes, though Mayhew estimated that 124 million were sold in the London streets annually. Probably the chief patrons of the stall-keepers were children and young people, street-walkers, and out-door workers such as porters and coal-heavers, but the availability of these cheap, savoury dishes was a not unimportant addition to the monotonous diet of ordinary working people in London and the larger provincial cities.

'Eating-out' was still highly unusual in working-class circles in this period, though here, too, provision at a modest price was growing. Single young men living away from home might eat at a pie or cook-shop, or take an 'ordinary' at a chop house or public house, where a slice of meat with vegetables, accompanied by cheese and beer, could be had for a few pence. When an evening meal was taken out it was usually among a party of male friends, and probably the dinner given by Mr Guppy at the *Slop Barn* was not untypical – veal and ham, and french beans, summer cabbage, pots of half-and-half, marrow pudding, 'three Cheshires', and 'three small rums'.[20] The culinary skill of the average landlord was not very high, but the stew prepared for the showmen at the Jolly Sandboys in *The Old Curiosity Shop* is still appetizing:

> 'It's a stew of tripe,' said the landlord, smacking his lips, 'and cowheel,' smacking them again, 'and bacon,' smacking them once more, 'and steak,' smacking them for the fourth time, 'and beans, cauliflowers, new potatoes and sparrowgrass, all working up together in one delicious gravy.'
>
> 'At what time will it be ready?' asked Mr Codlin faintly.
>
> 'It'll be done to a turn,' said the landlord, looking up at the clock, 'at twenty-two minutes before eleven.'
>
> 'Then,' said Mr Codlin, 'fetch me a pint of warm ale, and don't let nobody bring into the room even so much as a biscuit till the time arrives.'

On the rare occasions when a family ate out it was usually as part of a jaunt to one of the pleasure gardens, of which there were a dozen or more in London and the suburbs. By mid-century Vauxhall, Cremorne, and the rest had sunk far in the social scale, and now provided refreshment and entertainment at low cost. The working man who could not get home for dinner usually took cold food with him to eat at midday – bread with cheese, meat or dripping, and pie and potatoes were the most common – since the industrial canteen provided by the firm was still in its infancy at the end of the century. Perhaps the earliest pioneer in this direction was Sir Titus Salt who, at his model industrial village, Saltaire, provided a dining-hall where meals could be had at cost and where food brought in by the operatives of his woollen mills was cooked for them, though the printing firm Hazell, Watson, and Viney also provided a refreshment room for employees as early as 1878.[21] Other pioneers of the works canteen included Colman's, Cadbury's, Fry's, and Lever Bros. When J.E. Meakin compiled his account of industrial welfare schemes in 1905 he found that Cadbury's had the largest catering facilities of any firm in Britain: dining accommodation at Bournville was provided for 2,000 employees, who could buy a roast and two vegetables for 4d, pork pie 1½d, soup and bread 1d, eggs, sausages, bacon, and pudding 1d, tea, coffee, cocoa, milk, potatoes, bread, butter, cheese and cake at ½d.[22] More commonly, the larger firms by 1914 were providing merely a dining-room and facilities for food brought in by the worker to be warmed. Not all shared the sensitivity of the North-Eastern Railways Co. who, at their Gateshead works, had long deal dining-tables, each with a division ten inches high running down the middle 'so that without rising or leaning over, no one can see what his *vis-à-vis* has brought, and all can go home with the comforting hallucination that their neighbours supposed them to fare better than they did'.

Turning to the actual budgets of town workers, it is immediately clear that until the 1870s little change had taken place from the earlier part of the century. The strikingly wide differences in the standard of comfort were determined by the occupation of the husband, the number of dependent children and, less important, the part of the country in which the family lived – in London rents were substantially higher than elsewhere and a garden rare, whereas in some northern industrial towns a free house and fuel went with the job. Looking first at some budgets of comfortably-off workers in mid-century, we may take a Northumberland miner with three sons all working. The family's earnings per fortnight were:

	£	s	d
Father, two weeks	2	4	0
Putter, one boy, 17 years	1	16	8
Driver, one boy, 12 years		13	9
Trapper, one boy, 8 years		9	2
	£5	3s	7d

Outlay per fortnight

	£	s	d
Mutton, 14 lb		8	9
Flour, 5 stone		13	0
Maslin (mixed grain), 3 stone		7	6
Bacon, 14 lb		9	4
Potatoes, ½ boll		2	3
Oatmeal			6
Butter, 2 lb; milk, 3d per day		6	0
Coffee, 1¼ lb		3	0
Tea, ¼ lb		1	6
Sugar, 3 lb		2	0
Candles			6¼

Soap	1	8
Pepper, salt, mustard, etc.		6
Tobacco and beer	4	0

	£3 0s	$6\frac{1}{4}$d

Shoes, 9s per month	4	6
Clothes, stockings, etc.	17	6
Sundries	2	6

Total expenditure	£4 5s	$0\frac{1}{4}$d

The husband contributed 1s 3d per month to a benefit club; he had rent and fuel free.[23] With their 14 lb of meat each week this was an exceptionally fortunate family taken at the peak of its earning power: they could not have lived so well when the children were too young to work, nor would they do so when the sons married and left home. This budget compares with those of skilled workers collected by Le Play in 1855. A London cutler with four children occupied a house in Whitefriars Street, described as 'less insanitary than most, but damp and sunless'. It had water laid on in the cellar, and 'latrines'. His weekly expenditure was:[24]

	£	s	d
Rent		7	9
Food	1	0	0
Coal and light		2	10
Cleaning		1	0
School			10
Clothes		3	2
Sundries		1	2
	£1	16s	9d

But another working cutler in Sheffield is apparently better off. Though his wage is only 28s a week, he puts 1s a week in the church offertory, and has saved £46 through a building society. He has only one child and much lower rent. A foundryman in Derbyshire, with four children and a wage of 27s 8d, also lives fairly well. Spending 14s a week on food, the family typically had:

Breakfast at 7. Parents – tea or coffee, with milk and sugar. Bread and butter and cold meat. Children – bread and milk.
Dinner at noon. Meat, bread, potatoes, vegetables: fruit or cheese.
Tea at 4. Tea, sugar, bread and butter.
Supper at 8. Remains of dinner.

This man had a garden, as well as the advantage of lower northern prices.

At the other extreme lay the diets of what Dr Edward Smith describes as the 'lower fed operatives' in his Report to the Privy Council of 1863.[25] He selected for his investigation certain groups of indoor workers – silk-weavers and throwsters, needlewomen, kid-glove stitchers, stocking- and glove-weavers and shoemakers – whose earnings were known to be either low or uncertain (in fact they averaged 11s 9d per family per week), and by careful inquiry determined the average quantity of food which they received each week per person and per family. This was then set against his calculation of minimum subsistence. Smith found, not surprisingly, that the worst-fed class was needlewomen, of whom he investigated thirty-one London families. An adult worker ate on average each week:

Bread	$7\frac{3}{4}$ lb
Potatoes	$2\frac{1}{2}$ lb
Sugars	$7\frac{1}{4}$ oz
Fats	$4\frac{1}{2}$ oz
Meat	$16\frac{1}{4}$ oz
Milk	7 oz
Tea	2 oz per family

The total cost of this was 2s 7d per adult weekly. 'They are exceedingly ill-fed, and show a feeble state of health . . . the amount of money spent on food is very ill-spent.' Half the families never received any butcher's meat, and those who did made their Sunday's dinner from 1d of sheep's brains or 1d of black pudding. At much the same level were the kid-glove stitchers of Yeovil. They received weekly:

Bread	$8\frac{3}{4}$ lb
Potatoes	$5\frac{1}{4}$ lb
Sugars	$4\frac{1}{4}$ oz
Fats	7 oz
Meat	$18\frac{1}{4}$ oz
Milk	$18\frac{1}{4}$ oz
Tea	$1\frac{3}{4}$ oz per family

The larger quantity of milk and potatoes available in an agricultural district was the advantage here, but with a weekly expenditure on food of only 2s 9½d this class too was 'ill-fed and unhealthy'. Another group of workers whose trade was now badly depressed were the Derbyshire stocking- and glove-weavers: their wages ranged from 6s to 15s a week, and for a dozen pairs of gloves they received 1s 3d, half of which was taken for stitching and frame-rent. Spending 2s 6¼d a week, they received:

Bread	11.9 lb
Potatoes	4 lb

171

Sugars	11 oz
Fats	$3\frac{1}{2}$ oz
Meat	$\frac{3}{4}$ lb
Milk	$1\frac{1}{4}$ pints
Tea	2 oz per family
Cheese	$\frac{3}{4}$ lb per family

A typical diet of this group was:

No. 92, Horsley Woodhouse.
Breakfast. Milk and oatmeal for the children: coffee, bread, and sometimes bacon for the adults.
Dinner. Always hot, and with meat or bacon and vegetables or bread daily.
Tea. Tea, bread and butter or treacle.
Supper. Milk.

These workers, reported Smith, were 'moderately fed, but do not exhibit a high state of health'. The trade of the silk-weavers had also been depressed in recent years, though it was still carried on widely in Spitalfields and Bethnal Green, as well as in Coventry and Macclesfield. The class was 'insufficiently nourished, and of feeble health', as a specimen diet indicates:

No. 38, Coventry.
Breakfast. Children have bread and treacle, adults have tea or coffee and bread with lettuce perhaps.
Dinner. Bacon and potatoes, and in this case the bacon and potatoes are boiled together, and the water is thrown away!
Tea. Tea and bread.
Supper. Bread and cheese.

The best-paid group were the shoemakers of Northampton and Stafford, who could earn from 12s to £2 a week, according to skill. Their diet, however, was little better than that of the others, since, said Smith, 'shoemakers are not a thrifty and well-conducted class'. Adult workers ate:

Bread	11.2 lb
Potatoes	$3\frac{1}{2}$ lb
Sugars	10 oz
Fats	$5\frac{3}{4}$ oz
Meat	$15\frac{3}{4}$ oz
Milk	18 oz
Tea	$3\frac{1}{4}$ oz per family
Cheese	14 oz per family

A Stafford family's daily fare was as follows:

Breakfast. Tea, bread and butter, with milk added to the tea for the children.

172

Dinner. Meat, Sunday and Monday, with vegetables, and other days bacon and bread.
Tea. Same as breakfast.
Supper. Bread, cheese and beer for the parents, milk and bread for the children.

Putting all his results together, Smith discovered that these indoor workers were considerably worse fed than agricultural labourers, and were, indeed, below his estimate of minimum subsistence with respect to the nitrogen content of the diet:

	Carbonaceous foods	Nitrogenous foods
Minimum subsistence	28,600 grains	1,330 grains
English farm labourers	40,673 grains	1,594 grains
Indoor workers	28,876 grains	1,192 grains

For the first time, a quantitative calculation based on the best available scientific evidence had revealed the existence of what, in later years, became known as 'the submerged tenth' – a substantial proportion of the industrial community which could not maintain itself in a state of bare physical efficiency. Put into modern nutritional terms, the average diets of these indoor workers provided 2,190 kilocalories a day, 55 g of protein, 53 g of fat, 12.5 mg of iron, and 0.36 g of calcium; the poorest group, the needlewomen, received only 1,950 kilocalories and 49 g of protein. If, as Dr Smith was convinced, the adult male workers in the other occupations took the lion's share of the food, especially of the meat, bacon, and cheese, it follows that wives and children received less than the averages quoted here, and relied mainly on bread and potatoes smeared with dripping or treacle. Almost certainly their calorie intake would be low enough to affect the growth of children, and the protein intake inadequate for pregnant and lactating women as well as for children. The calcium intake was extremely low by modern standards but, unfortunately, the data do not exist for an estimate of vitamins.[26] These workers were considerably worse fed than the agricultural labourers examined by Smith, whose diets work out to 2,760 kilocalories, and 70 g of protein: the indoor workers consumed more sugar than the labourers, but less bread and meat, and much less milk and potatoes.

Such was the dietary condition of some of the poorest-paid, fully employed workers in the 'Golden Age' of Victorian prosperity. But the better-off sections above them could quite easily be pulled down to the same or to an even lower level by unavoidable misfortune – the death of the chief wage-earner, accident, sickness, old age, or infirmity. A dramatic example of the precariousness of life for reasonably well-paid workers is given by the Cotton Famine when, during the American Civil War of 1861–5, the northern states blockaded the southern ports and practically stopped the export of raw cotton to Lancashire, so depriving thousands of spinners and weavers of their livelihood. John Ward's *Diary* describes how the event affected the life of a Clitheroe weaver who had been used to living proudly and comfortably:

> 31st August 1861, this has been a fine day. We got notice at our mill this morning to run four days per week until further notice.
>
> November 16th . . . I read the newspaper, but there is nothing fresh from America nor any word from the naval expedition that has gone to the south. There is great distress all through the manufacturing districts: they are all running short time through the scarcity of cotton.
>
> April 10th, 1864. It is nearly two years since I wrote anything in the way of a diary. I now take up my pen to resume the task. It has been a very poor time for us all the time owing to the American war, which seems as far off being settled as ever. The mill I work in was stopped all winter, during which time I had three shillings per week allowed by the Relief Committee, which barely kept me alive. When we started work again it was with Surat cotton, and a great number of weavers can only mind two looms. We can earn very little. I have not earned a shilling a day this last month. . . . My clothes and bedding is wearing out very fast, and I have no means of getting any more. . . . The principal reason why I did not take any notes these last two years is because I was sad and weary. One half of the time I was out of work, and the other I had to work as hard as ever I wrought in my life, and can hardly keep myself living. If things do not mend this summer I will try somewhere else or something else, for I can't go much further with what I am at. . . . [27]

The plight of the Lancashire operatives naturally aroused public sympathy and concern, and voluntary relief committees at least kept most of the unemployed out of the workhouse. At the end of 1862 272,000 people were receiving out-relief from the boards of guardians, and almost as many again were being supported by charitable organizations.[28] Such was the national concern for these unfortunate victims of unemployment, to whom the usual Victorian explanation of moral failing could not be attached, that Dr Edward Smith was again commissioned to survey their diet, and to compare their present condition with that before the depression. He found that the average income of the families had fallen from a comfortable 39s 6d a week in 1861 to 14s in 1862, and the amounts spent per head on food from 3s 3d to 1s 11d. The consumption of meat and potatoes had fallen by 70 per cent, of fats by 50 per cent, and of bread by 35 per cent; sugar had only fallen by 25 per cent, and was partly replaced by treacle, while milk consumption had remained stable at 1.4 pints per person per week. In total, the intake of calories had fallen from 3,370 kilocalories a day to 2,220, and protein from 84 to 56 g a day (both still a little higher than the normal diets of the indoor workers previously discussed). The interesting observation here is that in a period of greatly reduced income, the cotton workers had not given up the more expensive or 'unnecessary' foods like meat and sugar in favour of cheap, filling sources of energy such as bread and potatoes, but had chosen to reduce their consumption of nearly all foods, though by different amounts. It illustrates the conservatism of food habits, and the desire to preserve a palatable diet albeit at the expense of quantity.[29]

Few of the budgets of the period mention expenditure on drink – probably because of a natural reluctance to admit to something which in the new climate of Victorian morality and temperance was regarded as one of the great national evils – although we know that the *per capita* consumption of beer was rising to its peak of 34 gallons per year in 1876. Thereafter, it remained at around 30 gallons until 1900, from which time it began a slow fall. Certainly, many families in the later nineteenth century lived in self-inflicted poverty because of what they spent at the public house. By 1850 beer had already lost whatever claim it had once had to be called the national drink: it was mainly a man's drink, women preferring tea, or spirits, or both. William Hoyle calculated that the expenditure per head of the population on drink was £2 18s 10d in 1850, rising to £4 7s 3d in 1875,[30] while Samuel Smiles estimated that in the later year the working classes spent £60,000,000 on drink and tobacco.[31] It seems likely, then, that the average working-class household was devoting between £15 and £20 a year to alcohol; and when allowance is made for the growing number of teetotallers, it means that some families must have spent a third, and possibly even half, of all their income on drink.[32] Hoyle wrote:

> We are acknowledged to be by far the richest nation in the world, and yet a great portion of our population are in rags. Why is this? Is it because they get insufficient wages that they are poor? No! For wages are relatively higher in England than almost in any country in the world; but it is because they squander their earnings improvidently upon things that are not only needless, but useless and hurtful.

By the end of the century temperance and Band of Hope movements were having some success, and the growth of new leisure pursuits was beginning to provide attractive alternatives to the public house, but on the eve of the First World War the national drink bill was still £164,000,000, or £3 10s 10d for every man, woman, and child in the country.[33] Rowntree and Sherwell calculated in 1900 that every male drinker consumed on average 73 gallons of beer a year and 2.4 gallons of spirits,[34] while in that year 182,000 people in England and Wales were convicted of drunkenness, almost a quarter of them women.[35] In London, one house in every seventy-seven was a public house[36] and *The New Survey of London Life and Labour*, which launched a searching inquiry into the matter, concluded that as much as one-quarter of the average poor family's income was still spent by the husband and wife on drink.[37] The interesting fact was, however, that heavy drinking had now sunk to the bottom of the social scale: the proportion fell off progressively as incomes rose, so that 'of all working-class family incomes, other than the poorest, from 10 per cent in the better-off to 15 per cent in the less prosperous, was spent on drink'. By 1914 the great brewery companies, who controlled a majority of the public house outlets for their beers, were seriously concerned about declining consumption and increasingly restrictive licensing policies. Much money had been spent in the 1880s and 1890s on rebuilding and refurbishing public houses to produce a 'glamorous and theatrical' effect,[38] but they faced growing competition from the Coffee House Companies, which offered food and entertainment as well as non-alcoholic drinks, and from the People's Refreshment House Association, founded in 1896, which was taking over public houses in small towns and country districts, and also providing refreshments and recreational facilities as rival attractions to the demon drink. These developments were giving rise to a Public House Reform Movement – an attempt to give licensed premises greater respectability by, on the one hand, providing comfort and amenities as well as liquor, and, on the other, by enforcing stricter order and managerial control.

During the last quarter of the century – the period which economic historians have designated the 'Great Depression' – improvements are observable in the general standard of working-class diet. More than anything else, these were due to the falling prices of basic foodstuffs like wheat and meat (see Chapter 6, pp. 111 ff.). Robert Giffen calculated in 1879 that there had already been a fall of 24 per cent in prices since the onset of the depression in 1873,[39] nor had the trough yet been reached; as it neared its end in 1895, A.L. Bowley made a pioneer study for the Statistical Society of the changes which had taken place in real wages (i.e. the purchasing power of earnings), and concluded that between 1860 and 1891 they had risen by no less than 92 per cent:[40]

> In so far as actual want is now only the lot of a small proportion of the nation (though intrinsically a large number) and comfort is within the reach of increasing masses of workmen, the greatest benefit of this prosperity has fallen to wage earners; but this is only the righting of injustice and hardship. In 1860 it was the working classes who were in most need of any benefit that might accrue to the nation, and it would have been only reasonable to expect that their progress in actual money (apart from better conditions of work) should be at least as rapid as that of the richer classes.[41]

Urban England: poverty and progress

The other principal factor which was enlarging the quantity and variety of working-class consumption at this time was the series of changes taking place in the supply and distribution of foodstuffs. Of the growth in imports of wheat, meat and other foods we have already spoken. Also significant were the changes which occurred in the supply of milk.

Before the outbreak of the cattle disease (rinderpest) in 1865 by far the larger part of the towns' milk was obtained from town dairies. The cattle which lent themselves best to this artificial town life were imported Dutch cows, but they were found to be much more susceptible to the disease than country animals: of 9,531 cows in the Metropolitan Board of Works area, 5,357 were attacked by the plague, and of these only 375 recovered.[42] The lesson so painfully learned of the unhealthiness of town-fed cows resulted in the imposition of such strict sanitary regulations on town dairies that very many closed down almost immediately, and from this time onwards the industrial town came to be supplied largely by country milk. In the case of London, this was soon being brought by rail from the west country and Derbyshire – distances up to 150 miles. Before many years, the wholesale milk trade was being concentrated into large firms who, through their contracts with farms, were able to control minutely the quality and condition of milk as well as the general sanitary condition of the farm. In the later years of the century a supply of milk purer than the townsman had ever known was becoming available, and milk consumption was slowly beginning to rise. At 2d a pint, however, it was still relatively expensive, and a survey carried out in 1902 showed that while the consumption of middle-class families was 6 pints per head a week, that in the lower middle class was 3.8 pints, among artisans 1.8 pints, and among labourers only 0.8 pints.[43] The economic gradients were still very steep, especially in the choice of foods not regarded as essential. In 1889 it was officially calculated that families with incomes of less than £40 a year spent 87.42 per cent of this on food while those with £100–£110 spent only 42.49 per cent on a wider range of foods.[44]

In 1902 the Statistical Society carried out a survey of the household budgets of 223 of its members with a view to calculating the level of consumption of some basic foods.[45] The Society's members were not so unrepresentative as might be imagined, including landed proprietors, merchants, railway directors, civil servants, doctors, lawyers, farmers, clerks, salesmen, electricians, compositors, printers, decorators, sugar boilers, shipwrights, labourers, and farm labourers from all parts of the country. For the purposes of the inquiry they were grouped into four classes:

Group 1: Wage-earners, 82 households.
Group 2: Lower middle class, 60 households.

177

Group 3: Professional classes, 46 households.
Group 4: Upper classes, 32 households.

Detailed returns had to be kept for a minimum of four weeks, which, in addition to the actual quantities of food consumed, took account of the number present at each meal and meals taken away from home. The survey therefore represented the first major attempt to compare the food consumption of different classes of the community. The results are illuminating. Although we are only concerned here with Groups 1 (wage-earners) and 2 (including clerks, insurance agents, trade union secretaries, small tradesmen), the other groups are included for comparison:

	Meat (lb per head per annum)	Milk (galls per annum)	Cheese (lb per annum)	Butter (lb per annum)
Group 1	107	8.5	10.0	15
Group 2	122	25.0	10.0	23
Group 3	182	39.0	8.5	29
Group 4	300	31.0	10.5	41

Apart from the striking differences in levels of consumption of most foods between the different classes, the figures for Group 1 suggest a major improvement since the time of Edward Smith's survey forty years earlier. In particular, meat consumption had more than doubled, and both butter and milk consumption had grown appreciably. The figures are, of course, not strictly comparable, since Smith was reporting on groups of poorer labouring families while the Statistical Society's survey reflected more the consumption patterns of better-paid workers, but both were at their different times reasonably typical of the working class as a whole. The 1902 survey also contained interesting international comparisons which showed that, while Britain was the heaviest meat-eater of all European countries, she was the smallest milk-drinker.[46]

By the end of Victoria's reign it seemed that large sections of the working class were making impressive strides towards comfort and prosperity. Even critics of the factory system were bound to admit that though wages still remained low they provided an infinitely higher standard than formerly: the earnings of Lancashire cotton operatives, wrote Allen Clarke in 1913, permitted 'a breakfast of coffee or tea, bread, bacon and eggs – when eggs are cheap – a dinner of potatoes and beef, an evening meal of tea, bread and butter, cheap vegetables or fish, and a slight supper at moderate price'.[47]

Because of these evidences of improvement, many contemporaries had assumed that all sections of labour were on the up-grade, that poverty and destitution were vanishing phenomena – perhaps inevitable during the early days of industrialization, but bound to disappear once the system in its maturity came to distribute its blessings throughout society. This complacency was rudely shaken towards the end of the century by a series of disclosures which, by dispassionate, sociological inquiry, showed that a vast and unsuspected amount of poverty still existed in English towns and villages, and that while it was true that some branches of labour had made significant gains in recent years, other sections had remained sunk in misery so abject as to be inaudible. The 'bitter cry of outcast London' was, in fact, only detected by the trained ear of the social investigator.

The work of discovery began with Charles Booth's great survey of life and labour in London, started in 1886 and completed, seventeen volumes later, in 1902. Undertaken initially in order to refute what he considered the exaggerated propaganda of the Social Democratic Federation about the extent of poverty in London, Booth discoverd that at a 'poverty-line' of 21s a week or less for a man, wife, and three children, 30.7 per cent of the population of London were in 'want' as against 69.3 per cent in comfort.[48] Booth collected detailed budgets from 55 working-class families in the East End. Assuming an equal distribution of food within the family, they provided 6.5 lb of bread per person per week, 2.1 lb of potatoes, 12 oz of sugar, 1.6 lb of meat, 3.9 oz of fats, and 1.4 pints of milk: in present-day nutritional terms this gives 2,620 kilocalories a day, 61 g of protein, 57 g of fat, 10.6 mg of iron, and 0.3 g of calcium.[49] These diets therefore compared closely, though rather unfavourably, with those of the indoor workers collected by Edward Smith a quarter of a century earlier.

In more polemical language William Booth, the founder of the Salvation Army, was at the same time writing of 'the disinherited' or 'the submerged tenth', those unfortunates who did not even qualify for the standard of comfort given to the London Cab Horse:

> The denizens in Darkest England for whom I appeal are (1) those who, having no capital or income of their own, would in a month be dead from sheer starvation were they exclusively dependent upon the money earned by their own work; and (2) those who by their utmost exertions are unable to attain the regulation allowance of food which the law prescribes as indispensable even for the worst criminals in our gaols.[50]

Within a few years, other writers had demonstrated that the proportion of poverty ascertained by Booth was not peculiar to the metropolis, but existed in industrial towns throughout the country. In his study of York, Seebohm Rowntree concluded that 9.9 per cent of the whole population was in 'primary' poverty and 17.9 per cent in 'secondary' poverty – no less than 28 per cent who were unable to afford the 3,500 kilocalories a day necessary for a man in moderate work; incidentally, Rowntree's minimum dietary included no fresh meat, and was therefore less generous than the workhouse regimen.[51] The labourer, he found, was particularly underfed during three phases of his life – in childhood, in early middle life when he had a family of dependent children, and lastly in old age. Twenty working-class budgets collected by Rowntree were very similar to Booth's London sample, providing an average of 2,050 kilocalories, 57 g of protein, and 59 g of fat per person per day. Rowntree also gathered some budgets from the 'servant-keeping' (i.e. middle-class) families of York, and a comparison of these with families earning less than 18s a week shows how wide was the dietary divide between classes. The poorest received only 1,578 kilocalories a day while the middle class had 3,526, only 42 g of protein compared with 96, and 40 g of fat against 139.[52] Rowntree observed that in these poor families it was expected that the husband should be reasonably well fed, even if at the expense of the rest of the family:

> We see that many a labourer, who has a wife and three or four children, is healthy and a good worker, although he earns only a pound a week. What we do *not see* is that in order to give him enough food, mother and children habitually go short, for the mother knows that all depends upon the wages of her husband.[53]

A few years later, a survey of the four towns – Northampton, Warrington, Stanley, and Reading – disclosed that 32 per cent of adult wage-earners received less than 24s a week, and that 16 per cent of the working classes were living in a condition of primary poverty. Large families were given as the chief cause of destitution, with the result that the proportion of infants and school children living below the poverty-line was alarmingly higher than the average; in Reading, for example, as many as 45 per cent of those under five, and 47 per cent of those under fourteen were in this condition.[54] Even among the relatively well-paid ironworkers of Middlesbrough, 125 out of 900 working-class households investigated were found to be 'absolutely poor', and another 175 'so near the poverty-line that they are constantly passing over it'. 'That's is,' wrote Lady Bell, 'the life of a third of these workers whom we are considering is an unending struggle from day to day to keep abreast of the most ordinary, the simplest, the essential needs.'[55] The verdict of these independent researches, and of three government inquiries which took place during the same period – the Report on the Aged Deserving Poor (1899), the Report on Physical Deterioration (1904), and the Reports of the Royal Commission on the Poor Law (1905–9) – were remarkably unanimous and unmistakable: below the outward prosperity and gaiety of Edwardian England, there persisted a degrading misery which blighted the lives of vast numbers of the people, which kept them, if not in actual starvation, at least in constant want, which sentenced young children to malnutrition and physical deficiency and consigned one-third of its old people to death in the workhouse.

Actual starvation was not unknown in 'darkest England'. Some of General Booth's shelter men saw a man stumble and faint in St James's Park in 1890, who died shortly afterwards in hospital: he had walked from Liverpool without food for five days, and the jury at the coroner's inquest returned a verdict of 'death from starvation'. Thousands of unemployed and casual labourers who lived and slept in the streets of London and provincial cities existed on the brink of this condition; some were drunks, loafers, and thieves, but if the records of the Salvation Army are to be credited, a high proportion were decent men and women who desperately wanted work but could not find it. One example must stand for many:

I'm a tailor. Have slept here [the Embankment]ifour nights running. Can't get work. Been out of a job three weeks. If I can muster cash I sleep at a lodging-house. . . . It was very wet last night. I left these seats and went to Covent Garden Market and kept under cover. There were about thirty of us. The police moved us on, but we went back as soon as they had gone. I've had a pen'orth of bread and pen'orth of soup during the last two days – often goes without altogether. There are women sleep out here. They are decent people, mostly charwomen and such who can't get work.[56]

For the growing problem of unemployment public relief and private philanthropy still did little despite the devoted work of such agencies as the Salvation Army and the charity organizations. A man might find temporary shelter in a casual ward, but here he was required to break 10 cwt of stones for an inadequate diet of 'bread and scrape' – breakfast 6 oz of bread and 1 pint of skilly, dinner 6 oz of bread and 1 oz of cheese, tea same as breakfast.[57] Below this there lay only the alternative of entering the workhouse proper, and it is significant that in 1912 the number of inmates reached an all-time peak of 280,000.

From the budgets and weekly menus collected by Rowntree in York in 1901,[58] it is possible to trace with some exactness the food of the regularly employed working class at this period. No detailed budgets were in fact received from households in Class A (earnings under 18s week), where the 2s 7d per person a week available for food would secure little more than bread, potatoes, tea, and margarine. Fairly representative of Class B (earnings 18s to 21s week), though with an unusually small family of only two children, was a carter receiving 20s a week: the family's food was starchy and monotonous, deficient in protein value by 18 per cent (Table 20).

A family in Class C (earnings 21s to 30s weekly) where the husband, a polisher, earned 25s a week, had somewhat more variety in its diet, though the additional child pulled down the total nutritional value to very

181

Plenty and Want

Table 20 *Menu of meals provided during the week ending 22 February 1901*

	Breakfast	Dinner	Tea	Supper
Friday	Bread, butter, tea	Bread, butter, toast, tea	Bread, butter, tea	
Saturday	bread, bacon, coffee	Bacon, potatoes, pudding, tea	Bread, butter, shortcake, tea	Tea, bread, kippers
Sunday	Bread, butter, shortcake, coffee	Pork, onions, potatoes, Yorkshire pudding	Bread, butter, shortcake, tea	Bread and meat
Monday	Bread, bacon, butter, tea	Pork, potatoes, pudding, tea	Bread, butter, tea	One cup of tea
Tuesday	Bread, bacon, butter, coffee	Pork, bread, tea	Bread, butter, boiled eggs, tea	Bread, bacon, butter, tea
Wednesday	Bread, bacon, butter, tea	Bacon and eggs, potatoes, bread, tea	Bread, butter, tea	
Thursday	Bread, butter, coffee	Bread, bacon, tea	Bread, butter, tea	

much the same level as the previous case: there was a deficiency of 25 per cent in protein and 7 per cent in energy value (Table 21).

Finally may be taken an example of a reasonably good dietary received by a Class D household (skilled workers, earnings over 30s weekly) where the husband was a foreman receiving 38s a week, and a teetotaller. Only 32 per cent of the York households fell into this income category (Table 22).

One of the difficulties is to know how representative these budgets were. In most cases, the family which was living reasonably well and where the housewife was eager to show off her thrifty management was the one to keep a budget satisfactorily, whereas those families about whose expenditure one would like to have details either could not or would not collect the information. We know that in many such households drink and betting seriously reduced what might otherwise have been an adequate wage to something well below the minimum requirement. Another difficulty is to know precisely how much of a weekly wage was available for food expenditure after making the necessary deductions for rent,

Table 21 *Menu of meals provided during the week ending 22 June 1901*

	Breakfast	*Dinner*	*Tea*	*Supper*
Friday	Bread, butter, pie, tea	Bread, beefsteak, coffee	Bread, cheese, tea	Bread, potted meat
Saturday	Bread, bacon, tea	Bread, beef, tea	Bread, butter, jam, tea	Bread, butter
Sunday	Light cake, butter, tea	Roast beef, potatoes, cabbage, Yorkshire, pudding	Bread, butter, jam, tea	Jam, bread
Monday	Bread, butter, jam, tea, cheese	Bread, beef, tea, potatoes, cabbage	Bread, butter, jam, tea	Jam, bread
Tuesday	Bread, butter, jam, tea	Meat pie, potatoes	Bread, butter, jam pie, tea	Shortcake
Wednesday	Bread, butter, jam, tea	Beef, hashed, bread, tea, rice pudding	Bread butter, shortcake, tea	Currant cake
Thursday	Bread, butter, tea	Bacon, bread, potatoes	Bread, butter, tea	Bread, butter

clothes, fuel, sundry expenses, and, all too often, repayment of debts. Lady Bell in her investigations in Middlesbrough found that a man earning 18s 6d spent only 7s 5d on food after paying rent 5s 6d, coal 2s 4d, clothing 1s, tobacco 9d, cleaning materials 8d, and insurance 7d, while a man earning 30s a week could afford to devote 16s 2½d to food. In a careful household like the first, the wife, on receiving the weekly wage, immediately set aside money for the recurrent out-goings and spent what she had left on food: the result was that the family passed as 'respectable' but was frequently inadequately nourished. The first family spent 3s 11d less each week on food than the amount allowed for maintenance in the York workhouse.[59]

In 1903, the Board of Trade published the results of 286 urban workmen's budgets, the average earnings of whom were 29s 10d a week. These showed that the expenditure on meat was now much heavier than that on bread – 6s 3¾d compared with 3s 6½d – the other items being, in order, butter (1s 8½d), milk (1s 5d), potatoes (1s 2d), other vegetables and fruit (1s 0½d), tea (11¾d), eggs (11½d), and sugar (10d).[60]

The change in the pattern of expenditure since Dr Smith's inquiry forty years earlier is noticeable and important, indicating a marked growth in protein as against carbohydrate foods, although fruit, green vegetables,

Table 22 *Menu of meals provided during the week ending*
30 September 1889

	Breakfast	*Dinner*	*Tea*	*Supper*
Friday	Toast, tea	Soup, dumplings, meat, bread, tea	Sardines, bread, milk, tea	Bread, cheese, cocoa
Saturday	Bacon, bread, toast, tea	Meat and potato pie, 2 bottles ginger ale	Bread, butter, pastry, tea	Bread and milk, meat, ginger ale
Sunday	Ham, bacon, mushrooms, porridge, bread, coffee	Roast beef, Yorkshire pudding, potatoes, beer	Bread, butter, pastry, tea	Bread and milk, meat, fried potatoes
Monday	Fried bacon, bread, porridge, tea	Cold meat, potatoes, rice pudding, tea, ginger ale	Bread, butter, pastry	Bread, butter, pastry, cocoa
Tuesday	Bacon, bread, porridge, tea	Hashed beef, potatoes, rice pudding	Bread, butter, pastry, tea	Bread and milk, fried fish, potatoes
Wednesday	Bacon, bread, tea, porridge	Meat, soup, bread, dumplings, tea	Bread, butter, cheese, pastry, tea	Bread and milk, fish, bread, beer
Thursday	Bacon, bread, butter, mushrooms, tea	Meat, potatoes, soup, cheese, bread, rice pudding	Bread, butter, pastry, tea	Sheep's 'reed' with sage and onions, potatoes

and fish were still comparatively insignificant items. In 1904 a much wider survey, embracing nearly two thousand families more representative of the whole country, gave a complete account of expenditure on food arranged under five income headings (Table 23).

Although even the poorest families (average income 21s 4½d) spent more on meat than on bread, and varied what was still a starchy, monotonous diet with cheese and pickles, jam and treacle, the highest-paid workers (average income 52s 0½d) spent three times as much on fruit

Table 23 *Average weekly cost and quantity of certain articles of food consumed by workmen's families in 1904*[61]

Limits of weekly income	Under 25s		25s and under 30s		30s and under 35s		35s and under 40s		40s and above		All incomes	
Number of returns	261		289		416		382		596		1,944	
	s	d	s	d	s	d	s	d	s	d	s	d
Average weekly family income	21	$4\frac{1}{2}$	26	$11\frac{3}{4}$	31	$11\frac{1}{4}$	36	$6\frac{1}{4}$	52	$0\frac{1}{2}$	36	10
Average number of children living at home	3.1		3.3		3.2		3.4		4.4		3.6	

	Cost											
	s	d	s	d	s	d	s	d	s	d	s	d
Bread and flour	3	$0\frac{1}{2}$	3	$3\frac{3}{4}$	3	$3\frac{1}{2}$	3	$4\frac{1}{4}$	4	$3\frac{3}{4}$	3	7
Meat (bought by weight)	2	8	3	$4\frac{3}{4}$	4	$3\frac{1}{2}$	4	$5\frac{1}{2}$	5	$10\frac{1}{2}$	4	$5\frac{1}{2}$
Other meat (including fish)	0	$7\frac{1}{2}$	0	$8\frac{3}{4}$	0	10	1	0	1	4	0	$11\frac{3}{4}$
Bacon	0	$6\frac{3}{4}$	0	9	0	$10\frac{1}{4}$	0	$11\frac{1}{2}$	1	$3\frac{3}{4}$	0	$11\frac{1}{2}$
Eggs	0	$5\frac{3}{4}$	0	$8\frac{1}{2}$	0	11	1	0	1	$4\frac{3}{4}$	1	0
Fresh milk	0	8	0	$11\frac{3}{4}$	1	$3\frac{1}{4}$	1	$4\frac{1}{4}$	1	$7\frac{3}{4}$	1	$3\frac{1}{4}$
Cheese	0	$4\frac{3}{4}$	0	$5\frac{1}{2}$	0	6	0	6	0	8	0	$6\frac{1}{2}$
Butter	1	2	1	7	1	$10\frac{1}{4}$	2	0	3	$0\frac{1}{2}$	2	$1\frac{1}{2}$
Potatoes	0	$8\frac{3}{4}$	0	$9\frac{3}{4}$	0	$10\frac{1}{2}$	0	$10\frac{1}{4}$	1	$1\frac{3}{4}$	0	11
Vegetables and fruit	0	$4\frac{3}{4}$	0	7	0	10	0	$11\frac{3}{4}$	1	$3\frac{3}{4}$	0	11
Currants and raisins	0	$1\frac{1}{2}$	0	$1\frac{3}{4}$	0	$2\frac{1}{4}$	0	3	0	$3\frac{3}{4}$	0	$2\frac{3}{4}$
Rice, tapioca, oatmeal	0	$4\frac{1}{2}$	0	5	0	6	0	$5\frac{3}{4}$	0	7	0	6
Tea	0	$9\frac{1}{4}$	0	$11\frac{1}{4}$	1	$0\frac{3}{4}$	1	$1\frac{1}{4}$	1	5	1	$1\frac{1}{2}$
Coffee and cocoa	0	2	0	$3\frac{1}{4}$	0	$3\frac{1}{2}$	0	$4\frac{1}{4}$	0	$5\frac{1}{2}$	0	$3\frac{3}{4}$
Sugar	0	8	0	10	0	$10\frac{3}{4}$	1	$11\frac{1}{4}$	1	3	0	$11\frac{3}{4}$

					Cost						
s	d	s	d	s	d	s	d	s	d	s	d
Jam, marmalade, treacle, syrup											
0	$4\frac{1}{4}$	0	$5\frac{1}{4}$	0	6	0	$6\frac{1}{2}$	0	$8\frac{3}{4}$	0	$6\frac{1}{2}$
Pickles and condiments											
0	2	0	$2\frac{1}{4}$	0	$3\frac{1}{4}$	0	$3\frac{1}{2}$	0	$4\frac{1}{4}$	0	$3\frac{1}{4}$
Other items											
1	$0\frac{1}{2}$	1	$3\frac{3}{4}$	1	$6\frac{1}{2}$	1	$10\frac{1}{2}$	2	$6\frac{1}{4}$	1	$9\frac{1}{2}$
Total expenditure on food											
14	$4\frac{3}{4}$	17	$10\frac{1}{4}$	20	$9\frac{1}{4}$	22	$3\frac{1}{2}$	29	8	22	6

			Quantities		
	lb	lb	lb	lb	lb	lb
Bread and flour	28.44	29.97	29.44	29.99	37.76	32.04
Meat (bought by weight)	4.44	5.33	6.26	6.43	8.19	6.50
Bacon	0.94	1.11	1.19	1.38	1.82	1.38
	pts	pts	pts	pts	pts	pts
Fresh milk	5.54	7.72	9.85	10.34	12.63	9.91
	lb	lb	lb	lb	lb	lb
Cheese	0.67	0.70	0.79	0.77	1.02	0.83
Butter	1.10	1.50	1.69	1.89	2.78	1.96
Potatoes	14.05	15.84	16.11	15.87	19.93	16.92
Currants and raisins	0.42	0.50	0.62	0.80	0.91	0.70
Rice, tapioca, oatmeal	2.54	2.64	2.93	2.55	3.38	2.95
Tea	0.48	0.55	0.57	0.59	0.72	0.60
Coffee and cocoa	0.15	0.18	0.20	0.23	0.29	0.22
Sugar	3.87	4.62	4.79	5.21	6.70	5.31

and vegetables, butter and eggs, and more than twice as much on milk. At a time when the term 'vitamins' had not yet been coined, the results of their deficiency in the diets of the poor were all too apparent. What food was like at *Round About a Pound a Week* – the income of between a quarter and a third of all families in Edwardian England – was well described by Mrs Pember Reeves in south London and by Robert Roberts in Salford, Lancashire. In 1913 Mrs Reeves described families of wage-earners in which there was less than 2d a day each for food, where 'the tiny amounts of tea, dripping, butter, jam, sugar and greens may be regarded rather in the light of condiments than of food'.[62] Here, bread was still unquestionably the staple, especially for children:

> Bread . . . is their chief food. It is cheap; they like it; it comes into the house ready cooked; it is always at hand, and needs no plate and spoon. Spread with a scraping of butter, jam or margarine, according to the length of purse of the mother, they never tire of it as long as they are in their ordinary state of health. . . .It makes the sole article in the menu for two meals a day.[63]

And from Salford in Lancashire comes a similar account:

> A treat for the smallest child consisted of a round of bread lightly sprinkled with sugar – the 'sugar butty'. But such was the craving for sweetness among the most deprived, some children I have known would take leaves from the bottom of their father's pot and spread them over bread to make the 'sweet tea-leaf sandwich'.[64]

National concern about the physical fitness of the population dated from at least as early as 1885, when James Cantlie published his book on *Degeneracy amongst Londoners*. He argued that a progressive deterioration occurred among town-dwellers, so that by the third generation the average male could achieve, at maturity, only 'height, 5 ft 1 in; chest measurement 28 in. His aspect is pale, waxy: he is very narrow between the eyes, and with a decided squint.'[65] These anxieties seemed to be confirmed by the South African War (1899–1902) when the Inspector-General of Army Recruiting reported that 37.6 per cent of volunteers had been found unfit for service or had subsequently been invalided out. How was our industry, our navy, and, above all, our Empire to be maintained if the cities, where three-quarters of the whole population now lived, were 'the nurseries of a degenerate race'?

Whether, in fact, the nation's health was in decline was unprovable, since no comparable data for an earlier period existed against which the findings of the Committee on Physical Deterioration could be matched, but there was abundant evidence of a generally low standard of health, particularly among the children of the working classes. In 1911, infant mortality, still high in the middle and upper classes at 77 deaths per thousand, doubled to 152 per thousand among unskilled labourers, while at age thirteen boys from this class were four inches shorter than the sons of middle-class parents.[66]

By the early twentieth century 'National Efficiency' had become a slogan which, for different reasons, almost all political parties could support. It fell to the Liberal government after 1906, spurred on by the emerging Labour party, to introduce a series of measures which have sometimes been hailed as the foundation of the Welfare State. Ever since the extensions of elementary schooling in the previous century teachers had been aware that hungry children made poor scholars and, beginning in 1864 with the

Destitute Children's Dinner Society, voluntary bodies had been providing free or 'penny dinners' for poor children in some cities.[67] In 1906 the Education (Provision of Meals) Act widened the coverage by allowing local authorities to levy a rate of a halfpenny in the pound to provide meals for children 'unable by reason of lack of food to take full advantage of the education provided for them'. By 1914 200,000 children out of a school population of 6,000,000 were receiving meals at the public expense. The Act was followed in 1907 by the Education (Medical Inspections) Act, providing for the medical examination of children three times during their school life, and extended in 1912 by Exchequer grants to education authorities providing medical treatment in school clinics. In 1908 non-contributory old age pensions of 5s a week were granted to poor people over the age of seventy, and three years later the National Insurance Act provided medical treatment for wage-earners (though not their dependants) through a 'panel' doctor scheme.

By 1914 the principles of state responsibility, particularly for the young and the old, were coming to be widely recognized, and the replacement of the old Poor Law by what the Webbs called a 'framework of prevention' was imminent. The unforeseen outbreak of war brought to an untimely end this first national attempt to raise the standards of those submerged millions of whom Britain became suddenly proud in the trenches of France.

Notes

1 Laing, Samuel (1844) Atlas Prize Essay: *National Distress. Its Causes and Remedies*, 8.
2 Report on the Sanitary Condition of the Labouring Population by the Poor Law Commissioners (E. Chadwick), HL, XXVI (1842).
3 Laing, op. cit., 27.
4 See Burnett, John, Vincent, David, and Mayall, David (eds) (1984/1987) *The Autobiography of the Working Class. An Annotated, Critical Bibliography, Vol. I, 1790–1900, Vol. II, 1900–1945*. Each volume locates and abstracts approximately 1,000 working-class autobiographies.
5 *The Autobiography of Thomas Wood, 1822–1880* (privately published, 1956).
6 A review by W.R. Greg of William Johnston's *England as it is; Political, Social and Industrial, in the Middle of the Nineteenth Century* in the *Edinburgh Review* CXC (April 1851), 305 et seq.
7 France, R. Sharpe, *The Diary of John Ward of Clitheroe, Weaver, 1860–1864. Transactions of the Historic Society of Lancashire and Cheshire*, 105 (1954), 137 et seq.
8 Smith, Edward (1864) *Practical Dietary for Families, Schools, and The Labouring Classes*, 196 et seq.

9 Hewitt, Margaret (1958) *Wives and Mothers in Victorian Industry.* See particularly chap. VII, 'The sacrifice of infants', chap. IX, 'Day nursing and its results', and chap. X, 'Infants' preservatives'.

10 Yarwood, Doreen (1983) *Five Hundred Years of Technology in the Home*, 60–2.

11 Burnett, John (1986) *A Social History of Housing, 1815–1985*, 215.

12 Daunton, M.J. (1983) *House and Home in the Victorian City. Working-Class Housing, 1850–1914*, 240.

13 Hewitt, op. cit., 80.

14 Smith, op. cit., 229 et seq.

15 Thompson, Sir Henry (1884) *Food and Feeding* (3rd edn), 173.

16 Francatelli, Charles Elmé (1852) *A Plain Cookery Book for the Working Classes*, 10–11.

17 Renner, H.D. (1944) *The Origin of Food Habits*, 220–2.

18 Quoted in Robert Blatchford (1908) *Merrie England*, 52.

19 Mayhew, Henry (1861) *London Labour and the London Poor: The Condition and Earnings of those that will work, cannot work, and will not work*, vol. I, *London Street-Folk*, 166 et seq.

20 Spencer, Edward (Nathaniel Gubbins) (1900) *Cakes and Ale. A Memory of Many Meals*, 255.

21 Gilman, Nicholas Paine (1899) *A Dividend to Labour*.

22 Meakin, J.E. Budgett (1905) *Model Factories and Villages*.

23 Quoted in Laing, op. cit., 39.

24 Quoted in G.M. Young (ed.) (1934) *Early Victorian England. 1830–1865* I, 133.

25 Sixth Report of the Medical Officer of the Privy Council, 1863: Report by Dr Edward Smith on the Food of the Poorer Labouring Classes in England, 'Indoor Occupations', 219 et seq.

26 Barker, T.C., Oddy, D.J., and Yudkin, John (1970) *The Dietary Surveys of Dr Edward Smith, 1862–3. A New Assessment*, 39–47.

27 Ward, op. cit., 167, et seq.

28 Longmate, Norman (1978) *The Hungry Mills. The Story of the Lancashire Cotton Famine, 1861–5*, 151. This contains many vivid contemporary accounts of the distress.

29 Barker, Oddy, and Yudkin, op. cit., 40–1.

30 Hoyle, William (1871) *Our National Resources and How They are Wasted. An omitted Chapter in Political Economy*. Series extended in *Hoyle and Economy* (1887).

31 Smiles, Samuel (1905) *Thrift*, 114.

32 Leone Levi in 1885 put the average weekly income of the working-class family at 32s. The annual expenditure on drink was therefore approximately £20 per family out of an income of £80. Levi, Leone (1885) *Wages and Earnings of the Working Classes*, a report to Sir Arthur Bass, MP, 12.

33 Wilson, George B. (1940) *Alcohol and the Nation*, Appendix F, Table 31.

34 Rowntree, J. and Sherwell, A. (1900) *The Temperance Problem and Social Reform*.

35 Johnston, James P. (1977) *A Hundred Years of Eating. Food, Drink and the*

Daily Diet in Britain since the late Nineteenth Century, 92.

36 Shadwell, Arthur (1902) *Drink, Temperance and Legislation*, 28.

37 *The New Survey of London Life and Labour* (1934) IX, 246 et seq.

38 Thorne, Robert (1985) 'The public house reform movement', in Derek J. Oddy and Derek S. Miller (eds) *Diet and Health in Modern Britain*, 234 et seq.

39 Giffen, Robert (1879) 'On the fall of prices of commodities in recent years', *Journal of the Royal Statistical Society* XLII, 39.

40 Bowley, A.L. (1895) 'Changes in average wages (nominal and real) in the United Kingdom between 1860 and 1891', *Journal of the Royal Statistical Society* LVIII, 225.

41 ibid., 251–2.

42 Bannister, Richard (1888) 'Our milk, butter and cheese supply', *Journal of the Royal Society of Arts* XXXVI, 967.

43 Cohen, Ruth L. (1936) *The History of Milk Prices – An analysis of the factors affecting the prices of milk and milk products*, 4–5.

44 Board of Trade Labour Statistics (1889) *Returns of Expenditure by Working Men*, pp. LXXXIV.

45 *Production and Consumption of Meat and Milk*, Second Report from the Committee appointed to inquire into the statistics available as a basis for estimating the production and consumption of meat and milk in the United Kingdom, published in *Journal of the Royal Statistical Society* LXVIII (1904), 368 et seq.

46 ibid., 426. Meat consumption (pounds per head per annum): United Kingdom 122, Germany 99, France 80, Belgium 70, Sweden 62. Milk consumption (gallons per head per annum): Saxony 46, Sweden and Denmark 40, France 16, United Kingdom 15.

47 Clarke, Allen (1913) *The Effects of the Factory System*.

48 Booth, Charles (1970) *Life and Labour of the People in London* II (First series: *Poverty*), 21.

49 Oddy, D.J. (1970) 'Working-class diets in nineteenth-century Britain', *Economic History Review* (2nd series) XXIII (1, 2, and 3), 319.

50 Booth, General (1890) *In Darkest England, and the Way Out*, 18.

51 Rowntree, B. Seebohm (1901) *Poverty. A Study of Town Life*.

52 Oddy, op. cit., 319.

53 Rowntree, op. cit., 135.

54 Bowley, A.L. and Burnett-Hurst, A.R. (1915) *Livelihood and Poverty. A study in the economic conditions of working-class households in Northampton, Warrington, Stanley and Reading*, 43 et seq.

55 Bell, Lady (Mrs Hugh Bell) (1907) *At the Works. A study of a manufacturing town*, 51.

56 Gen. Booth, op. cit., 27.

57 For a first-hand account of the parsimony of organized charity, see Jack London (1902) *The People of the Abyss*.

58 Rowntree, op. cit., chap. VIII, 'Family budgets', 222 et seq.

59 Lady Bell, op. cit., 56 et seq.

60 Memoranda, Statistical Tables, and Charts prepared in the Board of Trade

with reference to various matters bearing on British and Foreign Trade and Industrial Conditions, Cd. 1761 (1903), 212–14.
61 Second Series of Memoranda, Statistical Tables, and Charts prepared in the Board of Trade, etc., Cd. 2337 (1904), 5.
62 Reeves, Magdalen S.P. (1913) *Round About a Pound a Week*, 103.
63 ibid., 97–8.
64 Roberts, Robert (1971) *The Classic Slum. Salford Life in the First Quarter of the Century*, 85–6.
65 Cantlie, James (1885) *Degeneracy amongst Londoners*, quoted in G. Stedman Jones (1976) *Outcast London*, 127.
66 Oddy, D.J. (1982) 'The health of the people', in Theo Barker and Michael Drake (eds) *Population and Society, 1850–1980*, 123 (Table 1).
67 Hurt, John (1985) 'Feeding the hungry schoolchild in the first half of the twentieth century', in *Diet and Health in Modern Britain*, op. cit., 178 et seq.

9

High living

The characteristic feature of the English economy in the period from the Great Exhibition down to the outbreak of the First World War was continuing industrial expansion and increasing wealth for those who owned and controlled the means of production. Agriculture, the most basic and traditional industry, remained highly prosperous until the depression of the 1880s, when foreign competition began to shatter the near-monopoly of food supply which the English farmer had previously enjoyed: thereafter, the territorial aristocracy suffered some reduction in fortune as well as in political influence, though in 1914 they were still the undisputed leaders of social life. Their standard of conduct was the one imitated more or less closely and successfully by the new middle classes, called into increasing wealth and power by the growth of industry, commerce, and the professions. At the upper end of financiers, bankers, and railway directors they merged into, and not infrequently inter-married with, the landowning aristocracy: at the lower end of small shopkeepers and clerks they were scarcely distinguishable from the ranks of the skilled worker. For our purpose, however, they all had one thing in common which distinguished them from the working classes: an income which provided some margin over necessary expenditure and therefore permitted a choice in the selection of food.

Much of this margin, in both the middle classes and the aristocracy, was devoted to 'conspicuous expenditure' on things which would demonstrate the status of the owner. A large house, costly furniture and tableware were as much a sign of the husband's success in business as were the elaborate dresses of his wife and daughters: so, too, the employment of domestic servants on a lavish scale both relieved the housewife of unladylike drudgery and announced the prosperity of the establishment which could afford to employ ceremonial butlers, footmen, and coachmen as well as maids and kitchen staff. But it was at meal-times, and especially at the dinner-party, that wealth and refinement could be displayed most effectively. The dinner-party of the Victorian upper classes developed into a unique institution which had the great merit of combining business with pleasure: here the head of the family could entertain business associates

192

and talk 'shop' after the ladies had retired to the drawing-room to discuss fashion and arrange matches. Above all, the dinner-party provided a magnificent opportunity to show off the material possessions of the host – the solid furniture, ornate silver tableware and cutlery – and to demonstrate his good taste in the selection of expensive wines and food dressed according to fashionable *haute cuisine*. Traditional English dishes were now out of favour: to be smart, the menu had to be French and *recherché*. The acquisition of a French chef, or at the very least of a cook 'professed' in French practice, was now essential for the family with serious social aspirations.[1]

Adjustment to the new régime was not immediate or complete. Away from the influence of the towns, farmers small and large continued to eat, as they had for centuries, three hearty meals a day at breakfast, dinner, and supper: locally grown meat and vegetables, undisguised by fancy sauces, were good enough for them, though their daughters might acquire a taste for frivolous concoctions at the 'great house' or hunt balls. Even among some of the urban middle and professional classes, an older pattern of eating sometimes survived late in the century. Writing of these classes in 1886 a 'foreign resident' observed:

> Their hospitalities are of the solid rather than the advertising kind; their dinners, especially on Sunday afternoons, are Gargantuan repasts at which the table groans with good things. This is particularly the case with that peculiar festivity called 'high tea' – a meal still popular with the older members of the class – an informal, to many minds uncomfortable – medley of good things something like a picnic indoors – teacups and wine-glasses side by side, hot dishes and cold, the service intermittent and greatly dependent on self-help. Yet among the newer generation, the strict observance of modern society's rules gains ground. The evening meal is dinner à la Russe – evening dress de-rigueur, champagne the favourite wine, and cigarettes are smoked as unfailingly as at Marlborough House. Here too, balls, theatricals, musical evenings follow precisely the lines chronicled in *The Morning Post*. Costumes seen are as good, probably better: for the wives and daughters of the London bourgeois aspire to dress in the fashion, although their success is not invariably pre-eminently great.[2]

The writer's observation of the changing pattern was perceptive. The 1880s and 1890s were a crucial period in the development of middle-class attitudes and standards, and by the time Queen Victoria vacated the throne social imitation had largely imposed the newer pattern of dietary behaviour.

In a monarchical age it was natural that the standard should be set in the royal court. Though Queen Victoria was herself uninterested in food and liked only plain meals, her position as titular head of a vast Empire demanded that her dinner table should be at least as magnificent as that of any in Europe. It was, indeed, typical of her concept of Britain's imperial role that on every day of the year curry was prepared by Indian servants in the royal kitchens in case it should be asked for by visiting Orientals: usually it was sent back untouched. When the Queen was in residence at Windsor there was an indoor staff of over three hundred servants and a kitchen staff of forty-five, presided over, in the closing years of her reign, by the Royal Chef, M. Ménager. He received what was considered the princely salary of £400 a year, plus £100 a year living-out allowance: when in London, he lived in his own house, not with the other servants in the palace, and arrived each morning by hansom cab. His duty, and that of the eighteen chefs under him, was to prepare the usual meals of breakfast, luncheon, and dinner each day for the Royal Family and their guests – five courses for breakfast, ten to twelve courses for luncheon, and the same for dinner. By any other standard these meals were banquets, but for specially important occasions like the Diamond Jubilee celebrations in 1897, twenty-four extra French chefs were brought in since each of the fourteen elaborate courses required several days to prepare. Breakfast at court was still of the solid, traditional kind. The Queen herself usually had only a boiled egg, served in a gold egg-cup with a gold spoon, but the other members of the family ate heartily – a typical meal was an egg dish such as *œuf en cocotte*, bacon, grilled trout or turbot, cutlets, chops or steak and, to end, a serving of roast woodcock, snipe, or chicken. Dinner at Buckingham Palace lasted an hour-and-a-half, divided into two by the service of sorbets (water-ices flavoured with port, brandy, or rum) to cool and refresh the palate before the really solid part of the meal – the roast – was tackled. A typical dinner would consist of *consommé* and thick soup, salmon, cutlets of chicken, saddle of lamb, roast pigeons, green salad, asparagus in white sauce, *Macédoine en champagne*, mousse of ham, and lemon ice-cream: there would also be on the side-table hot and cold fowls, tongue, beef, and salad. With a luncheon of similar proportions, the Royal Family were adequately, if not excessively, nourished. Even on board the royal yacht *Victoria and Albert* the usual nine- or ten-course meals were served daily, though on some of the trips few of the party exhibited much appetite.[3]

Her Majesty's Dinner

Thursday, 28 June 1900

POTAGES

Consommé tortue   Potage des Rois

POISSONS

Saumon sauce roche   Eperlans frits sauce ravigotte

194

High living

ENTRÉES
Ris de veau à la Senn
Chaud-froid de volaille à la Reine

RELEVÉS
Bœuf braisé à la Richelieu
Selle d'agneau sauce menthe   *Petits pois à l'Anglaise*

RÔT
Cailles aux pommes de terre à l'Indienne

ENTREMETS
Asperges sauce Hollandaise
Babas au caraçao   ·   *Éclairs aux fraises*
Croûtes de Chantilly

GLACES
Créme au chocolat   *Eau de citron*

BUFFET
Hot and Cold Fowls   *Tongue*   *Cold Roast Beef*

Towards the end of the Queen's reign the length of the dinner-session was somewhat abbreviated due, according to one account, to the Prince of Wales's haste to reach the cigar stage.[4] But Edward VII came to the throne with a reputation as an epicure, and is given credit for the invention of numerous dishes; in his reign the luncheon and supper party, as well as that peculiarly English institution, the week-end, became the vogue, and a craze developed for rare and out-of-season foods. Writing in 1909, Lady St Helier describes 'plover's eggs at 2s 6d apiece, forced strawberries, early asparagus, petits poussins and the various dishes which are now considered almost a necessity by anyone aspiring to give a good dinner'. The new king and his queen, Alexandra, were, according to Gabriel Tschumi, who had first-hand knowledge of the royal kitchens during the reign, determined that the meals served at Buckingham Palace should be the best in the world. For the Coronation Banquet of 1902 – which had to be postponed because of the king's illness – fourteen memorable courses were prepared which included huge quantities of sturgeon, *foie gras*, caviare, and asparagus: other orders were for 2,500 plump quails, 300 legs of mutton, and 80 chickens. One of the desert dishes, *Caisses de fraises Miramare* – an elaborate strawberry dish – took three days to prepare. Much of the food which could not be preserved was ultimately distributed by the Sisters of the Poor to needy families in Whitechapel and the East End: their appreciation of such unaccustomed delicacies is not recorded. The amount of waste from such occasions, and from the kitchens of the wealthy generally, was so prodigious that General Booth, the founder of the Salvation Army, set up Household Salvage Brigades to collect and

195

distribute it to the poor. Baroness Burdett-Coutts started one such in Westminster, Lady Wolseley another in Mayfair:

> Sometimes legs of mutton from which only one or two slices had been cut were thrown into the tub. . . .It is by no means an excessive estimate to assume that the waste out of the kitchens of the West End would provide a sufficient sustenance for all the Out-of-Work who will be employed in our labour sheds.[5]

When in good health, Edward VII liked to begin the day with a substantial breakfast – haddock, poached eggs, bacon, chicken, and woodcock before setting out for a day's shooting or racing. When in residence, there would be the usual twelve-course luncheons and dinners, but Edward liked to get out a good deal to Ascot and Goodwood, and to Covent Garden. On these occasions hampers prepared in the royal kitchens followed him. At Covent Garden, for example, the king took supper in the interval from 8.30 p.m. to 9.30 p.m. served in a room at the back of the royal box: six footmen went down in the afternoon with cloths, silver and gold plate, and a dozen hampers of food followed later. For supper there were nine or ten courses, all served cold – cold *consommé*, lobster mayonnaise, cold trout, duck, lamb cutlets, plovers' eggs, chicken, tongue and ham jelly, mixed sandwiches, three or four desserts made from strawberries and fresh fruit, ending with French patisserie. A typical daily dinner menu at Buckingham Palace illustrates the luxury and plenty which was maintained in the Edwardian court.

MENU OF HIS MAJESTY KING EDWARD VII'S COURT

Buckingham Palace

Turtle Punch	*Tortue claire*
Madeira, 1816	*Consommé froid*
Johannesburg, 1868	*Blanchailles au Naturel et à la Diable*
	Filets de Truite froids à la Norvégienne
Magnums Moet et	*Ailerons de Volaille à la Diplomate*
Chandon, 1884	*Chaufroix de Cailles à la Russe*
Chambertin, 1875	*Hanche de Venaison de Sandringham, Sauce Aigre doux*
	Selle d'Agneau froide à l'Andalouse
Still Sillery, 1865	*Ortolans sur Canapés*
	Salade à la Bagration
Château Latour, 1875	*Asperges d'Argenteuil, Sauce Mousseline*
	Pêches à la Reine Alexandra
	Pâtisserie Parisienne
	Cassolettes à la Jockey Club
	Brouettes de Glacés assorties
	Gradins de Gaufrettes

High living

Royal Tawny Port
Royal White Port
Sherry, Geo. IV
Château Margaux, 1871
Brandy, 1800

4 *Juin* 1902

Some reduction in the extravagance of menus took place after the accession of George V in 1911. His Coronation Banquet of fourteen courses was, in fact, the last of the great traditional banquets to be served at Buckingham Palace: after the First World War, President Wilson was only honoured with ten courses.

In the highest social circles of the aristocracy and leisured classes the pattern of eating habits followed closely that of the royal example. At banquets, supper balls, and dinner-parties lavish meals on French lines were invariably provided, and the development of rapid transport facilities and of the new techniques of canning and refrigeration brought an ever greater variety to the tables of the rich. Public functions tended to serve more traditional English fare – a Lord Mayor's Banquet at the end of the last century, for example, consisted of turtle soup, fillets of turbot *Duglére*, mousses of lobster cardinal, sweetbread and truffles, baron of beef, salads, partridges, mutton cutlets *royale*, smoked tongue, orange jelly, Italian and strawberry creams, Maids of Honour, *pâtisserie Princesse*, and meringues: to this were drunk sherry, punch, hock, champagne, moselle, claret, port, and liqueurs. At a total cost of £2,000, the meal worked out at approximately £2 2s a head.[6] The ball supper, a favourite Victorian and Edwardian institution, gave more scope for originality. At one of the most fashionable of the Season, the Caledonian Ball given at the Hotel Cecil, more than 2,000 guests were served with an elaborate menu; even at this, the largest hotel in Europe, it was not always possible to cater for all the guests at one sitting.

Mrs Beeton's famous manual of domestic economy, written first in article form and published as a book in 1861, considered that for a private ball and supper for sixty persons there should be not less than sixty-two dishes on the table, as well as three *épergnes* of fruit, ices, wafers, wine, liqueurs, *Punch à la Romaine*, coffee, and tea. For a sit-down supper at the end of the century, the following was recommended (menu translated):[7]

BALL SUPPER MENU

Rich consommé in cups

Fried fillets of sole and tartar sauce
Cold salmon
Lobster mayonnaise

197

Plenty and Want

Lamb noisettes and green peas
Chatouillard potatoes

Truffled partridge pie
Ham and foie gras mousse

Cold lamb and fillet of beef
York ham   Ox tongue
Chicken galantine in aspic
Dressed quails and larks
Russian salad

Pears Melba
Chocolate Savarois
Coffee éclairs
Charlotte with whipped cream
Stewed fruit
Neopolitan ice
Wafers and friandises

Coffee and liqueurs

Such a menu would be served between 12 and 2 a.m., after which the guests might feel sufficiently refreshed to resume the waltz and the polka. Next morning the fortunate young man might find himself faced by a shooting-party luncheon, a typical menu for which included fillets of sole and iced lobster *soufflé*, braised beef with savoury jelly and dressed ox-tongues, fillets of duckling with goose-liver *farce*, braised stuffed quails, roast pheasant, Japanese salad, and the usual cheeses and desserts.[8] Such pleasures were not, of course, for men only, a fact made clear by the letter of a young lady who visited much at country houses in the 1890s:

> There was a big shoot yesterday, all of us very tweedy and thick booty, and we lunched in a barn near one of the farms. Such a set out: tables and folding chairs and flowers and fruit, liqueurs and coffee and all sorts of drinks. There were hot dishes too – hot-pot and beefsteak pudding and lots of cold things and puddings and cake.[9]

The most frequent and typical gastronomic occasion was, however, the dinner-party, which developed in the Victorian period into a highly formalized ritual. At the time Mrs Beeton was writing, fancy name cards had just been introduced. Guests were expected to arrive about half an hour before dinner, during which time the circulation of photograph or crest albums – not, of course, cocktails – helped to pass away the time. According to Richard Dana, a wealthy American who visited England in the 1870s and frequently dined with the aristocracy, one was invited for eight o'clock or even eight-thirty, 'and you are always expected to be punctually late to the extent of exactly quarter of an hour'. In the 1860s

198

and 1870s the dinner service was still *à la française* – that is, served in two or three parts with different services. Before it was announced to the host and hostess that 'Dinner is served', the soup was already in the plate of each guest: when these plates had been removed, two or three kinds of fish and of meat with the accompanying vegetables and sauces were placed on the table. Altogether, this made up the 'first service'; all the dishes so far served were, in fact, in Carême's strict use of the term, *entrées*, although they might include very substantial 'made dishes'. Their purpose was to lead up to and prepare the appetite for the roast. This contradicted Brillat-Savarin's dictum that the progression of dishes at dinner should be from the more substantial to those of a light and delicate nature, but this was not the practice at any rate in England. After the first service, the servants removed the plates and dishes and brought in the second service of three or four different roasts with their appropriate vegetables, gravies, sauces, and salads. The host usually carved and helped the guests himself, aided by his servants: the art of carving was therefore regarded as an important accomplishment. After this, the third course was brought on, consisting of various hot sweets such as flans, puddings, tarts, pies, and different kinds of dry or fresh fruit, cheeses, compotes, bon-bons, and so on. Since all this was put on the table at the same time, little room was left for floral decorations, and usually the only ornament was a massive silver centre-piece or *épergne*.

This was the classical dinner-menu which had emerged in France in the late eighteenth century, and survived in England until the 1870s and 1880s. One of Mrs Beeton's menus of 1861 is a typical example of it, though here the second and third courses have been combined:

Dinner of Twelve Persons

FIRST COURSE

Soupe à la Reine	*Julienne Soup*
Turbot and lobster sauce	*Slices of salmon à la Genevese*

ENTRÉES

Croquettes of Leveret	*Fricandeau de Veau*
Vol-au-vent	*Stewed mushrooms*

SECOND COURSE

Forequarter of Lamb	*Guinea Fowls*	*Charlotte à la Parisienne*
Orange Jelly	*Meringues*	*Ratafia Ice Pudding*
Lobster salad		*Sea kale*

Dessert and Ices

The traditional dinner underwent major modification in the later part of the century when service *à la Russe* was introduced, though the French service survived in old-fashioned households throughout the period. Service *à la Russe* was probably brought to England in the 1850s, but was by no means common until the 1870s and 1880s. The essential difference was that instead of being served in two or three great courses, each placed at the same time before the diners, the dishes were now placed in turn on the sideboard and served to guests by the waiters. The change made the menu more flexible: it resulted in reducing the number of dishes served, and shortened the function by accelerating the service. 'No dinner', declared Lady Jeune, 'should last more than an hour and a quarter if properly served. . . . Instead of this, dinners are constantly two hours long.'[10] The new style was clearly in accord with the age of speed and progress, and, moreover, it had the great advantage that dishes could be served direct from the kitchen while they were hot and palatable without the necessity of long delays unavoidable with the older method. This gave more scope to the skill of the chef, particularly in serving the elaborate hot entrées which, to a considerable extent, became the test of excellence in the Edwardian dinner.

A full dinner of the new pattern therefore consisted of the following courses: (1) *hors d'œuvre variés* (or oysters or caviare); (2) two soups (one thick and one clear); (3) two kinds of fish (one large boiled, the other small fried); (4) an *entrée*; (5) the joint, or *pièce de résistance*; (6) the sorbet; (7) the roast and salad; (8) a dish of vegetables; (9) a hot sweet; (10) ice-cream and wafers; (11) dessert (fresh and dry fruits); and (12) coffee and liqueurs.[11] Some of these courses might be omitted or combined, so that a typical menu of the new type would read as follows:[12]

SOUPS
Consommé Desclignac   Bisque of Oysters

FISH
Whitebait; Natural and Devilled   Fillets of Salmon à la Belle-Ile

ENTRÉES
Escalopes of Sweetbread à la Marne
Cutlets of Pigeons à la Duc de Cambridge

RELEVÉS
Saddle of Mutton   Poularde à la Crème
Roast
Quails with Watercress

ENTREMETS
Peas à la Française
Baba with Fruits   Vanilla Mousse
Croûtes à la Française

Here, the *hors d'œuvre* course is omitted because it was not yet generally given on the bills of fare of private houses. The idea of eating tasty trifles as a 'whet' or appetizer seems to have started in Russia, where guests took caviare, salt herring, anchovies, and other highly flavoured articles, followed by kümmel or brandy, in an anteroom before the announcement of dinner. Some English houses also served what was called an *hors d'œuvre* in the mid-century – at Lord Palmerston's banquets it came after the fish and at the Duchess of Sutherland's after the remove: in these cases, however, it took the form of 'pig's feet truffled', 'oyster patties', 'timbales', and 'croquettes', which were, properly, *entrées*. The *hors d'œuvre* in its subsequent (and present-day) form of sardines, anchovies, salamis, radishes, olives, smoked salmon, smoked ham, canapés, and so on was first introduced by hotels and restaurants towards the end of the century as a convenient way of amusing the customer while his dinner was being prepared: because of its popularity here it was adopted in private households and became usual in Edwardian times. Caviare, served very cold, either in the jar or in a silver timbale, or oysters served with brown bread and butter, lemon, mignonette (crushed cornpepper), and horseradish powder were the usual alternatives. Iced melon, served with castor sugar and powdered ginger, had also appeared before 1914. With the *hors d' œuvre* or oysters Chablis was served. After plates had been cleared, two soups, one thick and one clear, were offered by the waiters, and sherry served by the wine butler. When the fish course included a whole salmon or turbot as well as the fried whitebait, smelts or soles, the dish was first presented to the host with the cover raised at his left side. *Entrées*, consisting of jointed braised fowls, salmis of game, quails or anything of the kind requiring no carving, were then served in the dish as sent from the kitchen, followed by the joint which was carved on the *réchaud* and served with two or three green vegetables and potatoes. Immediately after this the sorbets appeared and, after them, a large box of Russian cigarettes would be passed round by the butler, followed by a waiter with a lighted spirit lamp or candle. After a few minutes' pause, the roast of poultry or game accompanied by salad served individually on half-moon plates was presented; with all these dishes champagne had become the fashionable drink by the end of the century. Finally, the puddings, ices, and savouries, served with fine Bordeaux and old port, the dessert, and, to conclude, coffee and liqueurs. In private houses these were generally not taken at the dinner-table:

> When the dessert is over, the hostess either nods or smiles at the lady at the right of her husband and rises; the rest of the ladies do the same and follow her to the drawing-room, where they are rejoined by the gentlemen half an hour later. During this half-hour or so, the gentlemen remain in the dining-room;

they draw close to the host and finish their wine, or drink coffee and smoke while one of them, perhaps, tells an after-dinner short story.[13]

In the two or three decades immediately before the outbreak of war other changes were taking place in the dinner of fashion which still further reduced elaboration and tended to make the meal lighter and more interesting. Lady Jeune, a well-known society hostess but also a 'modern woman' in revolt against extravagance and out-dated customs, believed that: 'No dinner should consist of more than eight dishes: soup, fish, *entrée*, joint, game, sweet, *hors d'œuvre* and perhaps an ice; but each dish should be perfect of its kind.'[14] Even this represented some reduction of the ten or twelve dishes of the traditional dinner. Equally important, the excessive meat-eating of earlier generations was gradually being replaced by dishes of a more vegetation nature, partly, at least, as a result of the new knowledge of nutrition which emphasized the dietary importance of fresh fruit and vegetables. London had several vegetarian restaurants at the turn of the century, and it is noticeable that the later editions of standard cookery books devoted increasing space to the preparation and service of vegetable dishes.[15] Kenney-Herbert urged that the importance placed in English menus on the joint and the *rôt* should be relegated, and, indeed, that the whole formal pattern of meals and the use of menu-cards should be abolished.[16] It was also in line with the new ideas of originality and variety in food that great importance was now attached to the *entrée* course, which gave great scope to the cook's talent in preparing and decorating 'made dishes'. '*Entrées*', wrote Herman Senn in 1907, 'are generally looked upon as the most essential part of a dinner. . . . There may be dinners without Hors d'œuvre, even without Soup, and without a Remove or Relevé, but there can be no well-balanced dinner without an Entrée course.'[17] His book gave a remarkable collection of more than three hundred dishes, divided between vegetable *entrées*, fish *entrées*, *entrées* of veal, beef, mutton, poultry (the largest category), and game, the essence of which was that they were all composed of more than one ingredient (as distinct from solid meats with a garnish) and were served in decorated shapes and moulds. They included such tempting items as *Huîtres au Jambon Dubarry, Timbales de Turbot Frascat, Chartreuse de Veau à la Crécy, Entrecôtes Grillées Édouard VII, Soufflé de Volaille à la Hollandaise* and *Escalopes de Venaison à la Polonaise*.

In late Victorian and particularly in Edwardian times, dining out in public at hotels and restaurants became a new and fashionable entertainment of the upper classes. Formerly only men had eaten at their clubs and chop houses: for society women to eat in public was partly a result of their growing emancipation and a desire for conspicuous expenditure, partly a result of the building of magnificent new hotels of the highest

202

standards of elegance and comfort which was taking place from mid-century onwards. One of the first was the Wellington, in Piccadilly, opened in 1853 with a lavishly decorated dining-room for two hundred guests, and two kitchens, one serving English, the other French dishes. Here, luncheon was still a simple, traditional meal, obviously intended for men in town on business or pleasure – a soup, followed by mutton chops, rump steak or cold joint with potatoes and pickles. The social occasion was the dinner, served from four o'clock until nine o'clock – either an English meal of five courses at 3s or French menus of six and seven courses at 5s or 8s.[18] But the great age of fashionable dining-out properly dates from the foundation of the Savoy Hotel by Richard D'Oyly Carte in 1889, where the connection with theatre-going was made explicit by after-theatre suppers served from 11 p.m. until 12.30 a.m. Music while dining, which opened with Johann Strauss's famous orchestra, was another innovation, but the great attractions were the lavish decor and outstanding cuisine, presided over by César Ritz as General Manager and Escoffier as Chef. In 1897 these two left for the new Carlton Hotel: in 1898 Claridges was rebuilt, also by the D'Oyly Carte Company, to be followed shortly by the Berkeley.[19]

The fabulous cuisine of a hotel like the Carlton could attract the Prince of Wales to its public rooms, and the clientele normally included a few European princes and princesses, ambassadors, a score or more of *marquis* and *marquises*, as well as the best-known authors, dramatists, and actresses of the day. Nor was it prohibitively expensive to eat the best dinner in the world among such company. Colonel Newnham-Davis, who wrote a series of articles at the end of the century for the *Pall Mall Gazette*, which was an early *Good Food Guide* to London hotels and restaurants, describes the occasion when he took the Princess Lointaine to dinner at the Carlton. He had first consulted with the chef in the morning, and the meal was to their order:

Royal Natives
Consommé Marie Stuart
Filets de Sole Carlton
Noisettes de Chevreuil Diane
Suprême de Volaille au Paprika
Ortolans aux Raisins
Pall Mall Salade
Soufflés aux Pêches à l'Orientale
Friandises
Bénédictines roses

All the dishes were, of course, elaborately dressed – the soup contained eggs and chopped truffles, the soles were served with vermicelli and crayfish tails with a flavour of champagne and parmesan, the *suprême de volaille*, a cold *entrée*, was served on a *socle* of clear ice, and so on. The bill was as follows:

'Couverts 1s; natives 5s; soup 2s; filet de sole 4s; noisettes 4s; suprême de volaille 6s; ortolans 10s (four were served, though only two eaten); salade 1s 6d; péches 4s; café 1s; champagne (Pommery Greno. 1889) £1 1s. Total: £2 19s 6d.'[20] In contrast with this, Newnham-Davis describes an excellent dinner at the Comedy Restaurant, Panton Street, where for only 2s 6d he had:

Hors d'œuvre variés
Consommé Caroline   Crème à la Reine
Sole Colbert
Filet Mignon Chasseur
Lasagne al Sugo
Bécassine Rôtie
Salade de Saison
Glace au Chocolat
Dessert

To find snipe on the menu of a half-crown dinner, even in 1901, was somewhat rare. But at the Restaurant Lyonnais in Soho an eatable meal could be had for as little as 8d: 'Soupe, 1 viande, 2 légumes, dessert, café, pain à discretion.' At the Hotel Russell the excellent *table d'hôte* dinner cost 5s; at the Café Royal an *à la carte* meal for two, cooked by Oddenino, which included caviare, *foie gras*, quails, champagne, and liqueurs, cost £2 4s 6d. Famous Italian restaurants like Gatti's and Romano's were still modest in price, while for a traditional English fish dinner at Simpson's one could begin with turbot, pass on to fried sole, then salmon or whitebait with cheese and celery to finish for 8s 6d for three persons; two good bottles of Liebfraumilch cost 12s. Still more traditional, the Cheshire Cheese offered its famous pudding of lark, kidney, oyster, and steak at 2s (helpings unlimited), stewed cheese at 4d, and a pint of the best bitter beer, 5d.

Eating out of doors also became a favourite occupation of Victorian and Edwardian society. 'The cult of the picnic', as Georgina Battiscombe points out, 'springs directly from the Romantic Movement,'[21] and it was natural enough that these romantic generations should take delight in organized expeditions into the countryside, especially if the picnic spot could be a ruined castle or abbey to be sketched and explored. Picnicking played a large part in Victorian literature, from Dickens to Surtees, Trollope to Jerome K. Jerome, and, from the amount of space devoted to it in recipe books, in actual life. The food provision on such occasions was lavish. In Mrs Beeton's first edition of 1861 a 'Bill of Fare for a Picnic for Forty Persons' includes:

A joint of cold roast beef, a joint of cold boiled beef, 2 ribs of lamb, 2 shoulders of lamb, 4 roast fowls, 2 roast ducks, 1 ham, 6 medium sized lobsters, 1 piece of collared calves head, 18 lettuces, 6 baskets of salad, 6 cucumbers, stewed fruit well sweetened and put into glass bottles well corked, 3 or 4 dozen plain pastry biscuits to eat with the stewed fruit, 2 dozen fruit turnovers, 4 dozen cheese cakes, 2 cold cabinet puddings in moulds, a few jam puffs, 1 large cold Christmas pudding (this must be good), a few baskets of fresh fruit, 3 dozen plain biscuits, a piece of cheese, 6 lb of butter (this, of course includes the butter for tea), 4 quartern loaves of household bread, 3 dozen rolls, 6 loaves of tin bread (for tea), 2 plain plum cakes, 2 pound cakes, 2 sponge cakes, a tin of mixed biscuits, ½ lb of tea. Coffee is not suitable for a picnic, being difficult to make.

The list ends with:

Beverages: 3 dozen quart bottles of ale, packed in hampers, ginger beer, soda-water, and lemonade, of each 2 dozen bottles, 6 bottles of sherry, 6 bottles of claret, champagne at discretion, and any other light wine that may be preferred, and 2 bottles of brandy.[22]

These quantities worked out at 122 bottles to be drunk by forty persons, plus an unspecified amount of champagne and light wine.

Later editions of Mrs Beeton, it is true, somewhat reduced these quantities. In 1906 a suitable menu for ten picnickers is given as:

5 lb cold salmon (price 8s 9d), 2 cucumbers, mayonnaise sauce, 1 quarter of lamb, mint sauce, 8 lb pickled brisket of beef, 1 tongue, 1 galantine of veal, 1 chicken pie, salad and dressing, 2 fruit tarts, cream, 2 dozen cheese-cakes, 2 creams, 2 jellies, 4 loaves of bread, 2 lb biscuits, 1½ lb cheese, ½ lb butter, 6 lb strawberries.

The total cost was £3 11s 1d.

The organization required for such excursions was considerable: in *Chambers Journal* for June 1857, the advice was given that:

A picnic should be composed principally of young men and young women; but two or three old male folks may be admitted, if very good-humoured; a few pleasant children; and one – only one – dear old lady; to her let the whole commissariat department be entrusted by the entire assembly beforehand; and give her the utmost powers of a dictatress, for so shall nothing we want be left at home. . . . Who else could have so piled tart upon tart without a crack or a cranny for the rich red juice to well through? Who else has the art of preserving Devonshire cream in a can? Observe her little bottle of cayenne pepper! Bless her dear old heart! She has forgotten nothing.

The food on such occasions was all-important, the venue of the picnic secondary. When the British Association held its meeting at Exeter in August 1869, an archaeological expedition was arranged for the members with the object of opening a barrow:

So large a slice of the afternoon, however, was consumed at the splendid collation in the tent near the six-mile stone, together with many other slices of a variety of good things, that there was no time left to complete the examination of the barrow or even to open the kistvaen. . . . It was intended to open the kistvaen in the presence of the visitors, but they did not visit the spot.[23]

The food of the professional and middle classes followed a similar pattern to that of the wealthy, suitably modified by the income of the household and the number of domestic servants kept. Dinner parties for them were a good deal less frequent – one a month was a common interval – and the daily fare was a good deal plainer than that previously described, but the kinds of dishes, the order of courses and service, were based on the model set from above, and approached more or less closely as means permitted. For present purposes we may define the middle classes of the later nineteenth century as those with incomes between £160 a year – the point at which income tax was payable – and around £1,000 a year; they and their dependants numbered about 15 per cent of the population at the end of the period. They were among the chief beneficiaries of Britain's increasing wealth, industrialization, and international trade. Although meat and dairy prices rose sharply in the 1860s during the cattle plague, the subsequent effects of free trade were greatly to reduce the costs of basic foods and to make more and more imported luxuries available to the class.

The result was probably not that the middle classes spent less of their incomes on food than formerly, but that they ate more luxuriously and were prepared to devote increasing amounts of money to enhance their style of living. Comparing life in 1875 with twenty-five years earlier, the author of 'Life at high pressure' summed up the change by saying, 'Locomotion is cheaper, but every middle-class family travels far more than formerly. Wine and tea cost less, but we habitually consume more of each.'[24] Social imitation, and what J.A. Banks has called 'the paraphernalia of gentility'; required a display of houses, servants, dress, and food which inflicted a growing burden on the resources of a class whose expansion was chiefly from the lower end. Near the bottom of the pile, with an income of only £250 a year, J.H. Walsh estimated that food and drink took £116 or 46.4 per cent (meat £30, drink £18): at £500 a year they needed £148 or 29.6 per cent (meat, £40, wine, beer, and spirits £27), while with an income of £1,000 a year food and drink took only £272 or 27.2 per cent (meat £75, drink £70).[25] The trend was clear – as income rose, the proportion going to food and drink declined, despite the use of more costly items and despite a larger household of domestic servants to be maintained.

Some ambivalence is discernible in the Victorian middle-class attitude to food. At the beginning of the period the accepted recipe book for those of moderate means was Eliza Acton's *Modern Cookery* (first edition, 1845),

206

the accent of which was on the importance of economy in contrast to the enormous waste of many English households:

> It may safely be averred that good cookery is the best and truest economy, turning to full account every wholesome article of food, and converting into palatable meals what the ignorant either render uneatable or throw away in disdain. . . . It is of the utmost consequence that the food which is served at the more simply supplied tables of the middle classes should all be well and skilfully prepared, particularly as it is from these classes that the men principally emanate to whose indefatigable industry, high intelligence and active genius we are mainly indebted for our advancement in science, in art, in literature and in general civilization.[26]

But despite the assurance that the book would concentrate on 'plain English dishes', many of the recipes required ingredients and skill which would place them beyond the reach of all but a tiny minority. Truffles boiled in half a bottle of champagne, a 'common English game pie' of venison and hare, and soles stewed in cream were expensive delicacies even in mid-Victorian England, scarcely economical by modern standards.

Mrs Beeton's famous work, which appeared a few years later and remained the accepted culinary compendium throughout the period, also suffered from the same ambivalence. It was, of course, far more than a mere cookery book – a manual of household economy for the domestic entrepreneur, as one writer has described it, containing much information on the management and duties of servants, the equipment of the kitchen, the storage of wine, and so on. Like Miss Acton, Mrs Beeton pleaded for economy in the use of materials while recommending dishes involving dozens of eggs, pounds of butter, and quarts of cream. Writing as she did before the new knowledge of nutrition had developed, it is not surprising that there is a noticeable lack of fresh fruit, vegetables, and salads in her menus, though there is an abundance of meat, fish, and solid foods. Recommended breakfast dishes included grilled steak, game pie, devilled turkey, broiled kidneys, fried soles, and ragout of duck, besides eggs, cold ham, and tongue. For dinner-parties and ball suppers Mrs Beeton's menus were as lavish as any of the day, but for the ordinary family dinner, such as would be eaten by the professional man on his return from office or counting-house, there were three or four courses: a soup or fish, a joint, vetetables, and pudding.

Plain Family Dinners

MONDAY	*Crimped skate and caper sauce. Boiled knuckle of veal and rice. Cold mutton. Stewed rhubarb and baked plum pudding.*
WEDNESDAY	*Fried soles. Dutch sauce. Boiled beef, carrots, suet dumplings, lemon pudding.*

207

THURSDAY   *Pea soup* (made from liquor that beef was boiled in). *Cold beef.*
            Mashed potatoes. Mutton cutlets and tomato sauce. Macaroni.

Later in the century recipe books appeared which were written more
specifically for middle- and lower-middle-class households and gave
serious attention to the question of cost. Mary Hooper's *Little Dinners:
How to Serve them with Elegance and Economy*, was clearly written with
the greatest female problem of the day in mind – the scarcity of husbands
for middle-class girls:

> It cannot be too strongly urged upon the ladies of the middle classes that there
> never was a time when it was so necessary for girls to be instructed in every
> branch of domestic economy. We cannot misread the signs of the times, or
> doubt that unless the men of the next generation can find useful wives,
> matrimony will become even a greater difficulty for them than it is now. . . . Let
> all be sure that she who in these days of expensive living shows how the best
> use can be made of cheap material, and who in any measure helps to revive
> what threatens to become a lost art in the home, does a work which far
> outweighs any within the power of woman.[27]

By the 1870s the middle classes were expanding rapidly, but while sons
went off to administer and missionize the Empire, daughters competed
keenly for those who remained; the dinner-party consequently became
even more important as a means of matrimonial introduction. Mary
Hooper's book gave complete specifications for a monthly dinner-
party throughout the year which could be provided at modest cost; for
example:

JANUARY   *Calf's Tail Soup*
                           Turbot à la Reine
                   Fillet of Beef – Roasted Artichokes
                           Stewed Pheasant
                   Lemon Omelets – Chestnut Cream

JUNE   *Lobster Soup*
                   Neck of Lamb à la Jardinière
                       Chicken aux Onions
                   Currant and Raspberry Tart
                           Cheese Fondu

OCTOBER   *Veal Broth*
                   Fillets of Cod   Caper Sauce
                   Roast Rump Steak   Tomato Sauce
                       Braised Partridges
                        Custard Pudding
                        Raspberry Jelly

Mrs J.E. Panton's *From Kitchen to Garret*, which appeared in 1888, is interesting as being written for 'little people' with incomes of from £300 to £500 a year, and for the full advantage which it took of the cheapened cost of food in recent years:

> Dress and house rent are the two items that have risen considerably during the last few years; otherwise, everything is much cheaper and nicer than it used to be before New Zealand meat came to the front, and sugar, tea, cheese, all the thousand and one items one requires in a house, became lower than ever they had been before; and therefore, if she be clever and willing to put her shoulder to the domestic wheel, she can most certainly get along much more comfortably in the way of food than she used to do. For example, when I was married [17 years earlier] sugar was 6d a pound and now it is 2d; and instead of paying 1s 1d a pound for legs of mutton, I give 7½d for New Zealand meat, which is as good as the best English mutton that one can buy. Bread, too, is 5½d – and ought to be considerably lower – as against the 8d and 9d of seventeen years ago . . . and fish and game are also infinitely less expensive, for in the season salmon is no longer a luxury, thanks to Frank Buckland, while prime cod at 4d a pound can hardly be looked upon as a sinful luxury.[28]

Two pounds, or at most £2 10s a week should keep 'Angelina, Edwin and the model maid' in comfort, thought the writer. This was calculated on the basis of meat 12s, bread and flour 4s, eggs 2s, milk 4s, ½ lb tea 2s 6d, 1 lb coffee 1s 7d, sugar 6d, butter (2 lb) 3s, and the remainder for fruit, fish, chickens, and washing:

> Should our bride have a small income of her own, this should be retained for her dress, personal expenses, etc., and should not be put into the common fund, for the man should keep the house and be the bread-winner.

But even on £2 a week for food, the household of three could live comfortably. For breakfast: fruit, preserves, slices cut from a tongue (3s 6d) or nice ham (8s 6d), sardines (6½d a box), eggs, fried bacon, curried kidneys, mushrooms, a fresh sole, 'an occasional sausage'; luncheon for Angelina and the maid might consist of cold beef followed by a lemon pudding, fish, a boiled rabbit, roast pork with apple sauce, and savoury pudding, or a stewed neck of mutton with pancakes to follow: 'Edwin's dinner requires, of course, more consideration' – but there ought always to be soup and fish before the joint, vegetables, puddings, and dessert to follow. On £2 a week for three adults this was good fare which would have been impossible before the 1880s. Occasionally – but only occasionally – a little dinner-party might be given with money saved from the housekeeping, but how expensive even the most carefully planned menu could be for such modest incomes is indicated by the following costing:

Plenty and Want

Menu No. 1 (for six persons)

White soup (1s)
Soles, Sauce Maître d'Hôtel (3s 6d)
Stuffed Pigeons (three at 10d each, total cost 2s 6d)
Roast Beef, Yorkshire Pudding (6s 6d)
Wild Duck (5s)
Mince Pies (1s 6d)
French Pancakes (8d)
Cauliflower au gratin (8d)
Dessert
(total cost of dinner not including wine, £1 1s 4d)

Other menus included pheasant (2s 6d each), salmon (2s 6d a pound), oysters (1d each), and turkey stuffed with chestnuts (8s).[29]

At the end of the century Mrs C.S. Peel, in one of her numerous works on housekeeping, estimated that a middle-class family of four or more could live plainly, but sufficiently, on 8s 6d per person per week: 'nice living' cost 10s, 'good living' 12s 6d, and 'very good living' 17s 6d.[30] On the evidence of household budgets it seems likely that the proportion of income going to food had risen somewhat since mid-century, despite the substantially lower costs of basic foods. G.S. Layard's article of 1888 on 'How to live on £700 a year' suggested £237 on food for two adults, two children and three servants, or 39 per cent,[31] while G. Colmore's estimate in 1901 for a household of only two adults and two servants with an income of £800 a year gave £299 on food, or 37.4 per cent:[32] both were substantially higher proportions than in Walsh's budgets of 1857. The difficulty is to know whether these 'ideal' budgets matched reality. We may test them against the actual experiences of two families.

In the 1880s a retired officer with £800 a year was living on the border of Wales with his wife, five children, four maids, and a gardener. The three nursery children were fed very plainly – for breakfast porridge, bread and milk, fried bread, toast or bread and dripping, sometimes jam; for lunch they joined the adults in hot or cold meat, vegetables, and a pudding, except that on Sundays it was invariably roast beef, Yorkshire pudding, roast potatoes, vegetables, apple-tart in summer and plum pudding in winter. When the children grew older the family moved to Clifton so they could have private, day-school education:

A household reduced to cook and house-parlourmaid, early dinner, high tea at six o'clock in order to save money and service. As I became older, I began to realize the constant planning, contriving and going without which is the lot of people, placed as my parents were placed, who strive to educate five children well and to live in the society of their equals.

210

High living

Her mother was allowed £5 5s a week for food, cleaning materials, and washing for the household of nine – about 10s each for food:

> Oh, the struggle to make it do, the constant anxiety that when the week's 'books' were set before him, more money would have to be demanded of my father. The introduction of quick steamships and cold storage enabled foreign meat to be brought into the English market, and excellent meat it was. The butchers scorned it – naturally – and told terrible tales of its origin to the servants, and frequently sold it as home-killed. The outcry against it became hysterical: our maids behaved as if they had been asked to eat rat poison. '*We* will eat it', decreed my father, 'and give English meat to the servants.' In the end what was good enough for 'the Captain' became good enough for them.
>
> About this time, factory-prepared foods, soups and sauces came into greater use: jams, jellies, potted meats, tinned and bottled fruits, also labour-saving foods such as ready-cut lump sugar and 'castor' sugar, stoned raisins, pounded almonds, prepared and chopped suet in packets, packet jellies, powdered gelatine, and all sorts of patent cleansers. Fewer and fewer people baked at home, except in the north.[33]

A second actual example is taken from York in 1901. B. Seebohm Rowntree's famous study of poverty extended as far upwards as 'Class C – Servant-keeping Class'; these were 'families who are comfortably off (keeping from one to four servants) but who live simply. . . . Only one of the [six] families dines in the evening, the male heads of the households are engaged either in professions or in the control of business undertakings.'[34] These were the tradesmen and managers, the cashiers and chief clerks who constituted the broad base of the middle classes, lived modestly in suburban villas, had an annual seaside holiday, and educated their children at the local grammar or private school. Case No. 22 is typical. The largish household of five adults and three children consumed £2 10s 6d worth of food a week, and what their meals during the week ending 23 May 1901 consisted of is given in Table 24.

The diet was somewhat heavy and deficient in fresh vegetables, though otherwise not unnutritious; it provided 4,009 kilocalories per man a day, well above the 3,500 required by those in moderate work. The inclusion of relatively recent introductions like brown bread (in fact, Hovis) and 'Frame food' is significant; other families in Class C ate 'Benger's Food', potted shrimps, pineapple, sardines, bananas, and stewed prunes. ('Frame food' and 'Benger's Food' are patent foods for infants/invalids.)

For the lower middle classes, probably more than for any other section of the community, the cheapness of food in the later nineteenth century had brought greater variety and palatability to the diet. In particular, cheaper meat allowed the Englishman to indulge his liking for a joint, while technology also contributed an important service by bringing tinned fish and fruit out of season to those who could afford to live above

211

Table 24 *Menu of meals of a household of 5 adults and 3 children, income £2 10s 6d in 1901*

	Breakfast	*Dinner*	*Tea*	*Supper*
Friday	Porridge, fried bacon and eggs, toast, white and brown bread, butter, marmalade, tea, coffee, milk, cream	Haricot mutton, carrots, potatoes, tapioca pudding	Brown and white bread, butter, cake, tea, milk	Boiled chicken, white sauce, bacon, potato chips, stewed rhubarb, bread, butter, cocoa
Saturday	Porridge, fried bacon and eggs, toast, white and brown bread, butter, marmalade, tea, coffee, milk, cream	Haricot mutton, cold chicken, sausages, boiled rice, stewed rhubarb	Bread, butter, tea-cake, cake, tea, milk, cream	Chicken, cheese, potatoes, bread, butter, milk
Sunday	Porridge, eggs, bread, butter, milk, coffee, tea, cream	Mutton, cauliflower, bread sauce, potatoes, rhubarb, custard, blancmange, oranges, biscuits, tea	Potted meat sandwiches, bread, butter, cake, marmalade, tea, milk	Potted meat cornflour mould, bread, butter, cake, rhubarb custard, cheese, hot milk
Monday	Porridge, fried bacon and bread, toast, bread, butter, marmalade, treacle, tea, coffee, milk, cream	Boiled mutton, carrots, turnips, potatoes, caper sauce, roly-poly pudding, rice pudding, oranges, tea	Bread, butter, tea-cake, cake, milk, tea	Fish, bread, butter, biscuits, cake, oranges, cocoa
Tuesday	Porridge, fried bacon and eggs,	Mutton, carrots, turnips,	Bread, butter, Frame food, marmalade,	Cutlets, stewed plums,

	Breakfast	Dinner	Tea	Supper
	bread, butter, toast, marmalade, coffee, tea, milk, cream	caper sauce, potatoes, hayrick pudding, lemon sauce, tapioca, pudding, tea	milk, cream, tea	bread, biscuits, cheese, cocoa
Wednesday	Frame food, fried eggs, bacon and bread, toast, white and brown bread, butter, marmalade, coffee, tea, milk, cream	Rissoles, poached eggs potatoes, bread pudding, bread, butter, tea	Bread, butter, tea-cake, Frame food, milk, tea	Baked haddock, stewed plums, biscuits, hot milk
Thursday	Frame food, bacon, eggs, toast, white and brown bread, butter, marmalade, tea, coffee, milk, cream	Roast mutton, greens, potatoes, chocolate mould, rhubarb and orange tart, bananas, coffee, cream	Bread, butter, tea-cake, seed-cake, Frame food, marmalade, milk, tea	Fish cakes, stewed rhubarb, biscuits, bread, butter, hot milk

subsistence level. The work of the housewife in preparing and cooking food had also become lighter – an important consideration as domestic servants were becoming scarcer and more expensive by the end of the century and 'the servantless house' was a respectable reality for those towards the lower end of the middle class. It was especially in such households that the new factory-made foods were appreciated, though canned and preserved foods might be scorned in wealthier establishments. Canning, in fact, was no new discovery, dating back at least to the 1820s when Moir and Son began canning lobster, salmon, and trout around Aberdeen; Crosse & Blackwell's had also established a salmon-canning factory at Cork in 1849, adding this to their thriving trade in pickles (200,000 gallons a year by the 1860s) and catsup (27,000 gallons). Canned Californian peaches, pears and pineapples were common by the 1880s, and by 1914 Britain was the world's largest importer of tinned foods.[35] Other useful innovations included baking powder, invented by

Alfred Bird in 1843, who then moved on to eggless custard and blancmange – available by the 1870s in fourteen flavours. Of even greater convenience were the breakfast cereals which began to rival the traditional, but time-consuming, porridge in the 1890s: the American Quaker Oats Company opened a London agency in 1893 and the Canadian Shredded Wheat Company a UK subsidiary around 1908.[36] The other great transatlantic food manufacturer, H.J. Heinz, was not yet a household name before the First World War, though his tomato ketchup and other products were sold by Fortnum and Mason from 1886; his baked beans, introduced to the United States in 1895 and piloted in Lancashire and Yorkshire in 1905–6, met 'no immediate response'.[37] English palates remained to be educated to some canned foods, but by 1914 the world food market was so organized as to place the cheapest wheat and meat, the best fish, tea, and coffee on English tables. The complacency with which we accepted this position of dependency was shortly to be rudely shattered.

Notes

1 For an excellent, general account of upper-class Victorian society, see Leonore Davidoff (1973) *The Best Circles: Society, Etiquette and the Season.*
2 *Society in London* by a 'Foreign Resident' (1886).
3 Full details of the organization of the royal cuisine in the later years of Queen Victoria's reign are given in Gabriel Tschumi (1954) *Royal Chef: Recollections of life in royal households from Queen Victoria to Queen Mary.*
4 Hampson, John (1944) *The English at Table*, 43.
5 Booth, General (1890) *In Darkest England, and the Way Out*, 118–19.
6 Rey, J. (nd, *c.* 1914) *The Whole Art of Dining*, 93.
7 ibid., 107
8 *The New Century Cookery Book. Practical Gastronomy and Recherché Cookery* (enlarged edn, 1904), 881.
9 Quoted in Mrs C.S. Peel (1929) *A Hundred Wonderful Years. Social and Domestic life of a Century, 1820–1920*, 113–14.
10 Jeune, Lady (1895) *Lesser Questions.*
11 Rey, op. cit., 71.
12 *Mrs A.B. Marshall's Cookery Book* (revised and enlarged edn, 1879), 474.
13 Rey, op. cit., 80.
14 Lady Jeune, op. cit.
15 Francatelli, Charles Elmé (1911) *The Modern Cook*, ed. C. Herman Senn.
16 Kenney-Herbert, A. (1894) *Common-Sense Cookery for English Households* (2nd edn), 22.
17 Senn, C. Herman (1907) *Recherchés Entrées. A collection of the latest and most popular dishes*, 7.
18 *London at Dinner, or Where to Dine* (1858, reprint 1969), Advertisements, 2–11.

19 MacKenzie, Compton (1953) *The Savoy of London*, chaps 2–5.
20 Newnham-Davis, Lieut.-Col. (1901) *Dinners and Diners. Where and How to Dine in London*, 6–10, 15–17, et seq.
21 Battiscombe, Georgina (1949) *English Picnics*, 11.
22 Beeton, Isabella (1861) *The Book of Household Management* (facsimile edn, 1968), 960.
23 Transactions of the Devonshire Association for the Advancement of Science, Literature and Art (1869); quoted in Battiscombe, op. cit., 101.
24 Greg, W.R. (1875) 'Life at high pressure', *The Contemporary Review* (March), 633. Quoted in J.A. Banks (1965) *Prosperity and Parenthood*, 67, which see generally for a discussion of the middle-class cost of living.
25 Walsh, J.H. (1857) *A Manual of Domestic Economy*, 606 et seq.
26 Acton, Eliza (1856) *Modern Cookery for Private Families*, VIII.
27 Hooper, Mary (1878) *Little Dinners, How to Serve them with Elegance and Economy* (13th edn), XIII–XIV.
28 Panton, J.E. (1888) *From Kitchen to Garret: Hints for Young Householders*, 19.
29 ibid., 212 et seq.
30 Peel, Mrs C.S. (1902) *How to Keep House*, 14.
31 Layard, G.S. (1888) 'How to live on £700 a year', *The Nineteenth Century* (February), 243.
32 Colmore, G. (1901) '£800 a year', *Cornhill Magazine* (June), 797.
33 Quoted in Peel, *A Hundred Wonderful Years*, op. cit., 143–9.
34 Rowntree, B. Seebohm (1901) *Poverty: A Study of Town Life*, 251 et seq.
35 Johnston, James P. (1977) *A Hundred Years of Eating. Food, Drink and the Daily Diet in Britain since the late Nineteenth Century*, 54.
36 Fraser, W. Hamish (1981) *The Coming of the Mass Market, 1850–1914*, 172–3.
37 Potter, Stephen (1959) *The Magic Number: The Story of '57'*, 56 and 117–18.

⇟10⇟
The quality of food

Food adulteration in the 1850s

In spite of the startling disclosures of the extent and seriousness of adulteration which had been made earlier in the century by Accum, Mitchell, Normandy, and other reliable observers, neither Parliament nor the nation was yet convinced that the problem was sufficient to warrant intervention by the state. Before 1850 it was still possible to have legitimate doubts – to believe that adulteration was not universal, but restricted to certain towns or, indeed, to certain parts of towns; that adulterations were not harmful, but, on the contrary, constituted improvements which lowered the cost of expensive foods to the poor; that most if not all sophistications were made in response to public taste and at the inconvenience of food manufacturers. The year 1850 marks a decisive turning-point in public attitudes about such matters. After this only the deluded, the perverse, and the wicked could continue to defend adulteration or see it as anything except a major social, economic, and public health problem.

Late in that year Thomas Wakley, the radical doctor-editor of the *Lancet* who, as coroner for West Middlesex, had already earned a reputation for fearless exposures of workhouse scandals, decided to institute a thorough and searching investigation into the methods and extent of food adulteration. Dr Arthur Hassall, physician and lecturer on medicine at the Royal Free Hospital, was appointed to conduct the inquiry with the assistance of Henry Letheby, later to become Medical Officer of Health for the City of London: between 1851 and 1854, the journal printed each week their reports on every major article of food and drink, reports so voluminous that at the end of four years they were separately published in a bulky treatise for wider circulation.[1] There were several new and distinctive features about what *Punch* described as 'the *Lancet*'s detective force'. For one thing, the survey was the most rigorous and advanced series of tests to which foods had ever been subjected; in all, some 2,400 analyses were carried out, and Hassall was the first investigator to make extensive use of the microscope as an aid to detection. By its means many previously unknown frauds were revealed, and suspected ones confirmed. For

216

another, Wakley took the bold step of publishing, after due warning, the names and addresses of manufacturers and traders whose samples were reported as impure. The complete accuracy of the analyses is confirmed by the fact that only one was ever challenged, and even this had to be withdrawn when the retailer discovered that his goods had in fact been adulterated without his knowledge.

Hassall examined some thirty of the commonest foods, drinks, and condiments, and compiled detailed classifications showing the various adulterants used for giving weight and bulk, for imparting colour, and for simulating taste, smell, and other properties. His findings, based on personal analyses of samples obtained indiscriminately from hundreds of shops all over London, proved beyond doubt that serious, and often dangerous, adulteration existed of practically every food which it would pay to adulterate; moreover, by comparing his with the earlier investigations it seems clear that adulteration had grown steadily throughout the first half of the century, to reach peak proportions in the 1850s. By now it had become impossible to obtain several basic foods in a pure state. For example, every one of forty-nine random samples of bread which Hassall analysed contained alum, including loaves sold by the League Bread Company, which had advertised the 'perfect purity' of its bread in *The Times* and warranted it 'free from alum and other pernicious ingredients'. In addition to this, half the samples of flour analysed by Hassall also contained alum, often unknown to the baker, so that in many cases bread was in fact receiving a double dose. In tea he found the leaves of sycamore, plum, and horsechestnut as well as exhausted tea-leaves, and concluded that 'there is reason to believe that the manufacture of spurious tea, both black and green . . . prevails extensively at the present time'.[2] Week by week the truth was uncovered. Oatmeal was cheapened with barley-meal and refuse known in the trade as 'rubble'; milk had added water in amounts ranging from 10 to 50 per cent; of twenty-nine tins of coffee examined, twenty-eight were adulterated with chicory, mangel-wurzel, and acorn, while several also contained red oxide of lead derived from a ferruginous earth used as a colouring adulterant of the chicory. By such detailed analyses Hassall amply demonstrated what others had only suspected – that many adulterations were not merely frauds on the pocket but constituted serious hazards to health. Poisonous colouring matters, chiefly mineral dyes, were widely used for 'facing' tea and colouring preserved meats and fish, while sugar confectionery, eaten mainly by children, contained a truly appalling collection of them: of a hundred samples of sweets analysed, fifty-nine were coloured with chromate of lead, twelve with red lead, eleven with gamboge, eleven with Prussian and Antwerp blue, six with vermilion, fifteen with artificial ultramarine, ten with Brunswick green, and nine with arsenite of copper. Many samples contained no fewer than seven different colours and four poisons. In many the sugar itself had been adulterated with hydrated sulphate of lime, and in four cases the colours had been painted on with white lead.[3]

If they had remained as articles in a learned journal, it is doubtful whether even Hassall's startling revelations would have achieved a very wide publicity. Fortunately, they were not only published in collected book form but, in popularized versions, were reprinted extensively in the daily press and periodical literature. The amount of public interest and concern was accurately expressed by one contributor to the *Quarterly Review*, who wrote:

> A gun suddenly fired into a rookery could not cause a greater commotion than did the publication of the names of dishonest tradesmen; nor does the daylight, when you lift a stone, startle ugly and loathsome things more quickly than the pencil of light, streaming through a quarter-inch lens, surprised in their native ugliness the thousand and one illegal substances which enter more or less into every description of food which it will pay to adulterate.

The *Lancet* articles at last compelled public recognition of an urgent social problem, and brought its reform within the sphere of practical politics. Throughout 1855 and 1856 a Select Committee of the House of Commons heard detailed evidence from doctors, chemists, traders, and manufacturers which completely endorsed Hassall's findings. Dr Alphonse Normandy, the author of a standard work on commercial products, summed up the position when he told the Committee: 'Adulteration is a widespread evil which has invaded every branch of commerce; everything which can be mixed or adulterated or debased in any way is debased.' The final report of the Committee, published in 1856, regretted that:

> we cannot avoid the conclusion that adulteration widely prevails. Not only is the public health thus exposed to danger and pecuniary fraud committed on the whole community, but the public morality is tainted and the high commercial character of the country seriously lowered, both at home and in the eyes of foreign countries.[4]

From the wide range of expert evidence which it took, the Committee of 1855–6 unearthed even more details of the methods and extent of adulteration than Hassall had been able to discover. Tea was one of the articles most heavily adulterated, both in China and after its arrival in England, and had been subjected to close examination by a chemist, Robert Warington:

> Two samples of tea, a black and a green, were lately put into my hands by a merchant for examination, the results of which he has allowed me to make public. The black tea was styled scented caper; the green, gunpowder; and I understand they are usually imported into this country in small chests called

catty packages. The appearance of these teas is remarkable. They are apparently exceedingly closely rolled, and very heavy, the reasons for which will be clearly demonstrated. They possess a very fragrant odour. The black tea is in compact granules, like shot of varying size, and presenting a fine, glossy lustre of a very black hue. The green is also granular and compact, and presents a bright pale-bluish aspect, with a shade of green, and so highly glazed and faced that the facing rises in clouds of dust when it is agitated or poured from one vessel to another; it even coats the vessels or paper on which it may be poured. . . . The greater part of the facing material was removed. It proved, in the case of the sample of green tea, to be a pale Prussian blue, a yellow vegetable colour which we now know to be turmeric, and a very large proportion of sulphate of lime. The facing from the sample of black tea was perfectly black in colour, and on examination was found to consist of earthy graphite, or black lead. It was observed that during the prolonged soaking operation to which these teas had been submitted, there was no tendency exhibited in either case to unroll or expand, for a reason which will be presently obvious. One of the samples was therefore treated with hot water, without, however, any portion of a leaf being rendered apparent. It increased in size, slightly, was disintegrated, and then it was found that a large quantity of sand and dirt had subsided (amounting to 37.5 per cent in the case of the black, and 45.5 per cent in the case of the green tea) . . . it was quite evident that there was no leaf to uncurl, the whole of the tea being in the form of dust. The question next presented itself as to how these materials had been held together, and this was readily solved; for on examining the infusion resulting from the original soaking of the sample, abundant evidence of gum was exhibited.[5]

These spurious teas were known openly in China as 'Lie flower caper' and 'Lie gunpowder', and to the English broker under the more accurate description of 'gum and dust'. They were bought by wholesale and retail dealers at from 8d to 1s a pound for mixing with teas which would sell at 6s and more a pound. Other cases were quoted to the Committee of teas which contained nearly half their weight in iron filings, of leaves rolled up to imitate tea which were not tea at all, and of chests which contained bricks, iron, and other refuse. But perhaps more important because less easily detectable than these crude frauds, a large proportion of the expensive green teas sold in England – the Hysons, Souchongs, and gunpowders – were made from common and damaged green tea, and sometimes ordinary black tea, 'treated' in the Canton factories by colouring and glazing with mineral dyes; one experienced dealer, Joseph Woodin, estimated that at least half of all the green teas imported, representing between four and five million lb a year, were 'Canton made'.[6] Woodin was the man who had founded the Co-operative Central Agency and had had his chests of pure uncoloured tea rejected by societies in the north and midlands because they looked less attractive than the highly coloured green teas generally sold there. Fortunately, Woodin persevered.

Lecturers were employed by the agency to go round the country and explain adulteration to the working classes; some at least were convinced, and sales gradually mounted.[7] But in the 1850s domestic adulteration by dyeing with dangerous colouring matters, the use of noxious 'tea improvers', and the mixing of damaged and spoiled teas with gum, sand, and other undesirable substances were all extensively carried on, and in May 1851, Londoners were alarmed to discover that the manufacture of completely spurious tea had not yet been suppressed. *The Times* reported that Edward South and his wife Louisa, of Camberwell, had been discovered

> busily engaged in the manufacture. There was an extensive furnace before which was suspended an iron pan containing sloe-leaves, and tea-leaves which they were in the habit of purchasing from coffee-shop keepers after being used. On searching the place they found an immense quantity of used tea, bay-leaves and every description of spurious ingredients for the purpose of manufacturing illicit tea, and they were mixed with a solution of gums and a quantity of copperas. . . . The prisoners had pursued their nefarious trade most extensively, and were in the habit of dealing largely with grocers, chandlers and others, especially in the country. . . .[8]

Those who preferred to drink beer rather than tea were even more exposed to harmful adulterations. Two official inquiries had recently been carried out into the liquor trade – one by a House of Lords Committee in 1850,[9] the other by a Select Committee on Public Houses in 1853–4;[10] both were bitter indictments of the Beerhouse Act of 1830, which had brought into existence no fewer than 123,000 beer-shops, virtually free from any control or supervision and notorious for the bad quality of the liquor they supplied. Before 1830 porter sold at 5d a quart. Now it was offered at 4d and even 3d a quart, but only by diluting and adulterating – there was an agreement among the London brewers to sell at 33s a barrel, and 3d a quart would only yield 36s. The brewers apparently had little interest in the quality at which their beer was ultimately sold in tied houses so long as a large 'draught' was kept up since this determined the selling-price of the property. According to George Ridley, an analyst, the most common adulteration by publicans was simple dilution, followed by the addition of sugar and salt to restore flavour and copperas or sulphate of iron to give a 'cauliflower head' by which ignorant customers judged strength. A favourite recipe of publicans recommended 'To a barrel of porter, 12 gallons of liquor (water), 4 lb of foots (coarse sugar), 1 lb of salt, and then there is something to bring a head up, a little vitriol, *cocculus indicus*, also a variety of things so very minute that . . . we cannot easily detect the small proportions.' In this way thirty-six gallons was turned into forty-eight, sold at 3d a pot, and yielded a profit of 15s a barrel.[11] Nor was this kind of practice restricted to London. The Chief Constable of Wolverhampton reported that he had made a number of convictions for narcotics such as grains of paradise in beer, and believed that much apparent drunkenness was due to this and the use of similar drugs.[12] The Report on Public Houses concluded by recommending the early initiation of a separate inquiry into the whole question of adulteration of food, drink, and medicines – a suggestion which resulted in the appointment of the Committee of 1855–6. Again, a mass of evidence was presented here about the malpractices of brewers, 'brewers' druggists', and publicans. George Phillips, the Chief Officer of the Chemical Department of the Inland Revenue stated that of forty samples of hops recently analysed thirty-five contained grains of paradise, quassia, gentian, chiretta, and coriander; *cocculus indicus* has been added to one, and tobacco to another.[13] Dilution with water, restoration of bitterness with quassia or gentian and of 'strength' with *cocculus indicus*, and the use of sulphate of iron for 'heading' were the stock-in-trade of most, if not all, publicans – in analysing two hundred samples of beer during the last nine years the chemist, John Mitchell, had not found one to be pure except some taken direct from the brewery.[14]

Similarly, Mitchell reported that every sample of bread he had examined, whether from poorer or wealthier districts, contained alum on an average of 40 grains to the 4-lb loaf; boiled potatoes and carbonate of ammonia were also used, and in flour he had found sulphate of lime and chalk used as whiteners and cheap additions to bulk. Bad as this was, Mitchell's evidence did perhaps do something to reassure public fears about one suspected adulteration. Ever since Accum's day there had been persistent rumours about the use by bakers of burnt or ground bones in bread; Mitchell testified that his analyses had never revealed their presence, and in fact no reliable witness either in 1855 or subsequently was able to prove their presence. In almost every other case, however, the worst fears of the Committee were realized and often exceeded. Chicory, ochre, roasted corn, and crusts of bread in coffee; butter, the greater part of which was merely curds; sulphuric acid, grains of paradise, *cocculus indicus*, and alum in gin; brick dust, tallow, peroxide of iron, ground shell, and ground biscuit in cocoa; green pickles, bottled fruits, and vegetables coloured with copper; anchovy sauce and potted meats coloured with *bole armenian* – these were only a few of the revelations which the Committee heard in an atmosphere of shocked incredulity which slowly turned to anger. By the end of the sitting it was certain that some form of general legislation against adulteration would be recommended, that a case for interference had been fully made out on grounds not only of public health but also of morality. The nation whose life depended on her trade was being made to look very like a nation of thieves.

Plenty and Want

Voluntary reform

For some years before legislation became effective in 1875 the quality of food and drink began to show noticeable improvement. Quite suddenly in 1855 adulteration had become news, and the widespread publicity given to the subject shaped and crystallized a public conscience which found expression in the press and the popular literature of the day as well as in Parliament and the columns of medical journals. The intervening years saw the spontaneous emergence of agencies of voluntary reform – societies instituted to campaign for legislative control, organizations avowedly established for the supply of unadulterated provisions, and a remarkable expansion of the co-operative retail of pure food. By the 1860s a climate of opinion had been formed which induced significant numbers of manufacturers and traders to put their own houses in order before they were compelled to do so; the measures of reform voluntarily undertaken by the trade therefore form an important prelude to the legislative suppression of adulteration.

In the creation of this public conscience the literature of adulteration played a fundamental part. Accum's *Death in the Pot* had fired the public imagination in the 1820s, but his subsequent 'disgrace' had allowed the subject to be conveniently forgotten, and in the intervening years it received only passing mention in commercial[15] and technical[16] treatises. John Mitchell's *Falsification of Food*, published in 1848, set a new standard by its original chemical analyses and detached style of expression, but its influence scarcely penetrated outside scientific circles. Widespread interest in adulteration had to be re-created in the 1850s, and the event which did this, and which precipitated a Parliamentary inquiry and, ultimately, legislation, was the *Lancet* series of articles between 1851 and 1854. Hassall had been immediately struck by the low quality of London food when he came to practise there in 1850, and within a few months had written a paper for the Botanical Society on the Adulteration of Coffee based on his own microscopical examination of random samples; shortly afterwards, Wakley wrote to him stating his opinion that mere exposure of the techniques of adulteration would achieve little unless accompanied by the names and addresses of the dealers who sold impure goods. This was the origin of the formidable, and hazardous 'Analytical Sanitary Commission' of the *Lancet*, which for four years conducted a weekly survey of every major article of food and drink and fearlessly published the names of hundreds of fraudulent traders. Hassall's insistence on detailed personal examination, his refusal to accept preconceptions derived from earlier writers, above all, his original development of the microscope as an aid to detection, ensured that there could be no mistake. Hassall represented the dispassionate scientist pre-eminently acceptable to the Victorian intelli-

222

gentsia, and his approach to a subject which had accumulated an assort-
ment of truth, half-truth, and legend was exactly what the situation
demanded.

Equally important, the somewhat indigestible material of Hassall's articles was popularized in a number of ways which brought the substance of
his discoveries to a far wider public. Several daily newspapers regularly
reproduced the current *Lancet* article in abbreviated and simplified form,
The Times especially being a consistent supporter. Of the journals the
Illustrated London News, Frazer's Magazine, Once a Week, the *Quarterly
Review*, and the *London Review* devoted considerable space to able articles by Andrew Wynter and others – the latter's *Our Peck of Dirt* for
example being an amusing account of the consternation of a party of
friends on discovering that the polony they had just 'enjoyed' for breakfast
was composed of highly flavoured putrid meat, the coffee contained dried
horse's blood supplied by the knacker's yard, and the cream was
thickened with calves' brains![17] Also, the *Lancet* articles were the source of
inspiration for a whole series of books and pamphlets whose object was to
inform and warn in a simple way about current frauds and dangers to
health; of these we may mention J.D. Burn's *The Language of the Walls*,
published in 1855, which devoted half its pages to adulteration, the anonymous *Tricks of Trade in the Adulterations of Food and Physic* and Dr
Marcet's *On the Composition of Food, and How it is Adulterated* of 1856,
and in 1857 Dr John Postgate's *A Few Words on Adulteration*. The same
year also saw the publication of a shorter treatise by Hassall, aimed at the
general reader, entitled *Adulterations Detected in Food and Medicine*,
while other contemporary works such as Dodd's *Food of London* and
Edward Smith's *Foods* and *Practical Dietary* also included substantial
references to the quality of food. Many of these achieved a large circulation
and ran into several editions, and there is no doubt that they diffused an
awareness of adulteration among a wide public who would never have
opened the pages of the *Lancet*, and, more particularly, produced a deep
effect on the middle-class conscience.

One immediate effect of the publicity of the 1850s was in the awakening
of interest among the medical profession. A list of those who began testing
samples and canvassing for reform would include the names of Henry
Letheby, Alphonse Normandy, John Simon, Robert Dundas Thomson,
John Mitchell, and Sir John Gordon, to mention only a few, but the man
who engaged himself most indefatigably and effectively in the campaign
was John Postgate, a Birmingham surgeon and lecturer on anatomy at
Sydenham College. His interest in the subject dated from 1853 when he
had to treat a patient who was suffering from the effects of adulterated
coffee, and this led him to examine the quality of Birmingham food
generally, and bread in particular. He had been astonished to discover

that, as in London, it was next to impossible to obtain a pure loaf – that nearly all contained alum and that potatoes, pea- and bean-meal were also frequently added. By 1854 he had become convinced that adulteration was one of the leading causes of disease in the great towns, and was in extensive correspondence with other doctors and chemists, was addressing public meetings, and forming local societies to campaign for suppression and control. It was, in fact, a letter which Postgate wrote to William Scholefield in January of that year suggesting a Committee of Inquiry which led to the appointment of the Select Committee of the House of Commons; by July 1855 the Committee was in session, and within another five years the first general Adulteration Act was on the statute-book.

Before this, however, a noticeable improvement in the quality of many foods had already taken place. When Hassall published his second volume in 1857 he was able to report that some manufacturers and traders had completely abandoned adulteration, many had at least given up the use of poisonous ingredients, and almost all had made some concessions to the growing public demand for purer food. The immediate effect of the *Lancet* disclosures was the emergence of a movement for voluntary reform, in which a considerable section of the trade joined in a determination to set their houses in order before legislation compelled them to do so. By the late 1850s 'pure and unadulterated' had become a stock advertising slogan of dealers anxious to cash in on the newly awakened fears of the public – all too frequently it was the same spirit of competition which had prompted adulteration in the first place which now made it more profitable to offer, usually at a somewhat higher price, a commodity which was 'guaranteed pure' and bore the certificate of a doctor or analyst. In other cases, however, traders who had previously been ignorant of the injury they were causing were now genuinely determined to redeem their names and reputations. In either case, the result to the consumer was much the same. Within a few years he was for the first time in a position to exercise a choice between pure and impure food; legislation was ultimately necessary principally because large numbers of people, for one reason or another, continued to choose wrongly.

One striking instance of voluntary reform was when Thomas Blackwell, of Crosse & Blackwell, announced to the Select Committee of 1855 that his firm had recently given up, at considerable cost to plant, the coppering of pickles and fruits and the colouring of sauces with *bole armenian*. 'After the articles which appeared in the "Lancet" four or five years ago we abandoned it. . . . We have had iron vessels made, which are coated with glass, and likewise we had one silver vessel made, but we found silver would not do.'[18] He understood that other 'respectable' manufacturers had followed suit, although the public did not at first like their pickles brown instead of green, and preferred their anchovy sauce to look bright red: Blackwell had taken pains to advertise the reasons for the change, and believed that most people now preferred the genuine articles.

Another example of the direct influence of the *Lancet* articles was the establishment in 1851 of the Metropolitan Brewing Company 'to supply the public with Genuine Beer'. It was launched with the considerable capital of £50,000, the prospectus stating that 'the increasing support to this Company, which is formed expressly to supply a pure beverage, affords satisfactory proof that with increased means a large and profitable trade may be done.' The baking trade was affected even more by the campaign for pure food, several large companies being formed to make bread free of alum and other adulterations; one, the Sanitary Commission Bread Company, was established in 1857 with Hassall as a director and a promise of a £50,000 investment from a single miller. Again, the grocery trade was similarly affected, several firms being set up for the supply of pure coffee and cocoa, uncoloured tea, genuine arrowroot, and so on. Horniman's packet tea trade showed a remarkable expansion about this time, and by the 1870s was easily the largest in the country with an annual sale of more than five million packets. In addition to numerous retailers, at least one large wholesaler – the Universal Purveyor Company – was set up 'for the supply of Articles of Domestic Consumption and Use Free from Adulteration and Fraud'. It undertook to provide groceries of all kinds, wines, spirits, and beer to a limited number of agents in London and the provinces: 'Unexceptional references as to character, as well as ample security, will be required.'

Such reformist activities were no doubt also inspired partly by the changes in public taste which were occurring in the middle of the century. In the case of beer, for example, there was a marked swing away from the 'hard, old beer' of coaching days towards paler, brighter, less alcoholic drinks, so that many of the adulterations formerly practised to artificially age, strengthen, and darken it were no longer relevant. The same is true of tea, where there was a declining demand for green – the more heavily coloured variety – and a growing preference for black, especially when Indian teas became available in quantity. In other directions, too, a similar trend against highly coloured and strongly flavoured foods is recognizable, born, no doubt, partly of suspicion but partly, also, of a more sophisticated public palate.

Finally, the important part played by the Co-operative Movement in making available to the working-class consumer food of a high standard of purity must not be undervalued. The measures of voluntary reform so far discussed affected almost exclusively the 'respectable' part of trade which catered for middle-class custom; for the poor, tied by debt to the local grocer and baker, there could be little improvement until the advent of effective legislation. In the intervening years, co-operation introduced a new ideal and a new practice into trade. Aiming as it did to restore economic and social purpose to buying and selling, the supply of pure goods was regarded as a principle as important as that of dividend on purchases – indeed, in numerous instances both before and after Rochdale it was pure food rather than cheap food which was the primary consideration. The earliest co-operative societies were isolated corn-mills and baking establishments formed towards the end of the eighteenth century in resentment against the frauds and extortions of millers and bakers – such was the Hull Corn-Mill Society established by local working men in 1795 to supply themselves with pure flour and bread, and numerous others came into existence after the end of the Napoleonic Wars. The modern form of co-operative retail society dates, as we have seen,[19] from the Rochdale Pioneers in 1844 and their numerous imitators; they too experienced great difficulty in obtaining supplies of pure food, which led them to revive the earlier idea of co-operative production. Already by 1850 the Rochdale society had its own mill, financed by the store, and others were in existence at Halifax, Leeds, and elsewhere.

The co-operative movement also illustrates the consumer-resistance which pioneers of pure food often had to meet and overcome. Holyoake himself had foreseen this difficulty, and had warned his audience at Rochdale in 1843: 'When you have a little store and have reached the point of getting pure provisions, you may find your purchasers will not like them, nor know them when they taste them. Their taste will require to be educated. They have never eaten the pure food of gentlemen.'[20] His words were prophetically true. The pure flour supplied by the Rochdale Flour Mill was darker in colour than members were accustomed to, and would not sell because of its brownness. The position was so critical for the society that for a time public pressure compelled it to produce white flour, but this involved such an abandonment of principle that a special Store Meeting shortly afterwards voted to return to purity, whatever the cost. Public confidence was gradually won and ultimately the unadulterated flour came to be greatly preferred. Another case in point was tea. The Co-operative Central Agency which was formed in 1850 to supply local societies with pure provisions, found that its green tea was unsaleable; the public, especially in the north of England, insisted that green tea should look bright and highly glazed, and at first rejected the dull, olive-coloured leaves which the Agency provided. Here too the good ultimately drove out the bad. Joseph Woodin, the Agency's manager, published a pamphlet on adulteration in 1852 'in order to undeceive consumers in the manufacturing districts', and lecturers were engaged 'to go round the country and explain the matter to the working-classes'.[21] The energetic and enterprising pursuit of such policies, often in the face of a hostile public, is a striking testimony to the faith of the early co-operators. Through them, and through them alone, some at least of the working classes were familiarized with a standard of purity they had never known, and were educated to an appreciation of the moral as well as the economic value of honest dealing.

The early food legislation

Although voluntary reform did something to raise the quality of food in higher-priced shops and co-operative stores, the diet of the majority of the population continued to be heavily adulterated until effective pure food laws could be passed through Parliament. Publicity changed the character of the problem, but did not solve it: it is noticeable, for example, that after 1850 several of the cruder (and more easily detectable) frauds were gradually abandoned in favour of newer and more subtle methods which had a run of success until they too were exposed. When Hassall extended his survey for the *Lancet* to provincial towns in 1857–8 he found that adulteration in Manchester, Birmingham, Leeds, and Liverpool was still rife, but not the almost universal practice it had been in the London of 1851. At the same time John Postgate published a collection of recent cases to show that fraudulent and even dangerous adulterations were still being carried on – his list included confectionery composed of twenty parts of sugar and ten of *terra alba*, which had caused the death of a child in Birmingham, and bread discovered in Hull which contained 5 per cent of silex or flint.[22] The inferior 'Cones' flour, which was itself often adulterated with rye, barley, Indian corn, and bean-flour, was extensively used by 'underselling' bakers throughout the 1850s and 1860s,[23] and, more serious still, Professor Odling discovered strong evidence of the deliberate addition of highly poisonous copper sulphate as a bread whitener.[24] It had been used in Belgium and France in minute quantities since about 1830 for the same purpose as alum, although its effect was far more drastic; it had often been suspected here, but never before proved. If this were not enough, in 1860 Dr Edward Lankester showed that poisonous colouring matters in food were still very common, and quoted recent cases in which three people had died after a public banquet at which they had eaten green blancmange containing arsenite of copper, and of yellow Bath buns which owed their colour to sulphide of arsenic. The next year, a lecture delivered to the Royal Society of Arts claimed that 87 per cent of the bread and 74 per cent of the milk sold in London were still adulterated.

Voluntary forces alone would not have provided a sufficient check to adulteration of this extent, and from the publication of the House of Commons Committee's final report in 1856 it was certain that legislation must shortly follow. But although Parliament and the nation had at last been convinced of the existence of a great and growing evil, wide differences of

227

opinion existed as to the remedy to be adopted. There were many still like Viscount Goderich who looked in the first place to voluntary reform by traders and an extension of co-operative retail of food,[25] while at the other extreme Hassall was demanding the creation of a central board of public analysts, with imprisonment and public exposure as the penalty for adulterators. Others again favoured the practice of France, where local *Conseils de Salubrité* harnessed the expert knowledge of doctors, chemists, and veterinary surgeons to guard the purity of all foods, drinks, and drugs.[26]

The first Adulteration of Foods Act which was passed in 1860[27] was therefore a compromise, steering an uncertain course between conflicting views. In common with much Victorian social legislation it suffered from all the failings of permissive adoption – the arguments of economy, the consideration due to vested interests, the sheer lethargy and inertia of much unreformed county administration. Under the terms of the Act various local authorities (the Commissioners of Sewers in the City of London, Vestries and District Boards in the Metropolis generally, and the Courts of Quarter Sessions in the counties) were empowered to appoint public analysts who would examine samples of food and drink (but not drugs) 'on complaint made' by private citizens. No provision was made for sampling; all the analyst could do was to wait for suspected articles to be brought forward by those public-spirited enough to pay a fee of up to 10s 6d for each analysis. No central authority was created. The responsibility for ensuring food quality was to be a local and purely optional one. A fine was to be the normal penalty for adulteration, with imprisonment only in default of payment, and a seller who could show evidence that he had himself been deceived, and was unaware of the adulteration, was not to be held liable.

To the bitter disappointment of radical reformers like Hassall and Postgate, the first Food Act passed onto the statute-book and into oblivion. All the evidence suggests that it was an utter failure. Trade opposition prevented the adoption of the Act over wide areas, and during the twelve years of its existence only seven analysts were appointed throughout Great Britain. Four of these did nothing at all. Two more had a few samples submitted to them during the first year or so, mainly by dealers who knew that their goods were pure and wanted an analyst's certificate for publicity purposes, but none subsequently. One of these, Dr Henry Letheby, the Public Analyst for the City of London, was called on to examine fifty-seven samples in the course of nine years; although twenty-six were reported as adulterated, in no case were proceedings brought before the magistrates in accordance with the provisions of the Act.[28] Only Dr Charles Cameron, the Medical Officer of Health and Public Analyst for Dublin, demonstrated how energy and initiative could transform a lame measure into effective operation. Between 1862 and 1874 he analysed 2,600 samples, reported nearly 1,500 as adulterated, and successfully obtained convictions in 342 cases.[29]

It should, however, be remembered that in 1860 legislative interference with the free workings of the economy was still exceptional and limited in scope. The mere attempt to place a law between seller and buyer was a major breach in the structure of *laissez-faire* and a significant contribution to the scanty public health provision of the day, and although the Act itself was ineffectual the important precedent had been established that it was within the proper role of the state to protect the consumer against injury to his pocket and his health. Throughout the 1860s a stream of criticisms and demands for more effective safeguards was kept up by the reformers. The *Lancet* continued to provide the spearhead of the attack, supported by the Royal Society of Arts, the National Association for the Promotion of Social Science, and individuals among whom Postgate and Letheby stand out, while Hassall himself demonstrated by a new series of investigations that, although some improvement had taken place since his first inquiry, an urgent problem still awaited solution in London and the leading provincial towns. On this occasion, half the samples of bread analysed contained alum in amounts ranging from 12 to 96 grains to the 4-lb loaf.[30] In 1868 John Postgate laid before Parliament a series of radical amendments to the 1860 Act which, after numerous delays and modifications, passed into law as the Adulteration of Food, Drink, and Drugs Act, 1872.

The most important legal changes in the new Act were that it now became an offence to sell a mixture containing ingredients for the purpose of adding weight or bulk (for example, chicory in coffee) unless its composition was declared to the purchaser, and that the sale of adulterated drugs now became punishable. Administratively, the Act extended the power of appointing analysts to boroughs having separate police establishments: the appointment was still to be optional 'save on the direction of the Local Government Board', an important, if ill-defined amendment which introduced an element of central control. Another valuable clause provided for the procuring of samples for analysis by Inspectors of Nuisances and other local officers, as well as by private persons. In all these respects the new Act was a great advance on its predecessor, more extensive in scope, and more vigorous in its enforcement. Within three years 150 out of the 225 districts empowered to appoint analysts had done so, and over 1,500 convictions for adulteration had been obtained. One of these newly appointed public analysts, Wentworth Lascelles Scott, has left a picture of the kind of work and the extent of adulteration at this period.[31] During fifteen months in north Staffordshire he took 937 random samples of food, drink, and drugs, of which 381 were adulterated and reported. The greatest problem was milk, more than half the samples of which were diluted with highly impure water, but twenty-six out of eighty-nine samples of beer were adulterated, six of them with the deadly *cocculus indicus*. More than half the samples of mustard were impure, containing flour and turmeric, while more than a third of the samples of pepper contained sand and a variety of vegetable matters. On the other hand, some foods already showed a marked improvement in quality: only two samples of bread were reported against, and only one out of twenty-two pieces of sugar confectionery now contained chromate of lead.

In other ways, however, the working of the new Act was still unsatisfactory. Its adoption was very uneven, and there was nothing to ensure that an analyst, once appointed, would have anything to do – the analyst for Somerset, for example, obtained 520 convictions in sixteen months while his colleague in Shropshire obtained two in twice as long. Many analysts were inexperienced, and even among the experts there were wide differences of opinion as to what constituted adulteration: a fundamental difficulty was that no agreed standards had yet been set, so that divergent opinions were held about the minimum percentage of 'fats' and 'total solids' in milk, whether the 'facing' of tea should be regarded as an adulteration, and so on. Analyst contradicted analyst, and confused magistrates gave conflicting decisions. After numerous petitions had been received from the larger towns complaining of these weaknesses, the Government appointed in 1874 a new Select Committee whose Report embodied most of the criticisms already mentioned.[32] The 1872 Act, the Report claimed, had been productive of much good in that 'people were now cheated rather than poisoned', but it was in need of amendment chiefly 'in order to give a clearer understanding as to what does and as to what does not constitute adulteration'. The result of this Report was the Sale of Food and Drugs Act, 1875, which, with numerous amendments, forms the basis of the present law.

The establishment of food purity

Within a decade of the passing of the new Act a remarkable improvement had been effected in the quality of basic foods – so much so that a good case may be made out for regarding the 1880s as the crucial period in the suppression of adulteration and the establishment of food purity. The most formidable penalty in the new Act lay in Section 3, which made any adulteration injurious to health punishable with a heavy fine and with imprisonment for a second offence, a remedy which food reformers had been urging ever since the time of Accum. In fact, however, for a seller to be liable under this section it was necessary to prove guilty knowledge on his part, and only in exceptional circumstances was such evidence forthcoming. The effective part of the Act lay in Section 6, which provided that no one should sell, to the prejudice of the purchaser, any article of food or any drug which was not 'of the nature, substance and quality of the article demanded': here it was not necessary to prove that the adulteration was injurious to health, or that the seller had knowledge of it.[33] There were, of course, difficulties of interpretation even here. If, for example, a seller notified the public that his goods were adulterated, could consumers still claim that they were 'prejudiced' in the meaning of the section? In the case of *Sandys* v. *Small* in 1878 whisky had been sold by a publican thirty degrees under proof, but conspicuous notices had been posted in the bar stating that 'All spirits sold here are mixed'. Nothing was said at the time of sale, and the customer had not in fact seen the notice. The Queen's Bench Division held that as the purchaser was 'informed' constructively beforehand of the mixture it was not to his prejudice and the publican had therefore committed no offence. Although difficulties arose in practice as to what constituted 'constructive notice', there was little quarrel with the principle of the ruling. The decision in *James* v. *Jones* (1 Q.B., 304, 1894) however, seems far less defensible, and represented a serious limitation on the working of the Act. In this case it was decided that baking-powder was not 'an article of food' within the meaning of the Act, apparently on the ground that it was never eaten alone although, of course, the sole purpose of its manufacture was for use in food. The seller of baking-powder containing 40 per cent of alum, which the judge himself admitted was 'injurious to health', was therefore not liable. The somewhat illogical conclusion followed that the sale of injurious baking-powder was not actionable, but the sale of bread which contained it was.

With this exception, adequate legal machinery for the suppression of adulteration now existed. Effective enforcement of the Act, however, depended upon two main factors – the readiness of local authorities to adopt what was still permissive legislation, and the skill and efficiency of the public analysts themselves. The Local Government Board achieved much by persuading and cajoling authorities to appoint analysts, although in its annual report for 1880 it had to admit that in several large towns including Derby, Durham, Hartlepool, Northampton, and Oxford no action had been taken, and 'we have too often been unable to obtain more than a general statement that as adulteration is not suspected to exist, the Town Council deems it unnecessary to harass the local tradesmen.'[34] During the decade, however, the tone of the Board's circular letters gradually became more authoritative, and within a few years nearly all authorities had fallen into line and had instituted regular sampling; by 1889 the Board's target of one sample per thousand of the population had been reached with a total of 26,954 analyses for the year. The public analysts themselves appear, on the whole, to have been a skilled and dedicated group of men, keenly anxious to make the Act work and to increase its efficiency. The Society of Public Analysts was founded in 1874, like many professional bodies, out of informal meetings of colleagues; within a few months it had enrolled almost every practitioner in the country, had laid down a definition of adulteration, was holding regular meetings and publishing its proceedings. There is no doubt that the activities of the Society gave a considerable stimulus to analytical chemistry in general and to the development of new tests and standards for food purity in particular,[35] and the Society played an especially important part in establishing limits outside which they would regard an article as adulterated, many of which were eventually adopted legislatively. The first statutory standards for spirits were laid down in 1879, for the new product 'margarine' in 1887, for milk in 1901, and for butter in 1902, and by 1914 a wide range of foods had become subject to legal minima.

One of the most valuable terms of the 1875 Act provided that public analysts were required to make quarterly statistical returns to the Local Government Board, and from these it is possible to compile an exact record of the gradual conquest and suppression of adulteration from this time onwards. As Table 25 shows, when returns were first published in 1877, 19.2 per cent of all the random samples analysed throughout the country were adulterated; by 1900 the figure had fallen to 8.8 per cent, and in 1913 it stood at 8.2 per cent. A spectacular improvement in the quality of many basic foods occurred during the 1880s, so that by the end of Victoria's reign the consumer generally received his bread and flour, his tea and sugar, as pure as he could wish. Some items, it is true, still presented an intractable problem which showed little improvement over the years – 13 per cent of all beer was still adulterated in 1900, 12.4 per cent of spirits, 10 per cent of coffee, and 9.9 per cent of milk, despite constant watch and repeated prosecutions by local authorities. But the chief offence in most of these cases was simple dilution with water, which remained easy, profitable, and difficult to detect. Deliberate, dangerous adulteration for the sake of gain had been all but eliminated.

Of the improvement of basic foods, that of bread was most marked. In the early years of the new Act, public analysts naturally concentrated much of their attention on it, and the paper read at the very first meeting of the Society was given by Professor Wanklyn 'On the detection of alum in bread'. The *Lancet* survey of 1872 had found that half of all the samples examined were still adulterated: in the first year of returns the figure had fallen to 7 per cent and by 1884 to as little as 2 per cent. This good result was partly due to an energetic drive by the authorities in tracking down and prosecuting offenders, partly to the improved quality of imported wheat and the introduction of roller-milling, which made the use of alum as a whitener unnecessary except to the lowest class of baker. Isolated cases of gross adulteration could, of course, still be found. In 1880, for example, the Public Analyst for Essex reported on one 4-lb loaf which con-

The quality of food

Table 25 *Statistics of bread and other articles adulterated 1877–1914 (compiled from the quarterly reports of public analysts to the Local Government Board)*

Year	Number of samples of bread analysed	Adulterated	Percentage adulterated	Percentage of all articles adulterated
1877	998	74	7.4	19.2
1878	921	66	7.1	17.2
1879	1,287	95	7.3	14.8
1880	1,096	70	6.4	15.7
1881	1,037	49	4.7	14.7
1882	1,204	77	6.4	15.1
1883	1,041	28	2.7	15.0
1884	1,217	24	2.0	14.4
1885	1,168	31	2.7	13.2
1886	991	32	3.2	11.9
1887	872	17	1.9	12.8
1888	689	4	0.6	10.8
1889	952	21	2.2	11.9
1890	689	5	0.7	11.2
1891	799	8	1.0	12.2
1892	804	3	0.4	12.4
1893	698	1	0.1	12.9
1894	653	9	1.4	10.3
1895	575	10	1.7	9.3
1896	625	1	0.2	9.2
1897	630	9	1.4	9.4
1898	717	6	0.8	8.7
1899	597	3	0.5	9.4
1900	437	3	0.7	8.8
1901	530	4	0.8	8.8
1902	552	2	0.4	8.7
1903	561	0	0	7.9
1904	473	1	0.2	8.5
1905	463	1	0.2	8.2
1906	373	1	0.3	9.3
1907	528	4	0.8	8.1
1908	394	4	1.0	8.5
1909	352	2	0.6	7.5
1910	327	0	0	8.2
1911	618	1	0.2	8.7
1912	414	0	0	8.4
1913	405	4	1.0	8.2
1914	No statistics available.			

tained the unprecedented quantity of 1,035 grains of alum, and would have been 'exceedingly harmful to anyone whom its nauseousness did not prevent from consuming it'.[36] Possibly this huge amount had gained access to the bread indirectly as a result of the use of alum in baking-powder where it was employed as a cheap substitute for tartaric acid,[37] and this continued to be a common practice until the Sale of Food and Drugs Act of 1899 widened the definition of food to include 'any article which ordinarily enters into or is used in the composition or preparation of human food'. Oatcakes containing 10 per cent of chalk were reported in 1880, and muffins which included plaster of Paris two years later,[38] but cases of this kind were now isolated survivals from an earlier epoch. The Local Government Board Report for 1892 could say with some satisfaction, 'It is now certain that the bread supplied to the people of England is practically pure.'

The quality of tea showed an even more dramatic improvement than that of bread under the influence of the 1875 Act. An investigation of 1872 had found thirty-six out of forty-one samples grossly adulterated with such things as sand, magnetic iron, China clay, Prussian blue, and spurious leaves,[39] but within a decade tea adulteration had all but disappeared, and from 1886 onwards it became a rarity to find even a single case reported in a year. Under the 1875 Act tea was subjected to a double scrutiny – once on arrival in the country by the Customs Department, and again by the public analysts if domestic adulteration was suspected – and it would be surprising if more than a fraction of impure tea had continued to slip through. Added to this, the declining popularity of green China teas, always the more highly adulterated, and the preponderance of Indian and Ceylon teas, whose purity had never been in question, finally put an end to what had been one of the most serious of all adulterations. By the 1880s grocers were finding it difficult to sell China teas unless they could guarantee them 'pure' or 'free from colouring matters', and even then, much was only sold at a loss, and not re-stocked.[40] By the end of the century, it seems, Chinese merchants had in fact stopped the colouring and 'facing' of tea, and only an occasional Caper was reported against for containing an excess of mineral matter. With the fall in price of imports and the vigilance of public analysts, the English grocer also abandoned his former mal-practices in the 1870s: the worst that can be said of him in the later nineteenth century is that he occasionally mixed cheap, inferior China teas with strong Indian varieties to lower cost or increase his profit. In any case, an Indian tea which contained 10 per cent of China 'rubbish' and sold at under 2s a pound was a far better buy than the heavily adulterated China tea for which mid-Victorian customers had paid three or four times as much.

Beer adulteration had also practically ceased to exist by 1880, except for

innocuous dilution. Fables continued to circulate, particularly at temperance meetings, about the poisonous ingredients allegedly used by
brewers – a speaker in 1883 made the unsupported statement that
245,000 cwt of 'chemicals' were annually used in English breweries,[41] and
a few years later a book purporting to be a serious study of drinks and
drinking habits stated that bitterness in beer was produced by strychnine,
absinthe, and *nux vomica*, and intoxication by belladonna, opium,
henbane, and picric acid.[42] In fact, *cocculus indicus* was last reported in
1864 and grains of paradise in 1878, and only rarely after this were old
adulterations such as 'heading', capsicum, and liquorice discovered by
public analysts as isolated curiosities. Narcotics disappeared from beer
with the vigilance of local authorities and a change in drinking habits: by
the closing decades of the century people no longer wanted to be stupefied
and had turned away from porter and 'hard beer' towards lighter, less alcoholic varieties. Dilution remained the outstanding problem, and a seem-
ingly intractable one: as late as 1900 one in five samples was watered, and
a great many of these salted in order to restore lost flavour and, no doubt,
increase thirst.

In the summer of that year, however, something far more serious
occurred. A mysterious disease, variously described as 'alcoholism' and
'peripheral neuritis', appeared in Manchester and Salford and spread into
the midlands as far south as Lichfield and Nottingham; by the end of the
year 6,000 cases had been reported, and seventy people had died. Those
affected were generally heavy drinkers, and it was not long before a
Manchester doctor traced the illness to arsenical poisoning in beer.[43] Ultimately the source was traced to a firm of brewing sugar manufacturers,
Bostock & Co., of Garston, who manufactured their glucose by a process
involving commercial sulphuric acid. It was this sulphuric acid, itself
made from arsenical iron pyrites and supplied by a Leeds firm, which was
responsible for the outbreak. One, if not both, manufacturers had been
morally guilty of criminal negligence in using, without testing, a substance
in the production of human food which is liable to contain poisonous
impurities. A Royal Commission on Arsenical Poisoning (1901–3) subsequently recommended that a legal maximum of not more than one-hundredth of a grain of arsenic per gallon of liquid or per pound of solid food be
enforced (up to four grains per pound of brewing sugar had been found)
but this was bolting the stable door after the horse had departed. The
arsenic scare of 1900 added considerable force to the arguments of those
food reformers who at the end of the century were urging that a new problem had now emerged and was awaiting solution – that of 'legalized
adulteration'.[44]

The bread debate

By the close of the century public anxiety was turning from traditional forms of adulteration, now apparently under effective control, towards wider issues of food quality and nutrition. The new science of dietetics, headed by such men as Drs Paton and Hutchinson, pointed to inadequate diet as a main cause of 'incapacitated manhood' which alarmed the nation at the time of the Boer War, though opinions differed as to whether the poor state of the nation's health was due to a deterioration in the quality of diet, to ignorance and laziness on the part of housewives, or quite simply, to poverty. Attention naturally focused on bread, still the staple food of the working classes. Although alum and other adulterants were virtually things of the past, almost all bread was now made from white, roller-milled flour of low extraction rate from which the bran and wheat-germ had been removed. Opposing this, a 'brown bread' lobby, initially composed mainly of middle-class vegetarians, socialists, and ascetics, dated from the 1880s, when May Yates founded the Bread and Food Reform League and Dr T.R. Allinson began campaigning on behalf of wholemeal bread. Their main obstacles were that the brown bread then available was more expensive than white, and tended to be unpalatable, with a thick crust and a moist, sodden interior.[45] However, further support was given to the League's cause in 1911 by F.G. Hopkins: although vitamins had not yet been discovered, he argued that the superior value of bran flour was due to 'unrecognized food substances, perhaps in very minute quantities, whose presence allows our systems to make full use of the tissue-building elements of the grain'.[46]

The same year, the Local Government Board commissioned Dr Hamill to investigate the bleaching and 'improving' of flour by millers. Bleaching by nitrogen peroxide gas had spread rapidly since the patenting of the process in 1901, as had the use of various chemical additives which were supposed to improve baking qualities. Hamill concluded that it was not desirable that 'such an indispensable foodstuff as flour, the purity and wholesomeness of which are of first importance to the community, should be manipulated and treated with foreign substances, the utility of which from the point of view of the consumer is more than questionable'.[47] No new legislation against such additives was forthcoming and, surprisingly, a test case brought in 1913 by Hull Corporation against a local firm of millers for adding potassium persulphate as an 'improver' was held by a magistrates' court not to be an adulteration under Section 6 of the Sale of Food and Drugs Act, 1875: apparently the case was not taken to appeal.

These anxieties about the composition of bread affected only a small minority of consumers, who tended to be regarded as cranks and faddists. Most people preferred the very white flour produced by the roller-mills, and by 1900 the white, wheaten loaf comprised at least 95 per cent of total bread consumption by weight.[48] From the 1880s, however, a small, specialist market for certain 'patent' breads claiming nutritional advantages began to grow, mainly among diet-conscious, middle-class consumers: they included Hovis (reinforced wheat-germ), Daren (wheat, wheat-germ, and rye), Triagon (wheat, maize, and rice), and Kermode's (wheat and maize). Only Hovis had achieved a national reputation by 1914, mainly as a result of successful advertising. The flour formula had been invented in about 1885 by Richard Smith, a miller of Stone, Staffordshire: the product was renamed 'Hovis' (from the Latin for 'strength of man') in 1891 and the Hovis Bread Company established in 1898. In fact, the company merely manufactured the flour, but did not bake bread: the strategy was to win over bakers – and, ultimately, consumers – by national advertising through brand-name packaging, sign-boards for delivery vans and cafes, and baking tins with the Hovis imprint. Country teashops displaying 'teas with Hovis', and serving it in specially designed Hovis tea-sets, became well-known to Edwardian cyclists and early motorists. It was the first successful attempt to exploit the new health food market on a national scale, and evidence of a growing dietary awareness among a small, though influential, section of the population.

Notes

1 Hassall, Arthur Hill (1855) *Food and its Adulterations; comprising the Reports of the Analytical Sanitary Commission of 'The Lancet' for the years 1851 to 1854 inclusive.*
2 ibid., 279.
3 ibid., 600 et seq.
4 Reports from the Select Committee on Adulteration of Food, etc., Third Report, HC 379 (1856), VIII, 1.
5 Warington, R. (1851) 'Observations on the teas of commerce', *The Memoirs of the Chemical Society* (May); Adulteration of Food, report cit., First Report, HC 432 (1855), VIII, 221: Appendix, 135.
6 Central Co-operative Agency. Instituted under Trust to counteract the system of adulteration and fraud now prevailing in the trade. Catalogue of Teas, Coffees, Colonial and Italian Produce, and Wines etc., with the Retail Prices affixed, sold by the Central Co-operative Agency at the Central Establishment, 76 Charlotte St, with Prefatory Remarks on Adulteration, arising from competition. J. Woodin. 1852, 28–9.
7 Adulteration of Food, op. cit., Third Report (1856): Evidence of J. Woodin, 270–3.
8 *The Times*, 27 May 1851.
9 Report from the Select Committee of the House of Lords appointed to consider the Operation of the Acts for the Sale of Beer, etc. (1850), (398) XVIII.

10 Report from the Select Committee on Public Houses, etc., together with the Proceedings of the Committee, Minutes of Evidence, Appendix and Index (1853–4), HC (367) XIV, 231.

11 ibid.: Evidence of George Ridley, Qs. 4681–4868.

12 ibid.: Evidence of Gilbert Hogg, Qs. 6523–6975. So also did the Rev. H. Fearon, B.D.: 'But is it really beer which our work people nowadays get to drink? . . . Look at that poor degraded man, reeling in his gait and now sinking helplessly down unconscious upon a doorstep in the street. You say he is intoxicated . . . I believe he is drugged. . . . Do not lay solely to the charge of malt and hops what is due to *cocculus indicus*, tinctured with tobacco and spiced with grains of paradise' – *Home Comfort: Working Life, how to make it happier*. A lecture given before the Young Men's Institution at Leicester (1857), 11–13.

13 Adulteration of Food, report cit., Second Report, HC 480 (1855), VIII, 373: Evidence of George Phillips, Q. 2304 et seq.

14 ibid., First Report: Evidence of John Mitchell, Q. 1073 et seq.

15 e.g. McCulloch, J.R. *A Dictionary, Practical, Theoretical and Historical, of Commerce and Commercial Navigation* (edns of 1834 and 1846); P.L. Simmonds (1846) *Commercial Products*.

16 e.g. Ure, Andrew (1835) *A Dictionary of Chemistry and Mineralogy* (4th edn); Jonathan Pereira (1843) *A Treatise on Food and Diet*.

17 Wynter, Andrew (1869) *Our Social Bees. Pictures of Town and Country Life, and other Papers* (10th edn), 76 et seq.

18 Adulteration of Food, op. cit., First Report (1855): Evidence of Thomas Blackwell, Qs. 1567 and 1602.

19 See chap. 6, pp. 125–6.

20 Holyoake, G.J. (1908), *The History of Co-operation*, 272.

21 Adulteration of Food, op. cit., Third Report (1856): Evidence of J. Woodin, 270–3.

22 Postgate, John (1857) *A Few Words on Adulteration*, 3 et seq.

23 Report relative to the Grievances of the Journeymen Bakers, etc., op. cit., 1862, XLI.

24 'On the composition of bread' by William Odling, Professor of Practical Chemistry at Guy's Hospital, in the *Lancet* I (1857), 137–8.

25 Goderich, Viscount, MP (1852) 'On the adulteration of food and its remedies', in *Meliora, or Better Times to Come*, Viscount Ingestre (ed.) (2nd edn).

26 The first *Conseil de Salubrité* was established in Paris as early as 1802, and most French provincial towns followed the example during the next two or three decades.

27 For a fuller examination of the Act and its historical setting, see John Burnett (1960) 'The Adulteration of Foods Act, 1860: a centenary appreciation of the first British legislation', *Food Manufacture* XXXV (November), 479 et seq.

28 Letheby, Henry (1868) *On Food: being the substance of four Cantor Lectures delivered before the Society for the Encouragement of Arts, Manufactures and Commerce, Jan. and Feb. 1868*, 71.

29 Scott, Wentworth Lascelles (1875) 'Food adulteration and the legislative enactments relating thereto', *Journal of the Royal Society of Arts* XXIII, 433.

30 *Lancet* I (1872), 26.

31 op. cit., 433 et seq.

32 Select Committee of the House of Commons on the Adulteration of Food Act (1872), HC 262 (1874), VI, 243.

33 Legal ingenuity practically nullified the working of this section in the first few years by the interpretation given to 'prejudice'. In a number of decisions immediately after 1875 it was held that if a sample was purchased by an inspector for analysis he was not 'prejudiced' by an adulteration since he had not bought the food for his own consumption. As practically all samples were taken in this way, and not by private purchasers, the provision became for a few years almost a dead letter. This unfortunate line of decisions and the narrow interpretation of 'prejudice' was brought to an end in the appeal case of *Hoyle* v. *Hitchman* in 1879.

34 Tenth Annual Report of the Local Government Board, 1880–81 (1881), 1XXXVI.

35 Dyer, Bernard and Mitchell, C. Ainsworth (1932) *The Society of Public Analysts: some reminiscences of its first fifty years, and a review of its activities*.

36 Local Government Board, op. cit., xc.

37 Robinson, H. M. and Cribbs, C. H. (1895) *The Law and Chemistry of Food and Drugs*, 337–46.

38 *The Analyst* 7 (1882), 115.

39 Liverseege, J.F. (1932) *Adulteration and Analysis of Food and Drugs. Birmingham methods and analyses of samples. Review of British prosecutions during half a century*, 318.

40 Anon (nd, *c.* 1884) *The Art of Tea Blending. A Handbook for the Tea Trade*, 37.

41 Quoted in John Bickerdyke (1886) *The Curiosities of Ale and Beer*.

42 Mew, J. and Ashton, J. (1892) *Drinks of the World*.

43 *British Medical Journal*, 24 November 1900.

44 See e.g. article by W. C. Quilter in 1887 in *Nineteenth Century*; and A. Gordon Saloman (1887) 'The purity of beer', *Journal of the Royal Society of Arts* 35, 246 et seq.

45 Hunt, Sandra *The Changing Place of Bread in the British Diet in the Twentieth Century*, series of upublished research papers sponsored by the Rank Prize Funds (Brunel University), 'The structure and economics of the baking and milling trades, 1880–1914', 17.

46 ibid., 19.

47 Hamill, J.M. (1911) *On the Bleaching of Flour*, Local Government Board, Food Reports no. 12 (Cd. 5613).

48 Collins, E.J.T. (1976) 'The "consumer revolution" and the growth of factory foods. Changing patterns of bread- and cereal-eating in Britain in the twentieth century', in Derek J. Oddy and Derek S. Miller (eds), *The Making of the Modern British Diet*, 28.

1a Pauper apprentices supplementing the factory rations

THE PIG AND THE PEASANT.

Peasant. "AH! I'D LIKE TO BE CARED VOR HALF AS WELL AS THEE BE!"

1b The pig and the peasant

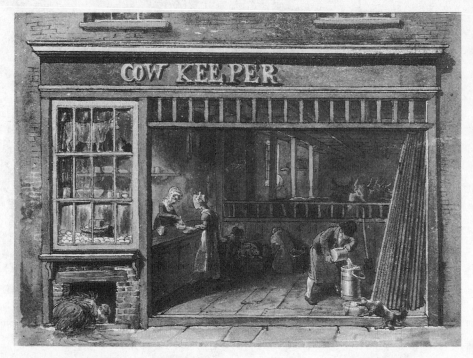

2a A London dairy or cowkeeper's shop, 1825

2b 'London
improvements' in
1845

LONDON IMPROVEMENTS.

3a The Great Tea Race

3b A visit to a brewery in 1847

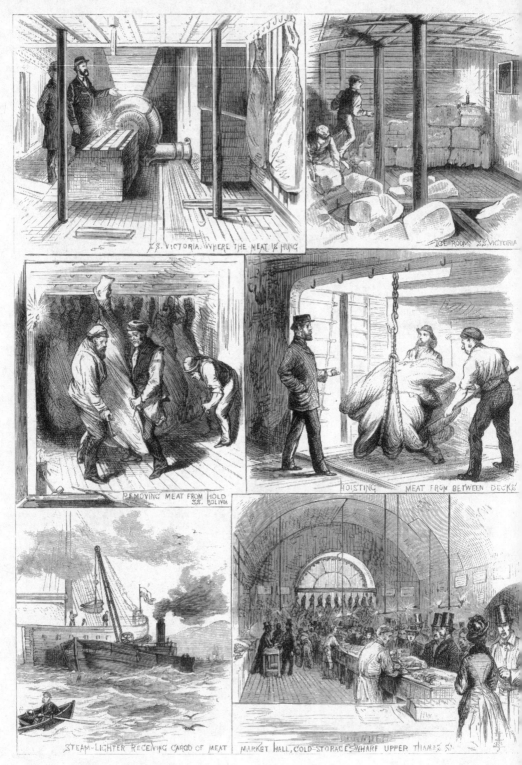

S.S. VICTORIA, WHERE THE MEAT IS HUNG

ICE ROOM, S.S. VICTORIA

REMOVING MEAT FROM HOLD S.S. BOLIVIA

HOISTING MEAT FROM BETWEEN DECKS

STEAM-LIGHTER RECEIVING CARGO OF MEAT

MARKET HALL, COLD-STORAGE WHARF UPPER THAMES ST.

4 The early frozen meat trade

5 Billingsgate fish market

6a Alexis Soyer

6b Isabella Beeton

6c The kitchen at the Reform Club

7 Cooking technology

(a) The cottager's stove

"The Cottager's Stove,"
WHICH REQUIRES NO BRICKWORK TO FIX IT.

A a Tin Kettle, holding seven quarts.
B an Iron Cover, which forms an additional oven on the top of the hot plate.
C Toaster.   D Saucepan to fit the top.

(b) a gas oven, c. 1855

(c) oil cooking stove, 1897

The Easiest
The Cheapest } Mode of Cooking.
The Cleanest

"Upwards of ONE MILLION of our Stoves in ACTUAL and SUCCESSFUL use at the present time
in all parts of the World!"

THE "ALBIONETTE" Is THE COOKER OF THE FUTURE!

THE "ALBIONETTE"

THE only perfect Oil Cooking Stove, performs every Cooking operation *at one and the same
time* at one-third the cost of COAL or GAS. Heat regulated to a nicety.
Lit and Extinguished in a moment.   "Our Latest and Best."
The result of 25 years' experience.
All other Oil Stoves are now old-fashioned.
Sold by all Stores and Ironmongers. Prices from 27s. to 90s. Illustrated Catalogue free, from
Rippingille's Albion Lamp Co., BIRMINGHAM.
ORIGINAL Inventors of Oil Cookers. Contractors to H.M. Government.
London Depôt and Show-rooms: 65, HOLBORN VIADUCT, E.C.

8a Distress in Coventry

A GALLANT REPLY.

Miss Lucy. "HERE'S WHERE YOU AND I ARE TO SIT, MAJOR!"   *Miss Lucy.* "WHAT—YOU A MAJOR, AND CAN'T STAND FIRE!"
The Major. "BY JOVE!—A—RATHER A WARM PLACE!"   *The Major.* "NOT AT MY BACK, YOU KNOW, MISS LUCY!"

8b A fashionable dinner party

9 Queen Victoria's dinner menu, 27 April 1882

HER MAJESTY'S DINNER

THURSDAY 27TH APRIL 1882

Potages.
A LA TORTUE.   AU PRINTANIER.
A LA CRÈME D'ORGES.

Poissons.
LE SAUMON, SAUCE HOMARD ET PERSIL.
LES FILETS DE SOLES FRITS.

Entrées.
LES RISSOLLES À LA D'ARTOIS.
LES COTELETTES D'AGNEAU AUX HARICOTS VERTS.
LES SUPRÈMES DE VOLAILLE AUX POIS.
LES FILETS DE BOEUF À LA FINANCIÈRE.

Relevés.
ROAST BEEF   ROAST MUTTON.
HAUNCHES OF VENISON.

Rôts.
LES POULETS GRAS   LES CAILLES BARDÉES.

Entremêts.
LES ASPERGES À LA SAUCE.
LES ESCALOPES DE FOIES GRAS À L'ASPIC
LA GELÉE AU VIN DE CHAMPAGNE.
LES CHOUX GLACÉS À LA DUCHESSE

Relevé.
LES SAVARINS AU CURAÇAO, SAUCE ABRICOT.

10 Menu on the *Mauretania*, 1907

CUNARD LINE

R.M.S. "MAURETANIA."

Thursday, December 5th, 1907.

MENU.

Hors d'Œuvres — Varies
Oysters—Half Shell

Green Turtle   Cream of Celery

(Queenstown) Fried Sole—Cardinal Sauce
(Queenstown) Boiled Codfish—Parsley Sauce

Sweetbreads—Toulouse
Noisettes of Mutton—Fines Herbs

Roast Quarters of Lamb (Queenstown)
Sirloin and Ribs of Beef   Roast (Celery-fed) Duckling
Boiled Chicken—Wiltshire Ham

(Queenstown) Brussels Sprouts   Grilled Tomatoes
Stuffed Peppers   Rice
Boiled and Mashed Potatoes

Sorbet—Moselle

Roast Pheasant—Chips—Bread Sauce

George Pudding a la Royal
Apricot Tart   Choux—Parisienne   Bavaroise au Citron

French Ice Cream and Wafers

Dessert

Tea   Coffee

11a A Maypole Dairy shop, Woolwich

11b Sainsbury's new Guildford branch, 1906

12 A jam factory, c. 1900

13a Lyons' first tea shop, 213 Piccadilly, London 1894

13b An ABC tea-room in 1900

14a The Cock Tavern, Fleet Street, c. 1880

14b The Savoy Restaurant, London, c. 1910

15a A young ladies' cookery school, 1880

15b Kitchen of the first British Restaurant, Hull, 1942

16 'Coupons required'. Weekly war rations for two, 1941

Part Three

---※—

1914 to the present day

⇒11⇐
The First World War

'The opening of the twentieth century', wrote Sir Jack Drummond, 'saw malnutrition more rife in England than it had been since the great dearths of medieval and Tudor times.'[1] The statement is almost certainly untrue. The fact is that in the years immediately before the outbreak of war social investigation was for the first time revealing the extent and effects of underfeeding, but appalling as these were, they would have been found greater still in the middle of the nineteenth century if anyone had cared to look or had known what to look for. What is astonishing is that, despite the dietary advances of the intervening years, the nation which went to war in 1914 was still so chronically undernourished that for millions of soldiers and civilians wartime rations represented a higher standard of feeding than they had ever known before.

The disclosures of poverty of Booth, Rowntree, and others had had little direct effect in government circles. More disturbing to Whitehall had been the admission by the Director-General of the Army Medical Service during the Boer War that the Inspector of Recruiting was having great difficulty in obtaining sufficient men of satisfactory physique for service in the forces: over the whole country, 38 per cent of volunteers were rejected for heart afflictions, poor sight and hearing, and bad teeth, and this despite a reduction in the minimum height for recruits to five feet. It was these fears, grounded upon concern for national safety rather than personal health, which led to the appointment of the Inter-Departmental Committee on Physical Deterioration and the beginning of some remedial action. A growing concern for the health of children, fortified by the complaints of teachers that hungry scholars were uneducable, led to the passing of the Education Act (Provision of Meals) in 1906 and the Medical Inspection Act in 1907.[2] By the outbreak of war some 200,000 children were benefiting from free meals, and many were receiving medical and dental treatment at school clinics. Mothers, too, were learning important lessons about the rearing of children through the activities of infant welfare centres which had started on a voluntary basis in St Pancras in 1907: by 1914 there were a hundred or more centres now receiving grants from the Local Government Board.[3] Another significant development was the establishment in

243

1913 of the Medical Research Committee, a body formed with government support to investigate the nature and causes of disease. It had barely begun a major study of rickets when war broke out.

In these measures, as in the introduction of Old Age Pensions in 1908 and of Health and Unemployment Insurance in 1911, the state was accepting a new responsibility towards the most urgent social problems of the day, poverty and disease. Certainly so far as children were concerned it was even beginning to accept the elements of a nutritional policy. Had knowledge not been so primitive, and if war had not intervened, it is likely that far-reaching advances might have been made towards national fitness. But the average general practitioner educated before the First World War had barely heard of proteins, let alone of vitamins, the recent discovery of an obscure Dutch biologist, Pekelharing. The science of nutrition was not yet established as a medical discipline, nor its relationship to disease in general recognized. Only the occurrence of a war involving the feeding of millions of fighting men, and ultimately, of the whole population, for the first time compelled the government to consider the dietary requirements necessary for human efficiency.

In August 1914 neither side expected that food supplies would play a major part in determining the issue of the conflict. Sir William Beveridge has argued that, for the first two years of war, the British government paid practically no attention to food supplies, nor, indeed, was it urgently necessary that it should.[4] Runciman, the President of the Board of Trade in the Liberal government, pursued a policy of 'business as usual' in the firm conviction that food imports would be best ensured by leaving merchants and traders free to obtain supplies in the normal, competitive way: as late as October 1916 he told the House of Commons that there was no need to establish a Ministry of Food or appoint a Food Controller. 'We want to avoid any rationing of our people in food.' Until then, the government had done no more than appoint a Sugar Commission (before the war two-thirds of all sugar consumed in Britain had come from Austria-Hungary) and a Royal Commission on Wheat which had the policy of building up a hidden reserve against emergencies. Four-fifths of Britain's wheat supplies were imported, mainly across the vulnerable Atlantic. Although supplies were not yet seriously interrupted, the price of imported wheat rose sharply from 36s a quarter in August 1914 to 70s by May 1915, well ahead of wage increases. Bread was still the staple diet in many working-class households, and it was rightly considered essential to accumulate stocks of wheat which would cover several weeks' consumption. Much more, of course, was done about military supplies. A new organization for victualling the vast armies was required, and was built up gradually: both the existence and the experience of this organization materially affected the later treatment of the civilian food problem.

244

By June 1916, however, the food situation was causing anxiety as the German submarine campaign threatened supplies. Prices were rising sharply, and complaints of profiteering led to the establishment of a Departmental Committee on Food Prices, which reported in September. Two months later there was established a Food Department at the Board of Trade exercising compulsory powers under the Defence of the Realm Act, which was elevated into ministerial status after the fall of the Asquith government in December. The first Food Controller was Lord Devonport, a businessman whose interests had been mainly in the food trade.[5] His appointment also coincided with the first public admission of the import-ance of expert, scientific opinion in the solution of food problems; a little earlier, a Committee of the Royal Society had been asked to advise on phy-siological matters relating to the war, and to draw up an accurate estimate of the minimum food requirements of the whole population. To do this, the Committee made a comparison with pre-war conditions, and found that over the years 1909–13 home production and imports of food had been sufficient to provide a reasonable margin over national dietary needs – 4,009 kilocalories per man a day against the 3,400 considered necessary for an average day's work, 113 g of protein against 100, and 517 g of carbohydrate against 500. The position when the Committee reported in 1916 was still fairly satisfactory: the food available was suffi-cient to provide the forces with 4,300 kilocalories and the civilian popula-tion with 3,859 per day, although the Committee warned that prices were rising and that steps would have to be taken to ensure an equitable distribution of the available food throughout the population.[6]

What Lord Beveridge describes as the second act of the drama covers the period from the appointment of Lord Devonport as Food Controller in December 1916 to his resignation in May 1917. The government was not yet prepared for effective control: food administration was still in the stage of inviting the public to avoid compulsion by voluntary sacrifices, and Devonport cannot be held solely responsible for all the failures of the period. In one or two directions there were, indeed, successes. The statu-tory powers of the Controller were reinforced, the Wheat Commission was developed and stocks of cereals increased, and their consumption dim-inished by restrictions on brewing and changes in the quality of flour. In April all the flour mills were taken over by the government, a step which indicated that the Wheat Commission could take decisive action when it considered it necessary. But Devonport's schemes for voluntary rationing were ill-conceived and, as Sir Jack Drummond has pointed out, drawn up without scientific advice about nutritional needs. For example, an appeal in February that purchases should be limited to 4 lb of bread, 2½ lb of meat and ¾ lb of sugar a head per week would have ensured only 1,200 to 1,300 kilocalories a day, which would have required a large supplement of foods by then becoming scarce and expensive.[7] In April his scheme for a 'meatless day' was attacked by the scientists on the ground that it would tend to increase the consumption of imported grain, so taking up precious carrying-space. By the spring of 1917 the German U-boat campaign was recognized as a serious threat: it was announced to a stunned House of Commons that two million tons of shipping had been lost and that the country had only three or four weeks' supply of food in stock. This news coincided with the Report of a Royal Commission on Industrial Unrest which emphasized the dangerous effects on morale of rising prices and faulty distribution of foodstuffs. One of the Controller's last actions was to submit to the War Cabinet a scheme setting up the machinery of rationing. He resigned in May, ostensibly because of ill-health induced by overwork and the constant attacks on his policies.

His successor, Lord Rhondda, was a very different Minister. He knew the importance of delegation, and was soon able to build up a brilliant team of assistants who completely reorganized the Department. Act Three of the story, in Lord Beveridge's words:

> witnesses the establishment of complete control over nearly everything eaten and drunk by 40,000,000 persons. The civilian population is catered for like an army; nothing is left to chance or private enterprise. The whole of the essential supplies, imported or home-grown, are bought or requisitioned by the Food Controller at fixed prices; the manufacturers, importers, and distributors become in various ways his agents on commission; they handle and distribute at fixed prices or fixed margins of profit under his directions.[8]

One of Rhondda's early measures was to introduce a bread subsidy, reducing the price of the quartern loaf from 1s to 9d: it was estimated that this saved approximately 2s a week in a working-class budget.[9] The price of milk was also fixed in October 1917, and in the following year a regular quota for all families with young children was ensured.

Civilian rationing began on 1 January 1918 with sugar: after an initial muddle as to whether registration should be on a household or individual basis (decided in favour of the latter), the scheme worked with complete success and assured everyone of ½ lb sugar a week. In the following weeks, however, the queues for meat, margarine, tea, and other foods grew alarmingly, and it became clear to a reluctant government that wider rationing would have to be introduced. In February, London and the home counties were rationed for meat (by value), for butter and margarine (by weight), and by April 1918 the scheme had been extended to the whole country. Not until the summer was control applied to other foodstuffs. The government had been deliberately cautious, half-fearing, it seems, an unfavourable response to the whole idea of rationing. In fact, public confidence was quickly won; the scientific advisers had been right in believing that rationing would be acceptable provided everyone was treated alike and evasion kept to a minimum.

The wartime rations fluctuated a little, but were usually on this scale: sugar, 8 oz per week; butter and margarine (combined), 5 oz; jam, 4 oz; tea, 2 oz; bacon, 8 oz, rising to 16 oz after July 1918. Fresh meat was rationed by price and registration with a particular butcher enforced: there was a famous *Punch* cartoon of the time which showed a labourer and a peer of the realm looking into a butcher's window. 'What's your choice, Guv'nor?' asks the labourer. 'Mine's a couple of sausages.' The peer answers sadly, 'I was just wondering how much shoulder of mutton I could get for fivepence.' Bread was not rationed. A cardinal principle of the scientists was that the people should be able to get as much as they wanted of cheap, energy-giving food to satisfy hunger, and although wartime bread was dark and unattractive[10] it was always available. Potatoes were also unrationed, though hard to come by unless one grew one's own, as many did. Probably the only food which people felt they had enough of was the fat American bacon which began to arrive in the summer of 1918: it was unpleasant stuff, but came at a time when the meat ration had to be reduced and so was endured.

Many civilians also benefited during the war from the greatly increased provision of factory canteens. Ever since the outbreak the government had pressed employers to recognize the importance of adequate nutrition for their workers, and in 1916 an official publication, *Feeding the Munition Worker*, laid down some important general principles:

> There is now an overpowering body of evidence and experience which proves that productive output in regard to quality, amount, and speed is largely dependent upon the physical efficiency and health of the worker. In its turn, such physical fitness is dependent upon nutrition, the purpose of which is to secure the proper development, growth, and energy of the human body. The human body calls for a constant supply of food, first for its growth, for the building up of its tissues and for repair, and secondly, as fuel for the production of heat and energy. Both requirements are indispensable and absolutely necessary. You cannot get health, work, and a reasonable output apart from good nourishing food; with increase in work there must be proportionate increases in quantity and in nutritive value of the food eaten. What is the necessary diet for the worker? Broadly, the answer is a dietary containing – a sufficient quantity of nutritive material in proper proportions, suitably mixed. Easily digestible, appetising, and attractive. Obtainable at low cost.[11]

By the end of the war, a thousand industrial canteens were supplying a million meals a day, and employers were benefiting from increased output, better time-keeping, and a lower sickness rate. The worker, for his part, was enjoying a usually well-cooked meal in surroundings which took him away from the shop-floor and at a price he could afford: a typical menu included soup at 1d, meat and two vegetables for 3d or a 'made' dish for 1½d, pudding at 1d, and tea at ½d.[12] Some dietary-conscious employers even provided free tea at an afternoon break, and free milk for juvenile workers.

Submarine warfare ended in November 1918, but not the Ministry of Food which it had called into life. Like many of the new departments created in 1916, the Ministry lived longer after the war than during it. For two-and-a-quarter more years and under two new Controllers the Ministry wrestled in an unsympathetic world with the difficulties of de-control: there were schemes for feeding Europe, lapses towards re-control during scarcities and rising prices in the summer of 1919 and the spring of 1920. During the rail strike of 1919 the organization of Lord Rhondda again briefly showed its value. 'The rest', says Lord Beveridge, 'is liquidation.'

The important question remains – what were the effects of the first food rationing and control on the British people? 'It does not follow', says Dorothy Hollingsworth, 'that because the British population did not suffer prolonged hunger, as did the civil populations of Germany and Austria, they were unaffected by the eighteen months or more of restricted diet.'[13] Drummond and Wilbraham continued:

> There is clear evidence that the general state of health did decline. The most obvious sign was the lowered resistance to infection. The people could not stand up to the terrible epidemic of influenza which swept across Europe in 1918. They died like flies; the mortality in London in some weeks was as high as 2,500 . . . we can see that vitamin deficiencies had prepared the way.[14]

British food control had three main aims: to maintain supplies, to ensure fair distribution, and to keep prices as low as possible, and its success can be measured by the extent to which it achieved these. As to the maintenance of supplies, Table 26 shows the weekly consumption per head of principal foods between 1909 and 1913 and in each of the war years: the figures represent not the domestic ration but total consumption in all forms, including food eaten outside the home and used in manufactured form. It brings out clearly the differing fortunes of different foods. Consumption per head of flour, bacon, ham, margarine, lard, and potatoes was materially greater in 1918 than before the war; that of butcher's meat, sugar, and butter materially less, by approximately 40 per cent in each case. Fresh milk, which is not shown in the table, was reduced by about one-quarter but more than compensated by increased supplies of dried and condensed milk. By and large, the gains balance the losses: the decline in fresh meat was made good by bacon, the reduction in butter balanced by an increase in margarine or, in 1918, of lard. The important consideration, however, is the calorific value of the diet, and Table 27

248

Table 26 *Weekly consumption of principal foods in the United Kingdom in 1909–13 and in each year from 1914 to 1918*

	1909–13	1914	1915	1916	1917	1918
	lb per head of the population					
Flour	4.28	4.23	4.15	4.33	4.69	4.80
Butcher's meat	2.04	1.97	1.91	1.81	1.68	1.27
Bacon and ham	0.34	0.34	0.42	0.44	0.36	0.46
Butter	0.31	0.30	0.27	0.23	0.20	0.17
Margarine	0.11	0.14	0.20	0.24	0.24	0.22
Lard	0.11	0.11	0.13	0.11	0.08	0.15
Potatoes	3.67	4.29	4.44	4.07	3.84	5.26
Sugar	1.46	1.49	1.58	1.21	1.00	0.93
	lb per 'man'					
Flour	5.13	5.07	5.01	5.22	5.67	5.80
Butcher's meat	2.44	2.36	2.31	2.19	2.01	1.53
Bacon and ham	0.41	0.41	0.50	0.53	0.44	0.56
Butter	0.37	0.36	0.33	0.28	0.24	0.20
Margarine	0.13	0.16	0.24	0.30	0.29	0.27
Lard	0.13	0.13	0.15	0.13	0.10	0.18
Potatoes	4.40	5.12	5.36	4.92	4.65	6.34
Sugar	1.74	1.78	1.90	1.46	1.20	1.11

shows that there was a negligible fall in the total value compared with pre-war days.

Even in 1917, the worst of the war years, there was a small excess over the 3,300 daily kilocalories specified by the Inter-Allied Commission, and at the end of the war the calories per day for all foods were only 2½ per cent below the pre-war level. The margin above requirements in the two last war years was not large, especially when unavoidable waste in preparation and distribution is taken into account, and it is likely that part of the population fell below the theoretical requirement of 3,300 kilocalories. There would, however, have been nothing unusual in this, since, as we have seen, a large part of the working population had been habitually underfed before 1914. To say that the nation's wartime diet was generally sufficient does not, of course, mean that there was no hardship. The forcible change to unfamiliar foods affected the more prosperous classes particularly and there were very few who enjoyed wartime bread or margarine and did not miss the sugar and butter. The important fact was that Britain was fed much better than her enemies, and somewhat better

Table 27 *Calorie value of weekly quantities of food consumed per 'man' in the United Kingdom in 1909–13 and in each year 1914 to 1918*

	1909–13	1914	1915	1916	1917	1918
Flour	8,464	8,365	8,266	8,613	9,355	9,570
Butcher's meat	3,086	2,988	2,891	2,692	2,332	1,710
Bacon and ham	1,036	1,054	1,263	1,336	1,181	1,426
Butter	1,346	1,285	1,177	1,011	845	732
Margarine	458	574	854	1,036	1,022	945
Lard	520	512	608	540	412	708
Potatoes	1,408	1,638	1,715	1,574	1,488	2,029
Sugar	3,236	3,311	3,534	2,716	2,232	2,065
Fresh milk	1,642	1,654	1,654	1,530	1,402	1,219
Other foods	2,895	2,797	2,892	2,879	2,971	3,102
Total weekly calories	24,091	24,178	24,854	23,927	23,240	23,506
Calories per day	3,442	3,454	3,551	3,418	3,320	3,358

than most neutrals, and that the rations, however small, were always available at a price which the poor could afford.

Retail food prices rose during the war, as did all commodity prices, from 100 points in July 1914 to 233 in November 1918. From the statistical evidence it seems that after 1917 the government's policy of food control, price fixing, and measures such as the subsidization of bread held back the rise in food prices compared with other articles, and so brought real benefit to the consumer.[15] The rate of price increase for controlled foods after July 1917 was only one-quarter of the rate before then, and less than half that for any other country. Food control, therefore, by fixing the prices paid to producers and the margins allowed to distributors, had a measurable effect on prices, which were lower than they would have been without it. The best evidence of the effect of the war on standards of living is, however, contained in a Report of a Committee under the chairmanship of Lord Sumner which was published in 1918. Besides furnishing the basis for a new index number of the cost of living, the Committee reached some striking conclusions of general interest:

> We have found in the evidence of budgets of working-class expenditure that in June 1918 the working classes, as a whole, were in a position to purchase food of substantially the same nutritive value as in June 1914. Indeed, our figures indicate that the families of unskilled workmen were slightly better fed at the later date, in spite of the rise in the price of food. This conclusion is more than confirmed by the reports we have obtained from the Medical Officers to the Education Authorities of the great cities. From London it is officially reported,

after inspection of all the children entering school, that 'the percentage of children found in a poorly nourished condition is considerably less than half the percentage in 1913'. A similar improvement is shown by the figures furnished by Birmingham, Bolton, Bradford, Bristol, Glasgow, and Nottingham. The general impression, especially of the poorer children, is favourable, and the view that parents are now better able to give their children the necessary food is borne out by the information we have received as to the number of meals provided to 'necessitous children' by the local education authorities. It is only in very exceptional cases that education authorities are supplying anything like as many meals as before the war; in most places the number has fallen to about half (Nottingham, Stoke, and Sheffield) and a quarter (London and Bolton), and in some places (as in Birmingham and Liverpool) it is hardly necessary to provide meals at all. The last available figures for England and Wales, those for 1917, compared with the estimated number of 1914, show a decline by about four-fifths in the country as a whole.[16]

Both contemporary observation and subsequent historical research appear to confirm this optimistic view of the effects of the war on civilian health. Commenting on changes in working-class life in Salford from the vantage-point of his mother's corner shop, Robert Roberts noted that:

By late 1916 abject poverty began to disappear from the neighbourhood. Children looked better fed. There were far fewer prosecutions for child neglect. Well before the end of the war the number of pupils taking free dinners at our school fell to one-fifth of the pre-1914 figures.[17]

Further, a recent study by J.M. Winter has contrasted Britain's experience of the effects of the war on public health with that of her European allies and enemies. In Britain, he argues, mortality rates among the civilian, working-class population fell during the war, and there was a reduction of 20 per cent in infant mortality, partly due to higher standards of maternal and child care but, importantly, to 'a major improvement in nutrition after 1914'.[18] The Great War, with its unparalleled loss of human life, undoubtedly stimulated a new concern for the numbers and health of children – in the words of R.M. Titmuss, 'the next generation of recruits'.[19] A rapid increase in infant welfare centres, a doubling in the number of health visitors from 600 to 1,355, and improvements in the training of midwives all contributed to the saving of lives of mothers and babies.

This paradox of improved living standards during the war was not, of course, due primarily to food rationing. The main factor was the virtual disappearance of unemployment, coupled with the extensive employment of women at relatively well-paid work and the separation allowance system. The wage-earning classes, for reasons unconnected with food control, had incomes more regular and better adjusted to their means than ever before. That there was food for them to buy, that it was fairly distributed, and that they were protected from exploitation of scarcity, was

251

the achievement of food control. If the Great Depression marks the first important step by the working classes of England towards material comfort, the First World War, for all its horrors and miseries, marks the second.

The commonly accepted view, derived largely from William Beveridge's account in 1928, has been critical of British food policy during the first total war – claiming that the country was badly unprepared for a threat to her food supplies, that little serious thought was given to the increasing shortages until 1916, that the first Food Controller was a disastrous appointment, and that food rationing, which began only in January 1918, was too little, too late. Dr Margaret Barnett has recently offered a convincingly argued, optimistic reassessment of all these, and other, assumptions about British bungles on the food front.[20] She shows that food policy in time of war had been the subject of a Royal Commission since 1905, and that Asquith, the Prime Minister, had created five *ad hoc* committees concerned with food supply as early as January 1915, which had successfully built up stocks of grain and sugar. Although it has been usual to criticize the campaigns for voluntary restraint, the strong opposition to suggestions of rationing and price controls, both of which were having bad effects in Germany, could only gradually be overcome and the nation won round to the idea of compulsion. Ultimately, under Lord Rhondda, an efficient bureaucracy of 26,000 civil servants was built up, rationing was made acceptable, and British agricultural output was greatly expanded – in the case of wheat a 59 per cent increase over 1914. These policies enabled Britain to survive a dangerous period without social revolution and with generally improved standards of civilian health.

Notes

1 Drummond, J.C. and Wilbraham, Anne (1957) *The Englishman's Food. A history of five centuries of English diet*, revised and with a new chapter by Dorothy Hollingsworth, 403.
2 See pp. 187–8.
3 McCleary, G.F. (1933) *The Early History of the Infant Welfare Movement*.
4 Beveridge, Sir William H. (1928) *Economic and Social History of the World War: British Food Control*.
5 He was Chairman of the International Stores. The Controller's wide powers included regulation of prices and methods of food production, the power to seize stocks and prevent waste.
6 *The Food Supply of the United Kingdom* (prepared originally as a confidential document, 9 December 1916, later published as Cd. 8421 in 1917).
7 The Royal Society pointed out how unrealistic these rations were when average consumption of bread in working-class households was around 10 lb a head a week.
8 Beveridge, op. cit., 2–3.

9   Hunt, Sandra *The Changing Place of Bread in the British Diet in the Twentieth Century*, series of unpublished research papers sponsored by the Rank Prize Funds (Brunel University), 'The First World War', 33–4.
10 The first 'war bread' was introduced in November 1916, with an extraction rate of 76 per cent compared with the normal 70–72 per cent. In February 1917 extraction of up to 81 per cent was allowed, plus a compulsory admixture of 5 per cent of flour of barley, oats, or rye. At the time of greatest scarcity in March and April 1918 extraction rose to 92 per cent. Soya, barley, and potato flour were also mixed with it.
11 Quoted in Curtis-Bennett, Sir Noel (1949) *The Food of the People, being the History of Industrial Feeding*, 211.
12 Proud, Dorothea (1916) *Industrial Welfare*.
13 Drummond and Wilbraham, op. cit., 439.
14 ibid., 529.
15 Bowley, A. L. (1921) *Prices and Wages in the United Kingdom, 1914–1920*, 35 et seq.
16 Report of the Sumner Committee on the Working Classes' Cost of Living (1918), Cd. 8980, para. 51.
17 Roberts, Robert (1971) *The Classic Slum*, 203.
18 Winter, J.M. (1977) 'The impact of the First World War on civilian health in Britain', *Economic History Review* (2nd Series) XXX (3), 499.
19 Titmuss, R.M. (1958) *Essays on the Welfare State*, 80.
20 Barnett, L. Margaret (1985) *British Food Policy during the First World War*.

≫12≪

Between the wars

The First World War demonstrated more clearly than any previous conflict the importance of adequate food supplies. Although the dietary needs of armies had long been recognized, the 'Kaiser's War' was the first to involve civilian populations no less than armies and the first to depend importantly on the civilian population's industrial efficiency and morale. 'The food question ultimately decided the issue of this war,' wrote Lloyd George at the end of the conflict. It was a justifiable exaggeration, for military experts regarded as one of the major causes of the Italian rout at Caporetto the reduction in the cereal ration of the Italian soldier some months earlier, and knew that the collapse of the Central Powers in the autumn of 1918 was due in part to the sheer hunger and fatigue of German workers and fighting men.

For another reason, too, the war had given a new importance to diet as a factor in national health. When in 1917–18 conscription involved the medical examination of two-and-a-half million men of military age, the results were summed up as follows:

> Of every nine men of military age in Great Britain, on the average three were perfect, fit, and healthy; two were on a definitely inferior plane of health and strength, whether from some disability or some failure of development; three were incapable of undergoing more than a very moderate degree of physical exertion, and could almost (in view of their age) be described with justice as physical wrecks; and the remaining man was a chronic invalid with a precarious hold on life.[1]

Altogether 41 per cent of men, supposedly in the prime of life, were graded C3 and unfit for service. By contrast a sample of 1,000 Cambridge undergraduates drawn from the middle classes showed 70 per cent to be above 'full stature' and only 10 per cent in Grades III and IV, equivalent to C3.[2] In the desire of politicians at the end of the war to construct a new world and a Britain 'fit for heroes' there was implicit, therefore, the recognition of a responsibility for adequate nutrition: for building health as well as houses and schools, and for raising the general standards of comfort of the generation which had suffered so much.

Food policy was also significant in 1918 for another reason. During the war British agriculture, after years of neglect, had been suddenly called upon to raise output in order to reduce precious carrying-space for essential imports; under government subsidization and price-fixing, the production of wheat and meat, as well as of potatoes, vegetables, and dairy produce had been greatly expanded to raise total food output by a third. What was to be the future of farming in peacetime? Was it to be allowed to return to the decay of pre-war days, which would inevitably follow the re-establishment of a free import policy, or should the government, for strategic, economic, and nutritional reasons, now accept a responsibility for the maintenance of a healthy home agriculture? This, it seems, had been in the mind of Lloyd George when he delivered his famous address on 'The Future of England' in November 1918:

> Agriculture was almost completely neglected by the state. During recent years very, very little was done – more, perhaps, than used to be, but very little. It was just like feeding a giant with a teaspoon. In 1913, £300,000,000 worth of the products of the soil were imported from abroad which could have been produced here.

In the post-war conditions of declining foreign markets for British manufactures, the burden of paying for food imports became an added reason for increasing domestic production. To farming enthusiasts like Sir Charles Fielding, the possibility even dawned of producing at home

> practically the whole of our food requirements. We have the area; we have the good land; we have the suitable climate; we have ample population, and, after we get into full swing, we can produce as cheaply as other countries. All that is needed is the enterprise, organization, goodwill, work, and inducement to get such a production from our own soil that this island will be independent of other nations, safe against submarines, and with a foreign trade balance in its favour.[3]

Britain's food supplies had, as we have seen, come to depend mainly on imports, and any hopes of returning to a policy of self-sufficiency were now utopian. Already by 1870 farmers had taken almost as much land into cultivation as was profitable under a free-trade régime; after the agricultural depression of the 1880s, the area had begun to shrink. Fortunately it had not been merely more of the same kinds of food that the consumer demanded, but different foods. If the diet of the mid-nineteenth century had remained unchanged, the growth in numbers would simply have meant an increased demand for wheat and the coarser foodstuffs, which English agriculture was ill-adapted to supply, but the rise in real incomes per head caused important changes in the type of food consumed. Over the whole period from 1866 to 1936 it is likely that real wages rose between 70 and 90 per cent,[4] a rise not uniformly distributed over the period, but concentrated into the years 1870–96 and those after 1924. Increased purchasing power resulted in a growing consumption of the 'protective' or health foods at the expense of, or in addition to, the cheaper cereals or energy foods: meat, butter, eggs, fruit, and vegetables were the foods for which demand increased most rapidly and these were precisely the foods which the British farmer could produce more easily in competition with agriculturists overseas. He enjoyed a clear advantage in producing meat of high quality; he had a similar advantage for most vegetables and temperate fruits. Even liquid-milk production proved capable of great expansion because, although *per capita* consumption grew only slightly, the total amount required almost doubled with population increase.

The other important feature of the food market between the wars, in addition to the change towards a more varied diet, was the improved service demanded by the consumer, particularly in respect of regularity and quality of supplies. The fruit-eating season, for example, was first extended by the importation of cheap tropical fruits, and later by the shipment of refrigerated apples and pears from the southern hemisphere. Eggs now came from an increasing number of foreign countries, which helped to relieve seasonal fluctuations in price. Such developments tended to make the consumer more critical in his demands for regular delivery and stable prices. He also came to expect supplies of uniformly high quality. Here, too, imports, because they were more easily graded, helped to educate the public, while the distributors, both wholesalers and retailers, who came to handle a far larger proportion of total food supplies than formerly, learned the convenience of dealing in dependable brands, of being able to repeat orders and receive the exact quantity and quality desired.

After the war a new phase of competition set in, more intense than before. In Canada, Australia, and the Argentine a vast expansion of wheat acreage occurred, while the invention of chilling now made it possible for the Argentine to export beef of a quality only slightly inferior to the finest British meat. New Zealand similarly expanded her lamb and butter exports at ever lower prices, while Denmark competed with butter, eggs, and bacon. The British farmer was forced to specialize, even more than before, on milk, eggs, fruit, and vegetables, where he could still enjoy a market protected by distance: if he continued to grow crops or rear stock in competition with imports he was forced to become more efficient, to economize labour, and to fertilize and mechanize far more than in the past.

The financial crisis of 1931 finally brought the policy of agricultural drift to an end. In the next year Britain abandoned free trade; tariffs and quantitative restrictions were imposed on a wide range of agricultural imports, while at home subsidies and marketing schemes helped the British farmer to survive a period of acute world depression. Imperial pre-

Table 28 *Annual average net imports into the United Kingdom (thousand cwt)*

Year	Sugar	Wheat and wheat flour	All grain and meal (excl. wheat)	Meat	Butter	Cheese
1861–5	11,814	34,652	25,585	1,553	1,031	771
1871–5	16,943	50,495	47,067	3,134	1,368	1,349
1891–5	28,288	96,583	78,475	10,437	2,409	2,150
1911–13	37,201	119,666	91,027	21,500	4,148	2,360
1925–9	36,200	109,500	69,472	31,043	6,600	3,020
1932–6	28,996	112,702	91,043	30,902	8,381	2,885

Table 29 *Index of volume of food imports*

Year	Meat (including bacon)	Dairy products	Eggs	Wheat	Vegetables	Fruit	All
1927–9	100	100	100	100	100	100	100
1930	106	109	107	99	101	99	105
1931	117	123	104	110	156	120	117
1932	112	127	84	96	142	118	111
1933	101	133	76	103	87	107	107
1934	94	142	81	95	81	88	104
1935	92	137	84	92	88	111	103
1936	92	138	102	92	100	88	105
1937	95	136	103	89	86	86	103
1937 Empire	144	161	63	130	136	174	142
Foreign	70	114	112	54	73	47	79

ference was also introduced to favour imports from Colonial and Commonwealth countries. These changes had important effects on the value of Britain's food imports, and on the sources from which they came (Table 29). It is clear that the tariff changes and the adoption of a policy of agricultural protection were, by 1939, having a steadying effect on the level of imports, at least preventing a flooding of the British market and noticeably increasing the proportion of imports coming from the Empire at the expense of foreign countries.

The British farmer's growing concentration on what were described as 'health protective' foods, aided by government subsidies and grading and marketing schemes as well as by the commercial development of canning and refrigeration, resulted in marked increases in the consumption of these foods between the wars. Between 1922 and 1936 the area under vegetables (not including potatoes) increased from 126,517 to 226,815 acres, the poultry population rose from 47 million in 1924 to 90 million ten years later, while the dairy herd increased by 36 per cent between 1913 and 1937.[5] Paying less than ever for his primary foods the consumer could devote more and more to the 'luxury' items – in fact, eggs at 1s a dozen and milk at 3d a pint were no longer luxuries for most people; at the same time technology made it possible to buy fresh apples and canned peas all the year round. No doubt the publicity given to 'the newer knowledge of nutrition' and the propaganda campaigns such as 'Eat More Fruit' helped in the process, though it is likely that the public would have eaten more of these foods, even before the discovery of the vitamins, had they been able to afford them.

The foods the British farmer produced were no longer the staple and bulky ones. For these, our reliance on imports was greater than ever: immediately before the outbreak of the Second World War we imported considerably more than half our total food supplies, providing more than two-thirds of the calories consumed. Between ten and fifteen food ships docked in English ports every day, bringing some twenty-two million tons of food and animal feeding-stuffs in the course of a year. Table 30 shows the totals of food consumed before the war and the proportions home-produced and imported.

In the manufacture and distribution of foodstuffs the most important change between the wars was the development of large-scale concerns which absorbed a growing share of the market. Tate & Lyle, for example, came to control a very high percentage of the sugar refining of the country; Marsh & Baxter by 1939 cured some 40 per cent of the bacon consumed in the country; milling firms and tea-blending firms, few in number, controlled their respective trades almost completely; in milk distribution United Dairies controlled, directly and indirectly, a large share of London's trade, while a few importers handled all the meat imported from South America. It is likely that food control during the First World War assisted the early growth of these large, semi-monopolistic enterprises[6] – certainly such firms as Lever Bros, Joseph Rank Ltd, and Spiller Ltd (flour millers), and Union Cold Storage (meat importers) all showed remarkable expansion in the years immediately after 1918.

Despite what was by now a steady decline in *per capita* consumption, bread still held a sentimental place as the staple of English diet, and flour-milling was an outstanding example of increasing industrial concentration in response to changes in the economic climate and in consumer demand.

Table 30 *Pre-war food consumption in the United Kingdom showing the percentages home-produced and imported*

Commodity group	Total (in thousands of tons)	Percentage home-produced	Percentage imported
	Annual average 1934–8		
Flour from wheat and other cereal products	4,428	12	88
Fats (butter, lard, margarine)	905	7	93
Sugar	2,184	18	82
Meat (including bacon)	2,707	45	55
Fish (including canned) (edible weight)	523	85	15
Eggs and egg products	500	60	40
Milk (liquid)	4,579	100	—
Condensed milk	260	70	30
Dried milk	35	61	39
Cheese	185	24	76
Potatoes	3,700	94	6
Other vegetables	2,715	92	8
Fruit (including tomatoes)	2,406	26	74

At the end of the First World War 300 large mills, mainly situated at the ports, produced 90 per cent of flour while 375 small mills were responsible for 10 per cent; one-third of total output was produced by the 'big three' millers – Rank and Spiller, each with 10–12 per cent of the market, and the Co-operative Wholesale Society with around 10 per cent. Rationalization of the industry was further encouraged by the establishment of the Millers' Mutual Association in 1929, and by the outbreak of the Second World War a series of mergers had given the 'big three' 66 per cent of total output: Rank was now the clear leader with 24–30 per cent of the market.[7] The mass-produced factory loaf, mechanically wrapped from the 1920s and sliced from the 1930s, was already on the way.

Large food manufacturers could also benefit from vertical integration, controlling their own supplies of raw materials and their own retail outlets. By 1939 Vestey's meat combine controlled more than 2,000 shops run under a variety of names; but it was in the grocery trades that concentration went furthest. In 1914 three chain grocers – Thomas Lipton Ltd, the Home and Colonial Stores, and the Maypole Dairy Co. – each had more than 500 branches, but at least 70 per cent of total retail trade was still in the hands of small shopkeepers. The inter-war years witnessed intense competition for the mass market of consumers, most of whom were enjoying increased purchasing power and able to afford a wider range of foodstuffs. The family firm of Sainsbury, aiming at the growing lower middle class of southern England, expanded from 123 branches in 1919 to 244 twenty years later: a typical publicity campaign in 1932 offered 'Back bacon, tea and Australian butter all at 8d a pound'.[8] The battle for the working-class customer was fought out between giant multiples to the accompaniment of mergers and takeovers. Ultimately, Lipton, the Home and Colonial, Meadow Dairy, and the Maypole all merged to form the Home and Colonial group, with over 3,000 branches, though each continued to trade under its own name. Its chief competitor was the International Tea group formed from mergers of a number of smaller companies. These inter-war multiples now dealt in a much wider range of foods than formerly – in fact, became distinguishable from the traditional family grocer mainly by their cut prices and aggressive salesmanship. Even the 'conservative' co-operative societies adopted some of the new marketing techniques, expanding their membership to eight-and-a-half million by 1939 and holding over 20 per cent of total retail trade in groceries and provisions. By then, they and the multiples controlled almost half of the nation's grocery business.[9]

The retail of food had become one of the biggest aspects of the nation's business, absorbing, according to Colin Clark, £1,305,000,000 a year, or nearly one-third of the national income.[10] Despite the growing share of the chain stores, there was still room for 80,000 grocers, 40,000 butchers, 30,000 bakers, and 30,000 greengrocers, the great majority of whom were single-shop owners: in the retail of fish, fruit, vegetables, and bread, the little shop was still all-important. The function of the small man was changing, however. He had less independence than formerly: more and more he was merely an agent selling the branded, packeted goods supplied by the large firms, often at a price which he was powerless to determine. Most small grocers, for example, no longer blended their own teas or weighed out sugar, butter, and salt. Instead they took their supplies from the tea blenders, the manufacturers of breakfast cereals, or the sugar refiners: only with eggs, bacon, and a few other articles could they now fix their own prices, and here the tendency was to sell at a low margin (sometimes, in the case of sugar, below cost) in order to attract custom for branded goods on which the margin was higher. A similar change was noticeable in the role of the meat retailer, who often ceased to be a butcher in the proper sense of the word and became a mere retailer buying joints from an importer or jobber. Many dairymen became agents of United Dairies, bound contractually not to sell above UD prices: bakers found their selling prices fixed by local agreements enforced by heavy sanctions.

In these circumstances of declining price competition, retailers tended to concentrate more on advertisement, on 'modern' shop fronts, and on services to the customer such as roundsman delivery and orders taken out in response to telephone calls.

All this made provisioning for the housewife very much easier. The advertising of branded goods meant that she could count on standard quality, while the growing sale of foods ready for the table or near to table-readiness simplified cooking problems and brought wider variety. The complicated processes of making custard, caramel, blancmange, jellies, and other sweets were reduced to a single short operation by the use of prepared powders. Porridge, the almost universal middle-class breakfast dish, could now be made in two minutes according to the Quick Quaker Oats recipe, but even so American-style cereals, taken with milk and sugar, soon rivalled the traditional food. The early products 'Force' and 'Grape-Nuts' were followed by a wide variety of 'corn flakes' and grains of wheat, rice, and barley 'puffed' by being fired at high velocity through a sort of air-gun. The range of canned foods introduced by Heinz, Crosse & Blackwell, and others also expanded enormously. When the war ended soup, salmon, corned beef, and Californian fruits were the only choice, but by the 1930s almost every kind of domestic and foreign fruit, meat, game, fish, and vegetable was available in tins at prices which many people could afford, at least occasionally. Canning provided a good outlet for English growers of peas and soft fruits, but what most people wanted was imported salmon and peaches for Sunday tea. Another sign of change, and of the improving standard of living, was in the enormous increase in the amount and variety of chocolate and confectionery sold to children and adults: before the war bars of chocolate had been 'plain' or 'milk', but subsequently a bewildering variety of creams and fillings appeared in 2d bars and 6d boxes, widely advertised and continually changing in order to stimulate demand. Potato crisps, at first merely a novelty, also became an important addition to the range of 'snack' foods; they were originally imported from France, but were now made in England and over a million packets were sold in 1928. People were also increasingly disposed towards foods which could claim some special 'health' property, especially when the now-fashionable 'vitamins' were invoked. Health-food shops (often connected with Theosophy, New Thought, or middle-class Socialism), selling exotic nuts, dried fruits, herb teas, breakfast cereals, grated carrots, vegetable cooking-fats, and so on came to be seen in the larger towns from about 1923 onwards. But the English public never became as nutrition-conscious as the American. Most people thought that 'health foods' and their advocates were slightly 'cranky' and were content to supplement their diet with a nourishing drink such as Bovril, which had a great success after its advertising campaign picturing historical giants from Julius Caesar

261

through Michelangelo to Cecil Rhodes: their secret, apparently, was that they were never tired – hence 'Don't get tired – drink Bovril'. If one still awoke fatigued in the morning, one was suffering from 'night-starvation', which could be remedied by taking a cup of Horlick's malted milk as a nightcap. It was a reflection of the increasing well-being of the nation, as well of changes in women's fashions, that the cult of 'slimming' appeared as a new phenomenon in the 1920s; some people began to cut down their consumption of bread and potatoes, and to eat a 'roughage' breakfast food which would give the vitamins full play.[11]

The sale of branded goods at fixed retail prices probably helped rather than hindered the co-operative societies between the wars, since the 'stores' customer still received dividends on the packet of Kellogg's Corn Flakes or the tin of Heinz Baked Beans. The societies continued to expand their share of total retail trade until, by 1939, they controlled 25 per cent of milk distribution and 40 per cent of the butter, 20 per cent of the tea, sugar, and cheese consumed in the country. Of other foods their share was not so great – 10 per cent of the bread and bacon, 8 per cent of the eggs, and 5 per cent of the meat eaten – while their share of vegetables, fruit, and fish was negligible.[12] Co-operation was losing something of its earlier social purpose, and for many members simply represented a convenient alternative to dealing at the local chain store; middle-class wives accepted the Co-op's milk delivery service but would not have entered the 'stores'. The fact remains that a growing section of the working class drew its food supplies from the societies, benefiting from both the high quality and the dividend which they received there.

Another important development was the growth, among all social classes except the lowest, of 'eating out'. Hotels and restaurants had suffered from wartime rationing and it was some years after 1918 before they revived. Writing in 1929, André Simon said, 'We are happily approaching the greatly to be desired stage when the art of good living is again receiving proper attention. Today, barely ten years after the Great War, we are not yet back to the pre-war level, but on our way there.'[13] Gourmets would doubt whether the heights of Edwardian cuisine were ever recaptured.

Not until some of the DORA restrictions were removed in 1921 did restaurant life really begin again. The Licensing Act of that year, permitting drinks to be served after 11 p.m. provided a sandwich was ordered with them, was seen as a concession to gaiety by a war-weary population, for many of whom war had at least brought higher profits and earnings than they had ever enjoyed before. The jazz atmosphere and the financial boom of the early 1920s were conducive to public entertainment and display, and one thing which many people wanted to do after years of austerity was to dine and wine lavishly. Restaurants like the Savoy were quick to see the advantage of combining eating with the dancing craze by installing a dance-floor in the middle of the crowded tables. Such attractions as dancing and cabaret turns made fashionable the habit of dining out, which had still been unusual for Englishwomen before the war. 'Private' drinking at bottle-parties and night-clubs was another popular way of evading the licensing restrictions: night-clubs like the 'Kit-Kat' club and Kate Meyrick's group – the '43', the 'Manhattan', and the 'Silver Slipper' – achieved an international fame partly from the distinguished and even royal clientele, and partly from the frequency of police raids and closures. All were expensive and essentially metropolitan; their middle-class, provincial counter-parts were the 'road-houses' which appeared in the suburbs and on the by-pass roads in the 1930s. They were elaborate inns which provided meals and drinks, dancing, a night's lodging, and an absence of awkward questions; in summer, tennis and swimming were alternative attractions. Every few miles on the Great West Road notices invited motorists to 'Swim, Dine, and Dance', but road-houses were also to be found on the outskirts of northern industrial towns, built in the contemporary concrete idiom and shrouded in an aura of local mystery and rumour. Many had a brief existence and were already shut down by 1939. The motorcar which had called them into existence also enabled people to drive out in the evenings and at the week-ends to village inns and the large, new public houses which dotted the arterial roads and roundabouts. Their bright, mock-Tudor or 'Modern Movement' lounges brought a new standard of comfort to the retailing of beer, which contrasted favourably with the Victorian gloom of most town pubs. In fact, beer consumption, which had been strictly controlled as part of the war effort, never returned to its high pre-war level. Heavy drinking in a single-sex, 'spit and sawdust' environment was increasingly uncommon or restricted to certain regions or occupations, many of which became casualties of depression and unemployment: at the worst time, in the early 1930s, national beer consumption was little more than one-third that of the late nineteenth century.

London restaurants may never have recovered quite the extravagance of Edwardian menus, but still provided very high standards of cuisine at prices which were not impossible for middle-class diners. In 1924 a 'good food guide' by Elizabeth Montizambert categorized London restaurants into four groups by price. The most expensive, offering table d'hôte menus at 5s to 10s, included the great hotels such as the Ritz, Savoy, and Carlton and famous restaurants like the Café Royal, whose luncheon cost 5s 6d and dinner 7s 6d. The second category (luncheon 3s 6d–5s) was represented by the leading restaurants of pre-war days – Frascati's, Gatti's, Hatchett's, the Trocadero, and the Criterion. Four- or five-course menus for 2s 6d were available at category three restaurants (Reggiori's, the Chantecler) and eatable meals at 1s 6d in category four – 'very cheap'.[14]

The spread of eating out to the lower middle classes was one of the important social phenomena of the time. It was due largely to the development of 'popular' catering by Lyons, the ABC, and others, at whose cafés a well-cooked meal could be had in comfortable surroundings, often to the accompaniment of a 'palm court' orchestra and for little more than a shilling. The London 'Corner Houses' set a more exotic standard in their 'Brasseries' with continental dishes like kebab and moussaka on the menu, while the 'Popular Café' was probably the first to allow its customers unlimited helpings on its famous 1s 6d teas. In 1929 J. Lyons and Co. declared a record profit of £909,000, and served seventeen-and-a-half million customers in its three London Corner Houses: there was little evidence here of the depression which had overtaken other regions of the country. The most expensive item on the Corner House tariff was lobster mayonnaise at 2s 6d, but hors d'œuvres ranged from 4d–9d, soups were 5d, whitebait 9d, mutton cutlet 8d, roast beef 11d, ices from 3d upwards, and meringue Chantilly 5d.[15] These were not exorbitant prices for an occasional treat in what passed for luxurious surroundings, but for daily fare with a more limited choice the ordinary Lyons' tea-shops were cheaper still. By the 1930s waiters and 'nippies' were giving way to the cafeteria, an American self-help idea which speeded up service and allowed the customer to see exactly what he was getting: big stores like Woolworth's installed them as a convenience for shoppers, although it was some time before they were generally accepted. Milk bars, on the other hand, were an immediate success. They were introduced during the 'Drink More Milk' campaign, and their chromium-plated interiors, high bar-counter stools, and glamorously named 'shakes' appealed particularly to the younger generation who could even find milk manly when served in this way. Milk bars and snack bars, cafeterias, cinema restaurants, and dance-hall buffets all contributed to a significant growth in eating outside the home for people whose horizons had previously been bounded by the public house and the fish-and-chip shop.

By contrast the dietary standards of the wealthier classes probably declined somewhat between the wars. This was partly a consequence of choice and partly of necessity. The taste for the solid, endless repasts of Victorian days was changing in favour of shorter, lighter meals more suited to the accelerated pace of life and to the new knowledge of nutrition which was beginning to influence people's tastes. The traditional dinner tended to be reserved for Lord Mayors' Banquets and similar survivals from a more leisured age, but at home the better-off now ate a mere three- or four-course lunch and dinner, and a breakfast on which the American influence was beginning to be noticeable. Grapefruit or breakfast cereals were increasingly popular alternatives to porridge, and not always followed by bacon and eggs; later in the day salads and fruit were displacing

boiled vegetables and baked puddings, often with good effects on diges-
tions and waist-lines. But the change was also partly one of necessity. The
middle class of the inter-war years, swollen by the growth of professional,
executive, and clerical functions, was larger than it had been in 1914, but
relatively poorer. The main growth came from the lower end of the
class – from the so-called 'white-collar' workers who increased from 18.7
per cent of the total labour force in 1911 to 23 per cent in 1931; by 1939
they comprised at least a quarter of all employed people.[16] Wartime and
post-war inflation had hit hardly those living on fixed incomes and
salaries, while greatly increased income tax cut earned incomes and profits substantially. Many middle-class families were having to economize on
domestic service, private education, and other luxuries which had formerly characterized the class. Changed expenditure patterns were resulting in a larger proportion of income devoted to food and other necessities,
less to the luxuries which had once made bourgeois life so pleasant. The
gulf between the classes was less wide and more easily bridged than it had
been, but the differences in standards of comfort had narrowed also.

Perhaps the greatest change was for the middle-class housewife who,
with the growing scarcity and cost of living-in domestic servants, now had
to do her own cooking and at least some housework. Mrs C.S. Peel, the
doyenne of writers on domestic economy, believed that the Great War had
brought great changes in the role of women both inside and outside the
home:

> During the years of the Great War many of us became very clever, and learned
> much which will be of permanent value to us. . . . Not only have we learned to
> use food with more care, but we have learned to economize fuel and labour.
> . . . Women are so disinclined to become domestic servants, and demand such
> high wages when persuaded to do so, that householders find themselves
> obliged to adopt labour-saving apparatus.[17]

Mrs Peel then proceeded to discuss 'the house of the future' where there
would be no basement kitchen and meals would be served through a but-
tery hatch directly into the dining-room. The kitchen would be tiled or
bricked so that it might be entirely hosed down:

> the floor being very slightly slanted and furnished with a gutter to take off the
> water. In the servantless house the scullery is abolished and replaced by a
> double sink in the kitchen: a 'cook's cabinet' such as is used in America takes
> the place of the open dresser, and all cooking is done either by gas or
> electricity.[18]

At the top of the social scale the pattern was still set by the monarchy.
Buckingham Palace had experienced 'austerity' during the war like every
other catering institution – meat could not be served at lunch, though

there were omelettes, scrambled eggs, rice and asparagus dishes and vegetable pie for the staff; mock cutlets of lamb and chicken deceived guests
by their size, but were made up of whatever scraps could be found.
Edwardian plenty never returned to Court. The big banquet given for
President Wilson at Christmas 1918 comprised ten courses instead of the
usual fourteen, and this became the pattern in subsequent years. In any
case, George V was no epicure. Breakfast was a standing order – on five
days a week egg, crisp streaky bacon and fish (trout, plaice, or sole); on
Saturdays and Sundays he had grilled sausages as well, except when Yar-
mouth bloaters were in season. The menu never varied except in sickness.
The wedding breakfast of the Duke and Duchess of York in 1923 was more
ambitious, though still only eight courses – half what it would have been
twenty years earlier. This meal lasted an hour. When the present Queen
was married in 1947 the wedding breakfast consisted of only four modest
courses, such as any suburban hotel might have provided, and was all
over within twenty minutes.[19]

If the dietary standards of the few tended to decline between the wars,
there is little doubt that those of the many rose. As Table 31 shows, a comparison of *per capita* consumption before the war with 1924–8 and 1934
shows substantial increases in practically every food, greatest in the case
of fruit, vegetables, butter, and eggs, least in that of potatoes and wheat
flour. In each case the rate of increase between 1924–8 and 1934 was
greater than in the previous fifteen years. In nutritional terms, the average
diet of 1934 showed an increase in total calories of 6 per cent compared
with pre-war: carbohydrate and vegetable protein fell, but animal protein
rose slightly, and there was a 25 per cent increase in animal fats. This,
together with the increased consumption of fruit and fresh vegetables,
represented a substantially increased intake of essential vitamins and
mineral salts. On these grounds, the 'average' diet of the 1930s was 'better'
than ever before.

Another cause for optimism was that it was not only 'better' but cheaper.
In 1934 the nation spent on food £1,075 a year out of a total national
income of £3,750, or 9s per head per week out of an average income of 30s.
Not only did food expenditure absorb less than one-third of personal
income but, compared with the nineteenth century, the proportion of
income devoted to the carbohydrate foods was far less, and that to protein
foods substantially more. In 1934 meat and fish accounted for 32 per cent
of food expenditure, eggs, milk, and cheese for 18 per cent, while bread
and cereals accounted for only 9 per cent. That twice as much was now
spent on fruit than on bread was a remarkable comment on the generally
improved standard of living (Table 32).

The 'average' consumer was, however, still a statistical abstraction in
the years between the wars. How widely wages could vary was demon-

Table 31 *Estimated annual consumption per head of certain foods in the United Kingdom at three periods*[20]

	1909–13	1924–8		1934	
		Quan-tity	As per-centage of 1909–13	Quan-tity	As per-centage of 1909–13
	lb	lb		lb	
Fruit	61	91	149	115	188
Vegetables (other than potatoes)	60	78	130	98	164
Butter	16	16	100	25	157
Eggs	No. 104	No. 120	115	No. 152	146
Cheese	7	9	128	10	143
Margarine	6	12	200	8	133
Sugar	79	87	110	94	119
Meat	135	134	99	143	106
Potatoes	208	194	93	210	101
Wheat flour	211	198	94	197	93

Table 32 *Estimated quantities and retail values of food supplies of the United Kingdom in 1934*

Commodity	Total supply	Total retail value	Per head per week	Per head per week
	Thousand tons	Million £	oz	d
Total meat	3,001	294.5	44.0	29.1
Fish	302	52.0	13.2	5.1
Bread	3,000	51.0	44.0	5.0
Flour	1,850	32.0	27.1	3.1
Other cereals	286	5.0	4.2	0.5
	Millions		No.	
Eggs	7,156	42.0	2.9	4.1
	Thousand tons		oz	
Egg products	41	2.5	0.6	0.2

Table 32 *Continued*

Commodity	Total supply	Total retail value	Per head per week	Per head per week
	Million gals	*Million £*	*pints*	*d*
Milk, fresh	860	89.0	2.8	8.7
	Thousand tons		*oz*	
Milk, condensed	240	10.0	3.5	1.0
Butter	533	54.5	7.8	5.4
Cheese	221	23.0	3.2	2.3
Cream	34	7.0	0.5	0.7
Margarine	164	8.0	2.4	0.8
Lard	187	11.0	2.7	1.1
Fruit	2,427	119.0	35.1	11.7
Potatoes	4,400	37.0	64.5	3.6
Other vegetables	2,085	40.0	30.2	3.9
Sugar	1,917	49.0	27.7	4.8
Tea, coffee, and cocoa	278	48.0	4.0	4.7
Total value of primary foodstuffs	—	974.5	—	95.8
Add for preparation of complex foodstuffs	—	100.5	—	9.9
Totals	—	1,075.0	—	105.7

strated by a Ministry of Labour inquiry in October 1935: although it did not cover all trades it showed a range of average weekly wages for adult males from 83s 8d in printing and book-binding down to 49s 9d in the clothing industry.[21] Below these were agricultural labourers (34s), the unskilled and casual trades and, in this period of acute depression, the unemployed. After a brief post-war boom the slump had begun; at the end of 1920 there were 850,000 out of work and in 1921, 1,500,000, and at the height of the crisis in 1931–2, 3,000,000, or 22 per cent of the total labour force. When the Second World War broke out over a million were still out of work, despite the employment which rearmament had already created, and over the whole period 1921–39 unemployment averaged 14 per cent. Moreover, the unemployed tended to be heavily concentrated in the 'depressed' or, as the government preferred to call them, 'special' areas – Glasgow, Tyneside, Lancashire, and south Wales – which were mainly dependent on one or two staple industries like cotton, coal, and shipbuilding. In these areas half or more of the entire population might be workless and wholly dependent on insurance benefits which in 1936 allowed 17s a week for men, 9s for a wife, 6s for juveniles, and 3s for children under fourteen.[22] Their poverty contrasted sharply with the relative prosperity of workers in the midlands and south, where the new light industries and consumer trades were often experiencing a boom.

Any estimates of dietary sufficiency in the inter-war years must take account of these variations in working-class income. John Boyd Orr in his investigation into *Food, Health and Income*, published in 1936, was the first to attach full importance to this comparison. His survey began by classifying the population into six groups by income, indicating the size of each group and the average expenditure of each on food (Table 33). His classification gave full weight to the size of family; thus, a man and wife earning £2 10s 0d a week with no children or dependants would fall into Group 4, with one child into Group 3, with four or more children into Group 1. The poorest 10 per cent of the population in 1934 consisted in the main of families in which there was a disproportionately high number of children or other dependants per earner – in fact Orr estimated that between 20 and 25 per cent of all children in the country were in the lowest income group.

Orr next constructed, on the basis of the best nutritional knowledge of the day, a diet which would give optimum requirements for health. Instead of discussing minimum requirements, about which there had been much controversy, he based his calculations of adequacy on a physiological ideal – 'a state of well-being such that no improvement can be

Table 33 *Classification of the population by income groups and average food expenditure per head in each group*

Group	Income per head per week	Estimated average expenditure on food	Estimated population of group	
			Numbers	Percentage
1	Up to 10s	4s	4,500,000	10
2	10s to 15s	6s	9,000,000	20
3	15s to 20s	8s	9,000,000	20
4	20s to 30s	10s	9,000,000	20
5	30s to 45s	12s	9,000,000	20
6	Over 45s	14s	4,500,000	10
Average	30s	9s	—	—

269

effected by a change in the diet'. He found that his standard of perfect nutrition was realized only at an income level above that of 50 per cent of the population. The meagre diet of Group 1 was inadequate for perfect health in all the constituents considered (calories, protein, fat, calcium, phosphorus, iron, and vitamins A and C); Group 2 was adequate only in proteins and fat; Group 3 in calories, protein, and fat; Groups 4 and 5 were deficient only in calcium; only in Group 6 were the standard requirements exceeded in every case. Of course, the absence of the requirements for perfect health in the three lower groups did not imply that half the population was starving or suffering from such a degree of ill-health recognized as clinical malnutrition. But there was abundant evidence that it was particularly in the lower groups that physical under-development, predisposition to rickets, dental caries, anaemia, and infective diseases such as tuberculosis were most marked, and that their incidence was due – at least in part – to the inadequacy of protein and vitamin intake. In the poorest group the consumption of milk was 1.8 pints per head a week, in the wealthiest 5.5 pints; the poorest consumed 1.5 eggs a week compared with 4.5 in the wealthiest, and spent only 2½d on fruit against 1s 8d.[23] Despite the general improvement in standards the nutritional inadequacy of the poorest in the 1930s was still vast and alarming.

Boyd Orr was only one among numerous workers in the early 1930s, who were investigating the extent of poverty, ill-health, and malnutrition, and the relationships between them. In an age of increasing affluence for some sections of the working class the condition of the unemployed excited particular concern, especially when visibly recorded in demonstrations and hunger-marches. Evidence of disease and malnutrition was forthcoming from a number of quarters. In the last year of the war 41 per cent of the men medically examined were in C3 condition, although in the prime of life. This might have been put down to wartime rationing, nervous strain, or other temporary causes, but these did not obtain in 1935 when no less than 62 per cent of volunteers were found to be below the comparatively low standard of physique required by the army. Were so many of the population living, if not in actual disease, at least 'below par', unable to lead wholly full and useful lives and always a potential liability to the community? The investigations carried out at the Peckham Pioneer Health Centre tended to confirm that they were. The centre was a social and recreational club restricted to entire families living within a limited area in south London, where the population was mainly artisan. On joining, each member of the family was given a medical overhaul and a series of laboratory tests. In a survey of 1,666 members it was found that only 144 adults and children and seventeen babies had no diagnosable disorder, and that although so many had something wrong with them, very few were under the care of a doctor.[24] In 1934 experiments by Lady Williams in the depressed Rhondda Valley showed that no improvement in ante-natal service reduced the high maternal mortality rate until food was distributed to expectant mothers – when this was done, it fell by 75 per cent. Again, despite the onslaught on the slums which many local authorities made in the 1930s, overcrowding and bad housing conditions remained a major cause of disease and ill-health. The Report on the Overcrowding Survey in England and Wales, published in 1936, revealed conditions which would have horrified Engels and Chadwick a century earlier; although the figure (on the basis of two rooms for three adults and three rooms for five) was only 3.8 per cent for the whole country, Durham had 12 per cent of over-crowding and Sunderland 20.6 per cent. In such areas a high infant mortal-ity rate and a high death rate from pulmonary tuberculosis still went hand in hand with poverty and insanitary living conditions: immediately before the Second World War Barrow-in-Furness had an infant mortality rate of ninety-eight per thousand while Hastings had one of thirty-five.[25] Nor did the solution simply lie in transferring slum-dwellers to model council-house communities. Dr G.C.M. McGonigle found disquieting evidence in Stockton-on-Tees that however good and sanitary the new houses might be there was no improvement in health if higher rents and travelling expenses involved a reduction in the income available for food: the death rate in the new housing estate went up while in the town as a whole, including the slum areas which still existed, it went down.[26] Malnutrition could be found in council houses as well as slum tenements.

For the first time in the 1930s the subject seriously occupied the atten-tion of government departments, local authorities, and the press, both serious and popular. In discussions of a term so inexact there were inevi-tably widely differing views. After the publication of Boyd Orr's researches, *The Times* had said, in February 1936, 'One-half of the population is living on a diet insufficient or ill-designed to maintain health.' Orr's calculations had, as we have seen, been concerned with a standard of perfect diet. Three years earlier, the British Medical Associa-tion had undertaken an inquiry 'to determine the minimum weekly expenditure on foodstuffs which must be incurred . . . if health and work-ing capacity are to be maintained'. This minimum diet in 1933 worked out at a cost of 5s 11d per man and 4s 11d for a woman. For a man there was not sufficient food for him to carry on moderately heavy work, and for a child, insufficient for proper development: it represented a bare minimum on which it was just possible to exist without very obvious deficiency. On this calculation Orr's Group 1 (representing 10 per cent of the population) and part of Group 2 (representing 20 per cent of the population) were below the minimum, and could be considered undernourished – some-thing under one-third of the whole population of the country. By 1939 there had probably been some improvement in this position. More milk was being drunk, and various health and welfare services had raised the standard of living of the very poor. But on the evidence of later surveys made between 1937 and 1939 Boyd Orr still estimated that on the outbreak of the Second World War 'The average dietary of about one-third of the population is above the standard required for health, the diet of about one-third nearly right, and the diet of the remaining third below the standard.'[27]

Even more revealing than national averages were the results of investigations into particular groups and regions. For example, a report for the Pilgrim Trust on *Men Without Work* in 1938 showed that 44 per cent of the families of the unemployed were existing on or below the bare subsistence level calculated on the BMA standard: in many cases parents, and particularly mothers, were literally starving themselves in order to feed and clothe their children reasonably. In Bristol, a city with a high standard of living and at a time (1937) of business revival, only one in ten families was below a 'poverty-line' approximately the same as the BMA standard, but of the families with four or more children, slightly over half were below it, and of families with three children a quarter were below. One child in every five in a prosperous city was living in poverty.

Three regional surveys, all carried out in 1936, are also iluminating. In Cardiff the Medical Officer of Health's Department investigated the nutrition of 9,467 schoolchildren, finding that of 2.7 per cent excellent, 90.6 per cent normal, 5.1 per cent slightly sub-normal, and 1.6 per cent bad. A detailed comparison was next made of the economic position and diet of families of children at the extremes of the nutritional scale. In Group A (excellent) the average size of the family was 5.4 persons and the gross weekly income £3 9s, while in Group D (bad) the average size was 6.1 and the income £2 13s 8d. Group A spent on food each week £1 10s 9d, Group D, £1 3s 1d. The important comparison, however, was between the amounts spent on different items of food (Table 34). The two groups spent almost identical amounts on cereals and bread, butter, fat and margarine, sugar, tea, and coffee, but Group A families spent practically twice as much on meat, fish, milk, eggs, fruit, and vegetables. The pattern of the nineteenth century was hardly changed. Poor families first satisfied their hunger with the cheap carbohydrate foods washed down with innumerable cups of tea, and only after this did they turn to the protein and vegetable foods high in vitamins, if money allowed.[28]

The nineteenth-century pattern had also survived in another respect. It was tempting to think in the 1930s that poor diet and malnutrition were essentially urban problems associated with unemployment, overcrowding, lack of fresh air, and other disadvantages of life in towns. A survey of nutrition in Cuckfield Rural District Council, a rural area with no unemployment problem, completely disproved this belief and showed

Table 34 *Budgets of Cardiff families, 1936*

Type of food	Average weekly expenditure			
	Group A (excellent)		Group D (bad)	
	s	d	s	d
Cereals and bread	5	6	5	9
Butter, margarine, and fat	4	11	4	10
Sugar	1	1	1	0
Meat, fish, and prepared meat foods	7	8	4	4
Vegetables and fruit	4	2	2	2
Milk, milk products, and eggs	5	3	3	0
Tea, coffee, etc.	2	2	2	0
Totals	£1 10s	9d	£1 3s	1d

that in 1936, as a century earlier, the agricultural labourer was among the worst-fed of English workers. Ninety-nine children out of 304 examined were of sub-normal nutrition – a proportion of 33 per cent. In the lowest income group with a weekly expenditure on food of from 2s to 2s 11d per head, 40 per cent of the children fell into the category. The average size of family in Cuckfield was 5.5 and the average income £2 4s 7d, with a range from £1 6s to £5 2s. Fifty-two out of the 120 families examined had less than £2 a week. The inquiry showed that the average consumption of fresh milk per day was 0.3 pints – well below the national average in a dairying county. Only 56 per cent bought fish, and only 54.4 per cent fresh fruit.[29] No doubt some families grew vegetables and kept hens, but it is certain that many rural families were very inadequately supplied with the health-protective foods.

Finally, in Newcastle upon Tyne, a rigorously controlled investigation into the diets of sixty-nine representative working-class families disclosed huge variations in the consumption of nutrients. The intake of calories per man-value varied from 1,846 to 5,261 a day, protein from 51 to 161 g, iron from 7.2 to 28.9 g. It was noticeable that the average diet of unemployed families was lower than that of employed, and that the average diet of the unemployed living on new council estates was lower than that of the unemployed in old houses. The amounts of energy and protein obtained per penny of money spent on food were 23 per cent higher in the unemployed than in the employed families – a fact which goes some way towards disproving the commonly made assertion that the poor allocated their resources extravagantly. But only 66 per cent of the unemployed bought fresh milk, and their average consumption was only 1⅓ pints per week. Nearly all families in Newcastle baked their own bread, and consumed 10 oz a day, providing over one-third of their calories. An average of 6 oz of potatoes and 2½ oz of sugar were eaten. Finally, an estimate of the extent of anaemia was made using the haemoglobin test: 5 per cent of the men, 21 per cent of the women, and 27 per cent of the children were found to be anaemic, and of the wives of unemployed men one-third were in this condition.[30]

Much the most wide-ranging dietary survey carried out at this time, however, was the investigation undertaken by Sir William Crawford in 1936–7 and published under the title *The People's Food*. Boyd Orr's survey had examined some 1,200 family budgets, with an undue proportion from the north of England and from families of low earnings: Crawford's was more fully representative, covering all social classes from wealthy business executives to the unemployed, drawn from 5,000 budgets of families in seven principal cities. The five-fold grouping used for marketing inquiries was adopted (Table 35). The survey was on a house-to-house interview basis and extended over six months from October to March, excluding the weeks preceding and following the Christmas holiday. The statistics were all related to a *per capita* figure in order to obviate differences in the size of family; the average weekly income and food expenditure of the five groups was found to be as in Table 36.

By the house-to-house method a great deal of hitherto unknown information about the composition and time of particular meals was assembled, so that the survey became not only one of nutrition but of eating habits generally. It was found that breakfast was now eaten by almost everyone before leaving home, whereas before the war many working

Table 35 *Income classification of the population*

	Approximate annual income	*Estimated percentage of total population of Great Britain in each group*
Class AA	£1,000 and over	1
A	£500 to £999	4
B	£250 to £499	20
C	£125 to £249	60
D	Under £125	15

Source:
Crawford 1938.

Table 36 *Weekly food expenditure by income groups*

	Estimated weekly per capita income		Estimated weekly expenditure on food		Food expenditure as a percentage of income
	s	d	s	d	
Class AA	159	6	18	9	11.8
A	88	4	16	2	18.3
B	43	0	12	6	29.0
C	20	3	7	11	39.2
D	12	6	5	10	46.6

Source:
Crawford 1938.

Table 37 *Foods eaten at breakfast*

	Class AA	Class A	Class B	Class C	Class D
Number of families	422	466	971	2,124	1,006
Bread, rolls, or toast	79.9%	85.8%	83.1%	82.8%	91.7%
Butter	36.7	41.8	54.0	60.5	56.6
Margarine	—	—	—	3.2	17.5
Dripping	—	—	0.1	0.1	2.7
Marmalade	58.5	50.6	36.6	13.1	5.2
Jam, honey, and syrup	4.3	2.6	2.9	8.0	7.3
Porridge	28.9	24.7	26.6	25.8	18.3
Other cereals	18.0	21.9	21.4	14.5	7.0
Eggs	70.4	67.4	64.9	52.8	31.6
Bacon and ham	62.3	59.9	58.3	53.0	31.7
Fish	12.3	6.4	5.3	2.4	2.7
Sausages	6.6	5.8	3.1	2.2	3.0
Fruit or fruit juice	31.0	22.3	15.9	4.6	1.3
Tomatoes	4.3	4.5	4.5	3.5	2.2

Source:
Crawford 1938.

men had often compressed breakfast into a short break two hours after starting work: shorter working hours now made it possible to eat at home in most cases. The time of breakfast was earlier in scattered cities like London where there was often a considerable journey to work, but even

275

Table 38 *Breakfast drinks*

	Class AA	Class A	Class B	Class C	Class D
Number of families	422	466	971	2,124	1,006
Tea	85.8%	88.6%	93.5%	97.6%	98.3%
Coffee	43.4	17.6	8.1	2.2	1.2
Cocoa	4.0	1.1	3.0	5.4	2.3
Milk	9.2	8.2	6.2	4.5	2.4

Source:
Crawford 1938.

here the surprising fact emerged that between a third and a half of London husbands lived sufficiently near their work to be able to go home for their midday meal. The peak breakfast-time was 8 a.m. – somewhat earlier in the poorer classes, somewhat later in the richer. The main foods eaten are listed in Table 37.

Bacon and eggs were by no means universal, especially in the lower groups, and 'other cereals' were now rivalling porridge. Marmalade, fruit, and fruit juice were evidently marks of social grading, as was the inclusion of fish, but butter consumption rose towards the bottom of the scale to go on the increased amount of bread eaten. Breakfast drinks also indicated social class, coffee declining rapidly below Class A (Table 38).

The midday meal – 'dinner' in all social classes except AA where 'lunch' was preferred – was concentrated around 1 p.m., again rather earlier in the lower groups and later in the higher. The foods eaten were as in Table 39. Several points are interesting: the fact that only one in five had roast beef for dinner, the steady decline in green vegetables, fish, salads, and fruit as the social scale descended, and the popularity of 'other meat dishes' (sausages, stews, meat pies, and 'pieces') in the lower groups. Clearly, the pattern of the British dinner was stereotyped and traditional – meat, potatoes, and sometimes 'greens', followed by pudding and helped down with a cup of tea or, more rarely, coffee. Additional items appeared in the upper income groups – soup and fish before the main course, fruit and cheese after the sweet. Although the American influence was noticeable on the breakfast menu it had had practically no effect on the midday meal. It is also noticeable that only a minority of husbands took lunch away from home (Table 40). Restaurant meals were not typical of the British public and in all social classes a majority of husbands ate their dinner with their families.

The next meal of the day, tea, was complicated by the division into 'afternoon tea' and 'high tea', two essentially different meals linked only

276

Between the wars

Table 39 *Foods eaten at midday meal*

	Class AA	Class A	Class B	Class C	Class D
Number of families	422	466	971	2,124	1,006
Soup	14.2%	12.9%	10.3%	5.6%	4.7%
Fish	14.9	13.7	9.9	4.8	5.0
Beef or veal	20.8	23.8	23.9	22.2	20.1
Mutton or lamb	22.8	16.7	16.5	10.5	8.3
Pork	2.3	2.5	3.2	5.2	2.5
Ham or bacon	4.0	2.5	1.3	1.3	2.0
Poultry	8.5	9.0	3.2	0.9	0.2
Other meat dishes	27.1	24.9	31.8	42.3	40.1
Potatoes	70.1	65.9	73.7	76.9	65.7
Green vegetables	50.7	45.7	41.5	43.8	32.3
Other vegetables	17.5	2.14	23.4	24.7	21.2
Salads	10.9	7.3	4.1	1.2	0.9
'Milk' puddings	23.0	20.3	26.9	25.0	13.8
Other puddings	15.7	15.8	16.1	13.1	5.3
Fruit and other tarts (including pies)	9.0	10.8	8.8	6.4	3.0
Fruit	36.7	41.4	30.7	14.1	6.4
Custard	9.5	10.3	11.9	6.1	5.5
Cream	15.2	12.0	5.6	0.7	—
Jellies, etc.	5.9	3.9	2.3	1.3	0.3
Cheese	15.9	13.7	7.5	2.7	2.5
Bread	7.8	12.2	8.2	8.3	10.6
Biscuits or cakes	12.6	10.5	8.8	4.1	1.5

Source:
Crawford 1938.

Table 40 *Place of husband's midday meal*

	Class AA	Class A	Class B	Class C	Class D
Number of families	422	466	971	2,124	1,006
In restaurant	39.3%	35.8%	25.7%	10.8%	4.7%
At home	52.9	53.9	61.1	50.6	59.5
Takes lunch with him	0.7	—	7.3	34.8	26.2
No information	7.1	10.3	5.9	3.8	9.6

Source:
Crawford 1938.

Table 41 *Foods eaten at tea*

	Class AA	Class A	Class B	Class C	Class D
Number of families	422	466	971	2,124	1,006
Bread and butter	56.6%	52.1%	58.8%	60.5%	52.9%
Bread	2.1	4.3	7.0	7.5	24.3
Butter	0.5	1.7	1.1	1.2	1.4
Margarine	—	—	—	1.9	13.8
Dripping	—	—	—	0.3	1.6
Toast	4.5	6.2	5.1	4.5	3.9
Sandwiches	5.0	4.9	2.0	0.4	0.3
Biscuits	12.8	15.9	9.3	5.2	1.1
Jam and preserves	29.4	21.7	29.1	33.8	33.9
Meat and fish pastes	0.9	1.5	2.0	3.1	0.7
Cakes, buns, and pastries	83.9	73.4	61.3	48.6	28.8
Eggs	2.1	4.1	5.5	6.3	2.5
Salads	1.9	4.5	7.0	5.6	1.8
Fruit	4.5	6.2	5.8	5.2	2.0
Cheese	0.9	2.4	3.7	5.1	3.6
Meat (poultry, sausages, and ham)	1.2	3.9	6.4	8.1	6.4
Fish	2.8	5.4	9.9	9.5	3.3
Potatoes	0.9	0.9	1.3	3.6	2.6
Vegetables	0.2	0.2	0.8	2.4	1.7
Puddings and sweets	0.9	2.6	2.1	5.5	3.4

Source:
Crawford 1938.

by the consumption of a common drink. 'Afternoon tea' was taken mainly by the AA and A groups at around 4 p.m., a light snack consisting of cakes, biscuits, and perhaps bread and butter. 'High tea' in the other classes was a substantial meal eaten on the return home of husband and children, usually between 5 and 6 p.m.; it usually included meat, potted meats, pies, or fish and chips, as well as a pudding or sweet. The wide variety of items eaten at tea is shown in Table 41. Cakes, buns, and pastries declined as 'afternoon tea' became 'high tea', giving way to meat, fish, potatoes, and vegetables in the more prosperous working-class homes (C); in the poorest grade (D), bread, margarine, and jam were most heavily consumed as the cheapest 'filling' foods. Regional variations were also noticeable. 'Afternoon tea' was more popular in London and the south, 'high tea' in the north, while, in particular towns, cooked meats, fish, or cheese held pride of place.

Table 42 *Foods eaten at evening meal*

	Class AA	Class A	Class B	Class C	Class D
Number of families	422	466	971	2,124	1,006
Soups	41.5%	25.5%	4.7%	1.6%	1.1%
Fish	35.3	21.9	13.5	10.3	9.4
Beef or veal	11.8	9.2	4.5	3.3	3.3
Mutton or lamb	15.1	11.1	5.6	1.7	1.1
Pork	1.4	1.9	0.8	0.6	0.7
Ham or bacon	2.1	1.7	1.8	1.9	1.3
Poultry and game	28.0	10.5	2.1	0.4	0.4
Other meat dishes	20.1	22.5	12.3	10.8	8.1
Potatoes	50.2	36.9	18.7	15.2	15.6
Green vegetables	39.1	26.2	10.2	4.1	3.4
Other vegetables	14.4	6.7	5.0	3.1	2.8
Salads	15.4	12.9	5.4	3.4	1.4
Milk puddings	9.4	6.9	5.8	2.7	1.1
Other puddings	12.6	9.2	3.3	0.8	0.8
Fruit and other tarts (including pies)	6.9	4.7	2.8	1.0	1.0
Fruit	40.3	32.2	14.1	2.8	1.3
Custard	3.3	5.6	3.1	1.0	0.6
Cream	14.7	7.5	2.2	0.1	—
Jellies, etc.	8.1	7.3	1.3	0.2	0.1
Cheese and cheese dishes	28.2	30.9	34.3	34.3	31.1
Bread	11.1	20.4	34.2	42.7	52.3
Butter	9.5	18.0	24.6	29.8	27.5
Biscuits and cakes	25.8	35.0	39.3	26.2	9.6
Egg dishes	5.0	6.9	3.7	2.7	1.7
Savouries	3.3	2.6	0.3	0.3	—

Source:
Crawford 1938.

A similar difficulty of nomenclature arose over the evening meal. In the upper-income groups this was 'dinner', the principal meal of the day, an expanded luncheon eaten between 7 and 8 p.m.: in the other groups 'supper' was a mere afterthought to 'high tea', eaten later in the evening between 9 and 10 p.m. Crawford's inquiry found that only in the AA class was 'dinner' in a clear majority, although in London most of the A class also used the term: elsewhere, even in the middle classes, 'supper' was the usual term until in the D group 94 per cent used it. The foods eaten indicate this variation (Table 42).

279

In the 'dinner'-eating classes soup and fish were considerably more popular than at lunch, meat and vegetables less so: in the poorest classes bread and cheese was easily the most common supper dish. In the AA group 26 per cent took alcohol with dinner and 58 per cent coffee after it: in group D cocoa (37 per cent) rivalled tea (39 per cent) as the last drink of the day. Surprisingly, perhaps, very little alcohol was consumed with the last meal of the day outside the AA class. In the C class only 2 per cent and in the D class only 1 per cent included beer with their supper, an indication that the pre-war habit of bringing home draught ale from the 'Jug and Bottle' department had all but disappeared. One reason for this was probably the increased attractiveness of public houses and working men's clubs, where women could be entertained in more comfort than formerly.

The tables quoted above also indicate something about food tastes and preferences. It is evident, for example, that tea was still the national drink, that beef was almost twice as popular as mutton and lamb, that, as a sweet, puddings had the highest percentage of preferences in all five social groups for men, women, and children alike. Fruit fell rapidly in popularity with social grading. The extent of variety in foods is, of course, not only a question of taste but of cost: the poorer classes in the 1930s were still unable to afford wide choice in their diet even if they had had the opportunity of acquiring preferences. This was borne out clearly by Crawford's findings (Table 43). But tradition was still an extremely powerful influence in English diet. Crawford's investigators asked housewives whether they were 'interested' in newspaper and magazine articles dealing with food, recipes, and diet generally, and the results were illuminating (Table 44). In the highest social classes only one-third of women were prepared to acknowledge even an interest in dietetic subjects, and this usually referred to slimming or the feeding of young children. 'Vitamins' and 'nutrition' were rarely mentioned.

On the question of dietary adequacy, the Crawford survey closely confirmed Boyd Orr's findings. In the C and D classes considerable numbers were spending less than the BMA minimum (Table 45). On this calculation

Table 43 *Number of items in meals*

	Midday meal	Evening meal
Class AA	4.15	4.52
A	3.97	3.74
B	3.70	2.54
C	3.21	2.02
D	2.53	1.76

Table 44 *Housewives interested in dietetic subjects*

	Class AA	Class A	Class B	Class C	Class D
Number of families	422	466	971	2,124	1,006
Interested	33.6%	33.5%	26.6%	17.0%	8.2%
Not interested	65.9	65.5	73.1	80.3	89.5
No reply	0.5	1.0	0.3	2.7	2.3

Source:
Crawford 1938.

Table 45 *Families with food expenditure below BMA minimum*

	Homes visited	Below minimum	Percentage
Class AA	415	—	—
A	458	—	—
B	962	4	0.42
C	2,121	361	17.02
D	996	480	48.19

Source:
Crawford 1938.

17.52 per cent of the population, or nearly 7,880,000 people, spent less on food than the figure regarded as minimal by the BMA. This does not necessarily mean that these people could not have raised their food expenditure to the minimum – only that they did not – but since the available income in the C and D classes was so small it allowed little scope for improvement. Moreover, this calculation presupposes that everyone able to spend the BMA minimum did so in the most nutritionally economic way – this was probably not the case. On the Crawford statistics of the actual kinds and quantities of foods purchased by the population, the numbers listed in Table 46 were found to be receiving inadequate amounts of different nutrients. Approximately one-third of the whole population was short of calories and protein and half or more than half was deficient in vitamins. For many millions the problem was not so much a financial as an educational one: a nutritionally adequate diet was probably possible in the 1930s for five-sixths of the population, but because of ignorance or prejudice, lack of time or lack of facilities, only half the population was actually receiving it.

Table 46 *Number of people consuming inadequate quantities of nutritive constituents*

	Compared with BMA diet (in millions)
Calories	15
Protein	18
Calcium	25
Phosphorus	20
Iron	33
Vitamin A	37
Vitamin B$_1$	24
Vitamin C	21

Source:
Crawford 1938.

Table 47 *Weekly* per capita *bread consumption*

	Weekly expenditure on bread	Quantity purchased	Flour equivalent
Class AA	7.6d	48.0 oz	36.9 oz
A	7.6d	48.2 oz	37.1 oz
B	7.8d	49.6 oz	38.2 oz
C	8.1d	54.9 oz	42.2 oz
D	8.7d	62.4 oz	48.0 oz

That there were wide variations in the amounts of different foods eaten by the five social classes was all too obvious. Bread, the cheapest energy-food, was consumed most heavily in Class D, where it represented 12 per cent of food expenditure, least in Class AA, where it accounted for only 3 per cent (Table 47). On the other hand, meat consumption showed the opposite trend, rising as income grew (Table 48). Forty per cent of the total meat consumption was of beef and veal, the rest being divided almost equally between mutton and pork. The consumption of fish also rose with income, from 4.8 oz per head in Class D to 10 oz in Class AA. Crawford's figures referred to domestic consumption, and took no account of what was eaten in fish-and-chip shops or in the street, but it is very unlikely that most of the population reached the 9 oz per week recommended by the

Table 48 *Total weekly* per capita *meat consumption*

	Amount spent per week	Quantity purchased per week
Class AA	58.4d	53.3 oz
A	51.1d	49.5 oz
B	38.1d	43.1 oz
C	23.6d	34.6 oz
D	16.7d	30.4 oz

Advisory Committee on Nutrition. Milk was an even better example of the fact that consumption of the nutritionally desirable foods varied inversely with income: in Class AA consumption (including condensed milk) was 5.3 pints per week, falling to 2.1 pints in Class D. For the whole population the figure was 3.26 pints per head a week, less than half of what nutritionists considered adequate. By contrast, the consumption of sugar was higher in all social classes than dieticians would approve. It had quadrupled over the preceding hundred years to reach an average of 110 lb per head a year, the highest of any country except Denmark. The Advisory Committee on Nutrition was concerned that a food of such little value was dulling the appetite and leading to a diminished consumption of more desirable foods, while other experts condemned its effects on children's teeth. Crawford's survey found that the weekly amounts purchased for home use by the five social classes were remarkably uniform – 17.6 oz in AA falling to 15.2 oz in D, with an average national figure of 16.7 oz. To be added to this was the sugar consumed indirectly in confectionery, cakes, biscuits, jam, syrup, and other forms, making up 11.9 oz per head per week, and a total consumption of 28.6 oz. Rising sugar consumption was certainly no indication of improving nutrition, nor was it necessarily a sign of a rising standard of living. It was so high in the poorer social classes partly because of their heavy use of cheap jams and syrups and the quantity that went into endless cups of tea: these, together with white bread, margarine, and an occasional kipper, were the hallmarks of the poverty-line diet which George Orwell observed in *The Road to Wigan Pier*.[31]

The judgement of historians on this period has inevitably been coloured by the Depression and mass unemployment. Hunger-marches and the dole seem inconsistent with a rising standard of living, yet probably the truth is that the proportion of very poor fell between the wars and that of the moderately prosperous increased. It is also true that the problem of poverty had changed – that although the numbers of the 'old poor', of miserably paid unskilled and casual workers, had diminished, there had arisen a 'new poor' of skilled workers whose skills had been made redundant by the processes of industrial change.[32] Unemployed and underemployed miners, shipyard workers, and cotton weavers made up the new 'submerged tenth', and their plight was all the more pitiful because it contrasted with the relative prosperity they had once known. But none of the numerous inter-war surveys disclosed a scale of poverty approaching that at the turn of the century when Rowntree and Booth had estimated 28–30 per cent of the population to be in that condition. The *New Survey of London Life and Labour* (1930) believed only 8 per cent to be below the poverty-line; Caradog Jones's *Social Survey of Merseyside* (1934) put the figure there at 14 per cent, while Ford's *Work and Wealth in a Modern Port* (1934) calculated that Southampton had 16 per cent in poverty. In 1936 Seebohm Rowntree carried out a second survey of York, this time using a somewhat more generous 'human needs' standard rather than one of 'mere physical efficiency', but even on this more liberal scale his estimate of poverty was 17.7 per cent of the population. No one could seriously doubt that the working classes on the eve of the Second World War were better fed, better clothed, and better housed than their parents had been a generation earlier.

This improvement was not wholly, or even mainly, a consequence of higher earnings. At the end of 1937 the average wage of an adult male was around 70s, though a London engineering labourer averaged 50s 3d, and his counterpart in Manchester 45s. Rowntree's new 'poverty-line' budget for a man, wife, and three children came to 53s (food on the BMA standard 20s 6d, rent 9s 6d, clothing 8s, fuel and light 4s 4d, household sundries 1s 8d, and miscellaneous expenses 9s).[33] This was still well ahead of the Unemployment Assistance Board scale which provided 37s 6d for an equivalent family. It could be argued, however, that the worker in the inter-war years benefited substantially from the growth of state and municipal welfare. Council housing rescued millions from the misery of industrial slums; medical services and insurance benefits gave a hope of better health and greater security, while the development of public utilities and recreational amenities was beginning to add to the richness of enjoyment of life. The state was at last beginning to provide for the working classes the conditions of civilized life which the middle classes had provided for themselves.

Not least important was the official recognition which the problem of malnutrition at last received from central and local authorities. A remarkable development of experimental research by such bodies as the Medical Research Council and the Food Investigation Board of the DSIR brought together invaluable empirical evidence about nutritional needs and the physiological effects of inadequacy, while at a local level the statistics assembled by Medical Officers of Health and others provided the necessary information on which the nutritional needs of particular areas and categories could be based. A survey of families in Hammersmith in 1931, for example, showed that there were many unemployed who had as little as 1s 7d a head to spend on a week's food, while even among those in work many could afford less than 4s: such findings made the BMA's minimum look utopian. They also underlined the need for remedial action by local authorities, especially so far as children and expectant mothers were concerned. By 1939 health departments were providing milk, cod-liver oil, iron, and vitamin products at low costs or free for clear cases of malnutrition in mothers and infants. The 'Milk in Schools' scheme which started in 1934 was supplying a third of a pint of milk daily to 50 per cent of elementary schoolchildren, either at half cost or none at all, and increased their consumption from nine to twenty-two million gallons a year. Necessitous children, and those clearly in need of extra nourishment, were provided with midday meals at school, 5 per cent of elementary schoolchildren benefiting from this.[34] By 1939 there were three thousand infant welfare centres under the supervision of the Ministry of Health. The results of these policies were already impressive. Twelve-year-old boys attending elementary schools in London were three inches taller and eleven pounds heavier than their fathers had been twenty years earlier: equally important, an experiment sponsored by the Milk Nutrition Committee in 1938–9 demonstrated that schoolchildren receiving supplementary milk not only showed a general improvement in health but derived greater benefit from their lessons.[35]

By 1939 the government was coming to recognize, at least in part, the need for a nutritional policy as an essential part of personal health services. Dieticians were urging that, just as the state in the nineteenth century had accepted responsibility for sanitary measures, it now had a similar duty to ensure nutritional adequacy for the population as a whole. Agricultural economists saw a greatly increased consumption of 'protective' foods, subsidized by the state, as the only way to restore the prosperity of British farming, while at the same time rescuing the health of the nation. What steps might have been taken in the next decades towards a nutritional policy is debatable. What no one foresaw in 1939 was that a unique opportunity for the improvement of national diet was to be afforded not by a continuance of peace, but by the outbreak of war.

Contemporary observers and subsequent historians have both been divided in their judgement of the inter-war years. Optimists can point to certain well-attested indicators of improvements in the standards of health – the general mortality rate fell from 14.7 per thousand in 1906–10 to 12.0 per thousand in 1936–8; infant mortality, widely regarded as a sensitive indicator of standards of living, fell from 105 per thousand in 1910 to 60 in 1930 and, less rapidly, to 56 by 1940; the great killer diseases of the past like diphtheria, tuberculosis, typhoid, scarlet fever, and measles were now on the retreat, while the proportion of schoolchildren diagnosed as suffering from malnutrition showed a dramatic improvement from 15–20 per cent before 1914 to 5 per cent in 1925, and a mere 1 per cent by 1925–32.[36] The generally improved fitness of the population also seemed to be proved by conscription during World War Two, when 70 per cent of men were graded as fully fit, twice the proportion in 1917–18. The official Reports of the Ministry of Health and of the local Medical Officers were almost unanimously optimistic, even about the state of health in the depressed areas. While it was recognized that infant mortality rates here could still be two or three times higher than in prosperous areas, this was put down mainly to ignorance rather than economic causes: remarkably, at Neath there was reported to be no 'real malnutrition', while at Ebbw Vale and Aberdare not a single child was classified as having 'bad nutrition'.

Such findings seem oddly at variance with popular images of the 1930s drawn from photographs of dole queues and hunger-marches, hollow-eyed men and stunted, rickety-looking children. The more polemical literature of the day painted a very different picture from the official reports. In *Hungry England* Fenner Brockway concluded that 'frequently, the allowances provided under the Means Test involve semi-starvation',[37] quoting budgets of the unemployed which provided only 16s 5d a week to feed a family of six. George Orwell believed that 'twenty million people are underfed',[38] and argued that 'the less money you have, the less inclined you feel to spend it on wholesome food'.[39] After a survey of 1,250 women and family budgets, Margery Spring Rice concluded that housewives were the chief victims of poverty and unemployment, almost always denying themselves food for the sake of their husbands and children.[40] Professor Oddy has calculated that some of the women's diets yielded as little as 1,305 kilocalories and 36 g of protein a day – far below even Boyd Orr's lowest Group 1 who averaged 2,320 kilocalories, and 63 g of protein.

In fact, both judgements of the inter-war years are true, and not incompatible. General standards of health improved though, significantly, less quickly in the 1930s than in the 1920s or 1940s. It is not impossible that at a time of national anxiety and international tension government departments felt under pressure to produce an optimistic picture and to play down the unpalatable. The national averages, accurate in themselves, concealed enormous variations in mortality and morbidity rates, and there continued to be gross class inequalities in health standards – inequalities which R.M. Titmuss believed actually widened in the 1930s compared with the 1920s. One of the unpalatable statistics was that the maternal mortality rate peaked in 1933 and 1934 at a higher level than at the beginning of the century, suggesting that there was some correlation with the worst years of the Depression and the height of unemployment. For most people the inter-war years were years of wider food choice, better health, and improved nutrition: for a minority – and in some years and some regions, a large minority – the progress was so frail, and started from so low a base, that it could easily revert to conditions of hunger, disease, and misery not seen since the turn of the century. England in the 1930s was still Disraeli's *Two Nations*.

Notes

1 Smith, Charles (1940) *Britain's Food Supplies in Peace and War*, a survey prepared for the Fabian Society by Charles Smith, 2.
2 Oddy, D.J. (1982) 'The health of the people', in Theo Barker and Michael Drake (eds), *Population and Society in Britain, 1850–1980*, 129.
3 Fielding, Sir Charles ('Agricola') (Late Director-General of Food Production) (1923) *Food*, 16.
4 Layton, W. T. and Crowther, Geoffrey (1935) *An Introduction to the Study of Prices*, 265–9.
5 *British Agriculture: The Principles of Future Policy* (1939), a Report of an Inquiry organized by Viscount Astor and B. Seebohm Rowntree.
6 *Britain's Food Supplies in Peace and War*, op cit., 240 et seq.
7 Hunt, Sandra *The Changing Place of Bread in the British Diet in the Twentieth Century*, series of unpublished research papers sponsored by the Rank Prize Funds (Brunel University), chap. 4, 1920–1939, 6–11.
8 Boswell, James (ed.) (1969) *JS 100. The Story of Sainsbury's*, 44.
9 Johnston, James P. (1977) *A Hundred Years of Eating. Food, Drink and the Daily Diet in Britain since the late Nineteenth Century*, 82–4.
10 Crawford, Sir William and Broadley, H. (1938) *The People's Food*, 8.
11 For a description of new foods and food habits see Graves, Robert and Hodge, Alan (1940) *The Long Weekend. A Social History of Great Britain, 1918–1939*, chap. 11, 'Domestic life', 171 et seq.
12 Walworth, George (1937) 'The organization of the co-operative movement' in W. A. Robson (ed.) *Public Enterprise*.
13 Simon, André L. (1929) *The Art of Good Living*, 3.
14 Montizambert, Elizabeth (1924) *London Discoveries*, quoted in S. Price (1986) *Eating Out in London. A Social History, 1900–1950*, Brunel University dissertation, Appendix V.
15 Richardson, D.J. *The History of the Catering Industry, with Special Reference to the Development of J. Lyons and Co. to 1939*, unpub. Ph.D. thesis quoted in ibid., Appendix VIII.
16 Constantine, Stephen (1983) *Social Conditions in Britain, 1918–1939*, 3.
17 Peel, Mrs C.S. (ed.) (1919) *The* Daily Mail *Cookery Book*, Introduction.
18 ibid., 1–2.
19 Tschumi, Gabriel (1954) *Royal Chef. Recollections of Life in Royal Households from Queen Victoria to Queen Mary*.

20 Orr, John Boyd (1936) *Food, Health and Income. Report on a Survey of Adequacy of Diet in Relation to Income*, 18.
21 Cole, G.D.H. and Postgate, Raymond (1938) *The Common People, 1746–1938*, 619.
22 When insurance benefit was exhausted the unemployed passed first onto 'transitional benefits' and then onto the 'dole' administered by the Public Assistance Committees. In 1936 this provided 23s a week for a man and wife, 4s for the eldest child, and 3s for other children: a quarter of the dole was regarded as rent.
23 Orr, op. cit., 49.
24 Herbert, S. Mervyn (1939) *Britain's Health*, prepared on the basis of the Report on the British Health Services by PEP, 171.
25 Titmuss, R.M. (1938) *Poverty and Population*.
26 McGonigle, G.C.M. and Kirby, J. (1936) *Poverty and Public Health*. On average, only 2s 11d per man per week was available for food in the council houses compared with 4s in the slums.
27 Orr, Sir John and Lubbock, D. (1940) *Feeding the People in Wartime*, 61.
28 Annual Report of the Medical Officer of Health for Cardiff for the year 1936, 148 et seq.
29 Cuckfield Rural District Council: Annual Report of the Medical Officer of Health for the year 1936 by William B. Stott, 5 and 10–12.
30 Annual Report of the Medical Officer of Health for the City and County of Newcastle upon Tyne on the Sanitary Condition of the City, 1936, Appendix A: A Study of the Diet of 69 working-class families in Newcastle upon Tyne, 23 et seq.
31 Orwell, George (1937) *The Road to Wigan Pier*.
32 Cole and Postgate, op. cit., 607.
33 Rowntree, B. Seebohm (1937) *The Human Needs of Labour*.
34 HMSO (1946) *How Britain Was Fed in Wartime. Food Control, 1939–1945*, 46.
35 *Milk Drinking in Schools*, Information Booklet No. 2, issued by the National Dairy Council's Information Service (nd), 3.
36 Webster, Charles (1982) 'Healthy or hungry thirties?', *History Workshop Journal* (Spring), 112. This article admirably analyses the opposing evidence and its interpretation.
37 Brockway, A. Fenner (1932) *Hungry England*, 223.
38 Orwell, *The Road to Wigan Pier* (1958 edn), 89.
39 ibid., 95.
40 Spring Rice, Margery (1939) *Working-Class Wives. Their Health and Conditions*.

❧ 13 ❧
The Second World War

There is a strange irony in the fact that the two crucial periods for the improvement of the diet of the majority of English people coincided with times of national crisis – the Great Depression of the 1880s and the wartime and post-war difficulties of the 1940s. In both cases the basic reason for improvement was the same – a rising standard of living resulting from an increase in the purchasing power of the population. But here the parallel ends. In the first period this increased spending power was due to external factors over which the government exercised no control – the emergence of great primary producing countries and developments in communications and technology which made possible the mass importation of cheap food; in the second, the state took a direct part by fixing prices, by rationing, and by deliberately pursuing a nutritional and social policy which succeeded in raising standards at a time of acute national peril. This was possibly the most remarkable, though least-publicized, achievement of wartime control.

The organization of food control was in some respects easier in 1939 than it had been in 1914. For one thing, British agriculture had been substantially expanded in the 1930s under the impetus of subsidies and marketing schemes, with the result that dependence on imported food was not quite as great as it had been formerly: land had been brought back into heart; mechanization and fertilization had both proceeded rapidly, so that in 1939 the soil of Britain proved capable of considerably increased production. Domestic agriculture was called on primarily to increase the output of foodstuffs for direct human consumption, so saving valuable shipping space, but also to provide feed for cows in order to maintain and even increase the supply of milk for liquid consumption. These objects were achieved with notable success, often with the unskilled labour of 'land girls' and schoolchildren at 'harvest camps'. In 1939 Britain was only 30 per cent self-sufficient in food (compared with 86 per cent in Germany): no less than 88 per cent of our wheat requirement was imported. By 1944 there had been, compared with pre-war production, a 90 per cent increase in wheat, 87 per cent in potatoes, 45 per cent in vegetables, and 19 per cent in sugar-beet; moreover, the output of barley and oats had doubled. All this made possible the halving of imported food, from a total of 22,026,000 tons before the war to 11,032,000 tons in 1944.[1]

Second, government planning of food control was far more advanced in 1939 than it had been on the outbreak of the First World War. As early as 1936 there had been set up the Food (Defence Plans) Department under the Directorship of Henry Leon French, who had been seconded from the Ministry of Agriculture and Fisheries: the Department at first reported to the Board of Trade, but became the nucleus of the new Ministry of Food which was established immediately on the outbreak of war under W.S. Morrison. In the 'Kaiser's War' the government had been reluctant to create a Ministry of Food, which it had not done until the end of 1916, and still more hesitant about introducing compulsory rationing. In 1939 the operational structure of rationing was already complete, and plans had been drawn up to create what was probably the largest state trading organization in the world: divisional food officers and local food executive officers had been appointed and instructed, all branches of the food trades had been taken into consultation and leading individuals from each selected to control the particular commodity in which they specialized, the details of rationing had been fully worked out, and the ration books themselves had been printed.[2] Britain's preparedness for war was, in this respect at least, remarkably well advanced, and it was the confidence which knowledge of this engendered that made public acceptance of food control relatively easy and complete.

Third, the science of nutrition had developed so much further by 1939 that it was now possible to plan a dietetically adequate rationing scheme far more precisely than during the First World War. In this connection the appointment of Professor J. C. Drummond as Chief Scientific Adviser to the Ministry was of the greatest significance. As an eminent nutritionist and student of the history of diet Drummond was uniquely qualified to apply scientific principles to nutritional strategy: equally important, his knowledge of the dietary inadequacy of the poorer sections of the pre-war population made him determined to use food control as an instrument not only to maintain but to improve the nutritional value of the diet. Thus, the 'welfare' aspects of rationing were largely the product of Drummond's fertile imagination and powers of persuasion. But his influence was also seen on many other aspects of food administration. He was quick to realize the important part which food technology could play in economizing shipping space, and it was partly because of this, and partly for nutritional reasons, that the extraction rate of flour for bread was raised to 85 per cent in March 1942, though bread itself remained unrationed throughout the war in order to provide unlimited quantities of a cheap energy-food. This had been no easy task against the vested interests of millers, who had a profit in the 'offals' sold as cattle food, and the long-established preference of the public for white bread. The change from a 70 per cent extraction rate before the war to 85 per cent produced a brownish-coloured 'National Wheatmeal Flour' which considerably increased the intake of iron and B vitamins but was by no means universally liked. One lady sieved the flour through some old silk stockings, and wrote triumphantly to Lord Woolton, Morrison's successor: 'I got all your vitamins out and gave them to the pigs.'[3]

Another of Drummond's major interests was the new process of dehydration, which brought such unfamiliar – though generally appreciated – foods to the British public as dried eggs, National Household Milk, and dehydrated vegetables. Again, shipping space was saved by new methods of packaging, by importing boneless meat, and by folding and compressing carcasses: the greatly increased import of American canned meats such as 'Spam' and 'Mor' after the introduction of Lend-Lease in 1942 also economized shipping by providing meat in a highly concentrated form. But Drummond also knew, better than most, that food habits were conservative and that the acceptance of little-known foods and the better use of known ones would require an organized programme of dietary education. Through the Food Advice Division of the Ministry, which worked under his guidance, information was given to housewives and caterers by radio, the press, posters, and leaflets which had considerable success in raising standards of cooking as well as nutritional knowledge.[4]

During the war years some degree of food control and rationing operated in almost every country in the world, from the richest agricultural countries like the USA and Australia to the poorest such as India and China. The combatants and the occupied countries naturally had more restrictions than the neutrals, and the German rationing scheme was probably the most complete of all, covering 95 per cent or more of the calories obtained in peacetime. Under this 'total' rationing the normal consumer in Germany received approximately 2,000 kilocalories a day, in the occupied Netherlands, Belgium, Finland, and Norway between 1,500 and 1,800, and in the Baltic States, France, Italy, Poland, and Greece, between 1,000 and 1,500.[5] Comparable statistics are not available for the USSR, but estimates suggest an average intake of approximately 1,800. These average figures are, however, misleading, since nearly all countries operated differential rationing schemes allowing more to manual workers and often supplementary protective foods to children, nursing and expectant mothers, and so on. In Germany in 1943 heavy workers received 2,685 and very heavy workers 3,435 kilocalories, a considerable improvement on the average figure though still less than nutritionists would specify.[6] Germany was, in fact, the best-fed of the continental countries. In Belgium a very heavy worker received 2,480 kilocalories, in Italy 1,915, and in France only 1,470. In Poland, Greece, parts of Yugoslavia, and occupied

Russia rations were so low in 1942 that actual famine was frequent, and although the situation improved subsequently, millions of people continued to live throughout the war in semi-starvation.

The British system of rationing was developed on lines different from those in other countries: in particular, it was less highly differentiated and rigid than the German, giving more flexibility and freedom of choice to the consumer. We succeeded in maintaining an adequate supply of calories of vegetable origin since, although some vegetables at first were scarce, bread and potatoes were not rationed, and all consumers were free to have as much of these as they wished. Price control and wage policies also ensured that they were within the reach of the population. Since total calories were unrationed, estimates of average intake serve little purpose, but it is believed that the figure remained at or above the standard of 3,000 a day. The rationing schemes were concerned mainly with protein foods, milk, and fats, the need for which varies less between different sections of the population than it does for other nutritive elements. The British scheme therefore rationed meat, bacon, cheese, fats, sugar, and preserves in fixed quantities per head[7] and made certain dietary modifications which were to the benefit of the population as a whole: raising the extraction rate of flour to 85 per cent, for example, increased the intake of iron, riboflavin, and nicotinic acid, while the fortification of margarine with vitamins A and D compensated to some extent for the scarcity of eggs. This was the basic system which applied to all. Nevertheless, it was recognized that certain categories of the population had special nutritional requirements, and therefore other schemes, many of them unique to Britain, were superimposed on this common basis.

Socially the most important of these were the distribution schemes which provided additional proteins, vitamins, and minerals to children of pre-school age, nursing and pregnant mothers. Children under one year had a priority right to two pints of milk a day, nursing and expectant mothers and children under five to one pint at the subsidized price of 2d a pint. The milk was supplied free if the parents' income fell below a certain minimum. For those over five, the milk-in-schools scheme, started before the war, was greatly expanded to include, in principle, all schoolchildren. One of the most remarkable achievements of domestic agriculture was to increase total milk production at a time when imports of animal feeding stuffs were greatly curtailed. Other important foods in the priority distribution schemes included eggs and the vitamins welfare scheme, which provided orange juice, cod-liver oil, and vitamin tablets to the same categories through an expanded clinic service.

These schemes undoubtedly contributed to the generally improved nutrition of mothers and children, though publicity and persuasion did not succeed in making their use universal: the maximum 'take-up' of fruit juices was 45.7 per cent of the potential issue, for vitamin A and D tablets 34.3, and for cod-liver oil only 21 per cent.⁸

Communal feeding was another special feature of the British system. While on the continent workers engaged in heavy labour received additional rations of certain foods, Britain adopted the policy of leaving useful additions to the diet outside the ration and available in centres where nutritious meals could be prepared economically. A few industrial canteens had existed before the war, but firms employing more than 250 were now required to operate them and smaller ones encouraged to do so: at the end of 1943 the impressive total of 10,577 factory canteens were in operation, besides another 958 on docks and building sites.⁹ Factory canteen advisers appointed by the Ministry of Food were valuable in ensuring that the meals were served as attractively and appetizingly as conditions allowed, and there can be little doubt that this bonus of good food contributed significantly to industrial morale. The provision of school canteens filled a similar need for a different category. Their object was to supply schoolchildren with one well-balanced meal a day at a subsidized price or, in cases of need, without charge: they were registered as priority catering establishments and received such special allowances as required. Before the war fewer than 200,000, or 4 per cent, of children took school dinners; by 1945 the figure had reached one-and-three-quarter millions, representing 36.3 per cent of children in attendance and, in addition, milk was now received by three-quarters of all schoolchildren.¹⁰ Both industrial and school canteens had existed before the war, although few in number. But the idea of British Restaurants (Churchill demanded the name in preference to the earlier Communal Feeding Centres) was entirely new. Originating as an emergency measure for 'blitzed' areas they eventually came to play an important part in wartime life, providing hot, nutritious meals at about 1s a head. By the middle of 1943, 2,115 restaurants were serving 615,000 midday meals each day: they were open to the general public, but the policy was to concentrate them in areas where there were many small factories without independent canteens so that industrial workers could benefit particularly.

A third successful peculiarity of the British system of food control was the points rationing scheme, introduced at the end of 1941. It applied to certain foods which were valuable but not essential additions to the basic diet and the supply of which was too small or erratic to permit of specific rationing – tinned meat, fish, and fruit and, later on, dried fruits, sugar, tapioca, rice, biscuits, dried peas and beans, breakfast cereals, and so on. Each consumer was entitled to so many 'points' each week, which he could spend on whichever items he chose; the foods concerned were 'priced' in ordinary currency and also in points. While giving flexibility of choice to the consumer, the scheme had the great merit of allowing the

Ministry to include or exclude foods as supplies varied, and also to steer demand in a desired direction by raising or lowering the points value of particular foods. When the scheme was first introduced, for example, the public rapidly bought up available supplies of tinned salmon at sixteen points and ignored the unfamiliar American pork sausage meat at the same value: when salmon was increased to twenty-four and sausage meat lowered to eight, demand quickly changed. The points system was a highly successful method of ensuring an equitable distribution of foods in short supply, and its originator, M.P. Roseveare, a Principal Assistant Secretary at the Ministry of Food, is an unrecognized genius.[11] In spite of the fact that it involved difficult explanations to the public and the co-operation of a quarter of a million retailers, its acceptance was surprisingly easy and the extent of the 'black market' surprisingly small. It is probably true, as A. Calder has stated, that nine out of ten housewives approved of the rationing schemes.[12]

Rationing worked as well as it did because it was not only just but could be seen to be just. The rations were small enough and domestic catering was difficult, particularly for single people living on their own who did not have the advantage of 'pooling' supplies as families did. Millions supplemented their diet by planting gardens and allotments with potatoes and green vegetables, and campaigns like 'Dig for Victory' had a substantial effect on raising domestic production. Much ingenuity was devoted to recipes which sound spartan by present standards but provided economical meals out of unrationed foods. The *Wine and Food Quarterly* was, in 1942, reduced to offering recipes for roast potatoes which 'are so delicious and satisfying that one hardly misses the beef or lamb of better days', and for *Carottes de Gaulle* (a patriotic variant of *à la Vichy*) as an entrée, 'not merely a "veg" to go with baked or grilled meats'. 'Many of us', continued the writer, 'sorely miss hot meat, such as a grilled steak or cutlet. An inadequate yet comforting substitute is nicely fried bread.'[13] The scarcity of meat gave some encouragement to the vegetarian movement, and to such dishes as lentil roast, butterbean cutlets, vegetable pie (a variant of the famous 'Woolton pie'), and buttered dandelion leaves.[14] Sheila Kaye-Smith believed that to give a dinner-party in wartime had to be a 'swindle' – evaporated milk instead of cream, rabbit instead of chicken,[15] while an adventurous Free Frenchman, the Vicomte de Mauduit, offered recipes for hedgehog, squirrel-tail soup, roast sparrows, and consommé of snails.[16] That housewives tired of dreary dishes after six years of war is undeniable, but husbands and children often got one good meal a day outside the home, and scarce rations could be kept for the evening and the week-end. It was also an important aid to morale that eating out in hotels and restaurants continued to be possible throughout the war, and many caterers did wonders within the maximum price limit of 5s a meal:[17] some deliberately kept prices low, and a three-course meal at a Corner House consisting of a substantial *hors d'oeuvre*, an interesting 'made' dish, and a sweet was astonishingly good value at 1s 9d.

The system of partial rationing no doubt suited the British public better than any scheme of complete control, however equitable, would have done: the feeling of independence and choice, though limited, was psychologically important. In 1944 the average household expenditure on rationed foods was only 31 per cent of total food expenditure. 'Points' rationing added another 11 per cent and 'controlled distribution' foods another 15 per cent, but the housewife was still left with almost half her budget to spend on completely unrationed foods, which included bread, flour, oatmeal, potatoes, fish, fresh vegetables, and fruit other than oranges.[18] The prices of these were strictly controlled in order to keep them within the reach of all consumers. With its virtual monopoly powers over the distribution of all imported and most home-grown foods, the Ministry was able to stabilize these at low levels and to fix the price of foods to the consumer according to considerations of social policy rather than economic cost.

Several attempts were made throughout the war to estimate the effects of food control on the nutritional standards of the population. In terms of kilocalories it appears that the pre-war average of 3,000 per head per day fell in 1940 and 1941 to 2,820, but increased to 3,010 by 1944. By this time, total protein intake was higher than pre-war by 6 per cent, due mainly to the increased use of potatoes and high extraction flour. But in mineral and vitamin intake, in which the pre-war population had been deficient, there were very substantial gains. Calcium and iron, vitamin B (thiamine), riboflavin, vitamin C (ascorbic acid), and nicotinic acid all increased considerably under rationing and the special distribution schemes, and only in vitamin A was there slight reduction.[19] These figures refer to averages, and do not take account of the differing physiological needs of various age and social groups. A more detailed investigation was attempted by the Wartime Food Surveys, which collected budgets from 600 to 700 working-class households each month: these also showed that on the whole the diet was up to nutritional requirements except possibly in respect of vitamin A. Similar data from middle-class households indicated that there was now little difference between their diets and those of the poorer families, reflecting the general levelling-up of standards and the small extent of rationing evasion. These surveys, together with continuous clinical investigations carried out by the Ministry of Health into particular groups, all indicate that the general health of the civilian population was good throughout the war.[20] The Ministry of Health's Report *On the*

State of the Public Health (1946) confidently stated that 'the average diet of all classes was better balanced than ever before. Luxury items soon disappeared, it is true, and meals tended to become monotonous, particularly in 1941 when the U-boat campaign was at its height, but it was nevertheless, always physiologically a better diet and more evenly distributed.'[21]

Particularly significant for the future were the improvements recorded in the birth rate, infant mortality, and the general health of children, which suggest that dietary standards for some categories of the population had notably risen. In the pre-war generations the birth rate had been falling in almost all western countries, and in Britain in the 1930s was below replacement level. It might be expected that the war would accentuate this decline. In fact births rose not only in the United States and Canada, but also in Sweden, New Zealand, and the United Kingdom, where the decline stopped in the early years of the war and the rate began to rise after 1941, reaching 17.7 per thousand in 1944 compared with 15.1 in 1938. By contrast Germany, which had been one of the few countries to pursue a positive population policy before the war, witnessed a decline in births from 20.4 per thousand in 1939 to 14.9 per thousand in 1942. Nativity is indirectly a measure of health in that it falls in a population deprived of the essentials of life, but mortality, and particularly infant mortality, is a better one. In fact infant mortality (deaths in the first year) fell in England and Wales from 53 per thousand in 1938 to 45 in 1944, and maternal mortality declined over the same period from 3.24 per thousand to 1.93:[22] in Germany, Belgium, France, Italy, and Hungary, on the other hand, infant mortality increased.

> In conclusion [said the League of Nations handbook on *Food Rationing and Supply*], data on mortality and morbidity point to a situation which, like nutrition, is becoming diversified on regional lines. The UK, Sweden, Switzerland, and Denmark have been able to retain their pre-war gains; they would even appear to have been able to register some further advances. Such reductions in nutrition and standard of living as the war has necessitated have been balanced by a more equitable distribution of available resources and by a scientifically improved composition of diets. The situation in Germany is less favourable. Without stressing the importance of any one factor, death rates of both infants and adults have increased to a marked degree.[23]

One further evidence of improvement is worth noting. Between 1940 and 1944 Dr E.R. Bransby of the Ministry of Health surveyed the growth of children in twenty-one areas of the country, comparing the heights and weights of standard age groups at the two dates. Despite the wartime dislocations of normal life, separated families, and evacuation (perhaps, because of it) the heights and weights of boys had improved in seventeen areas, and of girls in fourteen. Moreover, children identified by school

medical officers as having 'bad' nutrition (Grade D) fell nationally, and
especially in the pre-war depressed areas like Jarrow (1938 4.84 per cent,
1945 0.24 per cent) and Pontypridd (1938 2.03 per cent, 1945 0.52
per cent).[24]

The success of food control required an elaborate administrative
machinery which operated from the Minister of Food through nineteen
divisional food officers down to 1,250 local food officers. The local
administration was based on existing local government areas, the food
executive officer usually being the clerk to the local authority or his
deputy. Food control committees, consisting of trade representatives and
consumer members, advised him and had power to investigate and pro-
secute offenders against the Ministry's orders. The accounts suggest that
this machinery worked with remarkable efficiency and a minimum of
public criticism. But in the last resort the success of the administrative
schemes depended on the goodwill of thousands of traders and millions of
housewives. Retailers were burdened with forms and ration books in addition to shortages of provisions and staff, and the Ministry's policy of price-
fixing necessarily involved also the fixing of profit margins. This was done,
equitably on the whole, by first determining the gross profits earned in a
particular trade in peacetime and then adjusting for known changes in
cost. The Ministry possibly erred on the side of generosity to food manufacturers, but it was vital to ensure a continuance of distribution at almost
any cost. Housewives put up with queues and shortages because they
knew that all were being treated alike and because the government succeeded so well in keeping prices down: the food price index at the end of
1944 stood only 20 per cent higher than in September 1939. To keep bread
at 9d the 4-lb loaf (the pre-war price was 8d), eggs at 2s a dozen, meat at 1s a
pound and cheese at 1s 1d was a remarkable contribution to social policy,
and its cost, in the form of food subsidies which in 1944 totalled £152
million, was a relatively small price to pay. Coupled with almost full
employment and steadily rising wages, food control produced a marked
increase in the standard of living of the poorer third of the population
which, in the 1930s, had existed below nutritional adequacy: if the dietary
standards of the upper third had to be temporarily restricted there were
probably gains to their health also.

Notes

1 HMSO (1946) *How Britain was Fed in Wartime. Food Control 1939–1945*, 5.
2 Jones, Sir Thomas G. (1944) *The Unbroken Front. Ministry of Food, 1916–1944. Personalities and Problems*, 58 et seq.
3 Hunt, Sandra *The Changing Place of Bread in the British Diet in the Twentieth Century*, Series of unpublished research papers sponsored by the Rank Prize

Funds (Brunel University), 'The Second World War: Bread under government control, 1939–56', 21.

4 For a fuller account of Sir Jack Drummond's work at the Ministry of Food see Drummond, J.C. and Wilbraham, Anne (1957) *The Englishman's Food*, 448 et seq.

5 *Food Rationing and Supply*, Report of the Economic, Financial and Transit Department of the League of Nations (1944), 19.

6 It has been calculated that a shoemaker requires 2,000 to 2,400 kilocalories a day, a weaver 2,400 to 2,700, a carpenter or mason 2,700 to 3,200, a farm labourer 3,200 to 4,100 and a lumberman, 5,000 upwards. A seamstress needs 1,800 to 2,100 and a woman actively engaged in housework 2,300 to 2,900. An adolescent boy may need 3,500, while 1,500 to 2,000 may suffice for persons over seventy (ibid., 23 et seq.).

7 At the end of the war weekly rations for an adult were – meat (by price) 1s 2d (*c.* 1 lb); bacon and ham 4 oz; sugar 8 oz; butter and margarine 6 oz; cheese 2 oz; chocolate and sweets 3 oz; cooking fat 1 oz; tea $2\frac{1}{2}$ oz; preserves 4 oz.

8 HMSO (1946) *The State of the Public Health during Six Years of War*, 93.

9 Curtis-Bennett, Sir Noel (1949) *The Food of the People. The History of Industrial Feeding*, 278.

10 *State of the Public Health*, op. cit., 117.

11 Jones, op. cit., 42.

12 Calder, A. (1969) *The People's War: Britain 1939–1945*, 467.

13 Simon, André L. (ed.) *Wine and Food. A Gastronomic Quarterly*, no. 33 (Spring 1942), 29, and no. 34 (Summer 1942), 90.

14 White, W.H. (1940) *Food in Wartime. Over 200 Meatless Dishes*.

15 Kaye-Smith, Sheila (1945) *Kitchen Fugue*, 106.

16 Mauduit, Vicomte de (1941) *They Can't Ration These*.

17 The 5s maximum meal in hotels and restaurants was established by the Food (Restriction on Meals in Establishments) Order, 1941, which also limited the size of meals to three courses, including one main course. The price limit was circumvented to some extent by cover charges (10 per cent), charges for dancing or cabaret (2s 6d), and by the fact that although the retail prices of beer and whisky were controlled, those of wines and liqueurs were not. Christopher Driver (1983) *The British At Table, 1940–1980*, 33; Stephen Price, op. cit., 64. Driver quotes a Ritz story that crêpes Suzette were made compulsory at a high premium for the liqueur used.

18 *How Britain was Fed in Wartime*, op. cit., 42.

19 Compared with pre-war percentages, calcium intake in 1946 stood at 150 per cent, iron at 129 per cent, vitamin A at 95 per cent, vitamin D at 176 per cent, thiamin at 137 per cent, riboflavin at 114 per cent, nicotinic acid at 130 per cent and vitamin C at 112 per cent. Dorothy F. Hollingsworth (1983) 'Rationing and economic constraints on food consumption in Britain since the Second World War', *World Review of Nutrition and Dietetics* 42, 194 (Table III).

20 *How Britain was Fed in Wartime*, op. cit., 49.

21 Ministry of Health (1946) *On the State of the Public Health during Six Years of*

War, Report of the Chief Medical Officer of the Ministry of Health, 1939–1945, 115.
22 British Medical Association (1950) Report of the Committee on Nutrition, 93 (Table XXVII).
23 *Food Rationing and Supply*, op. cit., 78.
24 Oddy, D.J. (1982) 'The health of the people', in Theo Barker and Michael Drake (eds) *Population and Society in Britain, 1850–1980*, 130–2.

✦ 14 ✦
Want and plenty, 1945–85

When the first edition of *Plenty and Want* was published in 1966 it was justifiable to write:

> Since 1945 the British economy has remained on the whole buoyant and prosperous: although some traditional industries have lost ground to foreign competitors other, newer ones have largely taken their place, and unemployment has in most years been limited to the 2 or 3 per cent which some economists regard as necessary to ensure labour mobility. The nation has accepted from the sociologist the label of 'the affluent society' and from the politician the slogan 'we have never had it so good'.

Twenty years on little of that optimism remains. For much of the last decade economic growth has been sluggish, or stagnant, especially when viewed against the performance of some other industrialized countries. Mass unemployment, which we had thought never to see again, reappeared in the 1970s, the figure climbing slowly from 1.5 per cent in 1957 to 2.5 per cent in 1968, 3.4 per cent in 1971, then, dramatically, to 5.9 per cent in 1976 and 12 per cent in 1983: by then, over 3 million people were out of work, the highest number since the 1930s. Also exceptional and puzzling was the coincidence of high unemployment with high levels of inflation, the effects of which left no one untouched. Some degree of inflation had been with us ever since the end of the war, retail prices increasing on average by 5 per cent a year between 1945 and 1950, and by 2.6 per cent a year between 1954 and 1964. The 'take-off' towards double-figure inflation began in 1971 with a retail price increase of 9.4 per cent which, six years later and exacerbated by the oil crisis of 1973–4, had almost doubled to 17.9 per cent. In 1976 it required £1.82 to buy what £1 had bought in 1972, and *New Society* was reporting 'a revolution of falling expectations'. Not very long before, in 1962, the *Daily Express* had written of 'the rollicking revolution of merrie England'. Professor A.H. Halsey has recently argued that 'a post-war period can be identified as having come to an end in the mid-1970s, followed by a decade exhibiting a new form of polarization in British society'.[1]

In fact, until recent years the failings in the economy were disguised by a

300

continued advance in the standard of living for most English people – almost certainly a greater increase in the years 1945–70 than in any previous quarter-century. Until incomes restraint began to bite hard in 1974, price rises were more than balanced by wage and salary increases, which through the 1950s and earlier 1960s often ran at double the annual rate of inflation: in particular, powerful trade unions were able to take advantage of conditions of nearly full employment to narrow the gaps between semi-skilled and skilled earnings and between manual and professional earnings. Among the chief beneficiaries of rising standards were therefore some formerly low-paid groups of industrial, clerical, and women workers, while many professional and managerial salaries were squeezed by the combined effects of taxation and incomes policies. In the most recent years, with inflation under control and reduced to annual rates of 4 or 5 per cent, and with bargaining power reduced by weakened trade unions, the advance in standards of living has slowed, but over the whole period from 1951 to 1983 the average real weekly earnings (i.e. the purchasing power) of adult male manual workers almost doubled from £60 to £111.[2]

Until the economy moved into serious depression in 1974, rising real earnings meant that more people than ever before were able to afford a nutritionally adequate diet. The evidence of increasing prosperity has also been seen in the increase of home-ownership to 62 per cent in 1986, a similar growth of car-ownership (also to 62 per cent of households in 1986), and a spectacular increase in the ownership of domestic appliances, many of which would have been regarded as luxuries a few years earlier. In 1986 nine out of ten households had a television and a refrigerator, eight out of ten a washing-machine, seven out of ten central heating, and two out of three a freezer. The latest innovation in cookery technology, the microwave oven, introduced from the United States only in 1959, is already found in 26 per cent of households.[3]

Major social and demographic changes since the end of the last war have also had important effects on dietary patterns. Although the birth rate has generally been low, more people have married, and married younger, than in the past, while at the other end of the age-scale people have continued to live longer. The proportion of people over sixty was four times greater in 1985 than in 1901, and now represents 20 per cent of the whole population. One result of these changes has been a greatly increased number of separate households in Britain (currently 20.9 million), but of much smaller average size than in the past. In 1985 the average household in Britain consisted of only 2.56 people, compared with 3.1 in 1961: what was once considered the 'typical' family of husband, wife, and two children accounted for only 11.9 per cent of all households, while one-person households constituted 24 per cent in 1985, and two-person households a further 30 per cent. Large families having four or more children are now a mere 1.9 per cent of all households. Family eating and purchasing patterns, which were formerly dominated in all social classes by the large number of mouths to be fed, have had to adapt to catering for much smaller groups, often with specialized tastes or needs.

The increasing desire and ability of parents to limit family size, coupled with the growth of domestic technology, has released wives from many of the burdens of household drudgery. One of the most outstanding post-war social changes has been the increasing employment of married women outside the home – from 22 per cent of wives in 1951 to 52 per cent in 1985, either full-time or part-time. It may be speculated whether 'the kitchen revolution' of recent years, which has taken the form of better-planned use of space in the home as well as increased use of 'convenience foods' and labour-saving devices, is cause or effect of this change. According to a recent survey, two-thirds of all women spend between two and four hours a day in their kitchens, and only 16 per cent six hours or more.[4] In 41 per cent of married households washing the evening dishes is shared equally between men and women, though only 16 per cent share the preparation of the meal.[5] The trend towards women's liberation has apparently not reduced the centrality of the home and family-based activities in the lives of working women, many of whom give as a main reason for working the desire to improve their domestic circumstances.

In 1985 the average weekly household expenditure in the UK, not including taxes, insurance, betting, or savings, was £161.87 (1975, £54.58). Of this, food at 20.2 per cent was the largest item, followed by housing (16.1), transport and vehicles (15.2), clothing and footwear (7.4), durable household goods (7.2), fuel and light (6.1), alcoholic drink (4.9), and tobacco (2.7).[6] If we compare these statistics with those of 1953–4 when Britain was just emerging from the post-war period of scarcity and rationing, there have been some interesting changes. Then, food took 33 per cent of total expenditure – two-thirds more than in 1985, and tobacco 6.5 per cent, again substantially more. Most other items, however, accounted for less – transport and vehicles only 7 per cent, housing 9 per cent, and alcoholic drink 4 per cent. The long-term trend in Britain, as in the USA and other affluent societies, has been for food to absorb a smaller proportion of total personal income, while other categories, especially transport, have taken increasingly more. This major reduction in the proportion of expenditure on food reflects not only the growth in real incomes, but also the fact that food prices have risen more slowly in recent years than the prices of other items, while the volume of food consumed has increased only in line with population.[7]

In the nineteenth century and in the years before the Second World War, it was a well-observed phenomenon that as income fell the proportion devoted to food increased, that while the poor might have to spend half or two-thirds of their meagre wages merely to satisfy hunger, the richer classes could fare luxuriously on a much smaller fraction of their earnings. Although this characteristic still holds true today, the relative difference is considerably reduced. Thus, in 1985 the poorest 20 per cent of households allotted 29.4 per cent to food while the wealthiest 20 per cent devoted 15.5 per cent:[8] in money terms, the richest households spent £9.87 a head on food, the poorest £7.49.[9] Expenditure on alcoholic drink moves in the opposite direction, from 4.0 per cent in the poorest up to 5.1 per cent in the richest. Another variable in food consumption is now the most important – that of household size – although again less than formerly when, as we have seen, large families imposed great hardship on working-class budgets. Today, the one-adult household spends £11.38 a week on food while families consisting of two adults and four or more children spend on average only £5.91 a head. In these larger households the proportion of income spent on bread and other cereal products, dairy products, and milk rises with increasing numbers of children, while that on meat, fish, eggs, and beverages falls:[10] household size has now clearly emerged as the single most important determinant of food expenditure and choice.

In reviewing the dietary history of the last few decades it has to be remembered that food was rationed in all for fourteen years (1939–53) and that only after this did adjustment to free market conditions take place. In some respects the post-1945 diet was more frugal than the wartime ration, due principally to world shortages of foodstuffs, poor harvests, and the ending of 'Lend-Lease'. Supplies of fat fell noticeably, and their scarcity was especially felt during the arctic winter of 1946–7 when public complaints were loudest. In what amounted to a food crisis, the extraction rate of flour was raised to 90 per cent, bread itself was rationed from July 1946 to July 1948 (at two 2-lb loaves per adult a week), the meat ration was cut, and even potatoes were brought under a control system from November 1947 to April 1948, measures which had not been necessary even in the darkest days of war.[11] In fact, the nation's diet, at its worst from 1946–8, was still better than the average pre-war diet in most nutrients: measured as percentages of values before World War Two, energy fell to 97 per cent and fat to 84 per cent, but total protein was higher at 108 per cent and intakes of calcium, iron, and vitamins were all well above pre-war levels.[12] In 1949, as food supplies and the balance of payments improved, it was possible to begin a gradual de-control, apparently without losing the benefit to the lower income groups which wartime policies had brought. Losses had been more than made good by 1954, and the national diet was in every respect better then than in 1939.[13]

For a few years after the end of rationing increased consumers' expenditure went on foods formerly in short supply – meat, fats, sugar, eggs, canned fruits, and so on. But, clearly, an upper limit to food intake is set by physiological factors, and once these particular appetites had been satisfied by the later 1950s dietary habits settled down to a pattern which has changed only slowly over time. Table 49 compares average domestic food consumption at four dates – 1950, when rationing was still largely in force, 1960, typical of the 'affluent' years, 1983, and 1985, the most recent year for which full statistics are available: additionally, the final column gives average weekly expenditure per person in 1985. It should be noted that the data are drawn from the National Food Survey Reports, which record domestic food consumption and expenditure on a sample basis, but do not include food and drink consumed outside the home.

Over the period since 1950 certain trends in food consumption appear to have become clearly established. Overall, we now buy less food for consumption in the home, a trend particularly noticeable in the 1970s. By 1977 the energy value of household food met only 94 per cent of recommended intake compared with 111 per cent in 1970, though most, if not all, of this decline in eating at home was made up by increased use of meals and snacks outside the home and increased consumption of alcohol and sweets.[14] An interesting case in point is that of milk consumption, which has fallen markedly after rising during the Second World War as part of the deliberate national nutritional policy. At less than two-thirds of a pint a day it is now well short of the advertising slogan of the 1960s – 'Drinka Pinta Milka Day'. This has been only partly due to the changes in the provision of welfare milk and school meal schemes in 1971, which cut free milk except for children under seven; nor has it been due to cost, since the real price of milk has fallen relative to other foods. Probably more important have been changes in meal patterns, particularly at breakfast and tea, and the less favourable image which milk has recently acquired as a major source of fat. In this connection, it is notable that while household consumption of liquid whole milk fell by 8 per cent between 1983 and 1985, that of low fat milk more than trebled, and now accounts for 11 per cent of liquid milk purchases.[15] Curiously, however, similar concerns appear not to have influenced the consumption of cheese, which has continued to rise steadily and now stands at around 50 per cent higher than pre-war: as a relatively cheap source of protein and one of the earliest of all 'convenience foods', cheese has evidently adapted successfully to modern dietary patterns. The combined consumption of butter and margarine has fallen significantly, however, and in recent years margarine has moved ahead for the first time in peacetime. Butter reached a peak of 6.10 oz per head a week in 1958 and is now less than half as much, but margarine has gained from much improved quality and flavour, and from the growing preference of consumers for a 'soft-spread' product

Table 49 *Estimates of average household food consumption and expenditure, 1950–85*

	Consumption (oz per person per week)				Expenditure (pence per person per week)
	1950 (a)	1960 (b)	1983 (c)	1985 (d)	1985 (e)
Liquid milk (pints)	4.78	4.84	4.00	3.82	82.98
Other milk and cream	0.43	0.31	0.31	0.31	15.68
Cheese	2.54	3.04	4.01	3.91	31.32
Butter	4.56	5.68	3.27	2.83	15.03
Margarine	3.94	3.66	4.08	3.76	11.11
Lard and cooking fats	3.11	2.63	1.70	1.44	3.25
Other fats and oils	n.a.	n.a.	1.63	2.03	7.38
Eggs (number)	3.46	4.36	3.53	3.15	21.10
Preserves, syrup, treacle	6.30	3.21	2.05	1.87	5.73
Sugar	10.13	17.76	9.84	8.41	11.63
Beef and veal	8.06	8.74	6.57	6.51	65.26
Mutton and lamb	5.43	6.63	3.87	3.27	25.38
Pork	0.30	2.02	3.53	3.45	25.77
Bacon and ham	4.52	5.32	4.02	3.69	29.80
Poultry	0.35	1.68	6.69	6.57	33.16
Sausages }	4.01	3.52	13.47	13.29	94.14
Other meat products }	7.82	7.98			
(Total meat	30.49	35.89	38.13	36.77	273.51)
Fish, fresh and processed	6.18	4.69	1.82	1.78	16.30
Canned and prepared fish	0.44	0.95	1.76	1.46	15.48
Frozen fish and fish products	n.k.	0.29	1.55	1.67	12.77
Fresh green vegetables	13.81	15.34	10.78	9.78	14.46
Other fresh vegetables	16.16	13.88	15.71	15.70	30.60
Frozen vegetables	n.k. (0.2'56)	0.63	4.92	5.97	14.23
Canned and processed vegetables	4.55	6.21	12.44	12.51	36.13
Potatoes, excl. processed	62.04	56.14	39.88	40.96	17.62
Fruit, fresh	14.41	18.16	19.64	18.52	38.82
Canned and other fruit products	3.68	6.84	9.05	8.54	21.57
Flour	7.25	6.76	4.97	4.05	3.29

Table 49 *Continued*

	Consumption (oz per person per week)				Expenditure (pence per person per week)
	1950 (a)	1960 (b)	1983 (c)	1985 (d)	1985 (e)
White bread	50.91	36.63	20.81	19.37	27.62
Brown, wholewheat and wholemeal bread	2.55	3.35	5.89	7.33	13.63
Other bread	4.29	5.49	4.04	4.29	13.17
Cakes, buns, biscuits, etc.	10.37	11.98	9.06	8.71	44.75
Breakfast cereals	1.40	1.80	3.83	4.04	17.14
Tea	2.16	2.80	2.04	1.74	20.04
Coffee	0.21	0.39	0.69	0.68	19.59
Soups	1.31	2.10	2.83	2.86	7.04

Sources:
Table 49 based on the following Reports: (a) *Domestic Food Consumption and Expenditure, 1950. Annual Report of the National Food Survey Committee* (1952), Appendix D1, 103 et seq. (b) *Annual Report of the NFS Committee for 1960* (1962), Table 11, 19 et seq. (c), (d), (e) *Annual Report of the NFS Committee for 1985* (1987), Tables 2.3–2.10, 4–7, and Appendix B, Table 1, 60 et seq.

made from vegetable rather than animal fats. At around 13 lb a head a year, margarine consumption in Britain is still low compared with Norway (55 lb), the Netherlands (44 lb), or West Germany (28 lb).

Egg consumption grew from 104 a year in 1909–13 to 152 in 1934, and 227 in 1960, since when there has been a considerable contraction to 164. Much more spectacular was the long-term increase in the consumption of sugar, which grew five-fold in the hundred years after 1835, and rose extremely rapidly between 1950 and 1960 after rationing restrictions were removed: by then total consumption of raw sugar in the UK was estimated at 126 lb per person per year, and was exceeded only by that of Greenland, Gibraltar, Iceland, and Hawaii.[16] Since then, domestic purchases of sugar have fallen dramatically to $8\frac{1}{4}$ oz in 1985, though total consumption has declined less due to the heavy use of sugar in brewing, soft drinks, ice-cream, confectionery, and preserves. The doubling in retail sugar prices between 1974 and 1975 clearly sharpened the decline, although it seems that some swing in public taste away from sweets towards savouries,

306

encouraged by growing concern over the physiological effects of excessive sugar, is a more fundamental cause. A decline in home-baking and preserving is an additional factor.

Total meat consumption has not changed greatly since 1960 and in fact stands lower now than it did before the last war. Even in their years of affluence the British did not become the nation of meat-eaters that some forecast, and the traditional joint of beef or lamb has continued to slide in popularity, particularly the latter, probably because of its high fat content. Were it not for the increase in pork, and the much more spectacular rise in poultry consumption following the mass-production of broiler chickens, total meat consumption would now be less than in the rationed days of 1950. It is significant that 'convenience' products such as cooked, canned, and quick-frozen meats, pies and sausages, have increased, while purchases of carcase meat have fallen off. Its relative dearness in recent years, especially against poultry, has clearly been a major factor, but one authority has also suggested a lack of knowledge of meat cuts among younger housewives due to 'a break in the foodlore link between the generations', a reduction of face-to-face contact with butchers as a result of increased supermarket sales, and the reluctance of butchers to prepare cheaper cuts in a form more convenient for mid-week meals.[17] It may be that there are also more deep-seated reasons – that a society whose occupations are less laborious feels less need for animal protein, or even that the growing preference for 'white meats' (poultry, pork, cheese) rather than 'red' involves complex physiological and psychological factors.

In the immediate post-war period when meat supplies were scarce the consumption of fish increased sharply, but since then there has been a continuous decline, exacerbated by 'cod wars', herring scarcities, and vastly increased prices (white fish 1909–13 = 100, 1976 = 3396): by 1985 consumption was less than half that of the 1920s. The one exception to this has been the rapid growth of frozen fish and fish products, a successful innovation which began with the introduction of the fish finger in 1955. As everyone knows, the tasty and once cheap meal of fried fish and chips has lately become a luxury. After falling between the wars, potato consumption increased during the Second World War as part of national policy, and in 1947 was probably 50 per cent higher than in 1934–8: since then, it has fallen steadily, but has recently levelled out at around 40 oz a week. Fresh green vegetables have also fallen since 1960, but the great 'success story' of recent times has been the boom in quick-frozen vegetables, especially peas and beans: canned and processed vegetables, another form of 'convenience', have also continued to increase.

Probably the greatest change in recent years has been that of bread. Once the mainstay of the English diet, it is still the largest single source of energy and the second source of protein, but overall consumption has fallen greatly since 1950, and that of white bread dramatically from 50 oz a week to 20 oz. This has usually been explained as a natural result of rising standards of living and a shift away from cheaper energy foods, as well as of changes in domestic meal patterns – almost 20 per cent of bread is now eaten outside the home, much of it in the form of sandwiches. But recently, nutritional considerations have clearly had a major effect in stimulating a change to brown, wholemeal, and wholewheat breads, which now make up almost one-quarter of total bread consumption. The only other commodity in this range which has increased greatly since before the war is the group of breakfast cereals, which have trebled since 1950. Tea, of which the British are still the second heaviest consumers in the world after Australians, has been declining in popularity since 1960, but the steady rise in coffee consumption has now established it as a major competitor.

Summarizing these changes over the last quarter of a century, it appears that as a nation we now eat less beef, mutton, and bacon, less sugar, bread and potatoes, less butter and jam, less fish and fewer eggs, and drink less milk and tea – that is to say, less of many of the traditional articles of English diet. No simple pattern emerges. Some of these, like bread and potatoes, were basic foods of the past and had been experiencing decline for many years, except when interrupted by war: others, like sugar, butter, and eggs, were relative luxuries to which previous generations had aspired as their standard of living rose. Similarly, the foods which have increased in recent times – pork and poultry, brown breads, margarine, cheese, pasta, breakfast cereals, and frozen foods – do not fit into a single category or explanation.

Nevertheless, some trends seem fairly clear. Our diet is lighter and less bulky than it was: peak consumption was reached in 1970, from when there has been some reduction towards slightly more stringency.[18] Inflationary pressures in the 1970s appear to have had temporary effects on the consumption of some foods like beef, potatoes, and butter which experienced sharp, short-term price rises, but did not radically alter established trends. Similarly, although public awareness of the relationship between diet and health has become more widespread in recent years, since the publicity given to the COMA and NACNE Reports, this has not yet influenced eating habits profoundly or systematically. For example, visible fat consumption has remained at between 300 and 350 g a week throughout the last forty years: consumption of paté and salami, containing up to 40 per cent fat, has increased at the expense of lower-fat sausages; vegetable oil has increased little, while the consumption of sweets, confectionery, alcohol, and snack foods has shown marked growth recently. With the exceptions of wholemeal and wholewheat bread, and skimmed milk, it seems that, so far at least, nutritional arguments have not been a

Want and plenty, 1945–85

Table 50 *Changes in domestic consumption, 1962–76*[19]

	%		%
Pasta	+ 160	Carcase lamb	– 37
Poultry	+ 150	Sugar	– 34
Breakfast cereals	+ 69	Potatoes (new/old)	– 34
Carcase pork	+ 26	Preserves	– 30
Cheese	+ 221	Bacon	– 21
Rice	+ 3	Fish	– 21
		Bread	– 24
		Butter	– 17
		Carcase beef and veal	– 15
		Sausages	– 14
		Eggs	– 13
		Milk	– 5
		Margarine	– 3
		Flour	– 3

major determinant of food choice unless supported by some other consideration – economy, palatability, or convenience. In 1976 a market survey of the consumption trends of twenty food items since 1962 arranged them into two groups – those which had increased and those which had declined (Table 50): today, ten years later, it would be necessary to shift the category of only one item – margarine.

But what is now an outstanding and apparently irreversible trend in English diet in recent years is the growth in demand for 'convenience foods'. These are officially defined as 'processed foods for which the degree of culinary preparation has been carried to an advanced stage by the manufacturer, and which may be used as labour-saving alternatives to less highly processed products': they include cooked and canned meats and fish, a constantly expanding range of quick-frozen foods, canned vegetables, canned fruit, canned and dehydrated soups, breakfast cereals, cakes, puddings, pastries and biscuits, ice-cream, yoghurt, and 'desserts' of many kinds. Expenditure on the whole group averaged £3.20 per person per week in 1974, or more than a third of total food expenditure: while average household food expenditure rose by 27 per cent between 1980 and 1985, that on convenience foods increased by 48 per cent.[20] Because the consumer is buying services as well as food these commodities are a relatively expensive source of nutrients: they are bought because they require little time in preparation, give reliable results, and bring out-of-season foods and a wider choice within reach. Frozen peas and beans may not have the identical flavour of fresh, but most people are glad to have them in mid-winter and many eat them throughout the year. But the greatest advantage of convenience foods is that they enable the housewife to put a meal on the table within minutes rather than hours: they are part of women's liberation, adapted to working wives and small families, and giving greater flexibility in the choice and timing of meals.

The most spectacular aspect of 'the convenience revolution' has been the rapid growth during the last three decades of quick-frozen foods. In this, as in some other aspects of food technology, Britain followed US developments, where quick-freezing had begun just before the Second World War: in 1945 Bird's Eye began tentative operations in East Anglia, and in 1947 total UK output was valued at a quarter of a million pounds. In 1963 frozen food expenditure in the UK reached £80 million, by 1973 £345 million, and by 1986 £1,913 million,[21] of which one-seventh was bought by catering establishments. In terms of volume, household consumption of frozen foods has doubled since 1975 from 5 oz per person a week to 10 oz: frozen vegetables are the largest volume sector, followed by meat and meat products, fish, and cereals in that order, but the range has been continuously expanded into such things as sea-food, Chinese foods, cheesecake, and cauliflower florets where these 'luxury' items are reported to be booming. The expansion of this market has, of course, depended crucially on changes in retailing, which have brought more than 100,000 freezer cabinets into shops, self-service stores, and supermarkets, and on the rapid increase of home-freezers which are now found in 75 per cent of all homes, compared with 50 per cent in 1980.

It is tempting to speculate, though very difficult to know, whether British food tastes have changed radically since the end of the war. The factors which determine food choice are complex and still largely unexplained. Besides economic and physiological considerations, historical, psychological, ethical, religious, and status factors may exert powerful influences on food habits, yet why we select some foods and reject others is still largely unknown. 'We all recognize', writes Professor John Yudkin, 'that what determines our food choice are food preferences; what determines the other man's choice are food prejudices.' People eat for reasons which are satisfying to themselves – not to nutritionists. Through food choice, and the various rituals of cooking, serving, and consuming it, people are able to fantasize about a social status or life-style to which they aspire, to express personality, to honour their guests, or to worship their God, and it would be vain to expect too much rationality behind complicated and often unconscious objectives.

In the short term, food tastes are conservative and strongly resistant to change. Over a longer period one effect of increasing real income and increasing urbanization was to raise the consumption of animal protein, sugar, and fats and to lower that of foods of cereal origin: other, more recent effects have been to encourage the use of 'stress foods' with high sucrose, and 'snack' foods eaten between meals.[22] The latter have seen a spectacular growth recently to total sales of £1,000 million in 1986, of which potato crisps alone were valued at £585 million and savoury snacks at £242 million; the biscuit market added a further £930 million.[23] It is reported that snack-eating occasions in Britain have doubled in the last five years. Food choice is also obviously influenced by the number, variety, and accessibility of shops, and it is difficult to know whether the increasing concentration of retail outlets has widened or narrowed the customer's choice. The number of grocery outlets in Britain has fallen from 105,283 in 1971 to 50,500 in 1985: multiples now have a 70 per cent share of the grocery market, superstores 23 per cent, and in many small towns and suburban areas there may be no alternative to the single supermarket.

Again the diets of different countries still retain strong national characteristics determined by geographical, historical, and cultural factors, price movements, the incidence of wars, and so on, and there is little evidence as yet of a general trend towards a common 'European' diet. Thus, the UK has a milk consumption twice or three times higher than that of most European countries (usually explained by our unique doorstep delivery service). Italy consumes twice as much wheat per head as others, Britain has the lowest fruit and vegetable but almost the highest sugar consumption of the EEC, we drink an average of 12 litres of wine a head a year compared with 104 litres in France, and so on. Expressed in terms of total nutrients the differences become less but are still substantial – Belgium and Luxembourg have the highest fat content in their diets and Italians derive almost 40 per cent of their energy requirements from cereals, twice the proportion elsewhere in Europe.

In this respect, the British diet has historically been a 'richer' one than the Italian with an emphasis on more expensive animal sources of protein and fat. In 1973 a survey conducted by J. C. McKenzie into what foods housewives would buy more of if not limited by money showed meat at the top (chosen by 51 per cent) followed by chicken (40 per cent), apples, oranges, butter (21 per cent), fish (19 per cent), milk, and eggs.[24] It was noticeable that demand for more meat, chicken, and butter was strongest among the lower socio-economic groups and among families with children, and it has been observed that in recent years while overall meat consumption has remained largely static that of lower income groups has risen while that of wealthier groups has fallen. Obesity, until recently regarded as a disease of affluence, is currently increasing in the United States more rapidly among formerly poorer classes. In Britain in 1985 the difference in meat consumption between different income groups was marginal: households with earnings of over £300 a week ate 35.58 oz a head while those with incomes under £85 a week ate 34.08 oz.[25]

Deliberate restriction of some foods for cosmetic and physiological reasons has been a noticeable trend in British diets during the last decade or two, and is evidenced, among other things, by the substitution of green salads for potatoes, an increasing use of fruit, a preference for lean over fatty meats, and a drift away from butter towards margarine. The frequently observed preference of children at parties for savouries rather than sweets may well have a basis in some change in national taste: in a recent survey four out of ten housewives believed that their tastes had changed in the last ten years – that they and their families now ate more savoury foods and less sweet ones, that they had a wider variety in their diet and a liking for new dishes. This growing willingness to experiment by a people who were notorious for their conservatism and indiscrimination in food habits may be related to the belief of 63 per cent of housewives that food has less flavour now than it had twenty years ago.

A growing taste for foreign dishes has also been influenced by the huge expansion of overseas travel and holidays abroad, and by the proliferation of Chinese, Indian, Cypriot, and other restaurants throughout the towns and suburbs of Britain. The growth of modest eating-out in the 1950s and 1960s brought a knowledge and appreciation of new foods to less wealthy groups who in the past had rarely eaten a meal outside the home, and the time now seems remote (it was only in 1961) when a coach party of Welsh miners touring Spain thoughtfully brought their own chef with them – even then, he was sent home when they came to prefer Spanish cooking to his. By 1983 62 per cent of adults had had a holiday abroad at some time, compared with only 36 per cent in 1971: also, the fact that Britain's population now contains 3 million people who were born outside the UK, many of whom have opened food shops and restaurants, has had important effects on national food habits. The greatest success has gone to Chinese restaurants of which there are today over 5,000 and it is difficult to imagine that in the *Good Food Guide* of 1951 there were only nine oriental restaurants in London and four outside.[26] In a Gallup survey in 1976 into people's knowledge of foreign dishes, chow mein and sweet and sour pork were known by seven out of ten, pizza by eight out of ten, and ravioli by nearly as many; chilli con carne was familiar to only four out of ten, while moussaka, sole meunière, and wienerschnitzel had reached only one in three.[27] It is clear that canning and quick-freezing, coupled with mass advertising, have become important instruments of food change, and that the British eating public is less wedded to its 'meat and two veg.' than is commonly supposed. In recent times new foods have been introduced at an accelerating pace, and even in the recession year of 1975 'New Products in Grocers' reported a record 667 new lines on the market.

Despite the accumulation of food facts in recent years, what people actually eat at the different meals of the day is still a matter of some

Table 51 *Meal patterns, 1958*

	Men %	Women %
Early morning tea	40	47
Breakfast	93	91
'Elevenses'	48	50
Midday meal	95	98
Afternoon tea	45	50
Evening meal	92	91
Late supper	72	76

mystery. The National Food Survey, valuable as it is as a record of family food purchases, only takes us as far as the larder: it does not follow the food into meal patterns or into the mouths of individuals. The only extensive study of eating habits in recent times was carried out by the Market Research Division of W.S. Crawford Ltd in 1958 when for most people meal patterns were still 'traditional'. The results of this nation-wide survey are summarized in Table 51.

For just over half the population the day began with an early morning cup (or cups) of tea, the most popular time for which was between 7.0 and 7.30 a.m.: during the day, we each drank six cups. The first meal of the day, the British breakfast, had not then changed radically since before the war. More cold cereals as distinct from porridge were eaten, and slightly more fruit, but the light, continental breakfast had made little headway. Forty-seven per cent of people had a cooked course in summer and 51 per cent in winter, eggs and bacon heading the list (17 per cent of people had both), followed by tomatoes, sausages, and fish (only 1 per cent). As the breakfast drink, tea was taken by 85 per cent of people, coffee by only 4 per cent.

The midday meal – described as 'dinner' by 64 per cent and as 'lunch' by 34 per cent – was eaten by the majority between 12.30 and 1.30 p.m., though later at weekends. Surprisingly, in 1958 six out of every ten men went home for their midday meal: 21 per cent of men ate at work and 13 per cent at a cafe or restaurant. The courses eaten were soup (19 per cent in winter, 6 per cent in summer), a main dish (85 per cent), and a sweet (52 per cent): few people had more than two courses, and a quarter had only the main dish. Throughout the week no one dish dominated the menu – roasts, stews, ham, sausages, egg dishes, fish were all below 13 per cent of the total, but for Sunday lunch, the most traditional meal of the week, 32 per cent of all families ate roast beef and two vegetables. Roast lamb (15 per cent) and pork (12 per cent) were the only serious rivals. Two out of three homes had potatoes at midday, summer and winter alike, and 40 per cent had green vegetables, but salads reached only 13 per cent even in summer.

'Afternoon tea' was scarcely a meal, only half the consumers taking cake or biscuits with the drink. The only other meal of importance was the principal evening meal, variously described as 'tea' or 'high tea' (67 per cent), 'dinner' (23 per cent, mainly in the south-east), and 'supper' (2 per cent). The peak time was between 6.0 and 6.30 p.m., and it was remarkable that very few in any social class ate later than 7.0 p.m. The foods eaten did not fall into traditional courses: 30 per cent ate the 'high tea' type, consisting of a main dish (ham, bacon, sausages, cooked meats, eggs, etc.) with bread, butter, jam, and cakes; 24 per cent the 'dinner' type with a main dish, soup and/or sweet, but no bread, butter, and cakes; 23 per cent a main dish only; and 15 per cent an 'afternoon tea' type with no main dish. Only 3 per cent ate a soup in summer, 8 per cent in winter, but salads rose in popularity to 40 per cent on summer evenings. The most popular meats were ham, corned beef or luncheon meat, bacon, and sausages. Omelettes were so rare as to be unclassified. Only 1 per cent of families had alcohol with the evening meal, and only 4 per cent coffee after it. The day ended for three-quarters of all people with a supper drink – tea (36 per cent), coffee (16 per cent), 'health beverages' (15 per cent), or milk (8 per cent).

To what extent these meal patterns have changed during the last thirty years is unknown in the absence of an updated 'Crawford' survey, which is now overdue. One recent piece of research by Kellogg's into 'Who eats breakfast' suggests that an important change has taken place in the first meal of the day, however. An investigation in September and October 1976 covering 6,000 homes and 18,000 men, women, and children in all parts of the UK discovered that only 18 per cent of people ate a cooked breakfast: 40 per cent ate a cereal breakfast, twice the proportion of twenty years ago, and 25 per cent had bread, toast, or a roll, but neither cereal nor cooked dish. But perhaps the most surprising, and alarming, statistic in 1976 was that 17 per cent of the population, representing 9,000,000 people, had either nothing at all for breakfast, or only a drink. Not only had the cooked breakfast collapsed, but many people of all ages were going to work or to school 'on an empty stomach': they included half a million children under the age of twelve, a million teenagers, and seven-and-a-half million adults. No very convincing explanation of this change was offered. Working wives in a hurry to leave the house and reluctant to return to breakfast washing-up may be part of the answer, and it is known that children's breakfast is prepared in one-fifth of cases by children themselves. Deliberate slimming may also be a factor, especially by younger adults among whom no breakfast is most common.

The chief cause for concern highlighted by the Breakfast Survey is, no doubt, for schoolchildren, 9 per cent of whom were fasting for up to eighteen hours – from tea one day until school lunch the next – a problem exacerbated by the cuts in the school meals and milk programmes. In the East End of London 20 per cent of 10–11-year-old boys and 30 per cent of girls were found to be regularly fasting for eighteen hours, and there was strong evidence that this was tending to loss of scholastic performance. The opinion of nutritionists is that breakfast should supply one-quarter of the body's daily needs for energy and protein, and that children in particular cannot adapt successfully to the complete omission of the first meal of the day.[29] Anxieties about the health of schoolchildren were confirmed in the Black Report of 1980 on *Inequalities in Health*, which argued that under-nutrition existed in Britain, and would increase unless school meals and milk were now extended,[30] while a survey of the diets of people on low incomes carried out in 1984 found that 11.2 per cent had missed breakfast during the previous day, of which the highest proportion were young people on government schemes.[31]

In the absence of similar studies of the other meals of the day, we know much less about other possible changes. It must be the case, however, that for the midday meal the family is now much more dispersed than it was thirty years ago, and that lunch has lost much of its former primacy as the principal meal of the day. With longer journeys to work and the increased provision of works canteens to 35,000 in 1976, fewer men now return home for their midday meal: at the same time, the increase in the employment of married women has meant that fewer wives would be at home to prepare it anyway. Another principal change was the growth of the school meals service, first expanded during the war when 1,500,000 meals a day were provided and subsequently increased to cater for 6,000,000 pupils in 1973. The principle was established during the Second World War that the school dinner should provide at least 1,000 kilocalories and between 20 and 25 g of first-class protein: subsequently these requirements were redefined as 42 per cent of the child's recommended protein and 33 per cent of its energy needs.

A major change occurred in 1980, however, when control over the form and content of school meals passed from central government to local education authorities, with each adopting its own charging and catering policies: the great majority have instituted some form of cafeteria service, by which it is not possible to control the nutritional value of the meal. In 1984, 51 per cent of pupils at public sector schools in the UK took school meals, while 18 per cent received free school meals. For ten- and eleven-year-old children there seems to have been some marginal reduction to around 30 per cent of daily energy intakes supplied by school meals,[32] but a recent *Which* survey reports a marked trend towards healthier menus, with wholemeal quiches and pizzas, baked potatoes with fillings, cottage cheese, yoghurt, and fresh fruit replacing the traditional stew, over-cooked vegetables, and jam roly-poly.[33] The principal concern is for those older children eating out of school at cafés and take-aways and choosing meals low in many nutrients, especially iron.

These changes in the midday meal have had sequential effects on meals later in the day. The former pattern of an 'afternoon tea' of cakes, bread, and jam when children returned from school, followed by a later evening meal for parents and older children, has usually given way to a cooked family meal somewhere in time between the two. 'Afternoon tea' is now increasingly a meal restricted to the vanishing tea-shop, while the former importance of lunch as a family occasion has been transferred to the evening meal ('tea' or 'supper') where convenience foods come into their own. A new 'Crawford' survey would almost certainly reveal more cooking in the evening, more variety of dishes, and more catering for individual tastes particularly between adults and children. Ritual and conformism in family eating survive primarily at the Sunday lunch, but even this has lost some of its former pride of place: in a recent survey only 56 per cent of all housewives (and 66 per cent of those with children) rated it as the most important meal of the week, and many young housewives without children gave more importance to the weekday evening meal, Sunday being regarded as a day when they should be liberated from the kitchen.

One method of testing people's food tastes is to ask them to describe the contents of their ideal meal. On four occasions now – 1947, 1962, 1967, and 1973 – Gallup Poll has conducted enquiries on behalf of the *Daily Telegraph* which have asked a representative cross-section of people throughout Britain 'If expense were no object and you could have absolutely anything you wanted, what would you choose for a perfect meal?' Surprisingly, perhaps, lobster, quail, venison, caviar, asparagus, and other time-honoured delicacies did not appear significantly in the replies; more surprisingly still, the choices did not change in fundamental respects between the lean times of 1947 and the affluent ones of 1973.

A quarter of a century of revolutionary social change and an unprecedented rise in the standard of living had apparently resulted only in the substitution of shrimps for sole, steak for chicken, and the addition of a brandy to conclude the meal. But below the surface, some more significant changes in taste are demonstrated. Oxtail soup, second choice in 1947, had fallen badly in popularity by 1973: shrimp and prawn cocktail, scarcely mentioned in 1947 and claiming only 2 per cent of adherents in 1962, topped the fish course in 1973 and was especially the choice of middle-aged, middle-class southerners: by 1973 steak had become the 'luxury' meat choice and chicken so commonplace as to be chosen by only 9 per cent. Significantly, in the latest survey 20 per cent did not mention potatoes as part of their perfect meal compared with only 5 per cent six years

Table 52 *The perfect meal*[34]

1947	1973
Sherry	Sherry
Tomato soup	Tomato soup
Sole	Prawn or shrimp cocktail
Roast chicken	Steak
Roast potatoes,	Roast and/or chipped potatoes,
peas and sprouts	peas, sprouts, mushrooms
Red or white wine	Red or white wine
Trifle and cream	Trifle or apple pie
	and cream
Cheese and biscuits	Cheese and biscuits
Coffee	Coffee
	Liqueurs or brandy

earlier. Drinking before and with the meal had also changed notably. In 1947 one person in three chose a drink before the meal, now four in every five: at the earlier date only one in ten chose wine with the meal compared with half in 1973, while as the after-dinner drink coffee rose in popularity from 42 to 60 per cent. In these changes there appears to be some evidence of a demand for wider variety in food, possibly influenced by foreign travel, new marketing techniques, the growth of steak houses and 'take-away' restaurants, and certainly evidence of an increased taste for sherry, wine, and liqueurs. On the other hand, the fact that only 1 per cent chose turtle soup, 5 per cent roast duckling, 2 per cent crêpe suzette, and 2 per cent champagne suggests that the British eating public has not developed a taste for the more sophisticated delicacies of the past.

Unfortunately it is not recorded whether 'the perfect meal' was to be eaten at home or in a restaurant or hotel, but there has been a marked growth since the war in eating out in all forms, from the hamburger bar to the grand banquet in a City Livery Hall. But even at Grosvenor House, which can serve 1,500 guests, or at the Connaught Rooms where 700 fillet steaks can be grilled simultaneously, the three-course luncheon and four-course dinner are now general: only, it seems, at City functions and Jewish wedding receptions have anything approaching Victorian-sized meals survived, and even these have been somewhat curtailed in recent years. The rich, as we have seen, had been regular diners-out since Edwardian times: it is the growth of more modest eating outside the home by less wealthy salary-earners and wage-earners which is the more recent and interesting change.

In 1985 consumers' expenditure on meals outside the home was £9,393 million or 4.4 per cent of total expenditure, the same fraction as in 1980 but greater than in 1975 when it stood at 4.1 per cent: this huge amount was almost a third as much as the £29,950 million spent on food in the home.[35] Some of this, of course, went towards school dinners, meals in works canteens, and so on, and was not 'pleasure eating' in the strict sense, but nevertheless the proliferation of snack bars, foreign restaurants, and food counters in public houses is evidence of a large expansion of catering and its extension to groups of people who before the war rarely took a meal outside the home. In a recent survey of leisure activities, going out for a meal or entertaining friends to a meal at home were rated as the most popular occupations after watching television. In 1985 on average each person ate 3.23 meals a week outside the home and not from the household supply (e.g. sandwiches): 1.69 were midday meals in which institutional canteens played a major part, but the remaining 1.54 meals a week more accurately represented 'pleasure eating'.[36] A total of 130,000 catering establishments includes 61,000 public houses, 7,300 hotels, and 44,000 restaurants, cafés, and fish-and-chip shops.

English cooking has often been regarded as inferior to that of many European countries, due supposedly to our deficiency of creative imagination and lack of discernment. Professor John Fuller, Chairman of the National Catering Inquiry, has commented, 'The British are not very discriminating. They'll eat almost anything . . . they are often numb to taste through politeness. In many cases, "as good as mother's cooking" really means "as bad as mother's cooking".' But to turn the pages of *The Good Food Guide*, which lists memorable menus at several hundred restaurants, cafés, and pubs, all of which have been recommended by members, is to be made aware of the wealth and variety of good cooking to be found all over England at prices which compare favourably with many continental countries. Government control over meals in hotels and restaurants ended in 1950 and, combined with the gradual phasing-out of rationing, produced a revival of interest in cooking both in the home and in public places. Christopher Driver has pointed to two major influences on the regeneration of English gastronomy at this time – the founding of the Good Food Club by Raymond Postgate and the publication by Elizabeth David of *A Book of Mediterranean Food*, both in 1950.[37] 'Bon Viveur' could complain in 1953 that the days would never return when London was a gastronome's paradise, and that comparisons between his own guide to restaurants and that written by Lt.-Col. Newnham-Davies in 1901 were 'saddening', but he proceeded to name the Celebrité, Quo Vadis, La Châtelaine, and many more where good table d'hote lunches could be had for around 4s and recherché dinners for well under £1.[38] Until recently, at least, the general standard of British catering was undoubtedly improving: in the last few years steeply rising costs of food and labour appear to have halted progress, and many modest and not-so-modest eating places where individual cooking was once found now increasingly rely on packaged portions thrown from the deep-freeze to the grill and the microwave. Bland, stereotyped meals, eatable but unexciting, are too often the result. Fresh vegetables and freshly roasted joints of meat, home-made soups, pies, and puddings are rapidly becoming the luxuries of the rich, while frozen 'Aylesbury duckling' and 'escalope de veau' are on the menu of every mock-Tudor suburban pull-in.

After a long period during which public houses dispensed only beer, spirits, and packets of crisps, many are now returning to their earlier function of selling solid food with the drink. Cold lunch counters and 'meals in the basket' have spread in public houses up and down the country, and the licensed trade is increasingly aware of the fact that people frequently like to eat with their drink. But the sale of alcohol naturally remains the chief function of the English pub, and in recent years both the consumption and the proportion of expenditure on intoxicating drink have been increasing. In 1985 we spent £15,783 million on alcohol, representing 7.3 per cent of consumers' expenditure – half as much as household expenditure on food. Twenty years earlier, in 1965, alcohol took only 3.9 per cent of family expenditure.[39] Unlike food, the proportion of expenditure on alcohol rises with increasing income, but the upward trend in consumption in recent years after a long period of decline may be more a reflection of social factors than merely of an increase in purchasing power. Between 1960 and 1980 consumption of beer increased by 40 per cent to 270 pints a head a year, wine consumption grew by 250 per cent to 15 pints a head, and spirits by 135 per cent to 6 pints a head.[40] Since 1980 wine consumption has grown by a further 50 per cent and that of cider by almost as much. Teenage drinking and alcoholism have both emerged as serious socio-medical phenomena while the nutritional gain from alcohol consumption – 5.8 per cent of the average person's energy requirement – is small. Despite these clear upward trends in certain categories of liquor consumption, however, England has remained predominantly a country which takes its alcohol in the diluted form of beer, though here too there have been interesting changes in taste towards 'real ale' (initiated in 1971) on the one hand, and lager on the other.

It is a common assertion that present-day food is less natural than it used to be, that it is frequently processed and 'chemicalized' out of recognition, sometimes with dangerous substances, that flavour has been sacrificed in order to give foods a longer 'shelf-life', and that the widespread use of chemical sprays for pest-control on growing crops and fruits adds dangerous and even poisonous substances to our food.

Dear housewives [wrote an advocate of the 'natural school' in the 1950s], do you know that there is hardly an honest food left to buy . . .? Nearly all the foods that go on to our table are so changed, so processed and chemicalized that all their original goodness is either removed or killed. They are bleached, dyed, dehydrated, frozen, synthetic, tinned, sulphured, pasteurized, iodized, refined, adulterated and too often unclean as well. It seems a wonder that we are alive at all.[41]

Earlier chapters of this book have shown that the food of the nineteenth century was often highly impure, and that deliberate adulteration was then a well-organized and dangerous commercial fraud. Occasional examples of gross adulteration may still be found today: it is not long since a Blackpool firm of rock manufacturers was fined £150 for using a bright pink colouring material, Rhodamine B, which, in sufficient quantity, might induce cancer. It was held to be no defence that a person would have to consume a hundred tons of the rock in order for the amount to be critical. But the problem of food quality and composition today is generally much more subtle than this. Few people are aware that the majority of meringues sold by confectioners are made, not of egg white, but of a cellulose material, that 'orange' drinks may be manufactured without oranges, that 'dairy ice-cream' must contain at least 5 per cent of fat but 'ice-cream' need not contain any, and that while 'salmon spread' has to contain 70 per cent of salmon, 'salmon paste' need only have 25 per cent. With the growth of food technology since the war and the rapid expansion of convenience foods, additives of various kinds have come to play a major part in British diet, as in that of all industrialized, urbanized societies, and it is claimed we would not be able to enjoy the present variety and ease-of-preparation of foods without them. Additives fall into five main groups – preservatives and antioxidants, emulsifiers and stabilizers, colouring agents, flavourings, and solvents and nutritive additives (either required by government or voluntarily added by manufacturers).[42] All are subject to the general Food and Drugs Act, 1955, and, more particularly, to the recommendations of the Food Advisory Committee of the Ministry of Agriculture, Fisheries, and Food which specifies lists of permitted ingredients: in theory they must always satisfy the criteria that they are safe-in-use, never used with the intention of misleading the consumer, and not used in any greater quantity than is necessary to be effective.

No reasonable person can object in principle to the addition of some 'chemicals' to what is a chemical compound anyway, and housewives do it all the time in their cooking, but what legitimately concerns a number of experts is the 'safe-in-use' aspect. It is usually accepted that a substance is safe if it causes no detectable effects at a level of at least one hundred times the maximum amount likely to be added to food: commonly, therefore, the acceptable daily intake (ADI) for man is set at one-hundredth of the maximum no-adverse-effect level determined in the most sensitive

320

mammalian lifespan studies.[43] This is no doubt a sensible, pragmatic approach which safeguards the great majority of the population, but leaves unprotected some specially sensitive people who have suffered from allergies such as bleeding into the skin after exposure to certain colouring agents, and others who have experienced headaches, dizziness, and nausea from monosodium glutamate, used to enhance flavour (the 'Chinese Restaurant Syndrome'). Potentially more alarming is the fact that in the changing state of scientific knowledge opinions as to the possible toxic effects of substances can vary over time and between individual experts. The fact that a number of additives were permitted until recently in Britain, including agene (banned in 1955), cyclamates (banned 1969), brominated vegetable oils, and a range of colouring matters, cannot yet inspire total confidence about the safety of our foods.

Concern over additives has reached new levels in the last few years, partly because of accelerated growth in their use and partly because of disclosures which have had widespread publicity. It becomes difficult to believe that our diet is 'purer than it has ever been'[44] when it has been estimated that 3,850 additives are now in use, costing £225 million a year, and adding 4 kg a year to each person's 'food' intake.[45] The alternative view, expressed most forcibly by Caroline Walker and Geoffrey Cannon in a No. 1 bestseller, is that we are 'all at risk from the typical British diet':[46] to cite one example, the ingredients of 'Soup in a Cup' consist of:

Modified starch, dried glucose syrup, salt, flavour enhancers: monosodium glutamate, sodium 5-ribonucleótide: dextrose, vegetable fat, tomato powder, hydrolysed vegetable protein, yeast extract, dried oxtail, onion powder, spices, flavouring, colours: E150, E124, E102; caseinate, acidity regulator: E340; emulsifiers: E471, E472(b); antioxidant: E320.[47]

Similarly, a 'Raspberry Flavoured Trifle' consisted of thirty-eight ingredients, including twenty-two additives, but no raspberries. Following the introduction of the Food Act, 1984, 314 additives have been approved for use, and further regulations in 1986 have begun to bring Britain closer to EEC standards by requiring manufacturers to list certain colourings, preservatives, and antioxidants:[48] at present, these cover around 300, perhaps one-tenth of those in regular use, and in any case there is much doubt as to whether the public understand the meaning of chemical terms or E numbers. Criticizing the inadequacy of the present law, and the composition of the Food Advisory Committee, which gives strong representation to food companies, Dr Erik Millstone has concluded that: 'Additives are rarely necessary, hardly ever can we be certain that they are safe, and their presence frequently misleads consumers.'[49] However, the publicity given to the subject is clearly having an effect on some manufacturers. When Marks and Spencer removed colourings from their jams and canned peas in the early 1970s without informing their customers the immediate effect was to reduce sales by 50 per cent: in 1985 Birds Eye made a point of announcing that they would reduce their use of additives and altogether eliminate artificial colourings by 1986, apparently without any adverse sales effect on what is now a better informed and more discriminating public.[50]

How well-fed are we today? On the evidence of the National Food Survey Reports which have been published each year since 1949, the nation as a whole is well-nourished, and the major improvements in the diets of the poorer classes which came with rationing during the Second World War have been maintained. Already in the Report for 1950 it was observed that the pre-war differences in levels of nutrient intake between the richest and the poorest groups had been greatly reduced – that, for example, the range for calories was now only 11 per cent compared with 40 per cent in 1936–7, for vitamin A 34 per cent compared with 81 per cent and for vitamin B_1 9 per cent compared with 71 per cent.[51] Rationing, and the related policies of subsidies, welfare foods and price controls had considerably narrowed the nutritional gap between the social classes which had so concerned John Boyd Orr and others in the 1930s. On the whole, these gains survived the period of de-rationing in the early 1950s, and in 1962 total protein was 10 per cent above pre-war levels and energy value 4 per cent above, having remained unchanged since 1954. The range between the highest and the lowest social classes, expressed as a percentage of the average intake, had, however, tended to widen in the case of some nutrients, thiamine, nicotinic acid, and vitamin C.[52] Differences in the levels of consumption of foods continued to exist – there was still a steady decline in meat, milk, and fruit as income fell, and an increase in bread and potatoes – but it was possible for nutritionists to believe in the 1960s that as standards of living continued to rise the national diet would increasingly resemble the pattern set by the wealthiest socio-economic group.

The method commonly used for assessing the adequacy of the national diet is to compare the average intakes of nutrients with the amounts recommended for health by panels of medical experts (in Britain by the Department of Health and Social Security). Again, these comparisons show that through the 1960s the average consumer was generally well above the recommended allowances, especially since the data are derived from household consumption and do not take account of such things as alcoholic drink and sweets which would supplement the energy intakes.

A major change in this position dates from the mid-1970s, when a downturn in a number of nutrients became noticeable, and in 1976 average energy intake for the first time stood at 95 per cent of recommended value. This fall in energy value and, to a lesser extent in protein and iron, has accelerated in the last five years (Table 53), the energy value in 1985 being

Want and plenty, 1945–85

Table 53 *Energy value and nutrient content of domestic food consumption expressed as a percentage of recommended allowances (DHSS)*[53]

	1964	1969	1980	1985
Energy value	109	109	99	90
Total protein	126	126	129	119
Calcium	188	194	173	153
Iron	126	121	105	100
Thiamin	125	122	126	144
Riboflavin	128	130	139	127
Nicotinic acid equiv.	183	190	188	181
Vitamin C	176	181	200	179
Vitamin A	203	199	193	196

the lowest ever recorded. So far, the annual Reports of the Food Survey Committee have been relaxed about this change, pointing out that a more sedentary (and unemployed?) population needs less energy and that the deficit is compensated by meals and snacks eaten outside the home, and by sweets and alcoholic drinks. This may be so, but the fact that a joint MAFF/DHSS study has recently been initiated to assess the intake of nutrients by individuals and their relationship to indicators of health suggests that official circles are now aware of possible dangers.[54] Further concern arises from the fact that it has been known for some years that while the average diet may be satisfactory that of certain groups 'at risk' may not be. In particular, family size has emerged as one of the chief determinants of nutritional adequacy, and in families with two adults and four or more children (or children and adolescents) there are downward gradients for almost all nutrients. In 1976 such families were below the recommended levels for energy (91 per cent), iron (92 per cent), and vitamin D (70 per cent) and well below the national averages for protein (109 per cent) and vitamin C (138 per cent). By 1985 these levels had worsened considerably. Even in households with two adults and three children the energy value was only 78 per cent of that recommended and iron 83 per cent, while protein reached only 102 per cent compared with 117 in families with one child.[55]

The optimism of the 1950s about general standards of well-being of the population has also been shaken by the re-emergence of a problem of poverty in Britain. The belief of many politicians and social scientists that the Welfare State had all but eradicated this scourge was first seriously questioned in 1965 by Peter Townsend and Brian Abel-Smith who, using as an operational definition of poverty those living on less than 140 per cent of the basic National Assistance scale plus rent and/or other living costs, calculated that those in poverty had increased from 7.8 per cent of the population in 1953–4 to 14.2 per cent in 1960, representing $7\frac{1}{2}$ million people. The main causes of modern poverty, they believed, were low pay, particularly in public sector occupations, irregularity of work, old age, one-parent families, and above-average numbers of children, but since that time unemployment has reappeared as a principal constituent of the problem. The Child Poverty Action Group has recently produced statistics which suggest an alarming increase since that time. In 1983 they claim that 8,910,000 people were living on or below the Supplementary Benefit level (17 per cent of the population), and that 16,380,000 people (31 per cent of the population) were living in or on the margins of poverty, defined as 140 per cent of the Supplementary Benefit level or below: these numbers in 1983 included 3,490,000 unemployed. The effects on family income are illustrated by the fact that in 1987 a married couple with two children under eleven received on Supplementary Benefit £70.15 a week compared with the average expenditure of all households, excluding housing costs, of £166.60.[56] It should be noted that this is a relative definition of poverty, not the absolute one used by Rowntree and other earlier researchers, and many have questioned the validity of using the Supplementary Benefit scale as a poverty-line since it represents a moving target. Whatever the precise numbers of the poor there can now be little doubt that there are large groups in the population who are either in poverty or on the edge of it for whom marginal changes in income or a sudden crisis such as illness, death, or unemployment, can produce severe consequences. Evidence suggests that in such crises people tend to cut expenditure on food and drink rather than on fixed expenses such as rent, fuel, and hire-purchase payments.[57]

Particular concern has been expressed recently about the nutritional status and general health of children in large families, partly because these families account for a very large proportion of all children in the country, and partly because they tend to be concentrated in lower income groups where the money available for food is least. David Piachaud calculates that the number of children on or below the Supplementary Benefit level doubled between 1973 and 1983, that 1 in 6 children now live in families dependent on SB, and that 1 in every 3 live in families in poverty or on the margin of it.[58] If the top and bottom income groups in the National Food Survey are compared, there is clear evidence that wealth still affects the dietary pattern importantly – the poor spend 36p per person per week on fruit and fruit products compared with £1.16 by the rich, 26p on cheese compared with 46p, 36p on fish compared with 69p and £1.04p on vegetables compared with £1.35p: on the other hand, they spend more on bread, eggs, sugar, and preserves.[59] As we have seen, the National Food Survey is a fairly blunt instrument of research which can identify vulnerable groups in the population but cannot follow the food to individuals, and in the present state of knowledge we cannot know whether malnutrition has reappeared in Britain on a serious scale.

Nor is it possible from official sources to know in detail how the recent depression has affected the dietary standards of individuals on low incomes. In an attempt to discover this, a pilot study was carried out in 1984 by the Food Policy Unit of Manchester Polytechnic into the food consumption of a thousand people on low incomes in the north of England: they consisted of young people on government schemes, the unemployed, the old on state pensions, and people living in large families: two-thirds of all were living on personal incomes of less than £50 a week.[60] The study concluded that the unemployed was the group most hardly hit: they spent only £7.59 a week on food compared with £12.30 by pensioners, and 35 per cent of them said that they did not have a main meal every day compared with 27 per cent of the whole sample. The traditional pattern of three meals a day was enjoyed by only 62.6 per cent of all, and 51.9 per cent of the unemployed. When money was short, spending went on bread (21.8 per cent of all ate wholemeal only), sandwiches, chips, beans, and fried foods, but fresh meat, fish, fruit, and vegetables were cut: as in former times, the best food was reserved for men and children. There is much here which parallels the poverty of the 1930s, modified by the technological changes which now make frozen chips, fish fingers, and hamburgers convenient and relatively cheap substitutes for traditional dishes: similarly, new forms of snack foods and 'take-aways' have reappeared as part of youth street culture, as they were in Victorian times. Yet the charges of extravagance and improvidence levelled by some politicians and well-meaning dieticians scarcely seem justified. National Food Survey Reports show that the poor generally buy their food efficiently, getting a third more energy and protein per penny and twice as much vitamin A and D than wealthy families.[61]

Despite anxieties about the state of the economy and the reappearance of mass unemployment, most people in Britain eat enough to satisfy physiological requirements, and compared with a country like Brazil where the intake of calories by the poorest quartile of the population is only one-third that of the richest, we are still an affluent society. But do we eat the right foods – has free choice during the last thirty years, constrained as it has been for some by financial considerations, improved or deteriorated the national diet and the national health? Optimists would point to the fact that vital statistics have significantly improved. Since 1951 the male expectation of life has risen from 66.2 years to 71.4, the female from 71.2 to 77.2, while infant mortality, often regarded as the most sensitive health indicator, stands at its lowest-ever point of 9.4 per thousand.[62] Pessimists would argue that inequalities in health have actually widened over the last thirty years, that there is a 'social class gradient' in health which gives significantly better life chances to the better-off. A recent report claims, for instance, that manual workers have a 45 per cent higher risk of dying prematurely than non-manual workers, that babies born into social Class V (unskilled manual) are 59 per cent more likely to be stillborn or to die in their first year than those born into Class I (professional).[63] Further, the argument runs, such differences are due primarily to differences in diet rather than to environmental factors such as housing or working conditions. It has been suggested that possible reasons for higher mortality among those consuming 'poor' diets might include overweight due to the consumption of the wrong sort of calories, high sugar consumption and a lower intake of vitamins, and that heart disease and obesity may well have changed their social distribution since the 1950s. Simple assertions are best avoided in an area as complex as the relationship between diet and disease, yet there is good reason to believe that faulty diet is still a cause of much preventable ill-health – dental caries and diabetes due to heavy sugar consumption, coronary disease stimulated by high fat or sugar intake, and intestinal disease caused by lack of fibre in the diet are all urged by different authorities. Contemporary diet may not be best suited to contemporary living. As we have seen, the diet of many people in the past was predominantly a cereal one: with increasing affluence Britain, like other industrialized, urbanized societies, moved towards a 'richer' diet with more protein, fats, and sugar, and more 'stress foods' high in sucrose content. Anthropologically, a predominantly meat diet may have been the 'natural' food of man, but what was appropriate for a hunter may not suit the digestion of an office worker.

Until recently, the pessimists' case was often dismissed as that of cranks, faddists, and 'food Leninists',[64] and most people contented themselves with the old adage that 'a little of what you fancy does you good'. But opinion, both professional and lay, has changed much over the last decade, partly as a result of statistics which show alarming increases in diseases which many experts now accept to be diet-related (among men aged 50–54, 51 per cent of deaths were caused by circulatory diseases in 1984 compared with 29 per cent in 1951, and among women of the same age deaths from cancer increased from 34 to 53 per cent[65]), partly because of the wide publicity which a series of official and semi-official reports have received. The case for change in the national diet began to mount from around 1974 when a pressure group, TACC (Technology Assessment Consumerism Centre), strongly attacked the nutritional value of the white loaf and the removal of fibre and micronutrients during milling. Shortly afterwards, an article in *The Times* appeared under the title, 'Should Bread Carry a Government Health Warning?'.[66] In 1977 a Committee of the United States Senate chaired by George McGovern argued that the American diet had changed radically during the last fifty years 'with great and very harmful effects on our health. . . . Too much fat, too much sugar or salt can be and are linked directly to heart disease, cancer, obesity and stroke, among other killer diseases.'[67] In Britain in 1979 the government set up the National Advisory Council on Nutrition Education (NACNE), while in 1981 another advisory body to the DHSS, COMA (Committee on Medical Aspects of Food Policy), recommended that 'an increase in the cereal fibre content of the diet would be beneficial, and this could best be achieved by eating some bread baked from high extraction flour'.[68] By 1983 a draft of NACNE's long-awaited Report was ready but, it has been alleged, its publication was blocked until Geoffrey Cannon obtained a copy and leaked the contents in a series of articles in the *Sunday Times*: the full Report was then published in September 1983 as that of 'an *ad hoc* working party'.

The Report recommends long-term and short-term dietary goals for the whole population, not merely for groups 'at risk'. In summary, the long-term goals are to reduce consumption of fats by one-quarter, that of saturated fats by half, of sugars by half, of salt by half, and of alcohol by one-third: the total quantity of protein need not change, but the proportion of vegetable protein should rise at the expense of animal protein, and the consumption of fibre in the form of cereals, fruit, and vegetables should increase by a half. It is recognized that these changes could not be achieved quickly, and interim goals achievable in the 1980s are set at one-third of the ultimate changes.[69]

At present, when many people are confused about the controversy, there is need for more agreement among the experts and clearer guidelines to food manufacturers, doctors, and the general public. The need is now urgent both for reasons of health and economy. The era of cheap food from which Britain benefited in the past is no more, and the economic advantages of Britain's membership of the European Community are still in doubt when hundreds of millions of pounds are annually paid merely to stock-pile 'mountains' and 'lakes' of surplus produce. Scarcity of basic foods is not a problem in Britain – indeed, it is now seriously proposed that British agriculture, regarded as one of the most efficient in the world, should reduce its output by 20 per cent while remaining subject to pricing policies which favour less efficient European farmers. The arguments for a sensible food production policy seem irresistible. So too, many would claim, are the arguments for a sensible nutritional policy as part of a new public health programme.

It should be stressed that the NACNE proposals have not been officially adopted, that some eminent doctors and nutritionists accept them only in part and with varying emphases, and that, at a practical level, their implementation as national policy would have enormous implications

327

for agriculture, the food industries, and for government and EEC regulations. The case for change has been weakened by some exaggeration,
over-dramatization, and dubious appeals to history, such as the assertion
that 'we are now, amazingly, as badly fed as we were fifty years ago.
Indeed, in some important respects, we are actually worse off than before
the Second World War.'⁷⁰ A Welsh doctor recently reconstructed the agricultural labourer's diet of 1863 described by Edward Smith (see pp.
139–41 for examples) and fed it to mice, comparing the effects with those
fed on a present-day diet: the former survived longer, whereas the latter
developed high blood cholesterol and died younger. The doctor concluded
that 'People might well be advised to go back to the agricultural diet', and
that the 1863 diet had 'greater life-span potential than that currently consumed in Wales'.⁷¹ In fact, the average expectation of life (of men, not mice)
was then forty-one years, food adulteration with poisonous ingredients
was widespread and uncontrolled, and it is doubtful whether the inhabitants even of the remoter parts of Wales would now stomach the labourer's
coarse diet of 1863.

History has a legitimate and important part to play in the study of diet.
Over the century and a half reviewed in this book fundamental changes
occurred in the sources of our food supplies, the manufacture and distribution of products, and the diets of both richer and poorer classes. Trends in
consumption which had seemed firmly established in the past, like the
massive increase in the use of sugar during the last hundred years and the
more gradual rise in fats, have now been halted or reversed. Sometimes
changes were compelled by economic constraints or by war, but more
often they were due to the consumer's increasing power to choose the
foods he preferred. We did not usually choose foods because we believed
they were good for us, but because, for a variety of complex reasons, we
enjoyed them. There is perhaps now sufficient consensus among nutritionists as to what constitutes a healthy diet, and perhaps enough public
awareness about diet-related diseases, for a new element to have entered
into food choice. Food habits have changed much in the twenty years
since the first edition of this book, are still changing, and will change
further, but how influential the new considerations of health will be on
future trends is not a question for history.

Notes

1 Halsey, A.H. (1987) 'Social trends since World War II', *Social Trends* (Central
Statistical Office) 17, 11.
2 ibid., 12.
3 Birds Eye Report, *Frozen Foods: A Review of the Market in 1986*, 7; *Social
Trends*, ibid., 111 (Table 6.15).

4   Birds Eye Annual Review (1976) 'The kitchen revolution goes on', 5.
5   *Social Trends* 17, op. cit., 14 (Table A2).
6   ibid., 108 (Table 6.11).
7   *Household Food Consumption and Expenditure* (1985), Annual Report of the National Food Survey Committee, 1987, 2.
8   *Social Trends* 17, op. cit., 108 (Table 6.11).
9   *Household Food Consumption and Expenditure* (1985), op. cit., 13 (Table 2.20).
10 ibid., 16 (Table 2.22).
11 For a good account of the food situation at this time see Christopher Driver (1985) *The British at Table, 1940–1980*, chap. 3.
12 Hollingsworth, Dorothy F. (1983) 'Rationing and economic constraints on food consumption in Britain since the Second World War', *World Review of Nutrition and Dietetics* 42, 194 (Table III).
13 Drummond, J. C. and Wilbraham, Anne (1957) *The Englishman's Food. A History of Five Centuries of English Diet*, revised edn by Dorothy Hollingsworth, Appendix B, 468.
14 Buss, D.H. (1979) 'The resilience of British household diets during the 1970s', *Journal of Human Nutrition* 33, 49–50.
15 *Household Food Consumption and Expenditure* (1985), op. cit., 4.
16 Greaves, J. P. and Hollingsworth, Dorothy F. (1966) 'Trends in food consumption in the United Kingdom', *World Review of Nutrition and Dietetics* 6, 53.
17 Rose, Evelyn (1977) 'Consumer aspect of beef marketing', *Journal of Consumer Studies and Home Economics* 1 (2), June, 131 et seq.
18 Hollingsworth, op. cit., 207.
19 Birds Eye Annual Review (1977), 23. Data based on Taylor Nelson and Associates Family Food Panel.
20 *Household Food Consumption and Expenditure* (1985), op. cit., 40.
21 Birds Eye Report, *Frozen Foods*, op. cit., 4.
22 Miller, Sanford (1978) 'The kinetics of nutritional status: diet, culture and economics', in John Yudkin (ed.) *Diet of Man: Needs and Wants*, 191 et seq.
23 United Biscuits (1986) *The Grocery and Biscuit Market* and the 1986 *Snack Food Review*.
24 McKenzie, J. C. (1973) 'Factors affecting demand for protein products', in J. G. W. Jones (ed.) *The Biological Efficiency of Protein Production*.
25 *Household Food Consumption and Expenditure* (1985), op. cit., 13 (Table 2.20).
26 Driver, op. cit., 64.
27 Birds Eye Annual Review (1976), 3.
28 Warren, Geoffrey C. (1958) *The Foods We Eat. A Survey of Meals, Their Content and Chronology by Season, Day of the Week, Class and Age, Conducted in Great Britain by the Market Division of W. S. Crawford Ltd.*
29 *Who Eats Breakfast*. Breakfast Research Study Findings by John Birmingham, Director, British Market Research Bureau Ltd. Survey undertaken for The Kellogg Company of Great Britain Ltd, 1976.
30 The Commission chaired by Sir Douglas Black is reported in P. Townsend and N. Davidson (1982) *Inequalities in Health*, 182–3.

31 Lang, Tim, Andrews, Hazel, Bedale, Caroline, and Hannon, Ed (1984) *Jam Tomorrow. A Report of the First Findings of a Pilot Study of the Food Circumstances, Attitudes and Consumption of 1,000 People on Low Incomes in the North of England*, Food Policy Unit, Manchester Polytechnic, 30.
32 *Social Trends* 17, op. cit., 59.
33 Reported in the *Daily Telegraph*, 3 September 1987, 13.
34 'Meals in the mind', *Daily Telegraph Magazine*, 14 December 1973. Gallup Poll inquiries conducted on behalf of the *Daily Telegraph*: quoted by courtesy of Social Surveys (Gallup Poll) Ltd.
35 *Household Food Consumption and Expenditure* (1985), op. cit., 1.
36 ibid., 8.
37 Driver, op. cit., 49.
38 *Daily Telegraph Book of Bon Viveur in London* (c. 1953), XI.
39 HMSO (1966) *Family Expenditure Survey Report for 1965*, 26 (Table 1).
40 Driver, op. cit., 112.
41 Grant, Doris (1955) *Dear Housewives*, 21.
42 For example, when production of white flour was allowed in 1953 the government required the addition of vitamin B_1, nicotinic acid, iron, and calcium.
43 *Why Additives? The Safety of Foods* (1977), devised and edited by the British Nutrition Foundation, 53.
44 Johnston, James P. (1977) *A Hundred Years of Eating*, 67.
45 Millstone, Erik (1986) *Food Additives. Taking the Lid Off What We Really Eat*, 40.
46 Walker, Caroline and Cannon, Geoffrey (1985) *The Food Scandal. What's Wrong with the British Diet and How to Put it Right*, XXXI.
47 ibid., XXVII.
48 *Social Trends* 17, op. cit., 110.
49 Millstone, op. cit., 12.
50 Birds Eye (1985) *Frozen Foods Annual Report*, 1.
51 *Domestic Food Consumption and Expenditure, 1950*, Report of the National Food Survey Committee (1952), 49.
52 Greaves and Hollingsworth, op. cit., 74 (Table XVIII).
53 For the years 1964 and 1969 *Annual Report of the National Food Survey Committee for 1969* (1971), 114 (Table 34); for 1980 and 1985 *Annual Report for 1985* (1987), 81 (Table 11).
54 *Household Food Consumption and Expenditure* (1985), op. cit., 47 and footnote (2).
55 ibid., 83 (Table 13).
56 Child Poverty Action Group (1986) *Poverty: The Facts*, 5–6.
57 McKenzie, J. C. (1974) 'The impact of economic and social status on food choice', *Proceedings of the Nutrition Society*, 33, 67.
58 Piachaud, David (1986) *Poor Children: A Tale of Two Decades*, Child Poverty Action Group, 2–4.
59 *Social Trends* 17, op. cit., 109 (Table 6.12).
60 *Jam Tomorrow*, op. cit.
61 Hunt, Sandra (1985) 'And the poor? They shall eat carrots . . .', *Poverty*, Child Poverty Action Group, 60 (Spring).

62 *Social Trends* 17, op. cit., 115.
63 *Poverty: The Facts*, op. cit., 4.
64 Anderson, Digby (1985) 'The men who march on our stomachs', *Spectator*,
    17 August.
65 *Social Trends* 17, op. cit., 116.
66 *The Times*, 10 January 1976.
67 Quoted in *The Food Scandal*, op. cit., XVI.
68 Report of Committee on Medical Aspects of Food Policy, 1981, 53.
69 *The Food Scandal*, op. cit., 34–7.
70 Cannon, Geoffrey and Walker, Caroline (1985) 'Just how well do we eat?',
    Wheel of Health, Part I, *Observer* Review, 27 January, 45.
71 Quoted in ibid., 46.

Select bibliography

This bibliography lists the principal works used in this book, but not all the sources cited in the references to each chapter. It does not include Parliamentary Papers, which are listed under that heading in date order in the Index: nor does it include more ephemeral literature, whether in books, journals, or newspapers. The conventional distinction between primary and secondary sources is not appropriate in this bibliography: instead, books published before 1914 have been divided from those published subsequently.

Books published before 1914

Accum, Fredrick (1820) *A Treatise on Adulterations of Food, and Culinary Poisons.*

Acton, Eliza (1856) *Modern Cookery for Private Families*, new edn.

Acton, Eliza (1857) *The English Bread Book.*

'Alfred' (Samuel Kydd) (1857) *The History of the Factory Movement, from the year 1802 to the enactment of the Ten Hours Bill in 1847*, 2 vols, repub. 1966.

Anon (1795) *The Crying Frauds of London Markets, by the Author of the Cutting Butchers Appeal.*

Anon (c. 1830–1) *Deadly Adulteration and Slow Poisoning Unmasked, or Disease and Death in the Pot and Bottle, by an Enemy to Fraud and Villany*, n.d.

Anon (1850) *Doings in London; or Day and Night Scenes of the Frauds, Frolics, Manners and Depravities of the Metropolis.*

Anon (1824) *The Family Oracle of Health.*

Anon (1841) *The Guide to Trade: The Baker.*

Anon (1858) *London at Dinner, or Where to Dine*, repub. 1969.

Anon (c. 1850) *Memoirs of a Stomach. Written by Himself, that All who Eat may Read. Edited by 'A Minister of the Interior'*, n.d.

Anon (1757) *Poison Detected, by My Friend, a Physician.*

Anon (1856) *The Tricks of the Trade in the Adulteration of Food and Physic.*

Select bibliography

Arch, Joseph (1898) *The Story of his Life, Told by Himself*, edited, with a Preface, by the Countess of Warwick.

Ashton, John (1904) *The History of Bread.*

Bartley, George C.T. (1874) *The Seven Ages of a Village Pauper.*

Beeton, Isabella (1861 etc.) *The Book of Household Management.*

Bell, Lady (Mrs Hugh Bell) (1907) *At the Works. A Study of a Manufacturing Town.*

Bickerdyke, John (1886) *The Curiosities of Ale and Beer.*

Booth, Charles (1889) *Life and Labour of the People in London. First Series: Poverty.*

Booth, General (William) (1890) *In Darkest England, and the Way Out.*

Bosanquet, S.R. (1841) *The Rights of the Poor, and Christian Almsgiving Vindicated.*

Bourne, Stephen (1880) *Trade, Population and Food. A Series of Papers on Economic Statistics.*

Burn, J.D. ('One Who Thinks Aloud') (1855) *The Language of the Walls and a Voice from the Shop Windows, or the Mirror of Commercial Roguery.*

Caird, James (1852) *English Agriculture in 1850–51.*

Child, Samuel (1820 edn) *Every Man his own Brewer: A Practical Treatise, etc.*

Clarke, Allen (1913) *The Effects of the Factory System.*

Cobbett, William (1823) *Cottage Economy.*

Cobbett, William (1830) *Rural Rides.*

Copley, Esther (1849) *Cottage Cookery.*

Davies, Rev. David (1795) *The Case of Labourers in Husbandry, Stated and Considered.*

Davies, Maude F. (1909) *Life in an English Village. An Economic and Historical Survey of the Parish of Corsley in Wiltshire.*

Disraeli, Benjamin (1845) *Sybil, or The Two Nations.*

Dodd, George (1856) *The Food of London.*

Dolby, Richard (1830) *The Cook's Dictionary and Housekeeper's Directory. A New Family Manual, etc.*

Eden, Frederic Morton (1797) *The State of the Poor*, 3 vols.

Engels, Frederick (1844) *The Condition of the Working Class in England in 1844*, trans. by W.O. Henderson and W.H. Chaloner, 1958.

Family Economist (1848) *A Penny Monthly Magazine directed to the Moral, Physical and Domestic Improvement of the Industrious Classes.*

Fearon, Rev. H. (1857) *Home Comfort: Working Life, How to Make it Happier.*

'Foreign Resident, A' (1886) *Society in London.*

Francatelli, Charles Elmé (1852) *A Plain Cookery Book for the Working Classes*, repub. 1977.

333

Francatelli, Charles Elmé (1911) *The Modern Cook*, edited by C. Herman Senn.

Gilman, Nicholas Paine (1899) *A Dividend to Labour.*

Green, F.E. (1913) *The Tyranny of the Countryside.*

Greg, W.R. (1831) *An Enquiry into the State of the Manufacturing Population, and the Causes and Cures of the Evils Therein.*

Haggard, H. Rider (1902) *Rural England*, 2 vols.

Halsham, John (1897) *Idlehurst.*

Hassall, Arthur Hill (1855) *Food and its Adulterations: Comprising the Reports of the Analytical Sanitary Commission of the Lancet.*

Hassall, Arthur Hill (1857) *Adulterations Detected: or Plain Instructions for the Discovery of Frauds in Food and Medicine.*

Hayward, Abraham (1852) *The Art of Dining, or Gastronomy and Gastronomers.*

Heath, Francis George (1874) *The English Peasantry.*

Heath, Francis George (1911) *British Rural Life and Labour.*

Hill, Benson E. (1841) *The Epicure's Almanack, or Diary of Good Living.*

Holyoake, George Jacob (1908) *The History of Co-operation.*

Hooper, Mary (1878) *Little Dinners: How to Serve them with Elegance and Economy*, 13th edn.

Howitt, William (1862) *The Rural Life of England*, 3rd edn.

Hoyle, William (1871) *Our National Resources, and How they are Wasted. An Omitted Chapter in Political Economy.*

Hudson, W.H. (1902) *Hampshire Days.*

Ingestre, Viscount (ed.) (1852) *Meliora, or Better Times to Come*, 2nd edn.

Jackson, Henry (1758) *An Essay on Bread.*

Jeune, Lady (1895) *Lesser Questions.*

Kay, James Phillips (1832) *The Moral and Physical Condition of the Working Classes Employed in the Cotton Manufacture in Manchester.*

Kebbel, T.E. (1870) *The Agricultural Labourer: a Short Summary of his Position.*

Kenney-Herbert, A. (1894) *Common-Sense Cookery for English Households*, 2nd edn.

Kitchiner, William (1817 etc.) *The Cook's Oracle, containing Receipts for Plain Cookery on the most Economical Plan.*

Kitchiner, William (1824) *The Art of Invigorating and Prolonging Life, and Peptic Precepts*, new edn.

Laing, Samuel (1844) *National Distress: Its Causes and Remedies*, Atlas Prize Essay.

Letheby, Henry (1868) *On Food*, being the substance of Four Cantor Lectures.

Levi, Leone (1871) *The Liquor Trades.*

Levi, Leone (1885) *Wages and Earnings of the Working-Classes*, Report to Sir Arthur Bass, MP.

London, Jack (1902) *The People of the Abyss.*

Lovett, William (1876 etc.) *The Life and Struggles of William Lovett in his Pursuit of Bread, Knowledge and Freedom.*

McCulloch, J.R. (1834 etc.) *A Dictionary, Practical, Theoretical and Historical, of Commerce and Commercial Navigation.*

Mallock, W.H. (1896) *Classes and Masses, or Wealth, Wages and Welfare in the United Kingdom.*

Marshall, A.B. (1879) *Mrs Marshall's Cookery Book*, revised and enlarged edn.

Marshall, William (1817) *A Review of the Reports to the Board of Agriculture from the Southern and Peninsular Departments of England.*

Mayhew, Henry (1851) *London Labour and the London Poor*, vol. 1.

Meakin, J.E. Budgett (1905) *Model Factories and Villages.*

Mew, J. and Ashton, J. (1892) *Drinks of the World.*

Mitchell, John (1848) *A Treatise on the Falsifications of Food, and the Chemical Means Employed to Detect Them.*

Money, L. Chiozza (1911). *Riches and Poverty.*

Newnham-Davis, Lt.-Col. (1901) *Dinners and Diners. Where and How to Dine in London.*

Normandy, Alphonse (1850) *The Commercial Handbook of Chemical Analysis.*

Northcote, Stafford H. (1862) *Twenty Years of Financial Policy.*

Panton, Mrs J.E. (1885) *From Kitchen to Garret: Hints to Young Householders.*

Paris, J.A. (1826) *A Treatise on Diet.*

Peel, Mrs C.S. (1902) *How to Keep House.*

Peel, Mrs C.S. (1914) *The Labour-Saving House.*

Pereira, J. (1843) *A Treatise on Food and Diet.*

Porter, G.R. (1847/1851) *The Progress of the Nation in its Various Social and Economical Relations.*

Postgate, John (1857) *A Few Words on Adulteration.*

Pückler-Muskau, Prince (1830) *Tour in England, Ireland and France in the Years 1828–9.*

Read, George (1848) *The History of the Baking Trade.*

Reeves, Magdalen S.P. (1913) *Round About a Pound a Week.*

Rey, J. (*c.* 1914) *The Whole Art of Dining*, n.d.

Reynolds, M.E. (1848) *The Complete Art of Cookery.*

Robinson, H.M. and Cribb, C.H. (1895) *The Law and Chemistry of Food and Drugs.*

Rowntree, B. Seebohm (1901) *Poverty: A Study of Town Life.*

Rowntree, B. Seebohm and Kendall, May (1913) *How the Labourer Lives: a Study of the Rural Labour Problem*.

Rowntree, Joseph and Sherwell, Arthur (1900) *The Temperance Problem and Social Reform*, 8th edn.

Rundell, Mrs ('A Lady') (1824) *A System of Practical Domestic Economy*, new edn.

Shadwell, Arthur (1902) *Drink, Temperance and Legislation*.

Shaw, Charles (1903) *When I was a Child*, repub. 1977.

Smiles, Samuel (1905) *Thrift*.

Smith, Albert (1855) *The English Hotel Nuisance*.

Smith, Edward (1864) *Practical Dietary for Families, Schools and the Labouring Classes*.

Somerville, Alexander (1843) *A Letter to the Farmers of England on the Relationship of Manufactures and Agriculture, by One who has Whistled at the Plough*.

Somerville, Alexander (1848) *The Autobiography of a Working Man, by One who has Whistled at the Plough*.

Somerville, Alexander (1852) *The Whistler at the Plough*.

Soyer, Alexis (1849) *The Modern Housewife or Ménagère*.

Soyer, Alexis (1855) *A Shilling Cookery for the People*.

Spencer, Edward (1900) *Cakes and Ale. A Memory of Many Meals*.

Sturgeon, Launcelot (? pseud.) (1822) *Essays Moral, Philosophical and Stomachical on the Important Science of Good Living*.

Thompson, Sir Henry (1884) *Food and Feeding*, 3rd edn.

Tuck, John (1822) *The Private Brewer's Guide*.

Tuckwell, Rev. Canon (1895) *Reminiscences of a Radical Parson*.

Unwin, T. Fisher (ed.) (1905) *The Hungry Forties. Life under the Bread Tax*.

Ure, Andrew (1835) *The Philosophy of Manufactures, or an Exposition of the Scientific, Moral and Commercial Economy of the Factory System*, 3rd edn, 1861.

Ure, Andrew (1835) *A Dictionary of Chemistry and Mineralogy*, 4th edn.

Volent, F. and Warren, J.R. (eds) (1859) *Memoirs of Alexis Soyer*, rep. 1985.

Walsh, J.H. (1857) *A Manual of Domestic Economy*, new edn, 1873.

White, Arnold (ed.) (n.d.) *The Letters of S.G.O. (Sidney Godolphin Osborne)*, 2 vols.

Woodin, J. (1852) *The System of Adulteration and Fraud now Prevailing in Trade*.

Woodin, J. (1852) *The Central Co-operative Agency, ... with Prefatory Remarks on Adulteration*.

Select bibliography

Wynter, Andrew (1869) *Our Social Bees. Pictures of Town and Country Life, and other Papers*, 10th edn.

Books published since 1914

Note: Place of publication is London unless otherwise indicated.

Adams, James S. (1974) *A Fell Fine Baker. The Story of United Biscuits.*
Alexander, D. (1970) *Retailing in England during the Industrial Revolution.*
Ashby, M.K. (1974) *Joseph Ashby of Tysoe, 1859–1919.*
Ashley, Sir William (1928) *The Bread of our Forefathers*, Oxford.
Astor, Viscount and Rowntree, B. Seebohm (1939) *British Agriculture: The Principles of Future Policy.*
Banks, J.A. (1965) *Prosperity and Parenthood. A Study of Family Planning among the Victorian Middle Classes.*
Barker, Theo and Drake, Michael (eds) (1982) *Population and Society in Britain, 1850–1980.*
Barker, T.C., McKenzie, J.C., and Yudkin, John (eds) (1966) *Our Changing Fare. Two Hundred Years of British Food Habits.*
Barker, T.C., Oddy, D.J., and Yudkin, John (1970) *The Dietary Surveys of Dr Edward Smith, 1862–3. A New Assessment.*
Barker, T.C. and Yudkin, John (eds) (1971) *Fish in Britain. Trends in its Supply, Distribution and Consumption during the Past Two Centuries.*
Barnett, L. Margaret (1985) *British Food Policy during the First World War.*
Battiscombe, Georgina (1949) *English Picnics.*
Beveridge, William H. (1928) *Economic and Social History of the World War. British Food Control.*
'Bon Viveur' in London (the *Daily Telegraph*), n.d., *c.* 1950.
Boswell, James (ed.), (1969) *JS 100. The Story of Sainsbury's.*
Bowley, A.L. (1921) *Prices and Wages in the UK, 1914–1920.*
Bowley, A.L. and Burnett-Hurst, A.R. (1915) *Livelihood and Poverty. A Study in the Economic Conditions of Working-class Households in Northampton, Warrington, Stanley and Reading.*
Bridge, Tom (1983) *The Golden Age of Cookery*, Bolton, Lancs.
Brockway, A. Fenner (1932) *Hungry England.*
Burnett, John (1982) *Destiny Obscure. Autobiographies of Childhood, Education and Family from the 1820s to the 1920s.*
Burnett, John (1986) *A Social History of Housing, 1815–1985.*
Burnett, John, Vincent, David, and Mayall, David (eds) (1984/1987) *The Autobiography of The Working Class. An Annotated Critical Bibliography, vol. I, 1790–1900*, vol. II, 1900–1945, Brighton.
Burnett, R.G. (1945) *Through the Mill. The Life of Joseph Rank.*
Calder, A. (1969) *The People's War.*

Chambers, J.D. (1945) *Modern Nottingham in the Making.* Nottingham.

Clapham, J.H. (1926–38) *An Economic History of Modern Britain*, 3 vols. Cambridge.

Cohen, Ruth L. (1936) *The History of Milk Prices.*

Cole, G.D.H. and Postgate, Raymond (1938) *The Common People, 1746–1938.*

Cole-Hamilton, Isobel and Lang, Tim (1986) *Tightening Belts. A Report on the Impact of Poverty on Food*, The London Food Commission.

Constantine, Stephen (1983) *Social Conditions in Britain, 1918–1939.*

Cooper, Charles (n.d.) *The English Table in History and Literature.*

Corley, T.E.B. (1972) *Quaker Enterprise in Biscuits. Huntley and Palmers of Reading, 1822–1972.*

Crawford, Sir William and Broadley, H. (1938) *The People's Food.*

Curtis-Bennett, Noel (1949) *The Food of the People: The History of Industrial Feeding.*

Cutting, C.L. (1955) *Fish Saving. A History of Fish Processing from Ancient to Modern Times.*

Daunton, M.J. (1983) *House and Home in the Victorian City. Working-Class Housing, 1850–1914.*

Davidoff, Leonore (1973) *The Best Circles: Society, Etiquette and the Season.*

Davidoff, Leonore and Hall, Catherine (1987) *Family Fortunes. Men and Women of the English Middle Class, 1780–1850.*

Deerr, Noel (1949–50) *The History of Sugar*, 2 vols.

Derry, T.K. and Williams, Trevor I. (1960) *A Short History of Technology*, Oxford.

Dodds, John W. (1953) *The Age of Paradox: A Biography of England, 1841–1851.*

Driver, Christopher (1983) *The British at Table, 1940–1980.*

Drummond, J.C. *et al.* (1940) *The Nation's Larder, and the Housewife's Part Therein*, lectures delivered at the Royal Institution.

Drummond, J.C. and Wilbraham, Anne (1939) *The Englishman's Food. A History of Five Centuries of English Diet*, 2nd edn, revised and enlarged by Dorothy Hollingsworth, 1958.

Dyer, Bernard and Mitchell, C. Ainsworth (1932) *The Society of Public Analysts. Some reminiscences of its first fifty years.*

Ernle, Lord (1961) *English Farming Past and Present*, 6th edn with Introduction by G.E. Fussell and O.R. McGregor.

Fielding, Sir Charles ('Agricola') (1923) *Food.*

Filby, Frederick A. (1934) *A History of Food Adulteration and Analysis.*

Fussell, G.E. (1949) *The English Rural Labourer.*

Fussell, G.E. and Fussell, K.R. (1981) *The English Countryman.*

Select bibliography

Graves, Robert and Hodge, Alan (1940) *The Long Weekend. A Social History of Great Britain, 1918–1939.*

Grey, Edwin (1934) *Cottage Life in a Hertfordshire Village*, repub. 1977, Harpenden, Herts.

Hammond, J.L. and Hammond B. (1917) *The Town Labourer, 1760–1832.*

Hampson, John (1944) *The English at Table.*

Hanssen, Maurice and Marsden, Jill (1984) *E for Additives. The Complete E. Number Guide.*

Harrison, B. (1971) *Drink and the Victorians. The Temperance Question in England, 1815–1872.*

Hasbach, W. (1920) *A History of the English Agricultural Labourer*, trans. Ruth Kenyon.

Herbert, S. Mervyn (1939) *Britain's Health.*

Hewitt, Margaret (1958) *Wives and Mothers in Victorian Industry.*

Hilton, G.W. (1960) *The Truck System.*

Horn, Pamela (1980) *The Rural World, 1780–1850. Social Change in the English Countryside.*

Howe, Ellic (ed.) (1947) *The London Compositor. Documents relating to Wages, Working Conditions, etc., 1785–1900.*

Hugill, Antony (1978) *Sugar and all that. A History of Tate and Lyle.*

Hyde, H.M. (1951) *Mr and Mrs Beeton.*

Jefferys, James B. (1954) *Retail Trading in Britain, 1850–1950.*

Johnston, James P. (1977) *A Hundred Years of Eating. Food, Drink and the Daily Diet in Britain since the late Nineteenth Century.*

Jones, G. Stedman (1977) *Outcast London.*

Jones, Thomas G. (1944) *The Unbroken Front. The Ministry of Food, 1916–1944. Personalities and Problems.*

Kaye-Smith, Sheila (1945) *Kitchen Fugue.*

King, Frank A. (1947) *Beer has a History.*

Lang, Tim, Andrews, Hazel, Bedale, Caroline, and Hannon, Ed (1984) *Jam Tomorrow. Report of a Pilot Study of the food circumstances, attitudes and consumption of 1,000 people on low incomes in the north of England*, Food Policy Unit, Manchester Polytechnic.

Layton, W.T. and Crowther, Geoffrey (1935) *An Introduction to the Study of Prices.*

Lewis, R. and Maude, J. (1949) *The English Middle Classes.*

Liversedge, J.F. (1932) *Adulteration and Analysis of Food and Drugs. Birmingham methods. . . . Review of British prosecutions during half a century.*

Longmate, Norman (1968) *The Waterdrinkers. A History of Temperance.*

Longmate, Norman (1978) *The Hungry Mills. The Story of the Lancashire Cotton Famine, 1861–5.*

McCleary, I. (1933) *The Early History of the Infant Welfare Movement.*

339

McCord, Norman (1958) *The Anti-Corn Law Movement.*

McGonigle, G.C.M. and Kirby, J. (1936) *Poverty and Public Health.*

Mackenzie, Compton (1953) *The Savoy of London.*

Marx, Karl and Engels, Frederick (1953) *On Britain*, Moscow.

Mathias, P. (1959) *The Brewing Industry in England, 1700–1830.*

Mathias, P. (1967) *Retailing Revolution: A History of Multiple Retailing in the Food Trades, based on the Allied Suppliers Group.*

Mennell, Stephen (1985) *All Manners of Food. Eating and Taste in England and France from the Middle Ages to the Present.*

Millstone, Erik (1986) *Food Additives. Taking the Lid off what we really eat.*

Mingay, G.E. (ed.) (1981) *The Victorian Countryside*, 2 vols.

Mingay, G.E. (1986) *The Transformation of Britain, 1830–1939.*

Mitchell, B.R. and Deane, Phyllis (1962) *Abstract of British Historical Statistics*, Cambridge.

Morris, Helen (1938) *Portrait of a Chef. The Life of Alexis Soyer.*

Oddy, Derek J. and Miller, Derek S. (eds) (1976) *The Making of the Modern British Diet.*

Oddy, Derek J. and Miller, Derek S. (eds) (1985) *Diet and Health in Modern Britain.*

Orr, John Boyd (1936) *Food, Health and Income. Report on a Survey of Adequacy of Diet in Relation to Income.*

Orr, Sir John and Lubbock, D. (1940) *Feeding the People in Wartime.*

Orwell, George (1937) *The Road to Wigan Pier*, New York and London.

Palmer, Arnold (1952) *Movable Feasts. A Reconnaissance of the Origins and Consequences of Fluctuations in Meal-Times*, Oxford.

Peacock, A.J. (1965) *Bread or Blood. The Agrarian Riots in E. Anglia, 1816.*

Peel, Mrs C.S. (ed.) (1919) *The* Daily Mail *Cookery Book.*

Peel, Mrs C.S. (1929) *A Hundred Wonderful Years. Social and Domestic Life of a Century, 1820–1920.*

Pinchbeck, Ivy (1930/1985) *Women Workers and the Industrial Revolution, 1750–1850.*

Potter, Stephen (1959) *The Magic Number. The Story of '57' (H.J. Heinz).*

Powell, Horace B. (1956) *The Original has this Signature: W.K. Kellogg.*

Proud, Dorothea (1916) *Industrial Welfare.*

Renner, H.D. (1944) *The Origin of Food Habits.*

Rice, Margery Spring (1939/1981) *Working-Class Wives: Their Health and Conditions.*

Roberts, Robert (1971) *The Classic Slum. Salford Life in the First Quarter of the Century*, Manchester.

Rogers, R.G. (1961) *The Battle in Bossenden Wood. The Strange Story of Sir William Courtenay.*

Roussin, René (1960) *Royal Menus.*

Rowntree, B. Seebohm (1937) *The Human Needs of Labour.*

Salaman, R.N. (1949) *The History and Social Influence of the Potato*, Cambridge.

Samuel, Raphael (ed.) (1975) *Village Life and Labour*, History Workshop Series.

Simon, André L. (1929) *The Art of Good Living.*

Smith, Charles (1940) *Britain's Food Supplies in Peace and War. A Survey prepared for the Fabian Society.*

Spain, Nancy (1956) *The Beeton Story.*

Springall, L. Marion (1936) *Labouring Life in Norfolk Villages, 1834–1934.*

Stuyvenberg, J.H. van (ed.) (1969) *Margarine. An Economic, Social and Scientific History, 1869–1969*, Liverpool.

Tannahill, Reay (1973) *Food in History.*

Taylor, Arthur J. (1975) *The Standard of Living in Britain in the Industrial Revolution.*

Thompson, E.P. (1980) *The Making of the English Working Class*, Harmondsworth: Pelican.

Thompson, Flora (1973) *Lark Rise to Candleford*, Harmondsworth: Penguin.

Titmuss, R.M. (1938) *Poverty and Population.*

Titmuss, R.M. (1958) *Essays on the Welfare State.*

Tschumi, Gabriel (1954) *Royal Chef. Recollections of Life in Royal Households from Queen Victoria to Queen Mary.*

Twining, Stephen H. (1956) *Twinings. Two Hundred and Fifty Years of Tea and Coffee, 1706–1956.*

Unwin, George (1924) *Samuel Oldknow and the Arkwrights.*

Vaizey, John (1960) *The Brewing Industry, 1886–1951. An Economic Study.*

Walker, Caroline and Cannon, Geoffrey (1984) *The Food Scandal. What's Wrong with the British Diet.*

Warren, Geoffrey C. (1958) *The Foods we Eat. A Survey of Meals, their Content and Chronology, etc.*

Waugh, A. (1951) *The Lipton Story.*

Williams, Iola A. (1931) *The Firm of Cadbury (a centenary history).*

Wilson, George B. (1940) *Alcohol and the Nation.*

Wood, Thomas (1956) *Autobiography, 1822–1880*, privately printed.

Yarwood, Doreen (1981) *The British Kitchen.*

Yarwood, Doreen (1983) *Five Hundred Years of Technology in the Home.*

Young, G.M. (ed.) (1934) *Early Victorian England, 1830–1865.*

Yudkin, John (ed.) (1977) *Diet of Man. Needs and Wants.*

Journals, articles, and pamphlets

Bannister, Richard (1888) 'Our milk, butter, and cheese supply', *Journal of the Royal Society of Arts* XXXVI.

Barnsby, G. (1971) 'The standard of living in the Black Country during the nineteenth century', *Economic History Review* XXIV.

Blackman, Janet (1963) 'The food supply of an industrial town. A study of Sheffield's public markets, 1780–1900', *Business History* V (2).

Bowley, A.L. (1895) 'Changes in average wages (nomimal and real) in the UK between 1860 and 1891', *Journal of the Royal Statistical Society* LVIII.

British Association for the Advancement of Science (1881) *Report of the Committee . . . on the Present Appropriation of Wages*, 51st meeting.

British Nutrition Foundation (1977) 'Why additives? The safety of foods'.

——(1980) 'Snack meals, trends and effects' (October).

——(1982) 'Bread and potatoes: a perspective' (July).

——(1987) 'Food processing: a nutritional perspective' (September).

Browne, C.A. (1925) 'The life and chemical services of Frederick Accum', *Journal of Chemical Education* (New York) (October, November, December).

Burnett, John (1963) 'The baking industry in the nineteenth century', *Business History* V (2).

Burnett, John (1960) 'The adulteration of foods act. A centenary appreciation of the first British legislation', *Food Manufacture* XXXV (11).

Buss, D.H. (1979) 'The resilience of British household diets during the 1970s', *Journal of Human Nutrition* 33.

Chaloner, W.H. (1957) 'The hungry forties: a re-examination', *History Association*.

Cole, G.D.H. (1951) 'The social structure of England', *History Today* (February).

Colmore, G. (1901) '£800 a year', *Cornhill Magazine* (June).

Fay, C.R. (1923–5) 'The miller and the baker. A note on commercial transition, 1770–1837', *Cambridge Historical Journal* I.

France, R. Sharpe (ed.) (1954) 'The diary of John Ward of Clitheroe, weaver, 1860–64', *Transactions of the Historic Society of Lancashire and Cheshire* 105.

Giffen, Robert (1879) 'On the fall of prices of commodities in recent years', *Journal of the Royal Statistical Society* XLII.

Greaves, J.P. and Hollingsworth, Dorothy F. (1966) 'Trends in food consumption in the UK', *World Review of Nutrition and Dietetics* 6.

Greg, W.R. (1851) Review of William Johnston, 'England as it is, political, social and industrial', *Edinburgh Review* CXL (April).

Hollingsworth, Dorothy F. (1983) 'Rationing and economic constraints on food consumption in Britain since the Second World War', *World Review of Nutrition and Dietetics* 42.

Hunt, Sandra (1985) 'And the poor? They shall eat carrots . . .', *Poverty*, pub. by Child Poverty Action Group, 60 (Spring).

Jago, William (1890) 'Modern developments of bread making', *Journal of the Royal Society of Arts* 38.

Layard, G.S. (1888) 'How to live on £700 a year', *Nineteenth Century* (February).

McKenzie, J.C. (1962) 'The composition and nutritional value of diets in Manchester and Dukinfield in 1841', *Transactions of the Lancashire and Cheshire Antiquarian Society* 72.

McKenzie, J.C. (1974) 'The impact of economic and social status on food choice', *Proceedings of the Nutrition Society* 33.

Neild, W. (1841) 'Comparative statement of the income and expenditure of certain families of the working classes in Manchester and Dukinfield in the years 1836 and 1841', *Journal of the Statistical Society of London* IV.

Oddy, D.J. (1970) 'Working-class diets in late nineteenth-century Britain', *Economic History Review* (2nd series) XXIII.

Odling, William (1857) 'On the composition of bread', *Lancet* I.

Piachaud, David (1986) 'Poor children: a tale of two decades', *Poverty* (CPAG) (December).

Raistrick, Arthur (1938) 'Two centuries of industrial welfare', *Journal of the Friends' Historical Society*, Supplement no. 19.

Rose, Evelyn (1977) 'Consumer aspect of beef marketing', *Journal of Consumer Studies and Home Economics* 1 (2).

Salomon, A. Gordon (1887) 'The purity of beer', *Journal of the Royal Society of Arts* 35.

Scola, R. (1975) 'Food markets and shops in Manchester, 1770–1870', *Journal of Historical Geography* 1.

Scott, Wentworth Lascelles (1875) 'Food adulteration and the legislative enactments relating thereto', *Journal of the Royal Society of Arts* 23.

Webb, S. and Webb, B. (1904) 'The assize of bread', *Economic Journal* 14.

Webster, Charles (1982) 'Healthy or hungry thirties?', *History Workshop Journal* (Spring).

Winter, J.M. (1977) 'The impact of the First World War on civilian health in Britain', *Economic History Review* (2nd series) XXX.

Index

345

Index

Index

348

Index

Index

Reynolds, M.E. 70, 80
Rhondda, David Thomas,
Viscount 246, 248, 252
Rice, Margery Spring 286
Richardson, Dr T.L. 22
Ridley, George 220
riots, food 24, 35, 51
Ritz, César 203
road-houses 263
Roberts, Robert 186–7, 251
Rochdale Pioneers 125, 226
Roseveare, M.P. 294
Rowntree, B. Seebohm, studies:
agricultural labourers 154–5;
poverty line 109, 284; York
179–80, 181–2, 211
Rowntree, Joseph 115, 175
Runciman, Walter, Baron 244
Rundell, Mrs Maria Elizabeth 52–3,
70, 75–6, 79
Ruskin, John 4
Russia, influence on meal
service 200

Sadler, Michael 47
Sainsbury, J.J. 127, 260
St Helier, Lady 195
Salaman, Dr R.N. 9, 10, 11
Sale of Food and Drugs Act
(1875) 230–2
Sale of Food and Drugs Act
(1899) 234
Salford, diets 186–7, 251
Salvation Army 179, 181, 195
Sanitary Commission Bread
Company 225
schools: meals 188, 243, 293,
315–16; milk 285, 292
Scotland 29
Scott, Wentworth Lascelles 229
Senn, Herman 202
Shaw, Charles 49–50
Sheffield 7–8
Sherwell, Arthur 115, 175
shops, food 44–5, 125–8, 167,
259–60
Simmons, P.L. 99

Simon, André 262
slimming 314
Smiles, Samuel 175
Smith, Adam 94
Smith, Dr Edward, studies:
agricultural labourers'
diet 111–12, 140–4, 328
minimum subsistence
levels 139–40; national food
inquiry 139–44; publications
166, 223; Reports to Privy
Council 162–5, 171–4 town
workers' diet 162–5
Smithfield market 12
Social Democratic Federation 179
Society of Public Analysts 98–9,
231–2
Somerset 140, 147, 148, 230
Somerville, Alexander 11, 58–60,
138
Soyer, Alexis 74–5, 77–9;
publications 74, 166; soup
kitchens 42, 60, 74
Spencer, Edward 168
Spiller Ltd 258–9
spirits, consumption of 115, 175, 319
Staffordshire 49, 140, 153, 229
starvation 54, 180–1
state, food policy see government
Statistical Society surveys: household
budgets 176–8; Lancashire
cotton workers 56–9
stoves, cooking 42, 164–5
street-traders 167–8
Sturgeon, Launcelot 71
Suffolk 5, 32
sugar: adulteration of 218;
consumption of 14–15, 113–14,
142, 249, 266–8, 283, 305–7;
imports 257
Sugar Commission 244
Sumner, John Hamilton,
Viscount 250
supper 279, 314–15
supplies of food see agriculture;
imports; shops; etc., also bread;
meat; milk; etc.,

353

Index

Index

Woolton, Lord 291
workhouses 28, 31, 96, 216
working classes *see* agricultural
    labourers; town workers World
    War I 243–52; consumption
    248–50; food control 243–7, 250;
    munitions work 147; nutrition
    244, 247–8; unfit conscripts 61,
    254

World War II 289–97; food
    control 289–95; nutrition 295–6;
    prices 297

Yates, May 236
York, poverty in 179–80, 181–2, 211
Yorkshire 31, 34, 144
Young, Arthur 137
Yudkin, Prof. John 143, 310